THE ROLE OF RELIGION IN AMERICAN LIFE

An Interpretive Historical Anthology

Edited by
Robert R. Mathisen

UNIVERSITY
PRESS OF
AMERICA

LANHAM • NEW YORK • LONDON

Copyright © 1982 by **Robert R. Mathisen**

University Press of America,™ Inc.

4720 Boston Way
Lanham, MD 20706

3 Henrietta Street
London WC2E 8LU England

All rights reserved
Printed in the United States of America

Library of Congress Cataloging in Publication Data
Main entry under title:

The Role of religion in American life.

Includes bibliographical references.
1. United States–Church history–Sources. I.
Mathisen, Robert R.
BR515.R56   1982   209'.73   82-8568
ISBN 0-8191-2514-8 (pbk.)   AACR2

All University Press of America books are produced on acid-free
paper which exceeds the minimum standards set by the National
Historical Publications and Records Commission.

TO

My His200 Students

ACKNOWLEDGEMENTS

      I wish to thank the history department of Illinois State University for the intellectual stimulation they provided which resulted in the writing of this volume. Dean Vance A. Yoder and Dr. Myron D. Yeager of Grace College contributed to the completion of this work by providing the necessary time free from classroom responsibilities, and by helping with the correct placement of commas and periods. A special word of appreciation to Diane, Jeff, Jay, and Jill for their patience and understanding during the hours we spent apart while the volume was in preparation.

TABLE OF CONTENTS

PART 1   ESTABLISHING AMERICA: 1607-1820

1   RELIGION AND COLONIAL MASSACHUSETTS — 3

Bradford's History of Plymouth Plantation, 1606-1646, *William Bradford* — 3

A Modell of Christian Charity, *John Winthrop* — 9

The Last Will and Testament of Mr. Robert Keayne, *Robert Keayne* — 19

2   THE GREAT AWAKENING — 27

Some Thoughts Concerning the Present Revival of Religion in New England, *Jonathan Edwards* — 27

Seasonable Thoughts on the State of Religion in New England, *Charles Chauncy* — 36

The Testimony of Harvard College Against George Whitefield — 42

3   THE COMING OF THE AMERICAN REVOLUTION — 49

Discourse Concerning Unlimited Submission, *Jonathan Mayhew* — 49

A Calm Address to Our American Colonies, *John Wesley* — 53

1776 Election Sermon, *Samuel West* — 60

4   SOURCES AND IMPACT OF THE SECOND AWAKENING — 65

Attack on Infidelity, *Timothy Dwight* — 65

Forming the American Bible Society — 77

PART 2   EXPANDING AMERICA: 1820-1865

5   SLAVERY   91

Slavery, *William Ellery Channing*   91

Letters on Slavery, *James H. Hammond*   98

Address on Slavery, *James H. Thornwell*   102

6   RELIGION AND REFORM   109

The Church Must Take Right Ground, *Charles G. Finney*   109

The Bible Against Slavery, *Theodore D. Weld*   119

Six Sermons on the Nature, Occasions, Signs . . . of Intemperance, *Lyman Beecher*   126

7   MANIFEST DESTINY   135

Justification by Scripture, *John Q. Adams*   135

Letters to Rev. L. P. Judson, *Marcus Whitman*   142

Redeem Mexico from Misrule and Civil Strife, *Robert F. Stockton*   148

8   RELIGION AND THE CIVIL WAR   155

An Address to Christians throughout the World   155

Second Inaugural Address, *Abraham Lincoln*   168

Address at the Raising of the Union Flag over Fort Sumter, *Henry Ward Beecher*   171

PART 3   ENERGIZING AMERICA: 1865-1920

9   SCIENCE AND RELIGION — 183

What is Darwinism?, *Charles Hodge* — 183

Natural Science and Religion, *Asa Gray* — 192

Evolution and Religion, *Henry Ward Beecher* — 200

10   THE GOSPEL OF WEALTH AND BIG BUSINESS — 207

Wealth, *Andrew Carnegie* — 207

The Relation of Wealth to Morals, *William Lawrence* — 216

Acres of Diamonds, *Russell H. Conwell* — 222

11   THE SOCIAL GOSPEL — 227

Applied Christianity, *Washington Gladden* — 227

Social Aspects of Christianity, *Richard T. Ely* — 239

12   THEOLOGY — 251

The New Theology, *Theodore T. Munger* — 251

Present Day Theology, *Washington Gladden* — 258

A Theology for the Social Gospel, *Walter Rauschenbusch* — 264

13   RELIGION AND INTERNATIONAL RELATIONS — 273

Our Country, *Josiah Strong* — 273

The March of the Flag, *Albert J. Beveridge* — 280

America's Mission, *William Jennings Bryan* — 284

PART 4 EVALUATING AMERICA: SINCE 1920

14 AMERICA AND RELIGION IN THE UNCERTAIN TWENTIES   293

    The Man Nobody Knows, *Bruce Barton*   293

    The World's Most Famous Court Trial: Tennessee Evolution Case   303

    Up to Now, *Alfred E. Smith*   312

15 RELIGION IN THE AGE OF DEPRESSION   317

    A Christian Manifesto, *Edwin Lewis*   317

    Five Years of the New Deal, *Charles Coughlin*   325

16 EDUCATION, RELIGION, AND THE COURTS IN THE 20TH CENTURY   337

    Minersville School District v. Gobitis, and *West Va. State Bd. of Educ. v. Barnette*   337

    McCollum v. Bd. of Educ., and *Zorach v. Clauson*   345

    Engel v. Vitale   352

17 RELIGION DURING HOT AND COLD WARS   355

    The Churches and the Clergy in World War II, *Ray Abrams*   355

    The National Council of Churches and Our Foreign Policy, *Arthur H. Darken*   366

18 RELIGIOUS RESPONSES TO THE TURBULENT 60'S   381

    Communist America--Must It Be?, *Billy J. Hargis*   381

    Civil Religion in America, *Robert N. Bellah*   386

    The Jesus People, *Ronald M. Enroth*   394

PREFACE

"For the study and understanding of American culture, the recovery of American religious history may well be the most important achievement of the last thirty years." Writing these words in 1964, the eminent historian Henry F. May recognized that "even for those students of American culture who do not find religious thought and practice intrinsically interesting, knowledge of religious history has become a necessity." May realized that "the recovery of American religious history has restored a knowledge of the mode, even the language, in which most Americans, during most of American history, did their thinking about human nature and destiny."[1]

As May has suggested, a knowledge of religion's role in the progress of American history is necessary for a clear understanding of how America has developed. The purpose of the present volume is to provide historical documents which illustrate the role of religion in the emergence of American society. The vehicle used by the editor to achieve this purpose is the perceptive analysis of religion supplied by several sociologists of religion. Particularly helpful is sociology's functional approach to the study of religion which says that religion is not to be considered always as the independent variable that "causes" certain social and cultural developments; nor should religion be thought of as entirely a dependent variable which reflects its social environment.[2] Rather, religion should be looked upon historically as both an independent and a dependent variable. As part of a social structure, it is independent in that it performs certain functions and therefore _acts_ _upon_ society as a whole, but it is also dependent in that it is _acted_ _upon_ by the society within which it exists.

The documents collected in this volume demonstrate that from the colonial period through the first two-thirds of the nineteenth century, religion as an independent variable was more significant in the shaping of America than was religion as a dependent variable. During the last third of the nineteenth century, however, the trend reversed, so that since that time religion has been influenced by society in more significant ways than it has influenced society.

Each of the four parts of this volume focuses on a distinct segment of America's past. As the nation was established by pilgrims in search of a providential destiny, and then expanded by those seeking to quench their thirst for adventure and wealth, it was subsequently energized by forces that challenged the traditional values of America. Evaluation of America's journey thus far is still in progress.

While numerous definitions of religion have been suggested by social scientists, the definition by sociologist Ronald Johnstone is used here. Johnstone has stated that religion is "a system of beliefs and practices by which a group of people interprets and responds to what they feel is supernatural and sacred."[3]

The decisions involved in selecting documents for a reader are never easy; the present volume provided no exceptions. Each of the documents which appears here demonstrates the interaction of religion with other socio-cultural, economic, political, or diplomatic factors. It is hoped that the volume will enhance the reader's "knowledge of the mode . . . in which most Americans . . . did their thinking about nature and destiny."

---

[1]Henry F. May, "The Recovery of American Religious History," *American Historical Review* 70 (1964): 79.

[2]J. Milton Yinger, *The Scientific Study of Religion* (New York: Macmillan, 1970), p. 222.

[3]Ronald L. Johnstone, *Religion and Society in Interaction: The Sociology of Religion* (Englewood Cliffs, N.J.: Prentice-Hall, 1975), pp. 13-20.

PART 1 ESTABLISHING AMERICA
1607-1820

Religion played an important role in the establishment of most of the American colonies during the seventeenth and eighteenth centuries. Particularly noteworthy was the ever present religiously oriented sense of mission which guided people of all ranks to the New World early during the period between 1607 and 1820, and later preserved the nation during a time of philosophical doubt following the American Revolution. For reasons never fully understood, but nevertheless held as truth, a favoring Providence was seen as directing the destiny of His "chosen people" in the abundant wilderness called America.

In no colony is the significance of religion more clearly seen than in Massachusetts. The Pilgrims, the first group of Anglican dissenters who came to America, settled at Plymouth in 1620. Also known as Separatists, they were led by their political "Moses," William Bradford. In his account of Plymouth Plantation he reveals that the economic values and religious practices of the Pilgrims clashed, thus forcing settlers to reevaluate their goals. A short distance to the north from Plymouth, a second group of Anglican malcontents, the Puritans, settled the Bay Colony in 1630. Led by John Winthrop, this group of non-Separatists was urged to build their model society, the "city upon a hill," though as Winthrop indicates, the society would be noted for its divinely fixed social order in which some would be rich and others poor. One of the Bay Colony residents, Robert Keayne, reveals how he fell victim to the community's ceaseless striving in economic matters.

The Puritanism of the early decades underwent considerable change by the end of the seventeenth century due to both intra-colonial and extra-colonial influences. Much of the vitality and faith of the first Puritans in America was maintained by the next two generations. As the colonial population became increasingly heterogeneous, religious pluralism weakened the prestige of all church groups. Externally, the secular rationalism of the Enlightenment resulted in antagonism between it and Puritan revivalism. When by the early eighteenth century the vast majority of the population was outside of the church, a new approach was needed to revitalize the church and society. What resulted was the Great Awakening, which some, like Jonathan Edwards, defended for positive results, while others, like Charles Chauncy and critics at Harvard, denounced due to what was deemed its emotional excesses.

One of the social effects of the Great Awakening was the elevation of the common man and the advance of lay authority in the church. From this new significance of the individual in the church, it was only natural that the new experience in leadership would find its way to the political sphere where it stimulated the establishment of the United States as a nation. Jonathan Mayhew, who emerged from the Great Awakening as a theological liberal, denounced passive obedience to kings decades before the American Revolution. It is significant to note that the crux of his arguments was debated and disputed until 1776 by many clergy and laity alike, including the English Methodist John Wesley and the American Unitarian Samuel West.

The first several decades of the new, infant nation were fraught with difficulty from without and within. The popular deistic philosophy of the Revolutionary era had been hard on the churches, while the course of the French Revolution, with its excesses of the Reign of Terror, was looked upon by many Americans as the logical outcome of deism. Clergy like Timothy Dwight identified deism as the root of widespread infidelity, a prime target of Second Awakening preachers. The revivalism of the new awakening swept not only the East where it began, but also spread rapidly westward where migrant Americans were establishing new homes. The advance of people to the West was paralleled by the founding of missionary and Bible societies as well as new colleges by the 1840's.

RELIGION AND COLONIAL MASSACHUSETTS

Bradford's History of Plymouth Plantation, 1606-1646

WILLIAM BRADFORD

William Bradford (1590-1657) was the leading figure in the founding and early history of the Plymouth colony settled in 1620. His History of Plymouth Plantation remains as the most descriptive account of life in early Plymouth, where he served as governor from 1620 until his death. The following account published in 1908 in Bradford's History of Plymouth Plantation, 1606-1646, pp. 144-148, 292-294, edited by William T. Davis, describes some of the tensions experienced by the Pilgrim sect of the Puritans as they sought to reconcile their spiritual ideals with troublesome economic realities. What reasons does Bradford suggest for the introduction of individual plots? How did the appeal to economic advancement make more difficult the preservation of Plymouth society? What does Bradford find responsible for the decline of the Pilgrim spirit?

NOTE-- The spelling of the original has been retained.

This was the end of these that some time bosted of their
strength, (being all able lustie men), and what they would
doe and bring to pass, in comparison of the people hear, who
had many women and children and weak ons amongst them; and
said at their first arivall, when they saw the wants hear,
that they would take an other course, and not to fall into
shuch a condition as this simple people were come too. But
a mans way is not in his owne power; God can make the weake
to stand; let him also that standeth take heed least he fall.

Shortly after, Mr. Weston came over with some of the fisher-
men, under another name, and the disguise of a blackesmith,
were [where] he heard of the ruine and disolution of his
colony. He got a boat and with a man or 2. came to see how
things were. But by the way, for wante of skill, in a storme,
he cast away his shalop in the botome of the bay between
Meremek river and Pascataquack, and hardly escaped with life,
and afterwards fell into the hands of the Indeans, who
pillaged him of all he saved from the sea, and striped him
out of all his cloaths to his shirte. At last he got to
Pascataquack, and borrowed a suit of cloaths, and got means
to come to Plimoth. A strang alteration ther was in him to
such as had seen and known him in his former florishing condition; so uncertaine are the mutable things of this unstable
world. And yet men set their harts upon them, though they
dayly see the vanity therof.

After many passages, and much discourse, (former things
boyling in his mind, but bit in as was discernd,) he desired
to borrow some beaver of them; and tould them he had hope of
a ship and good supply to come to him, and then they should
have any thing for it they stood in neede of. They gave
litle credite to his supplie, but pitied his case, and remembered former curtesies. They tould him he saw their wants,
and they knew not when they should have any supply; also how
the case stood betweene them and their adventurers, he well
knew; they had not much bever, and if they should let him
have it, it were enoughe to make a mutinie among the people,
seeing ther was no other means to procure them foode which
they so much wanted, and cloaths allso. Yet they tould him
they would help him, considering his necessitie, but must doe
it secretly for the former reasons. So they let him have
100. beaver-skins, which waighed 170$\underline{li}$. odd pounds. Thus
they helpt him when all the world faild him, and with this
means he went againe to the ships, and stayed his small ship

and some of his men, and bought provissions and fited him
selfe; and it was the only foundation of his after course.
But he requited them ill, for he proved after a bitter
enimie unto them upon all occasions, and never repayed them
any thing for it, to this day, but reproches and evill words.
Yea, he divolged it to some that were none of their best
freinds, whilst he yet had the beaver in his boat; that he
could now set them all togeather by the ears, because they
had done more then they could answer, in letting him have this
beaver, and he did not spare to doe what he could. But his
malice could not prevaile.

All this whille no supply was heard of, neither knew they
when they might expecte any. So they begane to thinke how
they might raise as much corne as they could, and obtaine a
beter crope then they had done, that they might not still
thus languish in miserie. At length, after much debate of
things, the Gov (with the advise of the cheefest amongst them)
gave way that they should set corne every man for his owne
perticuler, and in that regard trust to them selves; in all
other things to goe on in the generall way as before. And
so assigned to every family a parcell of land, according to
the proportion of their number for that end, only for present
use (but made no devission for inheritance), and ranged all
boys and youth under some familie. This had very good success; for it made all hands very industrious, so as much
more corne was planted then other waise would have bene by
any means the Gov or any other could use, and saved him a
great deall of trouble, and gave farr better contente. The
women now wente willingly into the feild, and tooke their
litle-ons with them to set corne, which before would aledg
weaknes, and inabilitie; whom to have compelled would have
bene thought great tiranie and oppression.

The experience that was had in this commone course and condition, tried sundrie years, and that amongst godly and
sober men, may well evince the vanitie of that conceite of
Platos and other ancients, applauded by some of later times;
--that the taking away of propertie, and bringing in com-
munitie into a comone wealth, would make them happy and
florishing; as if they were wiser then God. For this com-
munitie (so farr as it was) was found to breed much confusion
and discontent, and retard much imployment that would have
been to their benefite and comforte. For the yong-men that
were most able and fitte for labour and service did repine

that they should spend their time and streingth to works for other mens wives and children, with out any recompence. The strong, or man of parts, had no more in devission of victails and cloaths, then he that was weake and not able to doe a quarter the other could; this was thought injuestice. The aged and graver men to be ranked and equalised in labours, and victails, cloaths, etc., with the meaner and yonger sorte, thought it some indignite and disrespect unto them. And for mens wives to be commanded to do servise for other men, as dresing their meate, washing their cloaths, etc., they deemed it a kind of slaverie, neither could many husbands well brooke it. Upon the poynte all being to have alike, and all to doe alike, they thought them selves in the like condition, and one as good as another; and so, if it did not cut of those relations that God hath set amongest men, yet it did at least much diminish and take of the mutuall respects that should be preserved amongst them. And would have bene worse if they had been men of another condition. Let none objecte this is men's corruption, and nothing to the course it selfe. I answer, seeing all men have this corruption in them, God in his wisdome saw another course fiter for them.

But to returne. After this course setled, and by that their corne was planted, all ther victails were spente, and they were only to rest on Gods providence; at night not many times knowing wher to have a bitt of any thing the next day. And so, as one well observed, had need to pray that God would give them their dayly brade, above all people in the world. Yet they bore these wants with great patience and allacritie of spirite, and that for so long a time as for the most parte of 2. years; which makes me remember what Peter Martire writs, (in magnifying the Spaniards) in his 5. Decade, pag. 208. <u>They</u> (saith he) <u>led a miserable life for 5. days togeather, with the parched graine of maize only, and that not to saturitie</u>; and then concluds, <u>that shuch pains, shuch labours, and shuch hunger, he thought none living which is not a Spaniard could have endured.</u> But alass! these, when they had maize (that is Indean corne) they thought it as good as a feast, and wanted not only for 5. days togeather, but some time 2. or 3. months togeather, and neither had bread nor any kind of corne. Indeed, in an other place, in his 2. Decade, page 94. he mentions how others of them were worse put to it, wher they were faine to eate doggs, toads, and dead men, and do dyed almost all. From these extremities they [the] Lord in his goodnes kept these his

people, and in their great wants preserved both their lives
and healthes; let his name have the praise. Yet let me hear
make use of his conclusion, which in some sorte may be applied
to this people: That with their miseries they opened a way
to these new-lands; and after these stormes, with what ease
other men came to inhabite in them, in respecte of the calamities these men suffered; so as they seeme to goe to a bride
feaste wher all things are provided for them.

****

Mr. Hatherley came over againe this year, but upon his owne
occasions, and begane to make preparation to plant and dwell
in the countrie. He with his former dealings had wound in
what money he had in the partnership into his owne hands, and
so gave off all partnership (excepte in name), as was found
in the issue of things; neither did he medle, or take any
care aboute the same; only he was troubled about his ingag-
mente aboute the Friendship, as will after appeare. And now
partly aboute that accounte, in some reconings betweene Mr.
Allerton and him, and some debts that Mr. Allerton otherwise
owed him upon dealing between them in perticuler, he drue
up an accounte of about 2000li., and would faine have in-
gaged the partners here with it, because Mr. Allerton had
been their agent. But they tould him they had been fool'd
longe enough with such things, and shewed him that it no way
belonged to them; but tould him he must looke to make good
his ingagment for the Friendship, which caused some trouble
betweene Mr. Allerton and him.

Mr. William Peirce did the like, Mr. Allerton being wound
into his debte also upon particuler dealings; as if they had
been bound to make good all mens debts. But they easily
shooke off these things. But Mr. Allerton herby rane into
much trouble and vexation, as well as he had troubled others,
for Mr. Denison sued him for the money he had disbursed for
the 6. part of the Whit-Angell, and recovered the same with
damages.

Though the partners were thus plunged into great ingagments,
and oppresed with unjust debts, yet the Lord prospered their
trading, that they made yearly large returnes, and had soone
wound them selves out of all, if yet they had otherwise been
well delt with all; as will more appear here after. Also
the people of the plantation begane to grow in their owtward

estats, by rea[son] of the flowing of many people into the
cuntrie, espetially into the Bay of the Massachusets; by
which means corne and catle rose to a great prise, by which
many were much inriched, and commodities grue plentifull;
and yet in other regards this benefite turned to their hurte,
and this accession of strength to their weaknes. For now as
their stocks increased, and the increase vendible, ther was
no longer any holding them togeather, but now they must of
necessitie goe to their great lots; they could not other wise
keep their katle; and having oxen growne, they must have land
for plowing and tillage. And no man now thought he could
live, except he had catle and a great deale of ground to keep
them; all striving to increase their stocks. By which means
they were scatered all over the bay, quickly, and the towne,
in which they lived compactly till now, was left very thine,
and in a short time allmost desolate. And if this had been
all, it had been less, thoug to much; but the church must
also be devided, and those that had lived so long togeather
in Christian and comfortable fellowship must now part and
suffer many divisions. First, those that lived on their
lots on the other side of the bay (called Duxberie) they
could not long bring their wives and children to the publick
worship and church meetings here, but with such burthen,
as, growing to some competente number, they sued to be dismissed and become a body of them selves; and so they were
dismiste (about this time), though very unwillingly. But
to touch this sadd matter, and handle things togeather that
fell out after ward. To prevent any further scatering from
this place, and weakning of the same, it was thought best
to give out some good farms to spetiall persons, that would
promise to live at Plimoth, and lickly to be helpfull to the
church or comonewelth, and so tye the lands to Plimoth as
farmes for the same; and ther they might keepe their catle
and tillage by some servants, and retaine their dwellings
here. And so some spectiall lands were granted at a place
generall, called Greens Harbor, wher no allotments had been
in the former division, a plase very weell meadowed, and
fitt to keep and rear catle, good store. But alass! this
remedy proved worse then the disease; for within a few years
those that had thus gott footing ther rente them selves away,
partly by force, and partly wearing the rest with importuni-
tie and pleas of necessitie, so as they must either suffer
them to goe, or live in continuall opposition and contention.
And others still, as they conceived them selves straitened,
or to want accommodation, break away under one pretence or

other, thinking their owne conceived necessitie, and the example of others, a warrente sufficente for them. And this, I fear, will be the ruine of New-England, at least of the churches of God ther, and will provock the Lords displeasure against them.

A Modell of Christian Charity

JOHN WINTHROP

John Winthrop (1588-1649) was as dominant in the founding and early history of Massachusetts Bay colony as William Bradford was in Plymouth. Moving from London where he had established a law practice, he served as governor of Massachusetts Bay for most of the years from 1630 until his death. The lay-sermon which follows is taken from the Winthrop Papers, 1623-1630, II, 282-295, published by the Massachusetts Historical Society and suggests the blueprint Winthrop wished his fellow passengers to follow as they carried out their mission in building "a city upon a hill" in New England. What evidence is there that Winthrop did not believe in total equality of all people? What emphasis did Winthrop place upon Christian charity as the Massachusetts Bay colony was about to establish itself? How important did Winthrop believe it was for the "city upon a hill" to succeed in its mission to the New World?

NOTE-- The spelling of the original has been retained.

God Almightie in his most holy and wise providence hath soe disposed of the Condicion of mankinde, as in all times some must be rich some poore, some highe and eminent in power and dignitie; others meane and in subjeccion.

THE REASON HEREOF.

1. REAS: *First*, To hold conformity with the rest of his workes, being delighted to shewe forthe the glory of his wisdome in the variety and differance of the Creatures and the glory of his power, in ordering all these differences for the preservacion and good of the whole, and the glory of his greatnes that as it is the glory of princes to have many officers, soe this great King will have many Stewards counting himselfe more honoured in dispenceing his guifts to man by man, then if hee did it by his owne immediate hand.

2. REAS: *Secondly*, That he might have the more occasion to manifest the worke of his Spirit: first, upon the wicked in moderateing and restraineing them: so that the riche and mighty should not eate upp the poore, nor the poore, and dispised rise upp against theire superiors, and shake off theire yoake; 2ly in the regenerate in exerciseing his graces in them, as in the greate ones, theire love mercy, gentlenes, temperance etc., in the poore and inferiour sorte, theire patience, obedience, etc.:

3. REAS: *Thirdly*, That every man might have need of other, and from hence they might be all knitt more nearly together in the Bond of brotherly affection: from hence it appeares plainely that noe man is made more honourable then another or more wealthy etc., out of any perticuler and singuler respect to himselfe but for the glory of his Creator and the Common good of the Creature, Man; Therefore God still reserves the propperty of these guifts to himselfe as Ezek: 16,17. he there calls wealthe his gold and his silver etc. Prov: 3.9 he claimes theire service as his due honour the Lord with thy riches etc. All men being thus (by divine providence) rancked into two sortes, riche and poore; under the first, are comprehended all such as are able to live comfortably by theire owne meanes duely improved; and all others are poore according to the former distribution.
There are two rules whereby wee are to walke one towards another: JUSTICE and MERCY. These are allwayes distinguished in theire Act and in theire object, yet may they both

concurre in the same Subject in eache respect; as sometimes
there may be an occasion of shewing mercy to a rich man, in
some sudden danger of distresse, and allsoe doeing of meere
Justice to a poore man in regard of some perticuler contract
etc. There is likewise a double Lawe by which wee are regulated in our conversacion one towardes another: in both the
former respects, the lawe of nature and the lawe of grace, or
the morrall lawe or the lawe of the gospell, to omitt the
rule of Justice as not propperly belonging to this purpose
otherwise then it may fall into consideracion in some
perticuler Cases: By the first of these lawes man as he was
enabled soe withall [is] commaunded to love his neighbour
as himselfe upon this ground stands all the precepts of the
morrall lawe, which concerns our dealings with men. To apply
this to the works of mercy this lawe requires two things
first that every man afford his help to another in every want
or distresse. Secondly, That he performe this out of the same
affeccion, which makes him carefull of his owne good according
to that of our Saviour Math: [7.12] Whatsoever ye would that
men should doe to you. This was practised by Abraham and
Lott in entertaineing the Angells and the old man of Gibea .
. . .

Having allready sett forth the practise of mercy according
to the rule of Gods lawe, it will be usefull to lay open the
groundes of it allsoe being the other parte of the Commaunde-
ment and that is the affeccion from which this exercise of
mercy must arise, the Apostle tells us that this love is the
fullfilling of the lawe, not that it is enough to love our
brother and soe noe further but in regard of the excellency
of his partes giveing any motion to the other as the Soule
to the body and the power it hath to sett all the faculties
on worke in the outward exercise of this duty as when we bid
one make the clocke strike he doth not lay hand on the
hammer which is the immediate instrument of the sound but
setts on worke the first mover or maine wheele, knoweing
that will certainely produce the sound which hee intends;
soe the way to drawe men to the workes of mercy is not by
force of Argument from the goodnes or necessity of the worke,
for though this course may enforce a rationall minde to some
present Act of mercy as is frequent in experience, yet it
cannot worke such a habit in a Soule as shall make it prompt
upon all occasions to produce the same effect but by frameing
these affeccions of love in the hearte which will as natively
bring forthe the other, as any cause doth produce the effect.

The diffinition which the Scripture gives us of love is this Love is the bond of perfection. First, it is a bond, or ligament. 2ly, it makes the worke perfect. There is noe body but consistes of partes and that which knitts these partes together gives the body its perfeccion, because it makes eache parte soe contiguous to other as thereby they doe mutually participate with eache other, both in strengthe and infirmity in pleasure and paine, to instance in the most perfect of all bodies, Christ and his church make one body: the severall partes of this body considered aparte before they were united were as disproportionate and as much disordering as soe many contrary quallities or elements but when Christ comes and by his spirit and love knitts all these partes to himselfe and each to other, it is become the most perfect and best proportioned body in the world Eph: 4.16. "Christ by whome all the body being knitt together by every joynt for the furniture thereof according to the effectuall power which is in the measure of every perfeccion of partes a glorious body without spott or wrinckle the ligaments hereof being Christ or his love for Christ is love I John 4.8. Soe this definition is right Love is the bond of perfeccion.

From hence wee may frame these Conclusions.

I. First all true Christians are of one body in Christ I. Cor. 12.12.13.17. [27.] Ye are the body of Christ and members of [your?] parte.

2ly. The ligamentes of this body which knitt together are love.

3ly. Noe body can be perfect which wants its propper ligamentes.

4ly. All the partes of this body being thus united are made soe contiguous in a speciall relacion as they must needes partake of each others strength and infirmity, joy, and sorrowe, weale and woe. I Cor: 12.26. If one member suffers all suffer with it, if one be in honour, all rejoyce with it.

5ly. This sensiblenes and Sympathy of each others Condicions will necessarily infuse into each parte a native desire and endeavour, to strengthen defend perserve and comfort the other.

To insist a little on this Conclusion being the product of
all the former the truthe hereof will appeare both by precept
and patterne i. John. 3.10. yee ought to lay downe your lives
for the brethren Gal: 6.2. beare ye one anothers burthens and
so fulfill the lawe of Christ.

For patterns wee have that first of our Saviour whoe out of
his good will in obedience to his father, becomeing a parte
of this body, and being knitt with it in the bond of love,
found such a native sensiblenes of our informities and
sorrowes as hee willingly yeilded himselfe to deathe to ease
the infirmities of the rest of his body and soe heale theire
sorrowes: from the like Sympathy of partes did the Apostles
and many thousands of the Saintes lay downe theire lives for
Christ againe, the like wee may see in the members of this
body among themselves. I. Rom. 9. Paule could have beene
contented to have beene seperated from Christ that the Jewes
might not be cutt off from the body: It is very observable
which hee professeth of his affectionate part[ak]eing with
every member: whoe is weake (saith hee) and I am not weake?
whoe is offended and I burne not; and againe. 2 Cor: 7.13,
therefore wee are comforted because yee were comforted. of
Epaphroditus he speaketh Phil. 2.30. that he regarded not his
owne life to [do] him service soe Phebe. and others are
called the servants of the Churche, now it is apparant that
they served not for wages or by Constrainte but out of love,
the like wee shall finde in the histories of the churche in
all ages the sweet Sympathie of affeccions which was in the
members of this body one towardes another, theire chear-
fullnes in serveing and suffering together how liberall they
were without repineing harbourers without grudgeing and helpfull without reproacheing and all from hence they had fervent
love amongst them which onely make[s] the practise of mercy
constant and easie.

The next consideracion is how this love comes to be wrought:
Adam in his first estate was a perfect modell of mankinde
in all theire generacions, and in him this love was perfected
in regard of the habit, but Adam Rent in himselfe from his
Creator, rent all his posterity allsoe one from another,
whence it comes that every man is borne with this principle
in him, to love and seeke himselfe onely and thus a man
continueth till Christ comes and takes possession of the soule,
and infuseth another principle love to God and our brother.
And this latter haveing continuall supply from Christ, as the

head and roote by which hee is united get the predominency
in the soule, soe by little and little expells the former
I John 4.7. love cometh of God and every one that loveth is
borne of God, soe that this love is the fruite of the new
birthe, and none can have it but the new Creature, now when
this quallity is thus formed in the soules of men it workes
like the Spirit upon the drie bones Ezek. 37. [7] bone came
to bone, it gathers together the scattered bones of perfect
old man Adam and knitts them into one body againe in Christ
whereby a man is become againe a liveing soule.

The third Consideracion is concerning the execise of this
love, which is twofold, inward or outward, the outward hath
beene handled in the former preface of this discourse, for
unfolding the other wee must take in our way that maxime of
philosophy, Simile simili gaudet or like will to like; . . .
this is the cause why the Lord loves the Creature, soe farr
as it hath any of his Image in it, he loves his elect because
they are like himselfe, he beholds them in his beloved sonne:
soe a mother loves her childe, because shee throughly conceives a resemblance of herselfe in it. Thus it is betweene
the members of Christ, each discernes by the worke of the
spirit his owne Image and resemblance in another, and therefore cannot but love him as he loves himselfe: Now when the
soule which is of a sociable nature findes any thing like to
it selfe, it is like Adam when Eve was brought to him, shee
must have it one with herselfe this is fleshe of my fleshe
(saith shee) and bone of my bone shee conceives a greate
delighte in it, therefore shee desires nearnes and familiarity
with it: shee hath a greate propensity to doe it good and
receives such content in it, as feareing the miscarriage of
her beloved shee bestowes it in the inmost closett of her
heart, shee will not endure that it shall want any good which
shee can give it, if by occasion shee be withdrawne from the
Company of it, shee is still lookeing towards the place where
shee left her beloved, if shee heare it groane shee is with
it presently, if shee finde it sadd and disconsolate shee
sighes and mournes with it, shee hath noe such joy, as to see
her beloved merry and thriveing, if shee see it wronged, shee
cannot beare it without passion, shee setts noe boundes of
her affeccions, nor hath any thought of reward, shee findes
recompence enoughe in the exercise of her love towardes it,
wee may see this Acted to life in Jonathan and David. Jonathan a valiant man endued with the spirit of Christ, soe
soone as hee Discovrs the same spirit in David had presently

his hearte knitt to him by this linement of love, soe that it is said he loved him as his owne soule . . . . other instances might be brought to shewe the nature of this affeccion as of Ruthe and Naomi and many others, but this truthe is cleared enough. If any shall object that it is not possible that love should be bred or upheld without hope of requitall, it is graunted but that is not our cause, for this love is allwayes under reward it never gives, but it allwayes receives with advantage: first, in regard that among the members of the same body, love and affeccion are reciprocall in a most equall and sweete kinde of Commerce. 2ly, in regard of the pleasure and content that the exercise of love carries with it as wee may see in the naturall body the mouth is at all the paines to receive, and mince the foode which serves for the nourishment of all the other partes of the body, yet it hath noe cause to complaine; for first, the other partes send backe by secret passages a due proporcion of the same nourishment in a better forme for the strengthening and comforteing the mouthe. 2ly the labour of the mouthe is accompanied with such pleasure and content as farre exceedes the paines it takes: soe is it in all the labour of love, among Christians, the partie loveing, reapes love againe as was shewed before, which the soule covetts more then all the wealthe in the world . . . . noething yeildes more pleasure and content to the soule then when it findes that which it may love fervently, for to love and live beloved is the soules paradice, both heare and in heaven: In the State of Wedlock there be many comfortes to beare out the troubles of that Condicion; but let such as have tryed the most, say if there be any sweetnes in that Condicion comparable to the exercise of mutuall love.

From the former Consideracions ariseth these Conclusions.

I First, This love among Christians is a reall thing not Imaginarie.

2ly. This love is as absolutely necessary to the being of the body of Christ, as the sinewes and other ligaments of a naturall body are to the being of that body.

3ly. This love is a divine spirituall nature free, active strong Couragious permanent under valueing all things beneathe its propper object, and of all the graces this makes us nearer to resemble the virtues of our heavenly father.

4ly. It restes in the love and wellfare of its beloved, for the full and certaine knowledge of these truthes concerning the nature use, [and] excellency of this grace, that which the holy ghost hath left recorded I. Cor. 13. may give full satisfaccion which is needfull for every true member of this lovely body of the Lord Jesus, to worke upon theire heartes, by prayer meditacion continuall exercise at least of the speciall [power] of this grace till Christ be formed in them and they in him all in eache other knitt together by this bond of love.

It rests now to make some applicacion of this discourse by the present designe which gave the occasion of writeing of it. Herein are 4 things to be propounded: first the persons, 2ly the worke, 3ly the end, 4ly the meanes.

I. For the persons, wee are a Company professing our selves fellow members of Christ, In which respect onely though wee were absent from eache other many miles, and had our imploymentes as farre distant, yet wee ought to account our selves knitt together by this bond of love, and live in the exercise of it, if wee would have comforte of our being in Christ, this was notorious in the practise of the Christians in former times, as is testified of the Waldenses from the mouth of one of the adversaries Aeneas Sylvius, mutuo [solent amare] pene antequam norint, they use to love any of theire owne religion even before they were acquainted with them.

2ly. for the worke we have in hand, it is by a mutuall consent through a speciall overruleing providence, and a more then an ordinary approbation of the Churches of Christ to seeke out a place of Cohabitation and Consorteshipp under a due forme of Government both civill and ecclesiasticall. In such cases as this the care of the publique must oversway all private respects, by which not onely conscience, but meare Civill policy doth binde us; for it is a true rule that perticuler estates cannott subsist in the ruine of the publique.

3ly. The end is to improve our lives to doe more service to the Lord the comforte and encrease of the body of christe whereof wee are members that our selves and posterity may be the better preserved from the Common corrupcions of this evill world to serve the Lord and worke out our Salvacion under the power and purity of his holy Ordinances.

4ly for the meanes whereby this must bee effected, they are 2fold, a Conformity with the worke and end wee aime at, these wee see are extraordinary, therefore wee must not content our selves with usuall ordinary meanes whatsoever wee did or ought to have done when wee lived in England, the same must wee soe and more allsoe where wee goe: That which the most in theire Churches maineteine as a truthe in profession onely, wee must bring into familiar and constant practise, as in this duty of love wee must love brotherly without dissimulation, wee must love one another with a pure hearte fervently wee must beare one anothers burthens, wee must not looke onely on our owne things, but allsoe on the things of our brethren, neither must wee think that the Lord will beare with such faileings at our hands as hee doeth from those among whome wee have lived, and that for 3 Reasons.

I. In regard of the more neare bond of mariage, betweene him and us, wherein he hath taken us to be his after a most strickt and peculiar manner which will make him the more Jealous of our love and obedience soe he tells the people of Israell, you onely have I knowne of all the families of the Earthe therefore will I punishe you for your Transgressions.

2ly, because the lord will be sanctified in them that come neare him. Wee know that there were many that corrupted the service of the Lord some setting upp Alters before his owne, others offering both strange fire and strange Sacrifices allsoe; yet there came noe fire from heaven, or other sudden Judgement upon them as did upon Nadab and Abihu whoe yet wee may thinke did not sinne presumptuously.

3ly When God gives a speciall Commission he lookes to have it stricktly observed in every Article, when hee gave Saule a Commission to destroy Amaleck hee indented with him upon certaine Articles and because hee failed in one of the least, and that upon a faire pretence, it lost him the kingdome, which should have beene his reward, if hee had observed his Commission: Thus stands the cause betweene God and us, wee are entered into Covenant with him for this worke, wee have taken out a Commission, the Lord hath given us leave to drawe our owne Articles wee have professed to enterprise these Accions upon these and these ends, wee have hereupon besought him of favour and blessing: Now if the Lord shall please to heare us, and bring us in peace to the place wee desire, then hath hee ratified this Covenant and sealed our Commission,

[and] will expect a strickt performance of the Articles contained in it, but if wee shall neglect the observacion of these Articles which are the ends wee have propounded, and dissembling with our God, shall fall to embrace this present world and prosecute our carnall intencions, seekeing greate things for our selves and our posterity, the Lord will surely breake out in wrathe against us be revenged of such a perjured people and make us knowe the price of the breache of such a Covenant.

Now the onely way to avoyde this shipwracke and to provide for our posterity is to followe the Counsell of Micah, to doe Justly, to love mercy, to walke humbly with our God, for this end, wee must be knitt together in this worke as one man, wee must entertaine each other in brotherly Affeccion, wee must be willing to abridge our selves of our superfluities, for the supply of others necessities, wee must uphold a familiar Commerce together in all meekenes, gentlenes, patience and liberallity, we must delight in eache other, make others Condicions our owne rejoyce together, mourne together, labour, and suffer together, allwayes haveing before our eyes our Commission and Community in the worke, our Community as members of the same body, soe shall wee keepe the unitie of the spirit in the bond of peace, the Lord will be our God and delight to dwell among us, as his owne people and will commaund a blessing upon us in all our wayes, soe that wee shall see much more of his wisdome power goodnes and truthe then formerly wee have beene acquainted with, wee shall finde that the God of Israell is among us, when tenn of us shall be able to resist a thousand of our enemies, when hee shall make us a prayse and glory, that men shall say of succeeding plantacions: the lord make it like that of New England: for wee must Consider that wee shall be as a Citty upon a Hill, the eies of all people are uppon us; soe that if wee shall deale falsely with our god in this worke wee have undertaken and soe cause him to withdrawe his present help from us, wee shall be made a story and a by-word through the world, wee shall open the mouthes of enemies to speake evill of the wayes of god and all professours for Gods sake; wee shall shame the faces of many of gods worthy servants, and cause theire prayers to be turned into Cursses upon us till wee be consumed out of the good land whether wee are goeing: And to shutt upp this discourse with that exhortacion of Moses that faithfull servant of the Lord in his last farewell to Israell Deut. 30. Beloved there is now sett before us life, and good, deathe and evill in that wee are commaunded this day to love the Lord our God, and to love one another to walke in his wayes and to keepe his Commaundements and his Ordinance, and his lawes, and the Articles of our Covenant with him that wee may live and be multiplyed, and that the Lord our God may blesse us in the land whether wee goe to possesse it: But if our heartes shall turne away soe that wee will not obey, but shall be seduced and worshipp other Gods our pleasures, and proffitts, and serve them; it is propounded unto us this day, wee shall surely perishe out of the good Land whether wee passe over this vast Sea to possesse it;

> Therefore lett us choose life,
> that wee, and our Seede,
> may live; by obeyeing his
> voyce, and cleaveing to him,
> for hee is our life, and
> our prosperity.

The Last Will and Testament of Mr. Robert Keayne

ROBERT KEAYNE

In 1635 Robert Keayne (1595-1656) made the trip to Boston from London, where he had been a prosperous merchant. He soon became a prominent political leader of the newly established New England community. In 1639 he was fined by the General Court for making excessive profits and was admonished by the Church. Fourteen years later and three years before his death in 1656, Keayne wrote his will in which he sought to justify his actions on the grounds that the same ethic which community founders had advocated to help build the model society had led him to err due to his compulsive drive for economic gain. Does Keayne feel it is his duty as a merchant to subordinate himself to the welfare of the community? How does he justify the behavior for which he was condemned? What indication is there that in colonial Massachusetts the temporal and the spiritual were seen as interrelated factors in a Puritan's life?

NOTE-- The spelling of the original has been retained.

. . . When that uncomfortable trouble & censure past upon me in the Court, I was indebted neare or altogeather Thirtie hundreth pounds which was sufficient to have broken the backe of any one man in the Country, though he had beene of a better estate then my selfe & so would have done me if God had not carryed me through it beyond my owne expectation or foresight. Now my care (and according to my dutie if I mistake not) hath beene first to pay these debts, that every man might have his due honestly & without trouble or just complaynt & withall to provide for my family which hath not beene smale nor carryed on with a light or easy charge & yet with no more prodigallitie then what necessitie & a wise Providence hath called for at my hands, considering also the great losses that I have had by sea & land, and had I beene wanting in care for the discharge of either of these I should have borne the burthen & reproach with little support or comfort from the Country, I must have stood upon my owne leggs or fallen into greater straights in respect of men whatsoever my publique good workes or bountie to others might have beene & in such a case they would not have beene so well esteemed but rather taken as fruites of my folly, prodigallity or vayne glory & would not have wanted for variety of censures, according to severall men fancyes & affections, but haveing now gott comfortably through or neare it, all those great debts and charges that I have beene at, so that I begin but now to breath as it were & through the great mercy & unexpected support & assistance of my good God to stand upon my owne leggs & doe but now as it were learne to goe alone I was not in a capacitie to doe it before, though God was pleased to give me a comfortable estate, but as soone as the Lord was pleased to carry me through my ingagements then God putt it into my minde to think what I might doe in acknowledging my thankfullnes towards him not only in words but in some reall actions or deeds, which purpose of myne I hope he will accept of. . . .

It may be some on the other side may marvell (especially some who have beene acquainted with some expressions or purposes of myne in former wills) that I should give away so much of my estate in private legacies & to private uses, which might better have beene spared & to give little or nothing to any publique use for the genn'all good of the country an comonwealth but what I have appropriated to our owne towne of Boston.

To answer which doubt or objection I must acknowledge that it hath beene in my full purpose & resolution ever since God hath given me any comfortable estate to doe good withall not only before I came into New England, but often since to study & endeavor both in my life & at my death to doe what I could doe to helpe on any publique profitable & genn'all good here, and what my thoughts & intents have beene about The Castle for publique defence, The Collidge & schooles for learning, the setting up of a Bridewell or Workehouse for Prisoners Malefactors & some sort of poore people stubborne idle & undutifull youth as children & servants to have beene kept at worke in either for correction or to gett there liveing & some other things that I need not mention, in which things though I could not have done so much as I desired, yet so much I should have done as might have proved an example & incouriagement to others of greater estates & willing mindes to have done more & to have helped to carry them on to more perfection for I have held it a great degree of unthankfullnes to God that when he hath bestowed many blessings & a larg or comfortable outward estate upon a man that he should leave all to his wife & children to advance them only, by makeing them great & rich in the world or to bestow it upon some freinds or kindred that it may be hath no great need of it & to dispose none or very little of it to publique charitable or good workes such as may tend to his glory & good of others in way of a thankfull acknowledgement to him for so great favors. . . .

I did submit to the censure, I payd the fyne to the uttermost, which is not nor hath beene done by many (nore so earnestly required as mine was) though for certaine & not supposed

offences of farr higher nature which I can make good not by
hearesay only but in my owne knowledge, yea offences of the
same kinde & which was so greatly agravated & with such indignation pursued by some, as if no censure could be too great or
too severe, as if I had not beene worthy to have lived upon
the earth, are not only now common almost in every shop & ware-
house but even than & ever since with a higher measure of
excesse, yea even by some of them that were most zealous & had
there hands & tongues deepest in my censure, since of buyers
which they were then, they are turned sellers & pedling merchants themselves so that they are become no offences now nor
worthy questioning nor takeing notice of in others & yet I
would say the great cry of oppression & excessive gaines then
considering the time that they kept the goods bought in their
hands, before they could or would pay & the quallity or rather
the business of there pay for kinde, yea contrary to theire
owne promisses in steed of gaynes there was apparent losse
without any gaynes to the seller, & the oppression lay justly
& truely on the buyers hand rather then on the seller, but then
the country being all buyers and few sellers though it would
not be seene on that syde then, for if the Lyon will say the
Lambe is a foxe, it must be so, the lambe must be content to
leave it, but now the country hath gott better experience in
merchandize, and they have soundly payd for there experience
since, so that it is now & was many years agoe become a common
proverb amongst the most buyers that knew those times, that my
goods & prizes were cheape peniworths in comparison of what hath
beene taken since & especially the prizes of these times, yet
I have borne this patiently & without disturbance or troubling
the Court with any petitions for remission or abatement of the
fyne, though I have beene advised by many friends yea & some
of the same court so to doe. . . .

. . . were it possible for me to know it [my vindication]
certainely before I dye (though it be not for the love of the
money, nor for addition to my estate by it, though it was a
considerable sume about Eighty pounds as I remember) it would
much ease & refresh my spirit in respect of the equity of it.
. . .

I did not then nor dare not now goe about to justify all my
actions. I know God is righteous & doth all upon just grounds,
though men may mistake in there grounds & proceedings, Counsell have erred & Courts may err & a faction may be too hard
& outvote the better or more discerning part, I know the

errors of my life, the faylings in my trade & otherwise have
beene many, therefor from God it was most just, though it had
beene much more severe I dare not so open my mouth against it,
nor never did as I remember but justify him, yet I dare not
say nor did I ever thinke (as farr as I can call to minde) that
the Censure was just & righteous from men, was the price of a
Bridle, not for takeing but only asking 2s for it which cost
here 20d such a haynous sine, which have since beene comonly
sould & are still for 2s 6d & 3s or more, though worse in
kinde, was the selling of 2 or 3 dozine of great gold buttons
for 2s 10d per dozine that cost 2s 2d ready money in London &
bought at the best hand (such a haynous sin) as I showed to
many by my Invoyce (though I could not at that instant finde
it when the Court desired to see it) & since was confirmed by
spetiall testimony from London & yet the buttons not payd for
when the complaynt was made, nor I thinke not yet, neither did
the complaynt come from him that bought & owed them nor with
his knowledge or consent as he hath since affirmed, but meerly
from the spleene & envy of another, whome it did nothing con-
cerne, was this so great an offence: Indeed that it might be
made so some out of there ignorance would needs say they were
coper & not worth 9d p dozine but these were weake grounds to
passe heavie censures upon, was the selling of 6d nayles for
8d p lb. & 8d nayles for 10d p lb. such a crying & oppressing
sine though as I remember it was about two years before he
that bought them payd me for them (& not payd for if I forgot
not) when he made that quarreling exception & unrighteous
complaynt in the Court against me (he then being of the Court
himselfe) as if I altered & corrupted my booke in adding more
to the prize than I had set downe, for them at first delivery,
which if I had set downe 8d for that after 2 years forbearance,
which I would have sould for 7d if he had payd me presently,
I thinke it had beene a more honest act in me than it was in
him that promissed or at least pretended to pay me presently
that he might git them at a lower prize than a man could well
live upon & when he had gott my goods into his hands to keepe
me 2 or 3 yeares without my money. . . .

. . . for my owne part as I did ever thinke it an ungodly act
in him so I doe thinke in my conscience that it had beene
more just in the Court to have censured him then me for this
thinge though this was the cheifest crime alleadged & most
powerfully carryed against me & other things drawne in to
make this the more probable & to helpe to make up a censure
as some farthing skeanes of thread & c. but the truth of the

thinge was this, this man sent unto me for 2 or three thousand of 6d nayles, I sent to him a bagg full of that sort just as them came to me from Mr. Ffoots in London. never opened nor altered by me, these I entered into my booke at 8d p lb. thinking he would have payd me in a very short time, it fell out that these nayles proved somewhat to little for his worke, he sent them againe & desired me to let him have bigger for them, I tooke them & sent him a bagg of 8d nayles of the same quantity at 10d p lb. now because I was loth to alter my booke & to make a new charge I only altered the figures in my booke & made the figure of 6 a figure of 8 for 8d nayles & the figure of 8 that before stood for 8d a lb. I made 10d. . . .

Now I leave it to the world to judge, or any impartiall man, or any that hath understanding in trade whether this was a just offence or so crying a sine that I had such cause to be so penitent for (this being the cheife & pressed on with so great agravation by my opposers) except it should be that my actions innocent in themselves were so misconstered & I knew not how to helpe my selfe, especially considering it was no oppresseing prize but usuall with others at that time to sell the like so & since for almost halfe as much more frequently, as I thinke all know & yet both given & taken without exception, or at least without publique complaint, yea & the same gentleman himself, since he hath turned Marcant & Trader seemes to have lost his former tendernes of conscience that he had when he was a buyer & not to be so scrupelous in his owne gaines. . . .

It is true that in any thinge wherein I might justly take shame or sorrow to my selfe God inclyned my heart not to withstand it for he that hydes his sines shall not prosper, but he that confesseth & forsaketh them shall finde mercy, in many this wee sinne all & who can say his heart is cleane, yet for the chiefe of the things that was most urged against me in Court & for which the sentence past against me, as the gould buttons, the bridle, the nayles, the falcyfying of my booke I did justify & stand to maintaine that they was evident mistakes & that I was wronged about them. . . . here I had no cause of penetency or confession of guilt except it was for that I had beene so used & reproached about them against all equitie, but if they should have cast me out of the church 20 times for this I should have chosen it rather then to have confessed my selfe guilty, for the satisfaction of any, wherein I knew my selfe (better then any else did) to be innocent.

Now haveing thus cleared my intentions plainely & really in all things as farr as I can remember which hath occasioned my will to be farr larger then I either intended or desired, there are 2 or 3 objections which doth lye in the way which being answered or removed I shall draw to an end. . . .

The objections are these

Ffirst if I value my estate to be worth 4000lb or thereabouts, how could I get such an estate with a good conscience or without oppression in my calling, seeing it is knowne to some that I had no portion from my parents or friends to begin the world withal which if none did know of I am bound to acknowledge that all may be attributed to the free mercy & kindnes of God alone who raiseth up & pulleth downe as he pleaseth. . . .

To which I answere I have now traded for myselfe about 40 or 50 yeares & through the favor of God though I had very little at first to begin with yet I had good creditt and good esteeme & respect in the place where I lived soe that I did ever drive a great trade not only since I came hither but especially in England

Now to gett 4000lb. in 40 or 50 yeares is not 100lb. a yeare cleare gaines one yeare with another which wee account to be no great matter in driving but a smale trade in an industrious & provident man especially where there is no great trusting of chapmen or giveing of creditt which usually is subject to great hazards & losses & a tradsman or marchant that hath a full trade may gett a 100lb. a yeare above his expences & a great deale more very honestly without hurting his owne conscience or wronging those that he deales with at all

Since I came into New England, it is well knowne to some that I brought over with me two or 300lb. in good estate of my owne & I have beene here in a way of trade & marchandize besides ffarming now this 18 yeares & he that hath a stocke of his owne of 2 or 3000 lb. to manage in a way of trade I thinke he may very lawfully & honestly gett 200lb. a yeare by it cleare if his expences be not very great & large, and yet with turning & managing this stocke of my owne (besides what goodes have beene sent me from England by other men to a considerable value from time to time) I have not cleared neare 100lb. a yeare above my expences since I came hither which is not 5lb.

p cent cleare gaines & yet I have beene no p'digall spender as I have beene no niggardly sparer in things needfull, as the accountt of my dayly & weekely expences will testifie or me when those bookes come to be viewed over. . . . though I have undergone many censures since I came hither according to mens uncharitable & various apprehentions some looking at me as an opresser in trading & getting unconsconably by what I sould & others as covetous & niggardly in housekeeping & not so liberall & bountifull as I should be (which how those two contraryes can justly be charged upon me & yet have increased my estate noe more in so long a time I yet see not) except it be by such as care not what they say of other men though never so false so they may lay others under reproach & magnifie themselves & theire wayes by disgracing of others but it is nothing for me to be judged of men, I have laboured to beare it with patience & to approve my hearte & wayes to God that judgeth righteously yet these things hath made me the more willing to cleare myselfe in all matteriall things in this my last testament though it be somewhat contrary to the nature of a will yet I am willing to leave this upon publique record as a just defence for my selfe knowing that a will wilbe read & made knowne & may be perused searched or coppied out by any when other writings wilbe more hid & obscured. . . .

But some may further object if I doe value my estate at so much as before mentioned how could I deale honestly in suffering myselfe to be valued in rated to the Country but after a 1000lb. estate at most or some times lesse.

To which I answer first that I doe not thinke a man is bound in conscience to make knowne his whole estate & suffer himselfe to be valued to the uttermost extent thereof, if he can honestly prevent it, it is not so in any nation in the world that I have heard or read of (except in case of great extremitie by an enemy in the Country or at the walls when all is in hazard to be lost) but quite contrary. In England I have knowne Knights, Aldermen, Marchants worth many thousands & have had lands worth some hundred pounds a yeare knowne, & yet to subsides & publique charges are not valued at halfe their estates & many reasons may be given why it should not be otherwise. . . .

THE GREAT AWAKENING 2

Some Thoughts Concerning the Present Revival of Religion in New England

JONATHAN EDWARDS

Jonathan Edwards (1704-1758), one of the greatest theologians in American history, was a key participant in the Great Awakening. His involvement in the Awakening began in 1734 with a series of sermons he delivered against the growing popularity of Arminianism. These sermons, the leading one of which was concerned with the doctrine of justification by faith, seem to have sparked the Northampton revival in the mid-1730's. In the 1740's much of Edwards' theological writing sought to encourage and defend the Awakening. The following excerpt was taken from a treatise which appeared in the fourth volume of Sereno E. Dwight's edited series of 1830, <u>The Works of President Edwards with a Memoir of His Life</u>. What answers does Edwards have for those who criticize the Awakening? How does Edwards distinguish between the good and bad effects of the Awakening? To what does Edwards point as being the real achievement of the Awakening? How did he describe what he believed would be the new role of America in the future?

I. Some make Philosophy, instead of the holy scriptures, their rule of judging of this work; particularly the philosophical notions they entertain of the nature of the soul, its faculties and affections. Some are ready to say, "There is but little sober solid religion in this work; it is little else but flash and noise. Religion now all runs out into transports and high flights of passions and affections." In their philosophy, the affections of the soul are something diverse from the will, and not appertaining to the noblest part of the soul. They are ranked among the meanest principles that belong to men as partaking of animal nature, and what he has in common with the brute creation, rather than anything whereby he is conformed to angels and pure spirits. And though they acknowledge that a good use may be made of the affections in religion, yet they suppose that the substantial part of religion does not consist in them, but that they are something adventitious and accidental in Christianity. . . .

If we take the scriptures for our rule, then the greater and higher our exercises of love to God, delight and complacency in him, desires and longings after him, delight in his children, love to mankind, brokenness of heart, abhorrence of sin, and self-abhorrence for it; the more we have of the peace of God which passeth all understanding, and joy in the Holy Ghost, unspeakable and full of glory: the higher our admiring thoughts of God, exulting and glorying in him; so much higher is Christ's religion, or that virtue which he and his apostles taught, raised in the soul.

It is a stumbling to some, that religious affections should seem to be so powerful, or that they should be so violent (as they express it) in some persons. They are therefore ready to doubt whether it can be the Spirit of God; or whether this vehemence be not rather a sign of the operation of an evil spirit. But why should such a doubt arise? What is represented in scripture as more powerful in its effects than the Spirit of God? which is therefore called "the power of the Highest," . . . So the Spirit is represented by a mighty wind, and by fire, things most powerful in their operation.

II. Many are guilty of not taking the holy scriptures as a sufficient and whole rule, whereby to judge of this work.-- They judge by those things which the scripture does not give as any signs or marks whereby to judge one way or the other. viz. the effects that religious exercises and affections of mind have upon the body. Scripture rules respect the state of the mind, moral conduct, and voluntary behavior; and not the physical state of the body. The design of the scripture is to teach us divinity, and not physic and anatomy. Ministers are made the watchmen of men's souls, and not their bodies; and therefore the great rule which God has committed into their hands, is to make them divines, and not physicians. . . . And therefore those ministers of Christ, and overseers of souls, who are full of concern about the involuntary motions of the fluids and solids of men's bodies, and who from thence are full of doubts and suspicions of the cause--when nothing appears but that the state and frame of their minds and their voluntary behaviour is good, and agreeable to God's word--go out of the place that Christ has set them in, and leave their proper business, as much as if they should undertake to tell who are under the influence of the Spirit by their looks or their gait. . . .

III. Another thing that some make their rule to judge of this work by, instead of the holy scriptures, is <u>history</u>, or former observation. Herein they err two ways:

First, If there be any thing extraordinary in the circumstances of this work, which was not observed in former times, theirs is a rule to reject this work which God has not given them, and they limit God, where he has not limited himself. And this is especially unreasonable in this case: For whosoever has well weighed the wonderful and mysterious methods of divine wisdom is carrying on the work of the new creation . . . may easily observe that it has all along been God's manner to open new scenes, and to bring forth to view things new and wonderful--such as eye had not seen, nor ear heard, nor entered into the heart of man or angels--to the astonishment of heaven and earth, not only in the revelations he makes of his mind and will, but also into the works of his hands. As the old creation was carried on through six days, and appeared all complete, settled in a state of rest on the seventh; so the new creation, which is immensely the greatest and most glorious work, is carried on in a gradual progress, from the fall of man to the consummation of all things. . . .

Secondly, Another way that some err in making history and former observation their rule instead of the holy scripture, is in comparing some external, accidental circumstances of this work, with what has appeared sometimes in enthusiasts.

They find an agreement in some such things, and so they reject the whole work, or at least the substance of it, concluding it to be enthusiasm. Great use has been made to this purpose of many things that are found amongst the Quakers; however totally and essentially different in its nature this work is, and the principles upon which it is built, from the whole religion of the Quakers. . . .

IV. I wold propose it to be considered, whether or no some, instead of making the scriptures their only rule to judge of this work, do not make their own experience the rule, and reject such and such things as are now professed and experienced, because they themselves never felt them. Are there not many, who, chiefly on this ground, have entertained and vented suspicions, if not peremptory condemnations, of those extreme terrors, and those great, sudden, and extraordinary discoveries of the glorious perfections of God, and of the beauty and love of Christ? Have they not condemned such vehement affections, such high transports of love and joy, such pity and distress for the souls of others, and exercises of mind that have great effects, merely, or chiefly, because they knew nothing about them by experience? Persons are very ready to be suspicious of what they have not felt themselves. It is to be feared that many good men have been guilty of this error: which however does not make it the less unreasonable. . . .

Another foundation error of those who reject this work, is, their not duly distinguishing the good from the bad, and very unjustly judging of the whole by a part; and so rejecting the work in general, or in the main substance of it, for the sake of some accidental evil in it. . . .

A great deal of noise and tumult, confusion and uproar, darkness mixed with light, and evil with good, is always to be expected in the beginning of something very glorious in the state of things in human society, or the church of God. After nature has long been shut up in a cold dead state, when the sun returns in the spring, there is, together with the increase of the light and heat of the sun, very tempestuous weather, before all is settled calm and serene, and all nature rejoices in its bloom and beauty. It is in the new creation as it was in the old: the Spirit of God first moved upon the face of the waters, which was an occasion of great uproar and tumult. Things were then gradually brought to a settled state, till at length all stood forth in that beautiful peaceful

order, when the heavens and the earth were finished, and
God saw every thing that he had made, and behold it was very
good. When God is about to bring to pass something great and
glorious in the world, nature is in a ferment and struggle,
and the world as it were in travail. . . .

Whatever imprudences there have been, and whatever sinful
irregularities; whatever vehemence of the passions, and heats
of the imagination, transports and ecstacies; whatever error
in judgment, and indiscreet zeal; and whatever outcries,
faintings, and agitations of body; yet, it is manifest and
notorious, that there has been of late a very uncommon influence upon the minds of a great part of the inhabitants of
New-England, attended with the best effects. . . . Multitudes
in all parts of the land, of vain, thoughtless, regardless
persons, are quite changed, and become serious and considerate.
There is a vast increase of concern for the salvation of the
precious soul, and of that inquiry, "What shall I do to be
saved?" . . . They have also been awakened to a sense of the
shortness and uncertainty of life, and the reality of another
world and future judgment, and of the necessity of an interest
in Christ. They are more afraid of sin, more careful and
inquisitive that they may know what is contrary to the mind
and will of God, that they may avoid it, and what he requires
of them, that they may do it, more careful to guard against
temptations, more watchful over their own hearts, earnestly
desirous of knowing, and of being diligent in the use of the
means that God has appointed in his word, in order to salvation. Many very stupid, senseless sinners, and persons of
a vain mind, have been greatly awakened.

There is a strange alteration almost all over New-England
amongst young people: by a powerful invisible influence
on their minds, they have been brought to forsake, in a
general way, as it were at once, those things of which they
were extremely fond, and in which they seemed to place the
happiness of their lives, and which nothing before could
induce them to forsake; as their frolicking, vain company-
keeping, night-walking, their mirth and jollity, their
impure language, and lewd songs. . . . It is astonishing to
see the alteration there is in some towns, where before
there was but little appearance of religion, or any thing
but vice and vanity. And now they are transformed into
another sort of people; their former vain, worldly, and
vicious conversation and dispositions seem to be forsaken,

and they are, as it were, gone over to a new world. Their thoughts, their talk, and their concern, affections and inquiries, are now about the favour of God, an interest in Christ, a renewed sanctified heart, and a spiritual blessedness, acceptance, and happiness in a future world.

Now, through the greater part of New-England, the holy Bible is in much greater esteem and use than before. . . . The Lord's day is more religiously and strictly observed. And much has been lately done at making up differences, confessing faults one to another, and making restitution: probably more within two years, than was done in thirty years before. It has been undoubtedly so in many places. And surprising has been the power of this spirit in many instances, to destroy old grudges, to make up long continued breaches, and to bring those who seemed to be in a confirmed irreconcilable alienation, to embrace each other in a sincere and entire amity. . . .

Multitudes in New-England have lately been brought to a new and great conviction of the truth and certainty of the things of the gospel; to a firm persuasion that Christ Jesus is the son of God, and the great and only Saviour of the world, and that the great doctrines of the gospel touching reconciliation by his blood, and acceptance in his righteousness, and eternal life and salvation through him, are matters of undoubted truth. . . .

And, under the influences of this work, there have been many of the remains of those wretched people and dregs of mankind, the poor Indians, that seemed to be next to a state of brutality, and with whom, till now, it seemed to be to little more purpose to use endeavours for their instruction and awakening, than with the beasts. Their minds have now been strangely opened to receive instruction, and been deeply affected with the concerns of their precious souls; they have reformed their lives, and forsaken their former stupid, barbarous and brutish way of living; and particularly that sin to which they have been so exceediingly addicted, their drunkenness. Many of them to appearance brought truly and greatly to delight in the things of God, and to have their souls very much engaged and entertained with the great things of the gospel. Any many of the poor Negroes also have been in like manner wrought upon and changed. Very many little children have been remarkably enlightened, and their hearts wonderfully affected and enlarged, and their mouths opened, expressing themselves in a manner far beyond their years, and to the just astonishment of those who have heard them. Some of them for many months, have been greatly and delightfully affected with the glory of divine things, and the excellency and love of the Redeemer, with their hearts greatly filled with love to, and joy in him; and they have continued to be serious and pious in their behaviour. . . .

It is not unlikely that this work of God's Spirit, so extraordinary and wonderful, is the dawning, or at least a prelude of that glorious work of God, so often foretold in scripture, which, in the progress and issue of it, shall renew the world of mankind. If we consider how long since the things foretold as what should precede this great event, have been accomplished; and how long this event has been expected by the church of God, and thought to be nigh by the most eminent men of God, in the church; and withal consider what the state of things now is, and has for a considerable time been, in the church of God, and the world of mankind; we cannot reasonably think otherwise, than that the beginning of this great work of God must be near. And there are many things that make it probable that his work will begin in America.--It is signified that it shall begin in some very remote part of the world, with which other parts have no communication but by navigation, in Isa. lx. 9. "Surely the isles shall wait for me, and the ships of Tarshish first, to bring my sons from far." It is exceeding manifest that this chapter is a prophecy of the prosperity of the church, in its most glorious state on earth, in the latter days; and I cannot think that any thing else can be here intended but America by the isles that are far off, from whence the first-born sons of that glorious day shall be brought. Indeed, by <u>the isles</u>, in prophecies of gospel-times, is very often meant Europe. . . . But this prophecy cannot have respect to the conversion of Europe, in the time of that great work of God, in the primitive ages of the Christian church; for it was not fulfilled then. The isles and ships of Tarshish, thus understood, did not wait for God first; that glorious work did not begin in Europe, but in Jerusalem, and had for a considerable time been very wonderfully carried on in Asia, before it reached Europe. An as it is not <u>that</u> work of God which is chiefly intended in this chapter, but some more glorious work that should be in the latter ages of the Christian church; therefore, some other part of the world is here intended by the isles, that should be, as Europe then was, far separated from that part of the world where the church had before been, and with which it can have no communication but by the ships of Tarshish. And what is chiefly intended is not the British isles, nor any isles near the other continent; they are spoken of as at a great distance from that part of the world where the church had till then been. This prophecy therefore seems plainly to point out America, as the first-fruits of that glorious day.

God has made as it were two worlds here below, two great habitable continents, far separated one from the other: The latter is as it were now but newly created; it has been, till of late, wholly the possession of Satan, the church of God having never been in it, as it has been in the other continent, from the beginning of the world. This new world is probably now discovered, that the new and most glorious state of God's church on earth might commence there; that God might in it begin a new world in a spiritual respect, when he creates the <u>new heavens</u> and <u>new earth</u>.

God has already put that honour upon the other continent, that Christ was born there literally, and there made the "purchase of redemption." So, as Providence observes a kind of equal distribution of things, it is not unlikely that the great spiritual birth of Christ, and the most glorious "application of redemption," is to begin in this. . . .

The other continent hath slain Christ, and has from age to age shed the blood of saints and martyrs of Jesus, and has often been as it were, deluged with the church's blood.-- God has, therefore, probably reserved the honour of building the glorious temple to the daughter that has not shed so much blood, when those times of the peace, prosperity and glory of the church, typified by the reign of Solomon, shall commence. . . .

The old continent has been the source and original of mankind in several respects. The first parents of mankind dwelt there; and there dwelt Noah and his sons; there the second Adam was born, and crucified, and raised again: And it is probable that, in some measure to balance these things, the most glorious renovation of the world shall originate from the new continent, and the church of God in that respect be from hence. And so it is probable that will come to pass in spirituals, which has taken place in temporals, with respect to America: that whereas, till of late, the world was supplied with its silver, and gold, and earthly treasures from the old continent, now it is supplied chiefly from the new; so the course of things in spiritual respects will be in like manner turned.--And it is worthy to be noted, that America was discovered about the time of the reformation, or but little before: Which reformation was the first thing that God did towards the glorious renovation of the world, after it had sunk into the depths of darkness and ruin, under the great anti-christian apostacy. So that, as soon as this new world stands forth in view, God presently goes about doing some great thing in order to make way for the introduction of the church's latter-day glory--which is to have its first seat in, and is to take its rise from that new world.

It is agreeable to God's manner, when he accomplishes any glorious work in the world, in order to introduce a new and more excellent state of his church, to begin where no foundation had been already laid, that the power of God might be the more conspicuous; that the work might appear to be entirely God's, and be more manifestly a creation out of nothing. . . . When God is about to turn the earth into a paridise, he does not begin his work where there is some good growth already, but in the wilderness, where nothing grows, and nothing is to be seen but dry sand and barren rocks; that the light may shine out of darkness, the world be replenished from emptiness, and the earth watered by springs from a droughty desert: agreeable to many prophecies of scripture. . . . Now as when God is about to do some great work for his church, his manner is to begin at the lower end; so, when he is about to renew the whole habitable earth, it is probable that he will begin in this utmost, meanest, youngest and weakest part of it, where the church of God has been planted last of all: and so the first shall be last, and the last first: and that will be fulfilled in an eminent manner in Isa. xxiv. 19. "From the uttermost part of the earth have we heard songs, even glory to the righteous." . . .

. . . And if we may suppose that this glorious work of God shall begin in any part of America, I think, if we consider the circumstances of the settlement of New-England, it must needs appear the most likely, of all American colonies, to be the place whence this work shall principally take its rise. And, if these things be so, it gives more abundant reason to hope that what is now seen in America, and especially in New-England, may prove the dawn of that glorious day; and the very uncommon and wonderful circumstances and events of this work, seem to me strongly to argue that God intends it as the beginning or forerunner of something vastly great.

I have thus long insisted on this point, because, if these things are so, it greatly manifests how much it behoves us to encourage and promote this work, and how dangerous it will be to forbear so doing. It is very dangerous for God's professing people to lie still, and not to come to the help of the Lord, whenever he remarkably pours out his Spirit, to carry on the work of redemption in the application of it; but above all, when he comes forth to introduce that happy day of God's power and salvation, so often spoken of. . . .

Seasonable Thoughts on the State of Religion in New England

CHARLES CHAUNCY

Charles Chauncy (1705-1787), a Boston minister, was the most formidable opponent Jonathan Edwards faced in the debate over the methods and accomplishments of the Great Awakening. In the following selection from Chauncy's Seasonable Thoughts on the State of Religion in New England published in 1743 in Boston, Chauncy disputes Edwards' defense of the Awakening in a point by point denunciation of the revival as a resurgence of heresies that had consumed the early Puritans. Chauncy's religious Universalism, an expression of eighteenth century Enlightenment thinking, was particularly critical of the appeal to emotion in revivalism. What was Chauncy's evaluation of the Great Awakening? What evidence is there that Chauncy was writing in direct response to what Edwards had written the previous year? What did Chauncy believe was the answer to the problems of society in the middle of the eighteenth century?

I have hitherto considered <u>Ministers</u> as the Persons, more especially obliged to discountenance the bad Things, prevailing in the Land; and now go on to observe.

That this is the Duty of <u>all in general</u>. Not that I would put any upon acting out of their <u>proper Sphere</u>. This would tend rather to Confusion than Reformation.--Good Order is the Strength and Beauty of the World.--The Prosperity both of <u>Church</u> and <u>State</u> depends very much upon it. And can there be <u>Order</u>, where Men transgress the Limits of their Station, and intermeddle in the Business of others? So far from it, that the only effectual Method, under GOD, for the Redress of <u>general Evils</u>, is, for <u>every one</u> to be faithful, in doing what is <u>proper</u> for him in his <u>own Place</u>: And even all may <u>properly</u> bear a Part, in <u>rectifying the Disorders</u> of this Kind, at this Day.

Civil Rulers may do a great deal, not only by their <u>good Example</u>, but a wise Use of their Authority, in their various Places, for the Suppression of every Thing hurtful to Society, and the Encouragement of whatever has a Tendency to make Men happy in the Enjoyment of their Rights, whether <u>natural</u> or Christian. And herein chiefly lies, (as I humbly conceive) a Duty of Rulers, at this Day. 'This true, as <u>private Men</u>, they are under the same Obligations with others, to make their Acknowledgments to CHRIST; and doubtless, if HE was visibly and externally (according to the Custom among <u>Kings</u> and <u>Governors</u>) to make his solemn Entry into the Land, as their SAVIOUR and LORD, "it would be expected they should, as <u>public Officers</u>, make their Appearance, and attend him as their <u>Sovereign</u> with sutable Congratulations, and Manifestations of Respect and Loyalty; and if they should stand at a Distance, it would be much more taken Notice of, and awaken

in Displeasure much more, than such a Behaviour in the
common People. But the Case is widely different, where his
supposed Entry is in this Sense, as that there is a great
Variety of Sentiments about it, among the best Sort of Men,
of all Ranks and Conditions: Nor does it appear to me, when
the Case is thus circumstanc'd, that it is either the Duty
of Rulers, or would be Wisdom in them, by any authoritative
Acts to determine, whose Sentiments were the most agreeable
to Truth. And as to their Appointment of Days of Thanksgiving,
or fasting, on this Account, there must be an Impropriety in
it, so long as that Complaint of God against the Jews is to
be seen in the Bible, Behold ye fast for Strife and Debate!
Their Duty rather lies in keeping Peace between those, who
unhappily differ in their Thoughts about the State of our
religious Affairs: And their Care in this Matter ought to
be impartial. Each Party, without Favour or Affection,
should be equally restrain'd from Out-rage and Insult. Those,
who may think themselves Friends to a Work of GOD, should
be protected in the Exercise of all their just Rights, whether
as Men, or Christians: So on the other Hand, those who may
be Enemies to Error and Confusion, have the same Claim to be
protected.

And if, on either Side, they invade the Rights of others, or
throw out Slander, at Random, to the Hurt of their Neighbour's
Reputation and Usefulness, and the bringing forward a State
of Tumult and Disorder; I see not but the civil Arm may justly
be stretched forth for the Chastisement of such Persons; and
this, though their Abuses should be offered in the Name of
the LORD, or under the Pretext of the most flaming Zeal for
the REDEEMER'S Honour, and serving the Interest of his Kingdom: For it ought always to be accounted an Aggravation of
Sin of Slander, rather than an Excuse for it, its being committed under the Cloak of Religion, and Pretence for the
Glory of GOD; as it will, under these Circumstances, be of
more pernicious Tendency. I am far from thinking, that any
Man ought to suffer, either for his religious Principles, or
Conduct arising from them, while he is no Disturber of the
civil Peace; but when Men, under the Notion of appearing
zealous for GOD and his Truths, insult their Betters, vilify
their Neighbours, and spirit People to Strife and Faction,
I know of no Persons more sutable to be taken in Hand by
Authority: And if they suffer 'tis for their own Follies;
nor can they reasonably blame any Body but themselves: Nor
am I asham'd, or afraid, to profess it as my Opinion, that

38

it would probably have been of good Service, if those, in these Times, who have been publickly and out-ragiously reviled, had, by their Complaints, put it properly in the <u>Magistrates</u> Power, to restrain some Men's <u>Tongues</u> with <u>Bit</u> and <u>Bridle</u>.

<u>Private Christians</u> also, of all Ranks and Conditions, may do something towards the Suppression of these <u>Errors</u>, by mourning before the LORD the Dishonour which has hereby been reflected on the Name of CHRIST, and Injury done to Souls; by being much in Prayer to GOD for the out-pouring of his SPIRIT, in all desirable Influences of Light, and Love, and Peace; by taking good Heed that they ben't themselves drawn aside, avoiding to this End, the Company and familiar Converse of those, who, by <u>good Words</u> and <u>fair Speeches</u>, might be apt to deceive their Hearts, but especially an Attendance on religious Exercises, where the <u>Churches</u> and <u>Ministry</u> are freely declaimed against by those who have gone out from them, under the vain Pretence of being more holy than they; and in fine, by a faithful Performance of those Duties, which arise from the various Relations they sustain towards each other: As thus, if they are <u>Children</u>, by hearkening to the Advice of their <u>Parents</u>, by counseling, reproving, warning, restraining, and commanding their <u>Children</u>, as there may be Occasion: If they are <u>Servants</u>, by pleasing their <u>Masters</u> well in all Things, not defrauding them of their <u>Time</u> or Labour, but accounting them worthy of all Honour, that the Name of GOD be not blasphemed; and, if they are <u>Master</u>, not only by providing for their <u>Servants</u> Things honest and good, but by keeping them within the Rules of Order and Decorum, not suffering them to neglect the Religion of the Family at home, under Pretence of carrying it on elsewhere; especially, when they continue abroad 'till late in the Night, and so as to unfit themselves for the Services of the following Day.

In these, and such like Ways, <u>all</u> may exert themselves in making a Stand against the Progress of Error: And all are oblig'd to do so; and for this Reason, among others I han't Room to mention, because the <u>last Days</u> are particularly mark'd in the <u>Prophecies of Scripture</u>, as the Times wherein may be expected, the Rise of SEDUCERS. . . .

'This true, we read of the coming on of a <u>glorious State</u> of Things in the LAST DAYS: Nor will the <u>Vision fail</u>.--We may rely upon it, the Prophesies, foretelling the Glory of the REDEEMER'S Kingdom will have their Accomplishment to the making this Earth of Paradise, in Compare with what it now is. But for the particular Time when this will be, it is not for us to know it, the Father having put it in his own Power: And whoever pretend to such Knowledge, they are wise above what is written; and tho' they may think they know much, they really know nothing as to this Matter.

It may be suggested, that "the Work of GOD'S SPIRIT that is so extraordinary and wonderful, is the dawning, or at lest, a Prelude of that glorious Work of GOD, so often foretold in Scripture, which, in the Progress and Issue of it, shall renew the whole world." But what are such Suggestions, but the Fruit of Imagination? Or at best, undertain Conjecture? And can any good End be answered in endeavouring, upon Evidence absolutely precarious, to instill into the Minds of People a Notion of the millenium State, as what is now going to be introduced; yea, and of AMERICA, as that Part of the World, which is pointed out in the Revelations of GOD for the Place, where this glorious Scene of Things, "will, probably, first begin?" How often, at other Times, and in other Places, has the Conceit been propagated among People, as if the Prophecies touching the Kingdom of CHRIST, in the latter Days, were NOW to receive their Accomplishment? And what has been the Effect, but their running wild? So it was in GERMANY, in the Beginning of the Reformation. The extraordinary and wonderful Things in that Day, were look'd upon by the Men then thought to be most under the SPIRIT'S immediate Direction, as "the Dawning of that glorious Work of GOD, which should renew the whole World;" and the Imagination of the Multitude being fired with this Notion, they were soon persuaded, that the Saints were now to reign on Earth, and the Dominion to be given into their Hands: And it was under the Influence of this vain Conceit, (in which they were strengthened by Visions, Raptures and Revelations) that they took up Arms against the lawful Authority, and were destroy'd, at one Time and another, to the Number of an HUNDRED THOUSAND. . . .

And 'tis well known, that this same Pretence of the near Approach of the MILLENIUM, the promised Kingdom of the MESSIAH, was the Foundation-Error of the French Prophets, and those in their Way, no longer ago than the Beginning of this Century: And so infatuated were they at last, as to publish it to the World, that the glorious Times they spake of, <u>would be manifest over the whole Earth, within the Term of THREE YEARS.</u> And what Set of Men have ever yet appear'd in the Christian World, whose Imaginations have been thorowly warmed, but they have, at length, wrought themselves up to a <u>full Assurance</u>, that NOW was the Time for the Accomplishment of the Scriptures, and the Creation of the <u>new Heavens</u>, and the <u>new Earth</u>? No one Thing have they more unitedly concurred in, to their own shameful Disappointment, and the doing unspeakable Damage to the Interest of Religion.--A sufficient Warning, one would think, to keep Men modest; and restrain them from Endeavours to lead People into a Belief of that, of which they have no sufficient <u>Evidence</u>; and in which, they may be deceived by their vain <u>Imaginations</u>, as Hundreds and Thousands have been before them.

There are unquestionably many Prophecies concerning CHRIST, and the <u>Glory of his Kingdom</u>, still to be fulfilled; and it may be of good Service to labour to beget in People a Faith in these Things; or, if they have Faith, to quicken and strengthen it: But it can answer no good End to lead People into the Belief of any <u>particular</u> Time, as the Time <u>appointed</u> of GOD for the Accomplishment of these Purposes of his Mercy; because this is one of those Matters, his Wisdom has thought fit to keep conceal'd from the Knowledge of Man. Our own Faith therefore upon this Head can be founded only on <u>Conjecture</u>; and as 'tis only the like <u>blind Faith</u> we can convey to others, we should be cautious, lest their Conduct should be agreeable to their Faith. When they have imbib'd from us the Thought, as if the glorious Things, spoken of in Scripture, were to come forward in their Day, they will be apt (as has often been the Case) to be impatient, and from their <u>Officiousness</u> in tendring their Help where it is not needed, to disserve the Interest of the Redeemer.

The Testimony of Harvard College Against George Whitefield

The Great Awakening gave birth to sharp hostilities in many parts of the colonies. The center of many of these controversies was the preacher, George Whitefield, who more than any other person was responsible for fanning the revival sparks started by others into a single flame. The religious cleavages which had emerged in New England, as seen in Edwards' and Chauncy's writings, intensified when Whitefield denounced the spiritual condition of Harvard College in terms which caused the school to oppose his planned return from England to America in 1744. The 1744 Harvard pamphlet which follows is one of the clearest criticisms leveled against the Great Awakening. Upon what bases did Harvard College oppose the ministry of George Whitefield among the people of New England? What evidence is there that there was definite tension between the mind and heart in eighteenth century New England? Earlier Whitefield had written, "As for the Universities, I believe it may be said, their Light is become Darkness." How might this statement have sparked the response by Harvard?

In regard of the Danger which we apprehend the People and Churches of this Land are in, on the Account of the Rev. Mr. George Whitefield, we have tho't ourselves oblig'd to bear our Testimony, in this public Manner, against him and his Way of Preaching, as tending very much to the Detriment of Religion and the entire Destruction of the Order of these Churches of Christ, which our Fathers have taken such Care and Pains to settle, as by the Platform, according to which the Discipline of the Churches of <u>New England</u> is regulated: And we do therefore hereby declare, That we look upon his going about, in an Itinerant Way, especially as he hath so much of an enthusiastic Turn, utterly inconsistent with the Peace and Order, if not the very Being of these Churches of Christ.

And now, inasmuch as by a certain Faculty he hath of raising the Passions, he hath been the Means of rousing many from their Stupidity, and setting them on thinking, whereby some may have been made really better, on which Account the People, many of them, are strongly attach'd to him (tho' it is most evident, that he hath not any superior Talent at instructing the Mind, or shewing the Force and Energy of those Arguments for a religious Life, which are directed to in the everlasting Gospel). Therefore, that the People who are thus attach'd to him, may not take up an unreasonable Prejudice against this our testimony, we think it very proper to give some Reasons for it, which we shall offer, respecting the Man himself, and then his Way and Manner of Preaching.

<u>First</u>, as to the Man himself, whom we look upon as an Enthusiast, a censorious, uncharitable Person, and a Deluder of the People; which Things, if we can make out, all reasonable Men will doubtless excuse us, tho' some such, thro' a fascinating Curiosity, may still continue their Attachment to him.

First then, we charge him, with <u>Enthusiasm</u>. Now that we may speak clearly upon this Head, we mean by an <u>Enthusiast</u>, one that acts, either according to Dreams, or some sudden Impulses and Impressions upon his Mind, which he fondly imagines to be from the Spirit of God, perswading and inclining him thereby to such and such Actions, tho' he hath no Proof that such Perswasions or Impressions are from the holy Spirit: For the perceiving a strong Impression upon our Minds, or a violent Inclination to do any Action, is a very different Thing from perceiving such Impressions to be from the Spirit of God moving upon the Heart: For our strong Faith and Belief, that such a Motion on the Mind comes from God, can never be any Proof of it; and if such Impulses and Impressions be not agreeable to our Reason, or to the Revelation of the Mind of God to us, in his Word, nothing can be more dangerous than conducting ourselves according to them; for otherwise, if we judge not of them by these Rules, they may as well be the Suggestions of the evil Spirit: And in what Condition must that People be, who stand ready to be led by a Man that conducts himself according to his Dreams, or some ridiculous and unaccountable Impulses and Impressions on his Mind?

* * * * * * * * * * * * * * * * * *

But we proceed to mention one Piece of <u>Enthusiasm</u> of a very uncommon Turn, which shews to what a great Length this unhappy pernicious Disposition of the Mind may carry a Man. When Pag. 32 of his Life, he personates our blessed Lord himself, when in his Passion, says he, <u>It was suggested to me, that when Jesus cried out, I thirst, his Sufferings were near at an end; upon this I threw myself upon the Bed, crying out, I thirst, I thirst: Soon after I felt my Load go off--, and knew what it was truly to rejoice in the Lord.</u> And certainly it is easy enough to conceive, from what Spirit such a <u>Suggestion</u> must come. To mention but one Instance more, tho' we are not of such Letter-learned as deny, that there is such an Union of Believers to Christ, whereby <u>they are one in him, as the Father and he are One</u>, as the Evangelist speaks, or rather the Spirit of God by him; yet so Letter-learned we are, as to say, that that Passage in Mr. W--'s Sermon of the <u>Indwelling of the Spirit</u>, p. 311: vol. of Sermons, contains the true Spirit of Enthusiasm, where he says, <u>to talk of any having the Spirit of God without feeling of it, is really to deny the Thing.</u> Upon which we say, That the Believer may have a Satisfaction, that he hath the Assistance of the Spirit of God with him, in so continual and regular a Manner, that he may be said to dwell in him, and yet have no feeling of it; for the Metaphor is much too gross to express this (however full) Satisfaction of the Mind, and has led some to take the Expression literally, and hath (we fear) given great Satisfaction to many an Enthusiast among us since the Year 1740, from the swelling of their Breasts and Stomachs in their religious Agitations, which they have tho't to be <u>feeling the Spirit</u>, in its Operations on them. But it is no way necessary to instance any further upon this Head; for the aforesaid Compositions are full of these Things.

The whole tends to perswade the World (and it has done so with respect to many) that Mr. W. hath as familiar a Converse and Communion with God as any of the Prophets and Apostles, and such as we all acknowledge to have been under the Inspiration of the Holy Ghost.

In the next Place, we look upon Mr. W. as an uncharitable, censorious and slanderous Man; which indeed is but a natural Consequence of the heat of Enthusiasm, by which he was so evidentally acted; for this Distemper of the Mind always puts a Man into a vain Conceit of his own Worth and Excellency, which all his Pretences to Humility will never hide, as long as he evidently shews, that he would have the World think he hath a greater Familiarity with God than other Men, and more frequent Communications from his Holy Spirit. Hence such a Man naturally assumes an Authority to dictate to others, and a Right to direct their Conduct and Opinions; and hence if any act not according to his Directions, and the Model of Things he had form'd in his own heated Brain, he is presently apt to run into slander, and stigmatize them as <u>Men of no Religion, unconverted</u>, and <u>Opposers of the Spirit of God</u>: And that such hath been the Behaviour of Mr. W. is also sufficiently evident. . . .

* * * * * * * * * * * * * * * * *

Again, We think it highly proper to bear our Testimony against Mr. W. as we look upon him a <u>Deluder of the People</u>. How he designs to manage in this Affair now, we know not: but we mean, that he hath much deluded them, and therefore suppose we have Reason in this respect to guard against him. And here we mean more especially as to the Collections of Money, which, when here before, by an extraordinary mendicant Faculty, he almost <u>extorted</u> from the People. As the Argument he then used was, the Support and Education of his dear Lambs at the Orphan-House, who (he told us, he hop'd) might in Time preach the Gospel to us or our Children; so it is not to be doubted, that the People were greatly encouraged to give him largely of their Substance, supposing they were to be under the immediate Tuition and Instruction of himself, as he then made them to believe; and had not this been their Tho't, it is, to us, without all Peradventure, they would never have been perswaded to any considerable Contribution upon that Head; and this, notwithstanding, he hath scarce seen them for these four Years; and besides hath left the Care of them with a Person, whom these Contributors know nothing of, and we ourselves have Reason to believe is little better than a <u>Quaker</u>; so that in this Regard we think the People have been greatly deceiv'd.

45

* * * * * * * * * * * * * * * * *

Secondly, We have as much Reason to dislike and bear Testimony against the Manner of his Preaching; and this in Two respects, both as an Extempore and as an Itinerant Preacher.

And first, as to his extempore Manner of preaching; this we think by no means proper, for that it is impossible that any Man should be able to manage any Argument with that Strength, or any Instruction with that Clearness in an extempore Manner, as he may with Study and Meditation. Besides, it is observable that your extempore Preachers give us almost always the same Things in the applicatory Part of their Sermons, so that it is often very little akin to their Text, which is just open'd in a cursory, and not seldom in a perverted Manner, and then comes the same kind of Harangue which they have often used before, as an Application; so that this is a most lazy Manner, and the Preacher offers that which cost him nothing, and is accordingly little Instructive to the Mind, and still less cogent to the reasonable Powers. Now Mr. W. evidently shows, that he would have us believe his Discourses are extempore, and indeed from the Rashness of some of his Expressions, as well as from the dangerous Errors vented in them, it is very likely; Hence, no doubt, were the many unguarded Expressions in his Sermons when he was here before; and since he has come again, he hath told us, "That Christ loves unregenerate Sinners with a Love of Complacency:" Nay, he hath gone rather further, and said, "That God loves Sinners as Sinners;" which, if it be not an unguarded Expression, must be a thousand times worse: For we cannot look upon it as much less than Blasphemy, and shows him to be stronger in the Antinomian Scheme than most of the Professors of that Heresy themselves; and that this is not unlikely, is to be suspected, because the Expression was repeated, and when he was tax'd with it, by a certain Gentleman, he made no Retractions.

But, lastly, We think it our Duty to bear our strongest Testimony against that Itinerant Way of preaching which this Gentleman was the first promoter of among us, and still delights to continue in: For if we had nothing against the Man, either as an Enthusiast, an uncharitable or delusive Person, yet we apprehend this Itinerant Manner of preaching to be of the worst and most pernicious Tendency.

Now by an <u>Itinerant</u> Preacher, we understand One that hath no particular Charge of his own, but goes about from Country to Country, or from Town to Town, in any Country, and stands ready to Preach to any Congregation that shall call him to it; and such an one is Mr. W. for it is but trifling for him to say (as we hear he hath) That he requires in order to his preaching any where, that the Minister also should invite him to it; for he knows the Populace have such an Itch after him, that when they generally desire it, the Minister (however diverse from their's, his own Sentiments may be) will always be in the utmost Danger of his People's quarrelling with, if not departing from him, shou'd he not consent to their impetuous Desires. Now as it is plain, no Man will find much Business as an <u>Itinerant</u> Preacher, who hath not something in his Manner, that is (however trifling, yea, and erroneous too, yet) very taking and aggreeable to the People; so when this is the Case, as we lately unhappily seen it, it is then in his Power to raise the People to any Degree of Warmth he pleases, whereby they stand ready to receive almost any Doctrine he is pleased to broach; as hath been the Case as to all the Itinerant Preachers who have followed Mr. W's. Example, and thrust themselves into Towns and Parishes, to the Destruction of all Peace and Order, whereby they have to the great impoverishment of the Community, taken the People from their Work and Business, to attend their Lectures and Exhortations, always fraught with Enthusiasm, and other pernicious Errors: But, <u>which is worse, and it is the natural Effect of these Things</u>, the People have been thence ready to despise their own Ministers, and their usefulness among them, in too many Places, hath been almost destroy'd.

Indeed, if there were any thing leading to this manner of Management in the Directions and Instructions given, either by our Saviour or his Apostles, we ought to be silent, and so wou'd a Man of any Modesty, if (on the other hand) there be nothing in the N. Testament leading to it. And surely Mr. W. will not have the Face to pretend he acts now as an <u>Evangelist</u>, tho' he seems to prepare for it in Journ. from N.E. to <u>Falmouth</u> in <u>England</u>, p. 12. where he says, <u>God seems to shew me it is my Duty to Evangelize, and not to fix in any particular Place</u>: For the Duty of that Officer certainly was not to go preaching of his own Head from one Church to another, where Officers were already settled, and the Gospel fully and faithfully preached. And it is without Doubt, that the Mind and Will of Christ, with respect to the Order

of his Churches, and the Business of his Ministers in them,
is plainly enough to be understood in the N. Testament; and
yet Mr. W. has said of late, in one of his Sermons, he thinks
that an Itinerant Manner of preaching may be very convenient
for the furtherance of the good of the Churches, if it were
under a good Regulation. Now we are apt to imagine, if such
an Officer wou'd have been useful, Christ himself wou'd have
appointed him; and therefore (under Favour) this is to <u>be
wise about what is written</u>, and supposes either that our
Lord did not know, or that he neglected to appoint all such
Officers in the Ministry, as wou'd further in the best manner the Truths of the Gospel: And it is from such Wisdom as
this, that all the Errors of <u>Popery</u> have come into the <u>Christian
Church</u>, while the Directions of the Word of God were not
strictly adhered to, but one tho't this Way or that Ceremony
was very convenient and significant and another another, till
they have dress'd up the Church in such a monstrous heap of
Appendages, that at this Day it can hardly be discern'd to be
a Church of Christ.

And now, upon the whole, having, we think, made it evident
to every one that is not prejedic'd on his Side (for such as
are so, we have little hope to convince) that Mr. W. is
chargeable with that <u>Enthusiasm</u>, <u>Censoriousness</u> and <u>delusive
Management</u> that we have tax'd him with; and since also he
seems resolv'd for that Itinerant Way of preaching, which we
think so destructive to the Peace of the Churches of Christ;
we cannot but bear our faithful Testimony against him, as a
Person very unfit to preach about as he has done heretofore,
and as he has now begun to do.

And we wou'd earnestly, and with all due respect, recommend
it to the Rev. Pastors of these Churches of Christ, to advise
with each other in their several Associations, and consider
whether it be not high Time to make a stand against the
Mischiefs, which we have here suggested as coming upon the
Churches.

<u>Harvard College</u>, Dec. 28, 1744.

    EDWARD HOLYOKE, <u>President</u>. . . .

THE COMING OF THE AMERICAN REVOLUTION

Discourse Concerning Unlimited Submission

JONATHAN MAYHEW

Jonathan Mayhew (1720-1766), one of the boldest exponents of the Enlightenment in America during the pre-Revolution years, was well known in the Boston area for his theological liberalism. Along with Charles Chauncy, Mayhew leveled a heavy attack against the traditional doctrines of Calvinism. Both men held that revelation must be validated by human reason. Thus for Mayhew, the use of Romans 13 to support the giving of passive obedience to kings under all conditions was unreasonable. The Discourse Concerning Unlimited Submission, from which the following excerpt is selected, was published in Boston twenty-six years before the Americans declared their independence from England. It was a clear foreshadowing of the arguments which were voiced by clergy of many theological persuasions on the eve of the American Revolution. What is Mayhew's opinion about unlimited submission to a civil authority? On what bases does he present his arguments?

If we calmly consider the nature of the thing itself, nothing can well be imagined more directly contrary to common sense than to suppose that millions of people should be subjected to the arbitrary, precarious pleasure of one single man (who has naturally no superiority over them in point of authority), so that their estates and everything that is valuable in life, and even their lives also, shall be absolutely at his disposal, if he happens to be wanton and capricious enough to demand them. What unprejudiced man can think that God made all to be thus subservient to the lawless pleasure and frenzy of one, so that it shall always be a sin to resist him! Nothing but the most plain and express revelation from heaven could make a sober impartial man believe such a monstrous, unaccountable doctrine, and, indeed, the thing itself appears so shocking -- so out of all proportion -- that it may be questioned whether all the miracles that ever were wrought, could make it credible, that this doctrine really came from God. At present, there is not the least syllable in scripture which gives any countenance to it. The hereditary, indefeasible, divine right of kings, and the doctrine of non-resistance which is built upon the supposition of such a right, are altogether as fabulous and chimerical as transubstantiation or any of the most absurd reveries of ancient or modern visionaries. These notions are fetched neither from divine revelation nor human reason; and if they are derived from neither of those sources, it is not much matter from whence they come, or whither they go. Only it is a pity that such doctrines should be propagated in society, to raise factions and rebellions, as we see they have, in fact, been both in the last and in the present reign.

But then, if unlimited submission and passive obedience to the higher powers, in all possible cases, be not a duty, it will be asked, "How far are we obliged to submit? If we may innocently disobey and resist in some cases, why not in all? Where shall we stop? What is the measure of our duty? This doctrine tends to the total dissolution of civil government; and to introduce such scenes of wild anarchy and confusion, as are more fatal to society than the worst of tyranny."

After this manner, some men object; and, indeed, this is the most plausible thing that can be said in favor of such an absolute submission as they plead for. But the worst (or rather the best) of it is that there is very little strength or solidity in it. For similar difficulties may be raised with respect to almost every duty of natural and revealed religion. To instance only in two, both of which are near akin, and indeed exactly parallel, to the case before us: it is unquestionably the duty of children to submit to their parents, and of servants to their masters. But no one asserts that it is their duty to obey and submit to them in all supposable cases; or universally a sin to resist them. Now does this tend to subvert the just authority of parents and masters? Or to introduce confusion and anarchy into private families? No. How then does the same principle tend to unhinge the government of that larger family, the body politic? We know, in general, that children and servants are obliged to obey their parents and masters respectively. We know also, with equal certainty, that they are not obliged to submit to them in all things, without exception, but may, in some cases reasonably, and therefore innocently, resist them. These principles are acknowledged upon all hands, whatever difficulty there may be in fixing the exact limits of submission. Now there is at least as much difficulty in stating the measure of duty in these two cases as in the case of rulers and subjects. So that this is really no objection, at least no reasonable one, against resistance to the higher powers. Or, if it is one, it will hold equally against resistance in the other cases mentioned.

It is indeed true, that turbulent, vicious-minded men may take occasion from this principle, that their rulers may in some cases be lawfully resisted, to raise factions and disturbances in the state; and to make resistance where resistance is needless and therefore sinful. But is it not equally true that children and servants of turbulent, vicious minds, may take occasion from this principle, that parents and masters may in some cases be lawfully resisted, to resist when resistance is unnecessary and therefore criminal? Is the principle in either case false in itself, merely because it may be abused and applied to legitimate disobedience and resistance in those instances, to which it ought not to be applied? According to this way of arguing, there will be no true principles in the world; for there are none but what may be wrested and perverted to serve bad purposes, either through the weakness or wickedness of men.

A people, really oppressed to a great degree by their sovereign, cannot well be insensible when they are so oppressed. And such a people (if I may allude to an ancient fable) have, like the hesperian fruit, a dragon for their protector and guardian. Nor would they have any reason to mourn if some Hercules should appear to dispatch him. For a nation thus abused to arise unanimously, and to resist their prince, even to the dethroning him, is not criminal, but a reasonable way of vindicating their liberties and just rights; it is making use of the means, and the only means, which God has put into their power, for mutual and self-defense. And it would be highly criminal in them not to make use of this means. It would be stupid tameness and unaccountable folly for whole nations to suffer one unreasonable, ambitious and cruel man to wanton and riot in their misery. And in such a case it would, of the two, be more rational to suppose that they that did not resist, than that they who did, would receive to themselves damnation.

A Calm Address to Our American Colonies

JOHN WESLEY

John Wesley (1703-91), the founder of Methodism and the most popular evangelical preacher of the day, first came to America in 1735, when he accompanied James Ogelthorpe to Georgia as a missionary to the Indians. He returned to England in 1738, and shortly thereafter joined George Whitefield in his open-air preaching. In "A Calm Address to Our American Colonies" which was first published in 1775 in London, Wesley calls upon the Americans to "fear God and honour the King." Does Wesley believe that Parliament has the power to tax the American colonies? What is the basis for his argument? Wesley states he is "unbiassed" in the debate between England and the American colonies. After having read his address, does that seem to be true? Why or why not? Whom does Wesley believe are really responsible for the opposition expressed by the colonies against England?

The grand question which is now debated (and with warmth enough on both sides) is this, Has the English Parliament power to tax the American colonies?

In order to determine this, let us consider the nature of our Colonies. An English Colony is a number of persons to whom the King grants a charter, permitting them to settle in some far country as a corporation, enjoying such powers as the charter grants, to be administered in such a manner as the charter prescribes. As a corporation they make laws for themselves: but as a corporation subsisting by a grant from higher authority, to the control of that authority, they still continue subject.

Considering this, nothing can be more plain, than that the supreme power in England has a legal right of laying any tax upon them for any end beneficial to the whole empire.

But you object, "It is the privilege of a Freeman and an Englishman to be taxed only by his own consent. And this consent is given for every man by his representative in parliament. But we have no representation in parliament. Therefore we ought not to be taxed thereby."

I answer, This argument proves too much. If the parliament cannot tax you, because you have no representation therein, for the same reason it can make no laws to bind you. If a freeman cannot be taxed without his own consent, neither can he be punished without it: for whatever holds with regard to taxation, holds with regard to all other laws. Therefore he who denies the English Parliament the power of taxation, denies it the right of making any laws at all. But this power over the Colonies you have never disputed: you have always admitted statutes, for the punishment of offences, and for the preventing or redressing of inconveniences. And the reception of any law draws after it by a chain which cannot be broken, the necessity of admitting taxation.

But I object to the very foundation of your plea. That "every freeman is governed by laws to which he has consented," as confidently as it has been asserted, it is absolutely false. In wide-extended dominions, a very small part of the people are concerned in making laws. This, as all public business, must be done by delegation, the delegates are chosen by a select number. And those that are not electors, who are for the greater part, stand by, idle and helpless spectators.

The case of electors is little better. When they are near equally divided, almost half of them must be governed, not only without, but even against their own consent.

And how has any man consented to those laws, which were made before he was born? Our consent to these, nay and to the laws now made even in England, is purely passive. And in every place, as all men are born the subjects of some state or other, so they are born, passively, as it were consenting to the laws of that state. Any other than this kind of consent, the condition of civil life does not allow.

But you say, You <u>are</u> <u>intitled</u> <u>to</u> <u>life</u>, <u>liberty</u> <u>and</u> <u>property</u> <u>by</u> <u>nature</u>: and <u>that</u> <u>you</u> <u>have</u> <u>never</u> <u>ceded</u> <u>to</u> <u>any</u> <u>sovereign</u> <u>power</u>, <u>the</u> <u>right</u> <u>to</u> <u>dispose</u> <u>of</u> <u>these</u> <u>without</u> <u>your</u> <u>consent</u>.

While you speak as the naked sons of nature, this is certainly true. But you presently declare, Our <u>ancestors</u> <u>at</u> <u>the</u> <u>time</u> <u>they</u> <u>settled</u> <u>these</u> <u>Colonies</u>, <u>were</u> <u>intitled</u> <u>to</u> <u>all</u> <u>the</u> <u>rights</u> <u>of</u> <u>natural-born</u> <u>subjects</u>, <u>within</u> <u>the</u> <u>realm</u> <u>of</u> <u>England</u>. This likewise is true: but when this is granted, the boast of original rights is at an end. You are no longer in a state of nature, but sink down to Colonists, governed by a charter. If your ancestors were subjects, they acknowledged a Sovereign: if they had a right to English privileges, they were accountable to English laws, and had <u>ceded</u> to the King and Parliament, <u>the</u> <u>power</u> <u>of</u> <u>disposing</u> <u>without</u> <u>their</u> <u>consent</u>, <u>of</u> <u>both</u> <u>their</u> <u>lives</u>, <u>liberties</u> <u>and</u> <u>properties</u>. And did the Parliament cede to them, a dispensation from the obedience, which they owe as natural subjects? Or any degree of independence, not enjoyed by other Englishmen?

<u>They</u> <u>did</u> <u>not</u> indeed, as you observe, <u>by</u> <u>emigration</u> <u>forfeit</u> <u>any</u> <u>of</u> <u>those</u> <u>privileges</u>: <u>but</u> <u>they</u> <u>were</u>, <u>and</u> <u>their</u> <u>descendents</u> <u>now</u> <u>are</u> <u>intitled</u> <u>to</u> <u>all</u> <u>such</u> <u>as</u> <u>their</u> <u>circumstances</u> <u>enable</u> <u>them</u> <u>to</u> <u>enjoy</u>.

That they who form a Colony by a lawful charter, forfeit no privilege thereby, is certain. But what they do not forfeit by any judicial sentence, they may lose by natural effects. When a man voluntarily comes into America, he may lose what he had when in Europe. Perhaps he had a right to vote for a knight or burgess: by crossing the sea he did not <u>forfeit</u> this right. But it is plain, he has made the exercise of it no longer possible. He has reduced himself from a voter to one of the innumerable multitude that have no votes.

But you say, <u>As the Colonies are not represented in the British Parliament, they are entitled to a free power of legislation</u>. For <u>they inherit all the rights which their ancestors had of enjoying all the privileges of</u> Englishmen.

They do inherit all the privileges which their ancestors had: but they can inherit no more. Their ancestors left a country where the representatives of the people were elected by men particularly qualified, and where those who wanted that qualification were bound by the decisions of men whom they had not deputed. You are the descendents of men who either had no votes, or resigned them by emigration. You have therefore exactly what your ancestors left you: not a vote in making laws, nor a chusing legislators, but the happiness of being protected by laws, and the duty of obeying them.

What your ancestors did not bring with them, neither they nor their descendants have acquired. They have not, by abandoning their right in one legislature, acquired a right to constitute another: any more than the multitudes in England who have no vote, have a right to erect a Parliament for themselves.

However the <u>Colonies have a right to all the privileges granted them by royal charters, or secured to them by provin-cial laws</u>.

The first clause is allowed: they have certainly a right to all the privileges granted them by royal charters. But as to the second there is a doubt: provincial laws may grant privileges to individuals of the province. But surely no province can confer provincial privileges on itself! They have a right to all which the King has given them; but not to all which they have given themselves.

A corporation can no more assume to itself privileges which it had not before, than a man can, by his own act and deed, assume titles or dignities. The legislature of a colony may be compared to the vestry of a large parish: which may lay a cess on its inhabitants, but still regulated by the law:

and which (whatever be its internal expenses) is still liable to taxes laid by superior authority.

The charter of Pennsylvania has a clause admitting, in express terms, taxation by Parliament. If such a clause be not inserted in other charters, it must be omitted as not necessary; because it is manifestly implied in the very nature of subordinate government: all countries which are subject to laws, being liable to taxes.

It is true, the first settlers in <u>Massachusetts Bay</u> were promised <u>an exemption from taxes for seven years</u>. But does not this very exemption imply that they were to pay them afterwards?

If there is in the charter of any Colony a clause exempting them from taxes for ever, then undoubtedly they have a right to be so exempted. But if there is no such clause, then the English Parliament has the same right to tax them as to tax any other English subjects.

All that impartially consider what has been observed, must readily allow, that the English Parliament has undoubted right to tax all the English Colonies.

But whence then is all this hurry and tumult? Why is America all in an uproar? If you can yet give yourselves time to think, you will see, the plain case is this.

A few years ago, you were assaulted by enemies, whom you were not well able to resist. You represented this to your Mother-country, and desired her assistance. You were largely assisted, and by that means wholly delivered from all your enemies.

After a time, your Mother-country, desiring to be reimbursed for some part of the large expense she had been at, laid a small tax (which she had always a right to do) on one of her Colonies.

But how is it possible, that the taking of this reasonable and legal step, should have set all America in a flame?

I will tell you my opinion freely; and perhaps you will not think it improbable. I speak the more freely, because I am unbiased: I have nothing to hope or fear from either side. I gain nothing either by the Government or by the Americans, and probably never shall. And I have no prejudice to any man in America: I love you as my brethren and countrymen.

My opinion is this. We have a few men in England, who are determined enemies to Monarchy. Whether they hate his present Majesty on any other ground, then because he is a King, I know not. But they cordially hate his office, and have for some years been undermining it with all diligence, in hopes of erecting their grand idol, their Commonwealth upon its ruins. I believe they have let very few into their design: (although many forward it, without knowing any thing of the matter), but they are steadily pursuing it, as by various other means, so in particular by inflammatory papers, which are industriously and continually dispersed, throughout the town and country: by this method they have already wrought thousands of the people, even to the pitch of madness. By the same, only varied according to your circumstances, they have likewise inflamed America. I make no doubt, but these very men are the original cause of the present breach between England and her Colonies. And they are still pouring oil into the flame, studiously incensing each against the other, and opposing under a variety of pretences, all measures of accommodation. So that although the Americans, in general, love the English, and the English, in general, love the Americans (all, I mean that are not yet cheated and exasperated by these artful men), yet the rupture is growing wider every day, and none can tell where it will end.

These good men hope it will end, in the total defection of North America from England. If this were effected, they who trust the English, in general, would be so irreconcilably disgusted, that they should be able, with or without foreign assistance, entirely to overturn the government: especially while the main of both the English and Irish forces are at so convenient a distance.

But, my brethren, would this be any advantage to _you_? Can _you_ hope for a more desirable form of government, either in England or America, than that which you now enjoy? After all the vehement cry for liberty, what more liberty can you have? What more religious liberty can you desire, than that which you enjoy already? May not every one among you worship God according to his own conscience? What civil liberty can you desire, which you are not already possessed of? Do not you sit without restraint, every man under his own vine? Do you not, every one, high or low, enjoy the fruit of your labour? This is real, rational liberty, such as is enjoyed by Englishmen alone; and not by any other people in the inhabitable world. Would the being independent of England make you more free? Far, very far from it. It would hardly be possible for you to steer clear, between anarchy and tyranny. But suppose, after numberless dangers and mischiefs, you should settle into one or more Republics: would a republican government give you more liberty, either religious or civil? By no means. No governments under heaven are so despotic as the Republican: no subjects are governed in so arbitrary a manner, as those of a Commonwealth. If any one doubt of this, let him look at the subjects of Venice, of Genoa, or even of Holland. Should any man talk or write of the Dutch government as every cobbler does of the English, he would be laid in irons, before he knew where he was. And then woe be to him! Republics shew no mercy.

"But if we submit to one tax, more will follow." Perhaps so, and perhaps not. But if they did; if you were taxed (which is quite improbable), equal with Ireland or Scotland, still were you to prevent this by renouncing connection with England, the remedy would be worse than the disease. For O! what convulsions must poor America feel, before any other government was settled? Innumerable mischiefs must ensue, before any general form could be established. And the grand mischief would ensue, when it was established; when you had received a yoke, which you could not shake off.

Brethren, open your eyes! Come to yourselves! Be no longer the dupes of designing men. I do not mean any of your countrymen in America: I doubt whether any of these are in the secret. The designing men, the Ahithophels are in England; those who have laid their scheme so deep, and covered it so well, that thousands who are ripening it, suspect nothing at all of the matter. These well-meaning men, sincerely believing that they are serving their country, exclaim against grievances, which either never existed, or are aggravated above measure, and thereby inflame the people more and more, to the wish of those who are behind the scene. But be not you duped any longer: do not ruin yourselves for them that owe you no good will, that now employ you only for their own purposes, and in the end will give you no thanks. They love neither England nor America, but play one against the other, in subserviency to their grand design, of overturning the English government. Be warned in time. Stand and consider before it is too late; before you have entailed confusion and misery on your latest posterity. Have pity upon your mother country! Have pity upon your own! Have pity upon yourselves, upon your children, and upon all that are near and dear to you! Let us not bite and devour one of another, lest we be consumed one of another! O let us follow after peace! Let us put away our sins; the real ground of all our calamities! Which never will or can be thoroughly removed, till we fear God and honour the King.

1776 Election Sermon

SAMUEL WEST

Samuel West (1730-1807), a graduate of Harvard in 1754, was a preacher of a theology that would later be known as Unitarianism. Shortly after the battle of Bunker Hill, he joined the American army as a chaplain, a position he held for several months. On the eve of the signing of the Declaration of Independence, he delivered a sermon to mark the anniversary of the election of the honorable council in Massachusetts. According to A Sermon Preached Before the Honorable Council, preached on May 29, 1776, in Boston, what is West's opinion of submission to civil authority? How does West use Scripture to support his position? What conclusion does West draw to his entire argument?

[In 1 Peter 2:13,14, we hear] "Submit yourselves to every ordinance of man," -- or as the words ought to be rendered from the Greek, submit yourselves to every human creation; or human constitution, -- "for the Lord's sake, whether it be to the king, or unto governors, -- for the punishment of evil-doers, and for the praise of them that do well." Here we see that the apostle asserts that magistrates are of human creation that is, that magistrates have no power or authority but what they derive from the people; that this power they are to exert for the punishment of evil-doers, and for the praise of them that do well.

The only reason assigned by the apostle why magistrates should be obeyed . . . is because they punish the wicked and encourage the good; it follows, that when they punish the virtuous we have a right to refuse yielding any submission to them; whenever they act contrary to the design of their institution, they forfeit their authority to govern the people, and the reason for submitting to them immediately ceases. . . . Hence we see that the apostle, instead of being a friend to tyranny . . ., turns out to be a strong advocate for the just rights of mankind.

David, the man after God's own heart, makes piety a necessary qualification in a ruler: "He that ruleth over men must be just, ruling in the fear of God."

To despise government, and to speak evil of dignitaries is represented in Scripture as one of the worst of characters; and it is an injunction of Moses, "Thou shalt not speak evil of the ruler . . ." Great mischief may ensue upon reviling the character of good rulers; for the unthinking herd of mankind are very apt to give ear to scandal, and when it falls upon men in power, it brings their authority into contempt, lessens their influence, and disheartens them from doing service.

But though I would recommend to all Christians to treat rulers with proper honor and respect, none can reasonably suppose that I mean that rulers ought to be flattered in their vices, or honored and caressed while they are seeking to undermine and ruin the state; for this would be wickedly betraying our just rights, and we should be guilty of our own destruction.

It is with a particular view to the present unhappy controversy . . . that I chose to discourse upon the nature and design of government . . . so that we stand firm in our opposition to tyranny, while at the same time we pay all proper obedience to our lawful magistrates; while we are contending for liberty, may we avoid running into licentiousness . . . I acknowledge that I have undertaken a difficult task; but, it appears to me, the present state of affairs loudly calls for such a discourse. Need I upon this occasion descend to particulars? Can any one be ignorant what the things are of which we complain? . . . And, after all this wanton exertion of arbitrary power, is there any man who is not fired with a noble indignation against such merciless tyrants. . . .

Let us treat our rulers with all that honor and respect which the dignity of their station requires; but let it be such an honor and respect as is worthy of the sons of freedom to give. Let us ever abhor the base arts used by fawning parasites and cringing courtiers, who by their flatteries obtain offices which they are unqualified to sustain. Oftentimes they have a greater number of places assigned them than any one person of the greatest abilities can properly fill . . . and the community becomes greatly injured . . . so many an important trust remains undischarged.

. . . In order to avoid this evil, I hope our legislators will always despise flattery as something below the dignity of a rational mind, and that they will ever scorn the man that will be corrupted . . . And let us all resolve with ourselves that no motives of interest, nor hopes of preferment, shall ever induce us to flattering men in power. Let the honor and respect which we show our superiors be simple and genuine. . . . Tyrants have been flattered in their vices, and have often had an idolatrous reverence paid them. The worse princes have been the most flattered and adored and many such, in the pagan world, assumed the title of gods, and had divine honors paid them. This idolatrous reverence has ever been the inseparable concomitant of arbitrary power and tyrannical government; even Christian rulers, if they have not been adored as gods, yet the titles given them strongly savor of blasphemy, and the reverence paid them is idolatrous. What right has a poor sinful worm of the dust to claim the title of his most sacred Majesty? Most sacred certainly belongs only to God alone, -- yet how common is it to see this title or ones like it given to rulers! And how often have we been told that the ruler can do no wrong! Even though he should be so foolish and wicked as hardly capable of ever being in the right, yet still it must be asserted and maintained that it is impossible for him to do wrong! The cruel, savage disposition of tyrants, and the idolatrous reverence paid them, are both most beautifully exhibited to view by the apostle John in Revelation, thirteenth chapter . . .

The apostle gives description of a horrible wild beast which he saw rise out of the sea, having seven heads and ten horns, and upon his heads the names of blasphemy. By heads are to be understood forms of government, and by blasphemy, idolatry; so that it seems implied that there will be a degree of idolatry in every form of tyrannical government. This beast is represented as having the body of a leopard, the feet of a bear, and the mouth of a lion; i.e., a horrible monster, possessed of the rage and fury of the lion, the fierceness of the bear, and the swiftness of the leopard to sieze and devour its prey. Can words more strongly point out, or exhibit in more lively colors, the exceeding rage, fury, and impetuosity of tyrants, destroying and making havoc of mankind? To this beast we find the dragon gave his power . . ., this is to denote that tyrants are the ministers of Satan.

Such a horrible monster, we should have thought, would have been abhorred and detested of all mankind, . . . that all nations would have joined their power and forces together to oppose and utterly destroy him from off the face of the earth; but, so far are they from doing this, that, on the contrary, they are represented as worshipping him (vers 8): "And all that dwell on the earth shall worship him" -- all those "whose names are not written in the Lamb's book of life;" . . . Those who pay an undue and sinful veneration to tyrants are properly the servants of the devil. . . . Hence that terrible denunciation of divine wrath against the worshippers of the beast . . .: "If any man worship the beast . . . the same shall drink the wine of the wrath of God." . . . We have here set forth in the clearest manner, God's abhorrence of tyranny, tyrants, and the idolatrous reverence that their subjects are wont to pay them . . . Does it not, then, highly concern us all to stand fast in the liberty wherewith Heaven hath made us free, to strive to get the victory over the beast and his image -- over every species of tyranny? Let us look upon a freedom from the power of tyrants as a blessing that cannot be purchased too dear, and let us bless God that he had delivered us from that idolatrous reverence which men are so apt to pay to arbitrary tyrants. Let not the powers of earth and hell prevail against liberty.

Honored fathers, we look up to you, in this day of calamity as the guardians of our invaded rights, and the defenders of our liberties against tyranny. You are called to save your country from ruin . . .

My reverend fathers and brethren in the ministry will remember that according to our text, it is part of the work of a gospel minister to teach his hearers the duty they owe to magistrates. Let us, then, endeavor to explain the nature of their duty faithfully, and show them the difference between liberty and licentiousness; and let us animate them to oppose tyranny and arbitrary power; and let us inculcate upon them the duty of yielding due obedience to lawful authority.

To conclude: While we are fighting for liberty, and striving against tyranny, let us remember to fight the good fight of faith, and earnestly seek to be delivered from that bondage of corruption which we are brought into by sin, and that we may be made partakers of the glorious liberty of the sons and children of God: which may the Father of Mercies grant us all, through Jesus Christ. "AMEN."

SOURCES AND IMPACT OF THE SECOND AWAKENING

4

Attack on Infidelity

TIMOTHY DWIGHT

Timothy Dwight (1752-1817), grandson of the famous theologian, Jonathan Edwards, has been referred to by some historians as "the father of the Second Awakening." After graduation from Yale in 1769, he remained there as a tutor, only to be greatly disappointed at not being named president of the college in 1777. Instead, he entered the army chaplaincy, serving during the Revolutionary War for a little over a year. For the next decade and a half, he divided his time between preaching, teaching, and writing poetry and hymns. In 1795, he was invited to become president of Yale. As president of the college, he was also pastor of the college church, where his solid doctrinal sermons attacked the scepticism rampant in the student body and defended the authenticity of the Bible, identifying "infidelity" as the enemy of faith. The following selection is taken from A Discourse, on Some Events of the Last Century, delivered in the Brick Church in New Haven, on Wednesday, January 7, 1801 (New Haven, 1801), pp. 17-23, 28-30, 32-34, 45-47. According to Dwight, what were the two great causes of infidelity in the late eighteenth century? What effect does Dwight say the supporters of France's revolution had on infidelity in the U.S.? As seen in this discourse by Dwight, what were some possible reasons for the coming of the Second Awakening?

In the course of this period, God has, in various instances, been pleased to revive his glorious work of sanctification, and to extend it through many parts of the land. I know that a number of men, and some of much respectability, have entertained unfavorable ideas of what are called revivals of religion; but I cannot help thinking their opinions of this subject rather formed in the closet than derived from facts, or warranted by the scriptures. Seasons of enthusiasm about various subjects have indeed often existed, and probably in every civilized country. In these seasons the human kind has not infrequently exhibited many kinds and degrees of weakness, error, and deformity. Hence, perhaps, sober men have, in some instances, been led to believe that wherever enthusiasm exists these evils exist also. As therefore revivals of religion have frequently been more or less accompanied by enthusiasm, they have, I think sufficient grounds, determined, that all which existed was enthusiasm, and that nothing would flow from it but these evils.

That the mind under the first clear, strong, and solemn views of its own sins should be deeply affected, and greatly agitated, is to be expected from the nature of man. He is always thus affected by the first strong view, taken of any object deeply interesting, and always thus agitated when such an object is seen in an uncertain, suspended state. No object can be so interesting, or more entirely suspended, than the state of the soul in the case specified.

When these emotions, thus excited by objects of such immense importance, and in so absolute a state of suspense, as the guilt, the condemnation, and the salvation, of an immortal mind, are attended with some degree of enthusiasm and extravagance; when they are followed by seasons of deep despondence, and successive transport; nothing takes place, but that, which sound philosophy must presuppose; as similar emotions are, in all similar cases, followed, especially in ardent minds, by the same consequences. All this, however, will go no length towards proving, that nothing exists beyond enthusiasm; and that, amid several irregular and excessive exertions of the mind, there is not to be found a real change of the disposition, a real assumption of piety. To me it is evident, that revivals of religion are often what they are called, if not always; and that the proof abundantly exists (where alone it ought to be looked for) in the real and permanent melioration of the moral character of multitudes, who then become serious and professedly religious.

Of the last of these revivals of religion, that which still extensively exists, it ought to be observed, that it has absolutely, or at least very nearly, been free from every extravagance, enthusiasm, and superstition, with them. But no man of common candour can hesitate to admit, that vice is not the only sober and rational state of a moral being; and that impiety is an unhappy proof of a real wisdom. In this great and auspicious event of which I have spoken, thousands have been already happily concerned, and thousands more will, it is hoped, hereafter claim a share.

But, with the rest of mankind, we have abused our blessings. Loose opinions and loose practices have found their place here also. The first considerable change in the religious character of the people of this country was accomplished by the war, which began in 1755. War is at least as fatal to morals, as to life, or happiness. The officers and soldiers of the British armies, then employed in this country, although probably as little corrupted as those of most armies, were yet loose patterns of opinion and conduct, and were unhappily copied by considerable numbers of our own countrymen, united with them in military life. These, on their return, spread the infection through those around them. Looser habits of thinking began then to be adopted, and were followed, as they always are, by looser conduct. The American war increased these evils. Peace had not, at the commencement of this war, restored the purity of life, which existed before the preceding war. To the depravation still remaining was added a long train of immoral doctrines and practices, which spread into every corner of the country. The profanation of the Sabbath, before unusual, profaneness of language, drunkenness, gambling, and lewdness, were exceedingly increased; and, what is less commonly remarked, but is perhaps not less mischievous, than any of them, a light, vain method of thinking, concerned sacred things, a cold, contemptuous indifference toward every moral and religious subject. In the mean time, that enormous evil, a depreciating currency gave birth to a new spirit of fraud, and opened numerous temptations, and a boundless field for its operations; while a new and intimate correspondence with corrupted foreigners introduced a multiplicity of loose doctrines, which were greedily embraced by licentious men, as the means of palliating and justifying their sins.

At this period Infidelity began to obtain, in this country, an extensive currency and reception. As this subject constitutes far the most interesting and prominent characteristic of the past Century, it will not be amiss to exhibit it with some degree of minuteness, and to trace through several particulars the steps of its progress.

Infidelity has been frequently supposed to be founded on an apprehended deficiency of the evidence, which supports a divine Revelation. No opinion can be more erroneous than this. That solitary instances may have existed, in which men did not believe the scriptures to be the word of God, because they doubted of the evidence in their possession, I am ready to admit; but that this has been the common fact, is, at least, in my view, a clear impossibility.

Our Saviour informs us, that "This is the condemnation, that light is come into the world, and men loved darkness rather than light, because their deeds were evil:" and subjoins, that "he who doth evil hateth the light, neither cometh to the light, lest his deeds should be reproved." Here one of the two great causes of Infidelity is distinctly and exactly alleged, viz. The opposition of a heart, which loves sin, and dreads the punishment of it, to that truth, which with infinite authority, and under an immense penalty, demands of all men a holy life. The other great cause of Infidelity is frequently mentioned by the inspired writers, particularly St. Paul, St. Peter, and St. Jude. In the following passages of St. Peter it is exhibited with peculiar force. "For when they speak great swelling words of vanity, they allure through the lusts of the flesh, through much wantonness, them that were clean escaped from them, that live in error. While they promise them liberty, they themselves are the servants (bond-slaves) of corruption." "There shall come in the last days scoffers, walking after their own lusts, and saying, Where is the promise of his coming? For since the fathers fell asleep, all things continue as they were from the beginning of the creation."

The Infidels, here referred to, are plainly philosophists; the authors of vain and deceitful philosophy; of science falsely so called; always full of vanity in their discourses: Scoffers, walking after their own lusts, and alluring others, through the same lusts, to follow them; promising them liberty, as their reward, and yet being themselves, and making their disciples, the lowest and most wretched of all slaves, the slaves of corruption. Philosophical pride, and the love of sinning in security and peace, are, therefore, the two great causes of Infidelity, according to the scriptures.

A more exact account of this subject, as existing in fact, could not even now be given. Infidelity has been assumed because it was loved, and not because it was supported by evidence; and has been maintained and defended, to quiet the mind of sin, and to indulge the pride of talents and speculation.

The form, which it has received, has varied in the hands of almost every distinguished Infidel. It was first Theism, or natural Religion, then mere Unbelief, then Animalism, then Scepticism, then partial, and then total Atheism. Yet it has, in three things at least, preserved a general consistency; opposition to Christianity, devotion of sin and lust, and a pompous profession of love to Liberty. To a candid and logical opposition to Christianity, consisting of facts fairly stated and justly exhibited, no reasonable objection can be made. It is to be wished, that this had been the conduct of the opposition actually made; but nothing has been more unlike that conduct. The war has been the desultory attack of a barbarian, not of a civilized soldier; an onset of passion, pride, and wit; a feint of conjectures and falsified facts; an incursion of sneers, jests, gross banter, and delicate ridicule; a parade of hints and insinuations; and a vigorous assault on fancy, passion, and appetite. These were never the weapons of sober conviction; this was never the conduct of honest men.

In the earlier periods of this controversy there were, however, more frequent efforts at argumentation, on the part of Infidels. For the last twenty or thirty years they seem to have despaired of success in this field, and have betaken themselves to that of action and influence. In this field they have wrought with a success totally unprecedented. Nor is this at all to be wondered at, if we consider the opportunity of succeeding presented to them, during the latter half of the last Century, by the state of society in Europe. The excessive wealth of that division of the eastern Continent has generated an enormous luxury, the multiplied enjoyments of which have become not only the ruling objects of desire, and the governing motives of action, but, in the view of a great part of the inhabitants, the necessary means of even a comfortable existence. On these life is employed, ambition fastened, ardour exhausted, and energy spent. Voluptuousness and splendour, formed on the Asiatic scale, engross men in public and private stations, in the university, the camp, the shop, and the desk, as well as the court and the cabinet. To glitter with diamonds, to roll in pomp, to feast on dainties, to wanton in amusements, to build palaces, and to fashion wildernesses of pleasure, are the supreme objects of millions, apparently destined to the grave, still, and humble walks of life, as well as of those, who were high born, and highly endowed. Science toils, ingenuity is stretched on the rack, and art is wearied through all her refinements, to satisfy the universal demand for pleasure; the mines of Golconda are ransacked, the caverns of Mexico emptied, and the mountains of Potosi transported across the ocean.

Of this universal devotion to pleasure and shew, modern Infidels have availed themselves to the utmost. To a mind, to a nation, dissolved in sloth, enervated by pleasure, and fascinated with splendour, the Gospel is preached, and heaven presented, in vain. The eye is closed, the ear stopped, and the heart rendered gross and incapable of healing. The soul is of course, unconscious of danger, impatient of restraint, and insensible to the demands of moral obligation. It is, therefore, prepared to become an Infidel, without research, and without conviction. Hence, more sagacious than their predecessors, the later Infidels have neither laboured, nor wished, to convince the understanding, but have bent all their efforts to engross the heart.

In the mean time other events, highly favourable to their designs, have taken place both in America and Europe. The American Revolution, an august, solemn, and most interesting spectacle, drew towards it at this time the eyes of mankind. The novelty of the scene, the enchanting sound of Liberty, to which the pulse of man instinctively beats, the sympathy ever excited for the feebler and suffering party, embarked deeply in the American cause a great part of the civilized world. Benevolent men, of all countries, hoped, when the contest was ended prosperously for us, and ardent men boldly pronounced, that a new era had arrived in human things, that "the iron rod of the oppressor was broken," and that "the oppressed would soon be universally set free."

Among the agents in the American Revolution, were many natives of France; men, in numerous instances, or ardent minds, and daring speculation; who either imbibed here new sentiments of liberty, or ripened those, which they had already adopted at home. These men, returning to their own country, diffused extensively the enthusiasm, which they had cherished here, and thus hastened the crisis, to which France was otherwise approaching. . . .

In this great moral convulsion Royalty and Christianity sunk in the kingdom of France. Emboldened beyond every fear by this astonishing event, Infidelity, which anciently had hid behind a mask, walked forth in open day, and displayed her genuine features to the sun. Without a blush she now denied the existence of moral obligation, annihilated the distinction between virtue and vice, challenged and authorized the indulgence of every lust, strode down the barriers of truth, perjured herself daily in the fight of the universe, lifted up her front in the face of heaven, denied the being, and dared the thunder, of the Almighty. Virtue and truth, her native enemies, and the objects of all her real hatred, she hunted from every cell and solitude; and, whenever they escaped her fangs, she followed them with the execrations of malice, the finger of derision, and the hisses of infamy.

Elevated now, for the first time to the chair of dominion, she ushered forth her edicts with the gravity of deliberation and the authority of law, and executed them by the oppressive hand of the jailor, the axe of the executioner, and the sword of the warrior. All rights fell before her, all interests were blasted by her breath, and happiness and hope were together swept away by her bosom of destruction.

In the midst of all this effrontery, Infidels forgot not their arts and impositions. As occasion dictated, or ingenuity whispered, they availed themselves of every disguise, and of every persuasive. As if they had designed to give the last wound to virtue, they assumed all her titles and challenged all her attributes to their own conduct. Daily forsworn, and laughing at the very distinction between right and wrong, they proclaimed themselves the assertors of justice, and the champions of truth. While they converted a realm into a Bastile, they trumpeted their inviolable attachment to liberty; while they "cursed their God, and looked upward," they announced themselves worshippers of the Supreme Being. With a little finger, thicker than the loins of both the monarchy and the hierarchy, encircled with three millions of corpses, and in the center of a kingdom changed into a stall of slaughter, they hung themselves over with labels of philanthropy. Nay, they have far outgone all this. Two of their philosophers, independently of each other, have declared, that, to establish their favourite system, the sacrifice of all the existing race of man would be a cheap price: an illustrious instance of Infidel benevolence, and of the excellence of their darling maxim, that "the end sanctifies the means."

These however, are but a small portion of their arts. They have, as the state of things required, disguised their designs; disavowed them; doubted their existence; wondered at those, who believed them real; ridiculed the belief; and professed themselves amazed at such credulity. This conduct has been reduced to a system, and taught and enjoined on their followers, as a code of policy, and as being often the most effectual means of spreading their opinions.

72

Nor have they less frequently resorted to the aid of obscure, unsuspected, and apparently undesigned communication. Their doctrines have, with great success, been propagated by remote hints; by soft and gentle insinuations; by half started doubts, and half proposed objections; and by the suggestion of a train of thoughts in which those doctrines are taken for granted, and considered as being so plain, and so generally received, that no person can be imagined to disbelieve, or even to doubt. The reader himself is presupposed to have long since admitted them, as the only doctrines of truth or common sense; as being too rational and candid to hesitate about things so clear and acknowledged; as unquestionably lifted above the reception of the contrary pitiful absurdities; and as thus prepared to act, as all other sensible and liberal persons have already acted. Thus their opinions steal upon his mind in methods equally unsuspected and imposing. . . .

Such is the astonishing state of moral things; in several parts of Europe, which, within a short time, has opened upon the view of our countrymen. The strong sympathy which, unhappily, and on no rational grounds, prevailed here towards those, who were leaders in the French Revolution, and towards the Revolution itself, prepared us to become the miserable dupes of their principles and declarations. They were viewed merely as human beings, embarked deeply in the glorious cause of liberty; and not at all as Infidels, as the abettors of falsehood, and the enemies of Righteousness, of Truth, and of God. Hence all their concerns were felt, and all their conduct covered with the veil of charity. They were viewed as having adventured, and suffered, together with ourselves, and as now enlisted for the support of a kindred cause. The consequences of these prejudices were such, as would naturally be expected. A general and unexamples confidence was soon felt, and manifested, by every licentious man. Every Infidel, particularly, claimed a new importance, and treated religion with enhanced contempt. The graver ones, indeed, through an affected tenderness for the votaries of christianity, adopted a more decent manner of despising it; but all were secure of a triumph and satisfied, that talents, character, and the great world, were on their side. The young, the ardent, the ambitious, and the voluptuous, were irresistibly solicited to join a cause, which harmonized with all their corruptions, pointed out the certain road to reputation, and administered the necessary opiates to conscience; and could not refuse to unite themselves with men, who spoke great swelling words of vanity, who allured them through much wantoness, and promised them the unbounded liberty of indulging every propensity to pleasure. The timid at the same time were terrified, the orderly let loose, the sober amazed, and the religious shocked beyond example; while the floating part of our countrymen, accustomed to swim with every tide, moved onward on obedience to the impulse. Thus principles were yielded, useful habits were relaxed, and a new degree of irreligion extensively prevailed.

Happily for us, the source, when these peculiar evils flowed, furnished us in some degree with a remedy. It was soon discovered, that the liberty of Infidels was not the liberty of New England; that France, instead of being free, merely changed through a series of tyrannies, at the side of which all former despotisms whitened into moderation and humanity; and that of the immeasurable evils, under which she and her neighbours agonized, Infidelity was the genuine source; the Vesuvius, from whose mouth issued those rivers of destruction, which deluged and ruined all things in their way. It was seen, that men, unrestrained by law and religion, is a mere beast of prey that licentiousness, although adorned with the graceful name of liberty, is yet the spring of continual alarm, bondage, and misery; and that the restraints, imposed by equitable laws, and by the religion of the scriptures, were far less burdensome and distressing than the boasted freedom of Infidels.

Even sober Infidels began to be alarmed for their own peace, safety, and enjoyments; and to which, that other men might continue still to be christians; while christians saw with horror their God denied, their Saviour blasphemed, and war formally declared against Heaven.

To all this was added a complete development of the base and villainous designs of the French government against our country, their piratical plunder of our property, and their inhuman treatment of our seamen. Persons, who thought nothing, who felt nothing, concerning religion, felt these things exquisitely; and rationally concluded, that men, who

could do these things, could, and would, do every thing
else, that was evil and unjust; and that their moral principles, which produced, and sanctioned, these crimes,
could not fail to merit contempt and detestation. Such
persons, therefore, began now to lean towards the side of
christianity, and to seek in it a safety and peace, which
they beheld Infidelity destroy.

Thus having in the midst of these enormous dangers obtained
help of God, we continue until the present time; and this
part of our country, at least, has escaped not only tributary bondage, but the infinitely more dreadful bondage of
Infidelity, corruption, and moral ruin.

It ought, here, and forever, to be remembered with peculiar
gratitude, that God has, during the past Century, often and
wonderfully interposed in our behalf, and snatched us from
the jaws of approaching destruction. The instances of this
interposition are too numerous to be now recounted, and are
happily too extraordinary to be either unknown or forgotten.
We have been frequently on the brink of destruction; but although cast down, we have not been destroyed. Perhaps we
have so often been, and are still, suffered to stand on this
precipice, that we may see, and feel, and acknowledge, the
hand of our Preserver. . . .

In the mean time, let me solemnly warn you, that if you
intend to accomplish anything, if you mean not to labour in
vain, and to spend your strength for nought, you must take
your side. There can be here no halting between two opinions. You must marshall yourselves, finally, in your own
defense, and in the defense of all that is dear to you.
You must meet face to face the bands of disorder, of falsehood, and of sin. Between them and you there is, there can
be, no natural, real, or lasting harmony. What communion
hath light with darkness? What concord hath Christ with
Belial? Or what part hath he that believeth with an Infidel? From a connection with them what can you gain? What
will you not lose? Their neighborhood is contagious; their
friendship is a blast; their communion is death. Will you
imbibe their principles? Will you copy their practices?
Will you teach your children, that death is an eternal
sleep? that the end sanctifies the means? that moral obligation is a dream? Religion a farce? and your Saviour the

spurious offspring of pollution? Will you send your daughters abroad in the attire of a female Greek? Will you enrol your sons as conscripts for plunder and butchery? Will you make marriage the mockery of a registers' office? Will you become the rulers of Sodom, and the people of Gomorrah? Shall your love to man vanish in a word, and evaporate on the tongue? Shall it be lost in a tear, and perish in a sigh? Will you enthrone a Goddess of Reason before the table of Christ? Will you burn your Bibles? Will you crucify anew your Redeemer? Will you deny your God?

COME out, therefore, from among them, and be ye separate, saith the Lord, and touch not the unclean thing; and I will receive you, and will be a father to you: And ye shall be my sons and daughters, saith the Lord almighty.

To this end you must coolly, firmly, and irrevocably make your determination, and resolve, that Jehovah is your God, and that you will serve him only. His enemies are the enemies of yourselves, and of your children; of your peace, liberty, and happiness; of your religion, virtue, and salvation,--Their principles abhor; their practices detest. Before your steady indignation, and firm contempt, they will fall of course. No falsehood can bear the sunbeams of truth; no vice can withstand the steady current of virtue. The motives to this opposition are infinite. Your all, your children's all, is at stake. If you contend manfully, you will be more than conquerors; if you yield, both you and they are undone. You are endeared by a thousand ties. Your common country is a land of milk and honey: In it a thousand churches are vocal with the praise of your Creator; and four thousand schools receive your children to their bosom, and nurse them to wisdom and piety. In this country you all sprang from one stock, speak one language, have one system of manners, profess one religion, and wear one character. Your laws, your institutions, your interests, are one. No mixture weakens, no strangers divide, you. You have fought and bled, your fathers have fought and died, together. Together they worshipped God; together they sat around the table of the Redeemer; together they ascended to heaven; and together they now unite in the glorious concert of eternal praise. With such an interest at hazard, with such bonds of union, with such examples, you cannot separate; you cannot fear.

Let me at the same time warn you, that your enemies are
numerous, industrious, and daring, full of subtlety, and
full of zeal. Nay, some of them are your own brethren, and
endeared to you by all of the ties of nature. The contest
is, therefore, fraught with hazard and alarm. Were it a war
of arms, you would have little to dread. It is a war of
arts, of temptations; of enchantments; a war against the
magicians of Egypt; in which no weapons will avail, but
"the rod of God." In this contest you may be left alone.
Fear not; "they that be for you will even then be more than
they that are against you." Almighty power will protect,
Infinite wisdom will guide, and Unchangeable goodness will
prosper, you. The Christian world rises daily in prayer to
heaven for your faithfulness and success; the host of
sleeping saints calls to you from the grave, and bids you
God speed. The spirits of your fathers lean from yonder
skies to survey the conflict, and your children of many
generations, will rise up, and call you blessed.

Forming the American Bible Society

The advent of the Second Awakening sparked
the growing interest in and demand for the distribution of Bibles. All along the east coast, local
and state Bible societies were organized during
the first fifteen years of the nineteenth century.
Then in May 1816, sixty representatives of these
scattered societies met in New York, where they
established the American Bible Society. The primary figure in the movement was Samuel J. Mills,
who was spiritually a child of the Second Awakening. The organization, deploring "local feelings,
party prejudices, sectarian jealousies," called
for cooperation in the great work of Bible distribution. In less than four years it had sent out

approximately a hundred thousand Bibles. The following statement which describes the purpose of the organization appeared in the Panoplist and Missionary Magazine, XII (1816), 271-73. Why was the American Bible Society formed? Why did its founders favor a national organization over local, independent associations? How does the formation of the American Bible Society reflect the religious concerns of a growing nation seeking to maintain its religious fervency?

Every person of observation has remarked that the times are pregnant with great events. The political world has undergone changes stupendous, unexpected, and calculated to inspire thoughtful men with the most boding anticipations.

That there are in reserve, occurences of deep, of lasting, and of general interest, appears to be the common sentiment. Such a sentiment has not been excited without a cause, and does not exist without an object. The cause is to be sought in that Providence, which adapts, with wonderful exactitude, means to ends; and the object is too plain to be mistaken by those who carry a sense of religion into their speculations upon the present and the future condition of our afflicted race.

An excitement, as extraordinary as it is powerful, has roused the nations to the importance of spreading the knowledge of the one living and true God, as revealed in his Son, the Mediator between God and men, Christ Jesus. This excitement is the more worthy of notice, as it has followed a period of philosophy falsely so called, and has gone in the track of those very schemes which, under the imposing names of reason and liberality, were attempting to seduce mankind from all which can bless the life that is, or shed a cheering radiance on the life that is to come.

We hail the reaction, as auspicious to whatever is exquisite in human enjoyment, or precious to human hope. We would fly to the aid of all that is holy, against all that is profane; of the purest interest of the community, the family, and the individual, against the conspiracy of darkness, disaster and death--to help on the mighty work of Christian charity--to claim our place in the age of Bibles.

We have, indeed, the secondary praise, but still the praise, of treading in the footsteps of those who have set an example without a parallel--an example of the most unbounded benevolence and beneficence: and it cannot be to us a source of any pain, that it has been set by those who are of one blood with most of ourselves; and has been embodied in a form so noble and so Catholic, as "The British and Foreign Bible Society."

The impulse which that institution, ten thousand times more glorious than all the exploits of the sword, has given to the conscience of Europe, and to the slumbering hope of millions in the region and shadow of death, demonstrates to Christians of every country what they cannot do by insulated zeal; and what they can do by co-operation.

In the United States we want nothing but concert to perform achievements astonishing to ourselves, dismaying to the adversaries of truth and piety; and most encouraging to every evangelical effort, on the surface of the globe.

No spectacle can be so illustrious in itself, so touching to man, or so grateful to God, as a nation pouring forth its devotion, its talent, and its treasures, for that kingdom of the Savior which is righteousness and peace.

If there by a single measure which can overrule objection, subdue opposition, and command exertion, this is the measure. That all our voices, all our affections, all our hands, should be joined in the grand design of promoting "peace on earth and good will toward men"--that they should resist the advance of misery--should carry the light of instruction into the dominions of ignorance; and the balm of joy to the soul of anguish; and all this by diffusing the oracles of God--addresses to the understanding an argument which cannot be encountered; and to the heart an appeal which its holiest emotions rise up to second.

Under such impressions, and with such views, fathers, brethren, fellow-citizens, the American Bible Society has been formed. Local feelings, party prejudices, sectarian jealousies, are excluded by its very nature. Its members are leagued in that, and in that alone, which calls up every hallowed, and puts down every unhallowed, principle--the dissemination of the Scriptures in the received versions where they exist, and in the most faithful where they may be required. In such a work, whatever is dignified, kind, venerable, true, has ample scope: while sectarian littleness and rivalries can find no avenue of admission.

The only question is, whether an object of such undisputed magnitude can be best obtained by a national Society, or by independent associations in friendly understanding and correspondence.

Without entering into the details of this inquiry, we may be permitted to state, in a few words, our reasons of preference to a national Society supported by local Societies and by individuals throughout our country.

Concentrated action is powerful action. The same powers, when applied by a common direction, will produce results impossible to their divided and partial exercise. A national object unites national feeling and concurrence. Unity of a great system combines energy of effect with economy of means. Accumulated intelligence interests and animates the public mind. And the Catholic efforts of a country, thus harmonized, give her a place in the moral convention of the world; and enable her to act directly upon the universal plans of happiness which are now pervading the nations.

It is true, that the prodigious territory of the United States--the increase of their population, which is gaining every day upon their moral cultivation--and the dreadful consequences which will ensue from a people's outgrowing the knowledge of eternal life; and reverting to a species of heathenism, which shall have all the address and profligacy of civilized society, without any religious control, present a sphere of action, which may for a long time employ and engross the cares of this Society, and of all the local Bible Societies of the land.

In the distinct anticipation of such an urgency, one of the main objects of the American Bible Society, is, not merely to provide a sufficiency of well printed and accurate editions of the Scriptures; but also to furnish great districts of the American continent with well executed Stereotype plates, for their cheap and extensive diffusion throughout regions which are now scantily supplied, at a discouraging expense; and which, nevertheless, open a wide and prepared field for the reception of revealed truth.

Yet, let it not be supposed, that geographical or political limits are to be the limits of the <u>American Bible Society</u>. That designation is meant to indicate, not the restrictions of their labor, but the source of its emanation. They will embrace, with thankfulness and pleasure, every opportunity of raying out, by means of the Bible, according to their ability, the light of life and immortality, to such parts of the world, as are destitute of the blessing, and are within their reach. In this high vocation, their ambition is to be fellow-workers with them who are fellow-workers with God.

People of the United States;

Have you ever been invited to an enterprise of such grandeur and glory? Do you not value the Holy Scriptures? Value them as containing your sweetest hope; your most thrilling joy? Can you submit to the thought that you should be torpid in your endeavors to disperse them, while the rest of Christendom is awake and alert? Shall you hang back, in heartless indifference, when Princes come down from their thrones, to bless the cottage of the poor with the Gospel of peace; and Imperial Sovereigns are gathering their fairest honors from spreading abroad the oracles of the Lord your God? Is it possible that <u>you</u> should not see, in this state of human things, a mighty motion of Divine Providence? The most Heavenly charity treads close upon the march of conflict and blood! The world is at peace! Scarce has the soldier time to unbind his helmet, and to wipe away the sweat from his brow, ere the voice of mercy succeeds to the clarion of battle, and calls the nations from enmity to love! Crowned heads bow to the head which is to wear "many crowns;" and, for the first time since the promulgation of Christianity, appear to act in unison for the recognition of its gracious principles, as being fraught alike with happiness to man and honor to God.

What has created so strange, so beneficient an alteration? This is no doubt the doing of the Lord, and it is marvelous in our eyes. But what instrument has he thought fit chiefly to use? That which contributes, in all latitudes and climes, to make Christians feel their unity, to rebuke the spirit of strife, and to open upon them the day of brotherly concord--the Bible! the Bible!--through Bible societies!

Come then, fellow-citizens, fellow-Christians, let us join in the sacred covenant. Let no heart be cold; no hand be idle; no purse reluctant! Come, while room is left for us in the ranks whose toil is goodness, and whose recompense is victory. Come cheerfully, eagerly, generally. Be it impressed on your souls, that a contribution, saved from even a cheap indulgence, may send a Bible to a desolate family; may become a radiatory point of "grace and truth" to a neighborhood of error and vice; and that a number of such contributions made at really no expense, may illumine a large tract of country, and successive generations of immortals, in that celestial knowledge, which shall secure their present and their future felicity.

But whatever be the proportion between expectation and experience, thus much is certain: we shall satisfy our conviction of duty--we shall have the praise of high endeavors for the highest ends--we shall minister to the blessedness of thousands, and tens of thousands, of whom we may never see the faces, nor hear the names. We shall set forward a system of happiness which will go on with accelerated motion and augmented vigor, after we shall have finished our career; and confer upon our children, and our children's children, the delight of seeing the wilderness turned into a fruitful field, by the blessing of God upon that seed which their father's sowed, and themselves watered. In fine we shall do our part toward that expansion and intensity of light divine, which shall visit, in its progress, the palaces of the great, and the hamlets of the small, until the whole "earth be full of the knowledge of Jehovah, as the waters cover the sea."

The Need for Western Colleges

Under the pressure of denominational rivalries which in part resulted from the Second Awakening, numerous church colleges were founded during the decades prior to the Civil War. The era has been termed by some as "the era of the church college." Many of these institutions did not survive for long, however, due to inadequate financial support and lack of sound planning. The former problem was particularly acute during the period of national economic distress in the late 1830's. To deal with the situation, the Society for the Promotion of Collegiate and Theological Education at the West was organized in 1843 in New York City. Shortly therafter the society printed the following report to answer the question as to why colleges were needed in the West. How does this article reflect the fact that one of the results of the Second Awakening was the founding of many new denominational colleges? What role did Catholicism play in the founding of new Protestant colleges? What contributions to society does the writer say that colleges can make which other Christian movements cannot make?

The considerations advanced in my last article go to show, that Colleges are a necessity of every extensive community, marked by nature as a social unity. We are now to look at some reasons why they are peculiarly needed at the West. First, then, we find such a reason in the fact that Rome is at this time making unprecedented efforts to garrison this valley with her seminaries of education. She claims already to have within it between fifteen and twenty colleges and theological schools; and this number is rapidly increasing.

To these permanency is ensured by the steadfastness of her policy, the constancy of her receipts from Catholic Europe, yearly increasing under the stimulating reports of her missionaries, and by her exacting despotism, moral if not ecclesiastic, over the earnings of her poor in this country. They are among the enduring formative forces in western society; and the causes which sustain them, will constantly add to their number. These institutions, together with numerous grades, under the conduct of their Jesuits and various religious orders, are offering (what professes to be) education almost as a gratuity, in many places in the West. Whatever other qualities her education may lack, we may be sure it will not want a subtle and intense proselytism, addressing not the reason but the senses, the taste, the imagination, and the passions; applying itself diversely to the fears of the timid, the enthusiasm of the ardent, the credulity of the simple, the affections of the young, and to that trashy sentiment and mawkish charity to which all principles are the same. Now the policy of Rome in playing upon all these elements through her educational enginery, is steadfast and profoundly sagacious. Her aim, in effect, is at the whole educational interest. The college is naturally the heart of the whole. The lower departments necessarily draw life from that. If Rome then grasps the college in the system of Western education, she virtually grasps the common school; she distills out the heart of the whole, if not a putrid superstition, at least that covert infidelity of which she is still more prolific.

Now a system so deep and so persistent, must be met by a correspondent depth and persistency of policy. Protestantism can no more counteract it by temporary and spasmodic efforts, than she could stop the Mississippi with a whirlwind. She can encounter it only by a system of permanent and efficient Protestant colleges. And this for two reasons. First, the Catholic seminaries in this country seem to meet a great and deeply felt social want, and can be displaced only by a supply for this want from another quarter. And secondly, in the nature of things, a college alone can counteract a college. The college acts upon the public mind in a manner so peculiar, through such ages and classes, and through influences so various and subtle, so constant, noiseless and profound, that it can be successfully combated only by a similar institution. Place efficient Protestant colleges in the proximity of the Catholic, and the latter will wither. For all purposes of severe intellectual discipline or masculine reason, their education is soon found to be a sham. A spiritual despotism dare not, cannot, teach true history or a free and manly philosophy. Again, other facts, which constitute a peculiar necessity for colleges in the West, are found in the circumstances and character of its population. First, the West is in its formative state. Never will impressions be made so easily and so enduringly for good or evil. Never will it be so important that its architect-minds--its plastic forces--should be endued with a broad and liberal intelligence. According to the elements now thrown in, it will soon permanently crystalize into dark and unshapely forms, or into order and beauty.

Another peculiar demand for colleges, may be found in the immense rapidity of our growth, and in the character of that growth, being a representative of almost every clime, opinion, sect, language, and social institute, not only of this country but of Christian Europe. Never was a more intense power of intellectual and moral fusion requisite to prevent the utter disorganization of society. Never was a people put to such a perilous proof of its power of assimilation, or required to incorporate with itself so rapidly such vast masses. We have in this fact, as well as in that of the Catholic aggression, dangers and trials put upon us, which our fathers never knew. Society here is new yet vast, and with all its forces in insulation or antagonism. Never was a community in more urgent need of those institutions, whose province it is profoundly to penetrate a people with a burning intelligence that shall fuse it into a unity with those great principles which are the organic life and binding forces of all society.

Again, in consequence of the incoherency of this element in a population thus heterogeneous, and broken off from the fixtures of old communities, without time to form new ones, all the social forces are shifting and mutable, and yield like the particles of liquid to the last force impressed. This quality of western society, combined with the bold, prompt, energetic and adventurous temperament impressed generally on it by common influences in the life of the emigrant, exposes it to vehement and brief excitements, to epidemic delusion and agitation. Upon this sea of incoherent and vehement mind, every wind of opinion has been let loose, and is struggling for the mastery; and the mass heaves restlessly to and fro under the thousand different forces impressed. The West is, therefore, peculiarly perturbed with demagogism and popular agitation, not only in politics, but in religion, and all social interests. Amid these shifting social elements, we want principles of stability, we want a system of permanent forces, we want deep, strong and constant influences, that shall take from the changefulness and excitability of the western mind, by giving it the tranquillity of depth, and shall protect it from delusive and fitful impulses, by enduing it with a calm, profound and pure reason.

Thus, while society with us has on the one hand to contend against a masked and political spiritual despotism entrenching itself in the educational interest, and on the other against a demagogic agitation, urged on too often by avarice, or ruffianism, or faction, or a sophistical but specious skepticism, or by fanatical or superstitious or shallow religionisms and socialisms of every hue, we find our defence against both to be the same, a thorough popular enlightenment and belief, anchored by permanent institutions gradually pervading the mass with great and tranquil and guardian truths, and adjusting the system to the fixed laws of intellectual and moral gravitation. It may perhaps be asked, "Why not, in such a community, immediately proceed by opposing to agitation for evil, agitation for good?" This may at times be expedient, but cannot be relied on permanently. First, because popular agitation, unless based on deep-wrought intellectual convictions, can only palliate, it cannot cure any evil. In the second place, in the germ of popular agitation, a freedom from the restraints of conscience and truth and honor, often gives a decisive advantage, and agitating movements springing forth immediately from the people to be moved, and possessing a quiet sympathy with its feeling, and a shrewd tact in dealing with its passions and prejudices, must ever out-general any countermovement originating from a different source. Especially, movements of this kind from abroad are liable to find themselves forestalled--the popular ear and mind preoccupied-- arguments closed--opposing tracts already in the hands of the people--and the Bible itself, under their elected interpreters, made to preach another gospel.

The above exigencies of Western society cannot be met without colleges. I am far from undervaluing over [other?] movements of Christian philanthropy towards the country. I am most grateful for them. I bless God for his Word broadcast by the American Bible Society amid this people; I am thankful for the interest the American Tract Society are directing hitherward, and hail with pleasure all the living truth and hallowed thought brought by it into contact with the popular mind. The attitude and history of the American Home Missionary Society in relation to the West, fill my mind with a sentiment of moral sublimity, and give it rank among the noblest and most sagacious schemes in the records of Christian benevolence. It will stand in history invested, to a great extent, with the moral grandeur of a civilizer and evangelizer of a new empire. But these are far from excluding the scheme of colleges. The permanency of their benefits can be grounded only on a thorough and liberal popular enlightenment. The educational interest, then, must underlie them all. But the only way in which the East can lay a controlling grasp on this, is by the establishment among us of permanent educational institutions. In a population, one tenth at least of which cannot read, it is plain that education is an essential prerequisite to bringing a large class--and that most necessary to be reached--within the influence of truth through the press. And no system of foreign supply of ministers, teachers or educated men, can obviate the necessity of institutions that shall constantly send forth those that shall be the educators of this people, in the school, the pulpit, the legislature, and the various departments of social life. Artificial irrigation cannot take the place of living waters. We are grateful for streams from abroad, but we feel there is need of opening fountains of life in the bosom of the people itself. The supplies from abroad we cannot rely on long. They are every day becoming more inadequate in numbers, and must to some extent be deficient in adaptation to our wants; a deficiency that often for years, sometimes for life, shuts one out from the people.

The common exigencies, then, of every extensive society, require colleges within itself. The peculiar evils to which that of the West is exposed, obviously cannot be permanently and successfully met by other means. The question then recurs in every aspect of this subject, Will the East assist the West in establishing a Protestant system of home education, or will she leave her to grapple single-handed with Romanism, and the other peculiar dangers to which she is exposed, in addition to the necessities that cluster around every infant community, or will she attempt by palliatives addressed to the symptoms, to heal a disease seated in the heart? A dangerous malady is on the patient. The peril is imminent and requires promptitude. Shall remedies be adapted to the disease or the symptoms, or with such fearful chances against it, shall the patient be abandoned to the conflict betwixt nature and death? Let the East remember the life thus hazarded involves her own--it is to her the brand of Meleager.

PART 2   EXPANDING AMERICA
1820-1865

The period from 1820 to 1865 was a time of unprecedented expansion not only for the American nation geographically, but also for religion as the churches confronted the problems and opportunities of the rapidly changing American society. The results of the Second Awakening included the establishing of new religious institutions in western areas recently populated by eastern migrants. These institutions--churches, schools, and missionary societies--would have to face the problems which would accompany the westward movement.

Of the problems facing the country in 1820, none presented a greater challenge than the institution of slavery. Since slavery influenced everything it touched, the church could not escape its impact, nor did slavery go unaltered when faced by the church. Such was the case long before 1820, however. For as early as the seventeenth century, and continuing through the eighteenth, churchmen argued the case and preached sermons which both supported and opposed human bondage. When the massive assault led by the abolitionists was leveled against slavery in the 1830's, those on both sides of the issue made new efforts in defense of their case. In the heat of the verbal battles which ensued, slaveowners were called "sinners," while their opponents were considered "biblical infidels." To no one's surprise, numerous individual churches and entire denominations experienced divisions. Antagonists like William Ellery Channing, James H. Hammond, and James H. Thornwell presented opinions on slavery which provided the basis for the ecclesiastical involvement in the slavery struggle.

During the first twenty years of the nineteenth century, many voluntary societies emerged that channeled the energy emitted by Second Awakening revivals into missionary, educational, and reform causes. In the years which followed, this activity was aided by changes in theology which placed greater emphasis on man's freedom to improve the human situation, as well as by a general atmosphere of optimism that favored the activism of the reform movement. With a touch of millennial expectancy, Charles G. Finney, the leading revivalist of the period, challenged the church to take the lead in cleaning up America's social sins. Theodore D. Weld, one of Finney's most famous converts, thundered against the ills of slavery, while preacher Lyman Beecher singled out the intemperate use of alcohol as a foremost threat to America's hopes of building a better society.

In this period of expansion, it was not uncommon for churchmen to provide theological arguments for the concept of American destiny. Such ideas lingered from seventeenth century New England Puritans who considered themselves God's chosen people, and continued to draw strength in the era of the Revolution when clergymen insisted God was conceiving a new nation to serve Him. During the decades just prior to the Civil War, this same God was expanding America's power so it could bring blessing to the world. If a journalist like John O'Sullivan could talk about America's "manifest destiny," certainly a seasoned politician like John Quincy Adams might expect a sympathetic hearing of his scriptural argument for American expansion. The growing home missions enterprise welcomed the attention focused on the national movement westward, as is suggested by the veteran medical missionary Marcus Whitman. Militarist Robert F. Stockton illustrates how the idealism of destiny was always in danger of being confused with opportunism.

When the Civil War came, the religious beliefs of those cloaked in both blue and gray led each to behave as though God were on their side in this "holy war." The aura of self-righteousness which exuded over the slavery issue during the antebellum years intensified during the war. Individuals, as well as groups of religious people, like those gathered at Richmond in 1863, insisted they were right. Toward the end of the war, President Lincoln found little reason for rejoicing, though clergymen Henry Ward Beecher detected numerous positive results from it.

SLAVERY

Slavery

WILLIAM ELLERY CHANNING

William Ellery Channing (1780-1842) was graduated from Harvard in 1796 and occupied the pastorate of the Federal Street Church in Boston from 1803 until his death. Early during his tenure at the Boston church he broke with Calvinist theology mainly over the doctrine of the depravity of man, preaching a gospel of the love and goodness of both God and man. Though reluctant for a number of years to sever his ties with the orthodox Calvinists, in 1819 he announced what were to become the basic beliefs of the new Unitarian movement. Along with being an influential religious leader, Channing was a significant literary figure and social critic, paving the way for the Transcendental movement and opposing strongly slavery and the idea of civil war. His essay on slavery which follows appears in The Works of William E. Channing, D.D., published in Boston by the American Unitarian Association in 1903. To what extent does Channing believe slavery is a moral issue? On what bases does he reject the idea that the

Apostle Paul sanctioned slavery? In 1835 when he writes this essay, is Channing optimistic or pessimistic concerning the issue of slavery and the churches' relationship to it?

The first question to be proposed by a rational being is, not what is profitable, but what is right. Duty must be primary, prominent, most conspicious among the objects of human thought and pursuit. If we cast down from its supremacy, if we inquire first for our interests, and then for our duties, we shall certainly err. We can never see the right clearly and fully but by making it our first concern. No judgment can be just or wise but that which is built on the conviction of the paramount worth and importance of duty. This is the fundamental truth, the supreme law of reason; and the mind which does not start from this, in its inquiries into human affairs, is doomed to great, perhaps fatal, error.

Of late our country has been convulsed by the question of slavery; and the people, in proportion as they have felt vehemently, have thought superficially, or hardly thought at all; and we see the results in a singular want of well-defined principles, in a strange vagueness and inconsistency of opinion, and in the proneness to excess which belongs to unsettled minds. The multitude have been called, now to contemplate the horrors of slavery, and now to shudder at the ruin and bloodshed which must follow emancipation. The word massacre has resounded through the land, striking terror into strong as well as tender hearts, and awakening indignation against whatever may seem to threaten such a consummation. The consequence is that not a few dread all discussion of the subject, and, if not reconciled to the continuance of slavery, at least believe that they have no duty to perform, no testimony to bear, no influence to exert, no sentiments to cherish and spread, in relation to this evil. What is still worse, opinions either favoring or extenuating it are heard with little or no disapprobation. Concessions are made to it which would once have shocked the community; whilst to assail it is pronounced unwise and perilous. No stronger reason for a calm exposition of its true character

can be given than this very state of the public mind. A
community can suffer no greater calamity than the loss of
its principles. Lofty and pure sentiment is the life and
hope of a people. There was never such an obligation to
disucss slavery as at this moment, when recent events have
done much to unsettle obscure men's minds in regard to it.
This result is to be ascribed in part to the injudicious
vehemence of those who have taken into their hands the
cause of the slave. Such ought to remember, that to espouse
a good cause is not enough. We must maintain it in a spirit
answering to its dignity. Let no man touch the great interests of humanity who does not strive to sanctify himself
for the work by cleansing his heart of all wrath and
uncharitableness, who cannot hope that he is in a measure
baptized into the spirit of universal love. Even sympathy
with the injured and oppressed may do harm, by being partial,
exclusive, and bitterly indignant. How far the declension
of the spirit of freedom is to be ascribed to the cause now
suggested, I do not say. The effect is plain, and whoever
sees and laments the evil should strive to arrest it.

But this subject has more than philosophical dignity. It has
an important bearing on character. Our interest in it is
one test by which our comprehension of the distinctive spirit
of Christianity must be judged. Christianity is the manifestation and inculcation of universal love. The great teaching
of Christianity is, that we must recognize and respect human
nature in all its forms in the poorest, most fallen. We
must look beneath "the flesh" to the "spirit." The spiritual
principle in man is what entitles him to our brotherly regard. To be just to this is the great injunction of our
religion. To overlook this, on account of condition or
color, is to violate the great Christian law. We have reason
to think that it is one design of God in appointing the vast
diversities of human condition, to put to the test, and to
bring out most distinctly, the principle of spiritual love.
It is wisely ordered that human nature is not set before us
in a few forms of beauty, magnificence, and outward glory.
To be dazzled and attracted by these would be no sign of
reverence for what is interior and spiritual in human nature.
To lead us to discern and love this, we are brought into
connection with fellow-creatures whose outward circumstances
are repulsive. To recognize our own spiritual nature and
God's image in these humble forms, to recognize as brethren

those who want all outward distinctions, is the chief way in which we are to manifest the spirit of him who came to raise the fallen and to save the lost. We see then, the moral importance of the question of slavery. According to our decision of it, we determine our comprehension of the Christian law. He who cannot see a brother, a child of God, a man possessing all the rights of humanity, under a skin darker than his own, wants the vision of a Christian. He worships the outward. The spirit is not revealed to him. To look unmoved on the degradation and wrongs of a fellow-creature, because burned by a fiercer sun, proves us strangers to justice and love in those universal forms which characterize Christianity. The greatest of all distinctions, the only enduring one, is moral goodness, virtue, religion. Outward distinctions cannot add to the dignity of this. The wealth of worlds is "not sufficient for a burnt-offering" on its alter. A being capable of this is invested by God with solemn claims on his fellow-creatures. To exclude millions of such beings from our sympathy, because of outward disadvantages, proves that, in whatever else we surpass them, we are not their superiors in Christian virtue.

Attempts are often made to support slavery by the authority of revelation. "Slavery," it is said, "is allowed in the Old Testament, and not condemned in the New. Paul commands slaves to obey. He commands masters, not to release their slaves, but to treat them justly. Therefore slavery is right, is sanctified by God's word." In this age of the world, and amidst the light which has been thrown on the true interpretation of the Scriptures, such reasoning hardly deserves notice. A few words only will be offered in reply.

This reasoning proves too much. If usages, sanctioned in the Old Testament and not forbidden in the New, are right, then our moral code will undergo a sad deterioration. Polygamy was allowed to the Israelites, was the practice of the holiest men, and was common and licensed in the age of the Apostles. But the Apostles nowhere condemn it, nor was the renunciation of it made an essential condition of admission into the Christian church. It is true that in one passage Christ has condemned it by implication. But is not slavery condemned by stronger implication, in the many passages which make the new religion to consist in serving one another, and in doing to others what we would that they should do to ourselves? Why may not Scripture be used to stock our houses with wives as well as with slaves?

Again. Paul is said to sanction slavery. Let us now ask, What was slavery in the age of Paul? It was the slavery, not so much of black as of white men, not merely of barbarians, but of Greeks, not merely of the ignorant and debased, but of the virtuous, educated, and refined. Piracy and conquest were the chief means of supplying the slave-market, and they heeded neither character nor condition. Sometimes the greater part of the population of a captured city was sold into bondage, sometimes the whole, as in the case of Jerusalem. Noble and royal families, the rich and great, the learned and powerful, the philosopher and poet, the wisest and best men, were condemned to the chain. Such was ancient slavery. . . .

Slavery, in the age of the Apostle, had so penetrated society, was so intimately interwoven with it and the materials of servile war were so abundant, that religion preaching freedom to the slave would have shaken the social fabric to its foundation, and would have armed against itselt the whole power of the state. Paul did not then assail the institution. He satisfied himself with spreading principles which, however slowly, could not but work its destruction.

Let me offer another remark. The perversion of Scripture to the support of slavery is singularly inexcusable in this country. Paul not only commanded slaves to obey their masters. He delivered these precepts: "Let every soul be subject unto the higher powers. For there is no power but of God: the powers that be are ordained of God. Whosoever, therefore, resisteth the power, resisteth the ordinance of God: and they that resist shall receive to themselves damnation." This passage was written in the time of Nero. It teaches passive obedience to despotism more strongly than any text teaches the lawfulness of slavery. Accordingly it has been quoted for ages by the supporters of arbitrary power, and made the stronghold of tyranny. Did our fathers acquiesce in the most obvious interpretation of this text? Because the first Christians were taught to obey despotic rule, did our fathers feel as if Christianity had stripped

men of their rights? Did they argue that tyranny was to
be excused because forcible opposition to it is in most
cases wrong? Did they argue that absolute power ceases to
be unjust because, as a general rule, it is the duty of
subjects to obey? Did they infer that bad institutions
ought to be perpetual because the subversion of them by force
will almost always inflict greater evil than it removes?
No; they were wiser interpreters of God's word. They believed that despotism was a wrong, notwithstanding the
general obligation upon its subjects to obey: and that
whenever a whole people should so feel the wrong as to demand its removal, the time for removing it had fully come.
Such is the school in which we here have been brought up.
To us, it is no mean proof of the divine original of
Christianity, that it teaches human brotherhood and favors
human rights; and yet, on the ground of two or three passages, which admit different constructions, we make
Christianity the minister of slavery, the forger of chains
for those whom it came to make free.

It is a plain rule of scriptural criticism, that particular
texts should be interpreted according to the general tenor
and spirit of Christianity. And what is the general, the
perpetual teaching of Christianity in regard to social duty?
"All things whatsoever ye would that men should do to you,
do ye even so to them; for this is the law and the prophets."
Now, does not every man feel that nothing, nothing, could
induce him to consent to be a slave? Does he not feel that,
if reduced to this abject lot, his whole nature, his reason,
conscience, affections, would cry out against it as the
greatest of calamities and wrongs? Can he pretend, then,
that, in holding others in bondage, he does to his neighbor
what he would that his neighbor should do to him? Of what
avail are a few texts, which were designed for local and
temporary use, when urged against the vital, essential spirit,
and the plainest precepts of our religion?

The work which I proposed to myself is now completed. I ask
and hope for it the Divine blessing, as far as it expresses
truth, and breathes the spirit of justice and humanity. If
I have written any thing under the influence of prejudice,
passion, or unkindness to any human being, I ask forgiveness
of God and man. I have spoken strongly, not to offend or
give pain, but to produce in others deep conviction corres-

ponding to my own. Nothing could have induced me to fix my
thoughts on this painful subject, but a conviction, which
pressed on me with increasing weight, that the times demanded
a plain and free exposition of the truth. The few last
months have increased my solicitude for the country. Public
sentiment has seemed to me to be losing its healthfulness
and vigor. I have seen symptoms of the decline of the old
spirit of liberty. Servile opinions have seemed to gain
ground among us. The faith of our fathers in free institutions has waxed faint, and is giving place to despair of
human improvement. I have perceived a disposition to deride
abstract rights, to speak of freedom as a dream, and of
republican governments as built on sand. I have perceived
a faintheartedness in the cause of human rights. The condemnation which has been passed on abolitionists has seemed
to be settling into acquiescence in slavery. The sympathies
of the community have been turned from the slave to the
master. The impious doctrine, that human laws can repeal
the divine, can convert unjust and oppressive power into
a moral right, has more and more tintured the style of conversation and the press. With these sad and solemn views of
society, I could not be silent; and I thank God, amidst the
consciousness of great weakness and imperfection, that I
have been able to offer this humble tribute, this sincere
though feeble testimony, this expression of heart-felt
allegiance, to the cause of freedom, justice, and humanity.

Having stated the circumstances which have moved me to write,
I ought to say that they do not discourage me. Were darker
omens to gather round us, I should not despair. With a
faith like his who came to prepare the way for the Great
Deliverer, I feel and can say, "The kingdom of heaven," the
reign of justice and disinterested love, "is at hand, and
all flesh shall see the salvation of God." I know, and rejoice to know, that a power, mightier than the prejudices
and oppression of ages, is working on earth for the world's
redemption,--the power of Christian truth and goodness. It
descended from heaven in the person of Christ. It was manifest in his life and death. From his cross it went forth
conquering and to conquer. Its mission is "to preach deliverance to the captive, and set at liberty them that are
bound." It has opened many a prison-door. It is ordained
to break every chain. I have faith in its triumphs. I do
not, cannot despair.

Letters on Slavery

JAMES H. HAMMOND

During the years prior to the Civil War, the accusation that slaveholders were sinful was resented by many Southerners. The South was a stronghold of orthodox religion, and slaveholding church members argued that the Bible defended their actions. James H. Hammond, a Christian owner of slaves from South Carolina, claimed it was presumptuous for those who attacked slavery to claim Divine support. His arugment is taken from his "Letters on Slavery," The Pro-Slavery Argument (Charleston, S.C., 1852), pp. 104-9. How does Hammond reconcile slavery with Scripture? Why does he think that abolitionists do the Bible more harm than freethinkers? How does Hammond use history to support his position on slavery?

If you were to ask me whether I am an advocate of Slavery in the abstract, I should probably answer, that I am not, according to my understanding of the question. I do not like to deal in abstractions. It seldom leads to any useful ends. There are few universal truths. I do not now remember any single moral truth universally acknowledged. We have no assurance that it is given to our finite understanding to comprehend abstract moral truth. Apart from revelation and the inspired writings, what ideas should we have even of God, salvation and immortality? . . . I might say that I am no more in favor of Slavery in the abstract, than I am of poverty, disease, deformity, idiocy, or any other inequality in the condition of the human family; that I love perfection, and think I should enjoy a millennium such as God has promised. But what would it amount to? A pledge that I would join you to set about eradicating those apparently inevitable evils of our nature, in equalizing the condition of all mankind, consummating the perfection of our race, and introducing the millennium? By no means. To effect these things, belongs exclusively to a higher power. And it would be well for us to leave the Almighty to perfect his own works and fulfil his own covenants. . . . On Slavery in the abstract, then, it would not be amiss to have as little as possible to say. Let us contemplate it as it is. And thus contemplating it, the first question we have to ask ourselves is, whether it is contrary to the will of God, as revealed to us in his Holy Scriptures--the only certain means given us to ascertain his will. If it is, then Slavery is a sin. And I admit at once that every man is bound to set his face against it, and to emancipate his slaves, should he hold any.

Let us open these Holy Scriptures. In the twentieth chapter of Exodus, seventeenth verse, I find the following words: "Thou shalt not covet thy neighbor's house, thou shalt not covet thy neighbor's wife, nor his man-servant, nor his maid-servant, nor his ox, nor his ass, nor anything that is thy neighbor's"--which is the tenth of those commandments that declare the essential principles of the great moral law delivered to Moses by God himself. Now, discarding all technical and verbal quibbling as wholly unworthy to be used in interpreting the Word of God, what is the plain meaning, undoubted intent, and true spirit of this commandment? Does it not emphatically and explicitly forbid you to disturb your neighbor in the enjoyment of his property; and more especially of that which is here specifically mentioned as being lawfully, and by this commandment made sacredly his? Prominent in the catalogue stands his "man-servant and his maid-servant who are thus distinctly <u>consecrated</u> <u>as</u> <u>his</u> <u>property</u>, and guaranteed to him for his exclusive benefit, in the most solemn manner. . . .

You cannot deny that there were among the Hebrews "bondmen forever." You cannot deny that God especially authorized his chosen people to purchase "bondmen forever" from the heathen, as recorded in the twenty-fifth chapter of Leviticus, and that they are there designated by the very Hebrew word used in the tenth commandment. Nor can you deny that a

"BONDMAN FOREVER" is a "SLAVE;" yet you endeavor to hang an argument of immortal consequence upon the wretched subterfuge, that the precise word "slave" is not be found in the translation of the Bible. As if the translators were canonical expounders of the Holy Scriptures, and <u>their words</u>, not <u>God's meanings</u>, must be regarded as his revelation.

It is vain to look to Christ or any of his Apostles to justify such blasphemous perversions of the word of God. Although Slavery in its most revolting form was everywhere visible around them, no visionary notions of piety or philanthropy ever tempted them to gainsay the LAW, even to mitigate the cruel severity of the existing system. On the contrary, regarding Slavery as an <u>established</u>, as well as <u>inevitable condition of human society</u>, they never hinted at such a thing as its termination on earth, any more than that "the poor may cease out of the land," which God affirms to Moses shall never be: and they exhort "all servants under the yoke" to "count their masters as worthy of all honor:" "to obey them in all things according to the flesh; not with eye-service as men-pleasers, but in singleness of heart, fearing God;" "not only the good and gentle, but also the froward:" "For what glory is it if when ye are buffetted for your faults ye shall take it patiently, but if when ye do well and suffer for it ye take it patiently, this is acceptable of God." St. Paul actually apprehended a runaway slave, and sent him to his master! Instead of deriving from the Gospel any sanction for the work you have undertaken, it would be difficult to imagine sentiments and conduct more strikingly in contrast, than those of the Apostles and the abolitionists. . . .

I think, I may safely conclude, and I firmly believe, that American Slavery is not only not a sin, but especially commanded by God through Moses, and approved by Christ through his apostles. And here I might close its defence; for what God ordains, and Christ sanctifies, should surely command the respect and toleration of man. But I fear there has grown up in our time a transcendental religion, which is throwing even transcendental philosophy into the shade-- a religion too pure and elevated for the Bible; which seeks to erect among men a higher standard of morals than the Almighty has revealed, or our Saviour preached; and which is probably destined to do more to impede the extension of

God's kingdom on earth than all the infidels who have ever lived. Error is error. It is as dangerous to deviate to the right hand as the left. And when man, professing to be holy man, and who are by numbers regarded, declare those things to be sinful which our Creator has expressly authorized and instituted, they do more to destroy his authority among mankind than the most wicked can effect, by proclaiming that to be innocent which has forbidden. To this self-righteous and self-exalted class belong all the abolitionists whose writings I have read. With them it is no end of the argument to prove your propositions by the text of the Bible, interpreted according to its plain and palpable meaning, and as understood by all mankind for three thousand years before their time. They are more ingenious at construing and interpolating to accommodate it to their new-fangled and etherial [sic] code of morals, than ever were Voltaire and Hume in picking it to pieces, to free the world from what they considered a delusion. When the abolitionists proclaim "man-stealing" to be a sin, and show me that it is so written down by God, I admit them to be right, and shudder at the idea of such a crime. But when I show them that to hold "bondmen forever" is ordained by God, <u>they deny the Bible, and set up in its place a law of their own making.</u> I must then cease to reason with them on this branch of the question. Our religion differs as widely as our manners. The great judge in our day of final account must decide beween us.

Address on Slavery

JAMES H. THORNWELL

While several denominations suffered splits prior to the Civil War (among them the Methodists and Baptists), others forestalled the inevitable until after the war had started. In May of 1861, the Old School Presbyterians met in Philadelphia, where the question of political loyalty emerged. Resolutions offered by northerners calling for a declaration of loyalty to the Federal Government were opposed vehemently by southern representatives. In December 1861, many of them met in Augusta, Georgia where they organized the General Assembly of the Presbyterian Church in the Confederate States of America. The Assembly approved an address composed by James H. Thornwell, which gave considerable attention to the moral issues of the peculiar institution of slavery. The address was entered into the minutes of the new denomination's initial meeting. How does Thornwell appeal to the Bible to support his position? How does he respond to the claim that "slavery is inconsistent with human rights?" What argument does the speaker use to refute the claim that the Scriptures oppose slavery?

The antagonism of Northern and Southern sentiment on the subject of slavery lies at the root of all the difficulties which have resulted in the dismemberment of the Federal Union, and involved us in the horrors of an unnatural war. . . .

And here we may venture to lay before the Christian world our views as a Church, upon the subject of slavery. We beg a candid hearing.

In the first place we would have it distinctly understood that, in our ecclesiastical capacity, we are neither the friends nor the foes of slavery, that is to say, we have no commission either to propagate or abolish it. The policy of its existence or non-existence is a question which exclusively belongs to the State. We have no right, as a Church, to enjoin it as a duty, or to condemn it as a sin. Our business is with the duties which spring from the relation; the duties of the masters on the one hand, and of their slaves on the other. These duties we are to proclaim and to enforce with spiritual sanctions. The social, civil, political problems connected with this great subject transcend our sphere, as God has not entrusted to His Church the organization of society, the construction of Governments, nor the allotment of individuals to their various stations. The Church has as much right to preach to the monarchies of Europe, and the despotism of Asia, the doctrines of republican equality, as to preach to the Governments of the South the extirpation of slavery. This position is impregnable, unless it can be shown that slavery is a sin. Upon every other hypothesis, it is so clearly a question for the State, that the proposition would never for a moment have been doubted, had there not been a foregone conclusion in relation to its moral character. Is slavery, then, a sin?

In answering this question, as a Church, let it be distinctly borne in mind that the only rule of judgment is the written word of God. The Church knows nothing of the intuitions of reason or the deductions of philosophy, except those reproduced in the Sacred Canon. She has a positive constitution in the Holy Scriptures, and has no right to utter a single syllable upon any subject, except as the Lord puts words in her mouth. She is founded, in other words, upon express <u>revelation</u>. Her creed is an authoritative testimony of God, and not a speculation, and what she proclaims, she must proclaim with the infallible certitude of faith, and not with the hesitating assent of an opinion. The question, then, is brought within a narrow compass: Do the Scriptures directly or indirectly condemn slavery as a sin? If they do not, the dispute is ended, for the Church, without forfeiting her character, dares not go beyond them.

Now, we venture to assert that if men had drawn their conclusions upon this subject only from the Bible, it would no more have entered into any human head to denounce slavery as a sin, than to denounce monarchy, aristocracy or poverty. The truth is, men have listened to what they falsely considered as primitive intuitions, or as necessary deductions from primitive cognitions, and then have gone to the Bible to confirm the crotchets of their vain philosophy. They have gone there determined to find a particular result, and the consequence is, that they leave with having made, instead of having interpreted, Scripture. Slavery is no new thing. It has not only existed for ages in the world, but it has existed, under every dispensation of the covenant of grace, in the Church of God. Indeed, the first organization of the Church as a visible society, separate and distinct from the unbelieving world, was inaugurated in the family of a slaveholder. Among the very first persons to whom the seal of circumcision was affixed, were the slaves of the father of the faithful, some born in his house, and others bought with his money. Slavery again re-appears under the Law. God sanctions it in the first table of the Decalogue, and Moses treats it as an institution to be regulated, not abolished; legitimated and not condemned. We come down to the age of the New Testament, and we find it again in the Churches founded by the Apostles under the plenary inspiration of the Holy Ghost. These facts are utterly amazing, if slavery is the enormous sin which its enemies represent it to be. It will not do to say that the Scriptures have treated it only in a general, incidental way, without any clear implication as to its moral character. Moses surely made it the subject of express and positive legislation, and the Apostles are equally explicit in inculcating the duties which spring from both sides of the relation. They treat slaves as bound to obey and inculcate obedience as an office of religion--a thing wholly self-contradictory, if the authority exercised over them were unlawful and iniquitous.

But what puts this subject in a still clearer light, is the manner in which it is sought to extort from the Scriptures a contrary testimony. The notion of direct and explicit condemnation is given up. The attempt is to show that the genius and spirit of Christianity are opposed to it--that its great cardinal principles of virtue are utterly against it. Much stress is laid upon the Golden Rule and upon the general denunciations of tyranny and oppression. To all this we reply, that no principle is clearer than that a case positively excepted cannot be included under a general law. Let us concede, for a moment, that the law of love, and the condemnation of tyranny and oppression, seem logically to involve, as a result, the condemnation of slavery; yet, if slavery is afterwards expressly mentioned and treated as a lawful relation, it obviously follows, unless Scripture is to be interpreted as consistent with itself, that slavery is, by necessary implication, excepted. The Jewish law forbade, as a general rule, the marriage of a man with his brother's wife. The same law expressly enjoined the same marriage in a given case. The given case was, therefore, an exception, and not to be treated as a violation of the general rule. The law of love has always been the law of God. It was enunciated by Moses almost as clearly as it was enunciated by Jesus Christ. Yet, notwithstanding this law, Moses and the Apostles alike sanctioned the relation of slavery. The conclusion is inevitable, either that the law is not opposed to it, or that slavery is an excepted case. To say that the prohibition of tyranny and oppression include slavery, is to beg the whole question. Tyranny and oppression involve either the unjust usurpation or the unlawful exercises of power. It is the unlawfulness, either in its principle or measure, which constitutes the core of the sin. Slavery must, therefore, be proved to be unlawful, before it can be referred to any such category. The master may, indeed, abuse his power, but he oppresses not simply as a master, but as a wicked master.

But, apart from all this, the law of love is simply the inculcation of universal equity. It implies nothing as to the existence of various ranks and gradations in society. The interpretation which makes it repudiate slavery would make it equally repudiate all social, civil and political inequalities. Its meaning is, not that we should conform ourselves to the arbitrary expectations of others, but that we should render unto them precisely the same measure which, if we were in their circumstance, it would be reasonable and just in us to demand at their hands. It condemns slavery, therefore, only upon the supposition that slavery is a sinful relation--that is, he who extracts the prohibition of slavery from the Golden Rule, begs the very point in dispute.

We cannot prosecute the argument in detail, but we have said enough, we think, to vindicate the position of the Southern

Church. We have assumed no new attitude. We stand exactly where the Church of God has always stood--from Abraham to Moses, from Moses to Christ, from Christ to the Reformers, and from the Reformers to ourselves. We stand upon the foundation of the Prophets and Apostles, Jesus Christ Himself being the Chief corner stone. Shall we be excluded from the fellowship of our brethren in other lands, because we dare not depart from the charter of our faith? Shall we be branded with the stigma of reproach, because we cannot consent to corrupt the word of God to suit the intuitions of an infidel philosophy? Shall our names be cast out as evil, and the finger of scorn pointed at us, because we utterly refuse to break our communion with Abraham, Isaac and Jacob, with Moses, David and Isaiah, with Apostles, Prophets and Martyrs, with all the noble army of confessors who have gone to glory from slave-holding countries and from a slave-holding Church, without ever having dreamed that they were living in mortal sin, by conniving at slavery in the midst of them? If so, we shall take consolation in the cheering consciousness that the Master has accepted us. We may be denounced, despised and cast out of the Synagogues of our brethren. But while they are wrangling about the distinctions of men according to the flesh, we shall go forward in our Divine work, and confidently anticipate that, in the great day, as the consequence of our humble labors, we shall meet millions of glorified spirits, who have come up from the bondage of earth to a nobler freedom than human philosophy ever dreamed of. Others, if they please, may spend their time in declaiming on the tyranny of earthly masters; it will be our aim to resist the real tyrants which oppress the soul--Sin and Satan. These are the foes against whom we shall find it employment enough to wage a successful war. And to this holy war it is the purpose of our Church to devote itself with redoubled energy. We feel that the souls of our slaves are a solemn trust, and we shall strive to present them faultless and complete before the presence of God.

Indeed, as we contemplate their condition in the Southern States, and contrast it with that of their fathers before them, and that of their brethren in the present day in their native land, we cannot but accept it as a gracious Providence that they have been brought in such numbers to our shores, and redeemed from the bondage of barbarism and sin.

Slavery to them has certainly been overruled for the greatest good. It has been a link in the wondrous chain of Providence, through which many sons and daughters have been made heirs of the heavenly inheritance. The Providential result is, of course, no justification, if the thing is intrinsically wrong; but it is certainly a matter of devout thanksgiving, and no obscure intimation of the will and purpose of God, and of the consequent duty of the Church. We cannot forbear to say, however, that the general operation of the system is kindly and benevolent; it is a real and effective discipline, and without it, we are profoundly persuaded that the African race in the midst of us can never be elevated in the scale of being. As long as that race, in its comparative degradation, co-exists, side by side, with the white, bondage is its normal condition.

As to the endless declamation about human rights, we have only to say that human rights are not a fixed, but a fluctuating quantity. Their sum is not the same in any two nations on the globe. The rights of Englishmen are one thing, the rights of Frenchmen another. There is a minimum without which a man cannot be responsible; there is a maximum which expresses the highest degree of civilization and of Christian culture. The education of the species consists in its ascent along this line. As you go up, the number of rights increases, but the number of individuals who possess them diminishes. As you come down the line, rights are diminished, but the individuals are multiplied. It is just the opposite of the predicamental scale of the logicians. There comprehension diminishes as you ascend and extension increases, and comprehension increases as you descend and extension diminishes. Now, when it is said that slavery is inconsistent with human rights, we crave to understand what point in this line is the slave conceived to occupy. There are, no doubt, many rights which belong to other men--to Englishmen [,] to Frenchmen, to his master, for example-- which are denied to him. But is he fit to process them? Has God qualified him to meet the responsibilities which their possession necessarily implies? His place in the scale is determined by his competency to fulfil its duties. There are other rights which he certainly possesses, without which he could neither be human nor accountable. Before slavery can be charged with doing him injustice, it must be shown that the minimum which falls to his lot at the bottom of the line is out of proportion to his capacity and culture--a thing

which can never be done by abstract speculation. The truth
is, the education of the human race for liberty and virtue,
is a vast Providential scheme, and God assigns to every man,
by a wise and holy decree, the precise place he is to occupy
in the great moral school of humanity. The scholars are distributed into classes, according to their competency and
progress. For God is in history.

To avoid the suspicion of a conscious weakness of our cause,
when contemplated from the side of pure speculation, we may
advert for a moment to those pretended intuitions which stamp
the reprobation of humanity upon this ancient and hoary institution. We admit that there are primitive principles in
morals which lie at the root of human consciousness. But the
question is, how are we to distinguish them? The subjective
feeling of certainty is no adequate criterion, as that is
equally felt in reference to crotchets and hereditary prejudices. The very point is to know when this certainty indicates a primitive cognition, and when it does not. There
must, therefore, be some eternal test, and whatever cannot
abide that test has no authority as a primary truth. That
test is an inward necessity of thought, which, in all minds
at the proper stage of maturity, is absolutely universal.
Whatever is universal is natural. We are willing slavery
should be tried by this standard. We are willing to abide
by the testimony of the race, and if man, as man, has everywhere condemned it--if all human laws have prohibited it as
crime--if it stands in the same category with malice, murder
and theft, then we are willing, in the name of humanity, to
renounce it, and renounce it forever. But what if the overwhelming majority of mankind have approved it, what if philosophers and statesmen have justified it, and the laws of all
nations acknowledged it; what then becomes of these luminous
intuitions? They are an _ignis fatuus_, mistaken for a star.

RELIGION AND REFORM 6

The Church Must Take Right Ground

CHARLES G. FINNEY

Charles G. Finney (1792-1875), the greatest antebellum revivalist in the nation, often linked religion with antislavery and other reforms in his sermons and lectures. At first a Presbyterian preacher, he later became a Congregationalist, serving as president of Oberlin College from 1851 to 1866. He was particularly influential in inspiring many other men and women to support the antislavery cause. In his view, America would experience a religious revival only when it abandoned sin in all forms. This abandonment of sin was a necessary prerequisite to Christ's second coming and the beginning of the millennial period of peace and justice. In a series of Lectures on Revivals of Religion which he delivered in 1835, Finney indicated the relationship between revivalism and reform. The following lecture, published in 1868 in Oberlin, Ohio was part of that series. What were some of the proper and improper ways, according to Finney, in which the church should respond to slavery? What role ought the church play in the attempt to reform those who "drink ardent spirits?" As seen by Finney, how was revival related to reform?

I proceed to mention things which ought to be done to continue this great and glorious revival of religion, which has been in progress for the last ten years.

There should be great and deep repentings on the part of ministers. WE, my brethren, must humble ourselves before God. It will not do for us to suppose that it is enough to call on the people to repent. We must repent, we must take the lead in repentance, and then call on the churches to follow . . . .

The church must take right ground in regard to politics. Do not suppose, now, that I am going to preach a political sermon, or that I wish to have you join and get up a Christian party in politics. No, you must not believe that. But the time has come that Christians must vote for honest men, and take consistent ground in politics, or the Lord will curse them. They must be honest men themselves, and instead of voting for a man because he belongs to their party, bank or anti-bank, Jackson or anti-Jackson, they must find out whether he is honest and upright, and fit to be trusted. They must let the world see that the church will uphold no man in office who is known to be a knave, or an adulterer, or a Sabbath-breaker, or a gambler. Such is the spread of intelligence and the facility of communication in our country, that every man can know for whom he gives his vote. And if he will give his vote only for honest men, the country will be obliged to have upright rulers. All parties will be compelled to put up honest men as candidates. Christians have been exceedingly guilty in this matter. But the time has come when they must act differently, or God will curse the nation, and withdraw his Spirit. As on the subjects of slavery and temperance, so on this subject, the church must act right, or the country will be ruined. God cannot sustain this free and blessed country, which we love and pray for, unless the church will take right ground. Politics are a part of religion in such a country as this, and Christians must do their duty to the country as a part of their duty to God. It seems sometimes as if the foundations of the nation were becoming rotten: and Christians seem to act as if they thought God did not see what they do on politics. But I tell you, he does see it; and he will bless or curse this nation, according to the course they take.

The churches must take right ground on the subject of slavery. And here the question arises, what is right ground? And first, I will state some of the things that should be avoided.

1. First of all, a bad spirit should be avoided. Nothing is more calculated to injure religion, and to injure the slaves themselves, than for Christians to get into an angry controversy on the subject. It is a subject upon which there needs to be no angry controversy among Christians. Slaveholding professors, like rumselling professors, may endeavor to justify themselves, and may be angry with those who press their consciences, and call upon them to give up their sins. Those proud professors of religion, who think a man to blame, or think it is a shame to have a black skin, may allow their prejudices so far to prevail, as to shut their ears, and be disposed to quarrel with those who urge the subject upon them. But I repeat it, the subject of slavery is a subject upon which Christians, praying men, need not and must not differ.

2. Another thing to be avoided is an attempt to take neutral ground on this subject. Christians can no more take neutral ground on this subject, since it has come up for discussion, than they can take neutral ground on the subject of the sanctification of the Sabbath. It is a great national sin. It is a sin of the church. The churches, by their silence, and by permitting slave-holders to belong to their communion, have been consenting to it. All denominations have been more or less guilty; although the Quakers have, of late years, washed their hands of it. It is in vain for the churches to pretend it is merely a political sin. I repeat it, it is the sin of the church, to which all denominations have consented. They have virtually declared that it is lawful. The very fact of suffering slave-holders quietly to remain in good standing in their churches, is the strongest and most public expressions of their views that it is not sin. For the church, therefore, to pretend to take neutral ground on the subject, is perfectly absurd. The fact is that she is not on neutral ground at all. While she tolerates slave-holders in her communion she justifies the practice! And as well might an enemy of God pretend that he was neither a saint nor a sinner, that he was going to take neutral ground, and pray, "good Lord and good devil," because he did not know which side would be the most popular.

3. Great care should be taken <u>to avoid a censorious spirit on both sides</u>. It is a subject on which there has been, and probably will be for some time to come, a difference of <u>opinion</u> among Christians, as to the best method of disposing of the question: and it ought to be treated with great forbearance on both sides. A denunciatory spirit, impeaching each other's motives, is unchristian, calculated to grieve away the Spirit of God, and to put down revivals, and is alike injurious to the church, and to the slaves themselves.

In the <u>second</u> place, I will mention several things, that, in my judgment, the church is imperatively called upon to do, on this subject:

1. Christians, of all denominations, should lay aside prejudice, and <u>inform themselves</u> on this subject, without any delay. Vast multitudes of professors of religion have indulged prejudice to such a degree, as to be unwilling to read and hear, and come to a right understanding of the subject. But Christians cannot pray in this state of mind. I defy any one to possess the spirit of prayer, while he is too prejudiced to examine this, or any other question of duty. If the light did not shine, Christians might remain in the dark upon this point, and still possess the spirit of prayer. But if they <u>refuse to come to the light</u>, they cannot pray. Now, I call upon all you who are here present, and who have examined this subject because you were indisposed to examine it, to say whether you have the spirit of prayer. Where ministers, individual Christians, or whole churches, <u>resist truth</u> upon this point now, when it is so extensively diffused and before the public mind, I do not believe they will or can enjoy a revival of religion.

2. Writings, containing temperate and judicious discussions on this subject, and such developments of facts as are before the public, should be quietly and extensively circulated, and should be carefully and prayerfully examined by the whole church. I do not mean by this, that the attention of the church should be so absorbed by this, as to neglect the main question of saving souls in the midst of them. I do not mean that such premature movements on this subject should be made, as to astound the Christian community, and involve them in a broil; but that praying men should act judiciously, and that, as soon as sufficient information can be diffused

through the community, the churches should meekly, but firmly, take decided ground on the subject, and express, before the whole nation and the world, their abhorrence of this sin.

The anti-masonic excitement which prevailed a few years since, made such desolations in the churches, and produced so much alienation of feeling and ill-will among ministers and people, and the first introduction of this subject has been attended with such commotions, that many good ministers, who are themselves entirely opposed to slavery, dread to introduce the subject among their people, through fear that their churches have not religion enough to take it up, and consider it calmly, and decide upon it in the spirit of the gospel. I know there is danger of this. But still, the subject must be presented to the churches. And if introduced with discretion, and with great prayer, there are very few churches that have enjoyed revivals, and that are at the present time anywhere near a revival spirit, which may not be brought to receive the truth on this subject.

Perhaps no church in this country has had a more severe trial upon this subject, than this. They were a church of young, and for the most part, inexperienced Christians. And many circumstances conspired, in my absence, to produce confusion and wrong feeling among them. But so far as I am now acquainted with the state of feeling in this church, I know of no ill-will among them on this subject. The Lord has blessed us, the Spirit has been distilled upon us, and considerable numbers added to our communion every month since my return. There are doubtless in this church those who feel on this subject in very different degrees: and yet I can honestly say that I am not aware of the least difference in sentiment among them. We have from the beginning, previous to my going on my foreign tour, taken the same ground on the subject of slavery, that we have on temperance. We have excluded slaveholders, and all concerned in the traffic, from our communion. By some, out of this church, this course has been censured as unwarrantable and uncharitable, and I would by no means make my own judgment, or the example of this church, a rule for the government of other ministers and churches. Still, I conscientiously believe, that the time is not far distant, when the churches will be united in this expression of abhorrence against this sin. If I do not baptize slavery by some soft and Christian name, if I call it SIN, both consistency and conscience conduct to the inevitable conclusion, that while this sin is persevered in, its perpetrators cannot be fit subjects for Christian communion and fellowship.

To this it is objected, that there are many ministers in the Presbyterian church, who are slave-holders. And it is said to be very inconsistent that we should refuse to suffer slaveholders to come to our communion, and yet belong to the same church with them, sit with them in ecclesiastical bodies, and acknowledge them as ministers. To this I answer, that I have not the power to deal with those ministers, and certainly I am not to withdraw from the church because some of its ministers or members are slave-holders. My duty is to belong to the church, even if the devil belong to it. Where I have authority, I exclude slave-holders from the communion, and I always will as long as I live. But where I have no authority, if the table of Christ be spread, I will sit down to it, in obedience to his commandment, whoever else may sit down or stay away.

I do not mean, by any means, to denounce all those slave-holding ministers and professors as hypocrites, and to say that they are not Christians. But this I say, that while they continue in that attitude, the cause of Christ and of humanity demands that they should not be recognized as such, unless we mean to be partakers of other men's sins. It is no more inconsistent to exclude slave-holders because they belong to the Presbyterian church, than it is to exclude persons who drink or sell ardent spirits; for there are a great many rumsellers belonging to the Presbyterian church.

I believe the time has come, and although I am no prophet, I believe it will be found to have come, that the revival in the United States, will continue and prevail no further and faster than the church takes right ground upon this subject. The churches are God's witnesses. The fact is, that slavery is, pre-eminently, the sin of the church. It is the very fact that ministers and professors of religion of different denominations hold slaves, which sanctifies the whole abomination in the eyes of ungodly men. Who does not know that on the subject of temperance, every drunkard in the land will skulk behind some rum-selling deacon, or wine-drinking minister? It is the most common objection and refuge of the intemperate, and of moderate drinkers, that it is practiced by professors of religion. It is this that creates the imperious necessity for excluding traffickers in ardent spirit, and rum-drinkers, from the communion. Let the churches of all denominations speak out on the subject of temperance, let them close their doors against all who have anything to do with the death-dealing abomination, and the cause of temperance is triumphant. A few years would annihilate the traffic. Just so with slavery.

It is the church that mainly supports this sin. Her unified testimony upon the subject would settle this question. Let Christians of all denominations meekly, but firmly, come forth, and pronounce their verdict, let them clear their communions, and wash their hands of this thing, let them give forth and write on the head and front of this great abomination, SIN!, and in three years, a public sentiment would be formed that would carry all before it, and there would not be a shackled slave, nor a bristling, cruel slave-driver, in this land.

Still it may be said, that in many churches, this subject cannot be introduced, without creating confusion and ill-will. This may be. It has been so on the subject of temperance, and upon the subject of revivals too. In some churches, neither temperance nor revivals can be introduced without producing dissension. Sabbath schools, and missionary operations, and everything of the kind, have been opposed, and have produced dissensions in many churches. But is this a sufficient reason for excluding these subjects? And where churches have excluded these subjects for fear of contention, have they been blessed with revivals? Everybody knows that they have not. But where churches have taken firm grounds on these subjects, although individuals, and sometimes numbers, have opposed, still they have been blessed with revivals. Where any of these subjects are carefully and prayerfully introduced, where they are brought forward with a right spirit, and the true relative importance is attached to each of them, if in such cases, there are those who will make disturbance and resist, let the blame fall where it ought. There are some individuals, who are themselves disposed to quarrel with this subject, who are always ready to exclaim, "Do not introduce these things into the church, they will create opposition." And if the minister and praying people feel it their duty to bring the matter forward, they will themselves create a disturbance, and then say, "There, I told you so; now see what your introducing this subject has done; it will tear the church all to pieces." And while they are themselves doing all they can to create a division, they are charging the division upon the subject, and not upon themselves. There are some such people in many of our churches. And neither Sabbath schools, nor missions, nor revivals, nor anti-slavery, nor anything else that honours God or benefits the souls of men, will be carried in the churches, without these careful souls being offended by it.

These things, however, have been introduced, and carried, one by one, in some churches with more, and others with less opposition at all. And as sure as God is the God of the church, as certain as that the world must be converted, this subject must be considered and pronounced sin by the church. There might infinitely better be no church in the world, than she should attempt to remain neutral, or give a false testimony on a subject of such importance as slavery, especially since the subject has come up, and it is impossible from the nature of the case, that her testimony should not be in the scale, on the one side or the other.

Do you ask, "What shall be done; shall we make it the all-absorbing topic of conversation, and divert attention from the all-important subject of the salvation of souls in the midst of us?" I answer, No. Let a church express her opinion upon the subject, and be at peace. So far as I know, we are entirely at peace upon this subject. We have expressed our opinion, we have closed our communion against slaveholders, and are attending to other things. I am not aware of the least unhealthy excitement among us on this subject. And where it has become an absorbing topic of conversation in a place, in most instances, I believe it has been owing to the pertinacious and unreasonable opposition of a few individuals against even granting the subject a hearing.

If the church wishes to promote revivals, she must sanctify the Sabbath. There is a vast deal of Sabbath-breaking in the land. Merchants break it, travellers break it, the government breaks it. A few years ago an attempt was made in the western part of this state, to establish and sustain a Sabbath-keeping line of boats and stages. But it was found that the church would not sustain the enterprise. Many professors of religion would not travel in these stages, and would not have their goods forwarded in canal boats that would be detained from travelling on the Sabbath. At one time, Christians were much engaged in petitioning Congress to suspend the Sabbath mails, and now they seem to be ashamed of it. But one thing is most certain, that unless something be done, and done speedily, and done effectually, to promote the sanctification of the Sabbath by the church, the Sabbath will go by the board, and we shall not only have our mails running on the Sabbath, and post-offices open, but, by and by, our courts of justice, and halls of legislation, will be kept open on the Sabbath. And what can the church do, what will this nation do, <u>without</u> <u>any</u> <u>Sabbath</u>?

The church must take right ground on the subject of temperance, and moral reform, and all the subjects of practical morality which come up for discussion from time to time.

There are those in the churches who are standing aloof from the subject of moral reform, and who are as much afraid to have anything said in the pulpit against lewdness, as if a thousand devils had got up into the pulpit. On this subject, the church need not expect to be permitted to take neutral ground. In the providence of God, it is up for discussion. The evils have been exhibited; the call has been made for reform. And what is to reform mankind but the truth? And who shall present the truth if not church and the ministry? Away with the idea, that Christians can remain neutral, and yet enjoy the approbation and blessing of God.

In all such cases, the minister who holds his peace is counted among those on the other side. Everybody knows that it is so in a revival. It is not necessary for a person to rail out against the work. If he only keep still and take neutral ground, the enemies of the revival will all consider him as on their side. So on the subject of temperance. It is not needful that a person should rail at the cold-water society, in order to be on the best terms with drunkards and moderate drinkers. Only let him plead for the moderate use of wine, only let him continue to drink it as a luxury, and all the drunkards account him on their side. If he refuse to give his influence to the temperance cause, he is claimed, of course, by the other side, as a friend. On all these subjects, when they come up, the churches and ministers must take the right ground, and take it openly and stand to it, and carry it through, if they expect to enjoy the blessing of God in revivals. They must cast out from their communions such members, as, in contempt of the light that is shed upon them, continue to drink or traffic in ardent spirits.

<u>There must be more done for all the great objects of Christian benevolence</u>. There must be much greater effort for the cause of missions, and education, and the Bible, and all the other branches of religious enterprise, or the church will displease God. Look at it. Think of the mercies we have received, of the wealth, numbers, and prosperity of the church. Have we rendered unto God according to the benefits we have received, so as to show that the church is bountiful, and willing to give their money, and to work for God? No. Far from it. Have we multiplied our means and enlarged our plans, in proportion as the church has increased? Is God satisfied with what has been done, or has he reason to be? Such a revival as has been enjoyed by the churches of America for the last ten years! We ought to have done ten times as much as we have for missions, Bibles, education, tracts, free churches, and in all the ways designed to promote religion and save souls. If the churches do not wake up on this subject, and lay themselves out on a larger scale, they may expect that the revival in the United States will cease.

The Bible Against Slavery

THEODORE D. WELD

Theodore D. Weld (1803-95) was perhaps the most famous of the converts of Charles Finney. Immediately upon his conversion in 1825, Weld came under the influence of numerous lay workers who devoted much of their time to various social reforms. One of these was James G. Birney, a prominent lawyer and planter, with whom he exchanged views on slavery in 1832. About this time the newly formed Lane Seminary in Cincinnati gained the famed Lyman Beecher as its president, a move which led Weld to enter Lane in the fall of 1833. He soon converted Lane into a hotbed of abolitionism and would gain a reputation for his radical anti-slavery crusades. In 1837 he wrote one of abolitionism's most powerful tracts, The Bible Against Slavery, which was published the next year by the American Anti-Slavery Society in New York. How did Weld distinguish slavery (persons reduced to property) from other relationships characterized by subjection? How did Weld bring religious principles to bear upon the moral issue of slavery? Which of the Ten Commandments does Weld say that slavery violates?

The spirit of slavery never seeks refuge in the Bible on its own accord. The horns of the altar are its last resort--seized only in desperation, as it rushes from the terror of the avenger's arm. Like other unclean spirits, it "hateth the light, neither cometh to the light, lest its deeds should be reproved." Goaded to frenzy in its conflicts with conscience and common sense, denied all quarter, and hunted from every covert, it vaults over the sacred inclosure and courses

up and down the Bible, "seeking rest, and finding none."
THE LAW OF LOVE, glowing on every page, flashes around it an
omnipresent anguish and despair. It shrinks from the hated
light, and howls under the consuming touch, as demons quail-
ed before the Son of God, and shrieked, "Torment us not."
At last, it slinks away under the types of the Mosaic system,
and seeks to burrow out of sight among their shadows. Vain
hopes! Its asylum is its sepulchre; its city of refuge, the
city of destruction. It flies from light into the sun; from
heat, into devouring fire; and from the voice of God into
the thickest of His thunders.

Definition of Slavery

If we would know whether the Bible sanctions slavery, we
must determine what slavery is. An element, is one thing;
a relation, another; an appendage, another. Relations and
appendages presuppose other things to which they belong. To
regard them as the things themselves, or as constitutent
parts of them, leads to endless fallacies. Mere political
disabilities are often confounded with slavery; so are many
relations, and tenures, indispensable to the social state.
We will specify some of these.

1. PRIVATION OF SUFFRAGE. Then minors are slaves.

2. INELIGIBILITY TO OFFICE. Then females are slaves.

3. TAXATION WITHOUT REPRESENTATION. Then slaveholders in
   the District of Columbia are slaves.

4. PRIVATION OF ONE'S OATH IN LAW. Then atheists are
   slaves.

5. PRIVATION OF TRIAL BY JURY. Then all in France are
   slaves.

6. BEING REQUIRED TO SUPPORT A PARTICULAR RELIGION. Then
   the people of England are slaves.

7. APPRENTICESHIP. The rights and duties of master and
   apprentice are correlative. The claim of each upon the
   other results from his obligation to the other. Apprenticeship is based on the principle of equivalent for
   value received. The rights of the apprentice are secured, equally with those of the master. Indeed while

the law is just to the former it is benevolent to the latter; its main design being rather to benefit the apprentice than the master. To the master it secures a mere compensation--to the apprentice, both a compensation and a virtual gratuity in addition, he being of the two in greatest fainer. The law not only recognizes the right of the apprentice of a reward for his labor, but appoints the wages, and enforces the payment. The master's claim covers only the services of the apprentice. The apprentice's claim covers equally the services of the master. Neither can hold the other as property; but each holds property in the services of the other, and BOTH EQUALLY. Is this slavery?

8. FILIAL SUBORDINATION AND PARENTAL CLAIMS. Both are nature's dictates, and intrinsic elements of the social state; the natural affections which blend parent and child in one, excite each to discharge those offices incidental to the relation, and are a shield for mutual protection. The parent's legal claim to the child's services is a slight return for the care and toil of his rearing exclusively of outlays for support and education. This provision is, with the mass of mankind, indispensable in the preservation of the family state. The child, in helping his parents, helps himself--increases a common stock, in which he has a share; while his most faithful services do but acknowledge a debt that money cannot cancel.

9. CLAIMS OF GOVERNMENT ON SUBJECTS. Governments owe their subjects protection: subjects owe just governments allegiance and support. The obligations of both are reciprocal, and the benefits received by both are mutual, equal, and voluntarily rendered.

10. BONDAGE FOR CRIME. Must innocence be punished because guilt suffers penalties? True, the criminal works for the government without pay; and well he may. He owes the government. A century's work would not pay its drafts on him. He will die a public defaulter. Because laws make men pay their debts, will those be forced to pay who owe nothing? The law makes no criminal, PROPERTY. It restrains his liberty, and makes him pay something, a mere penny in the pound, of his debt to the government; but it does not make him a chattel. Test it. To own property, is to own its product. Are children born of convicts, government property? Besides, can

property be guilty? Can chattels deserve punishment?

11. RESTRAINTS UPON FREEDOM. Children are restrained by parents, pupils by teachers, patients by physicians, corporations by charters, and legislatures by constitutions. Embargoes, tariffs, quarantine, and all other laws, keep men from doing as they please. Restraints are the web of civilized society, warp and woof. Are they slavery; then a government of LAW is the climax of slavery!

12. INVOLUNTARY OR COMPULSORY SERVICE. A juryman is impannelled against his will, and sit he must. A sheriff orders his posse; bystanders must turn in. Men are compelled to remove nuisances, pay fines and taxes, support their families, and "turn to the right as the law directs," however much against their wills. Are they therefore slaves? To confound slavery with involuntary service is absurd. Slavery is a condition. The slave's feelings toward it cannot alter its nature. Whether he desires or detests it, the condition remains the same. The slave's willingness to be a slave is no palliation of the slaveholder's guilt. Suppose he should really believe himself a chattel, and consent to be so regarded by others, would that make him a chattel, or make those guiltless who hold him as such? I may be sick of life, and I tell the assassin so that stabs me; is he any the less a murderer? Does my consent to his crime, atone for by my partnership in his guilt, blot out his part of it? The slave's willingness to be a slave, so far from lessening the guilt of his "owner," aggravates it. If slavery has so palsied his mind that he looks upon himself as a chattel, and consents to be one, actually to hold him as such falls in with his delusion, and confirms the impious falsehood. These very feelings and convictions of the slave (if such were possible) increase a hundredfold the guilt of the master, and call upon him in thunder, immediately to recognize him as a MAN, and thus break the sorcery that cheats him out of his birthright--the consciousness of his worth and destiny.

Many of the foregoing conditions are appendages of slavery, but no one, nor all of them together, constitute its intrinsic unchanging element.

ENSLAVING MEN IS REDUCING THEM TO ARTICLES OF PROPERTY--making free agents, chattels--converting persons into things--sinking immortality into merchandise. A slave is one held in this condition. In law, "he owns nothing, and can acquire nothing." His right to himself is abrogated. If he say my hands, my body, my mind, myself, they are figures of speech. To use himself for his own good, is a crime. To keep what he earns, is stealing. To take his body into his own keeping, is insurrection. In a word, the profit of his master is made the END of his being, and he, a mere means to that end--a mere means to an end into which his interests do not enter, of which they constitute no portion. MAN, sunk to a thing! the intrinsic element, the principle of slavery; MEN, bartered, leased, mortgaged, bequeathed, invoiced, shipped in cargoes, stored as goods, taken on executions, and knocked off at a public outcry! Their rights, another's conveniences; their interests, wares on sale; their happiness, a household utensil; their personal inalienable ownership, a servicable article or a plaything, as best suits the humour of the hour; their deathless nature, conscience, social affections, sympathies, hopes-- marketable commodities! We repeat it, THE REDUCTION OF PERSONS TO THINGS! Not robbing a man of privileges, but of himself; not loading him with burdens, but making him a beast of burden; not restraining liberty, but subverting it; not curtailing rights, but abolishing them; not inflicting personal cruelty, but annihilating personality; not exacting involuntary labor, but sinking man into an implement of labor; not abridging human comforts, but abrogating human nature; not depriving an animal of immunities, but despoiling a rational being of attributes--uncreating a MAN, to make room for a thing!

That this is American slavery, is shown by the laws of slave states. Judge Stroud, in his "Sketch of the Laws relating to Slavery," says, "The cardinal principle of slavery, that the slave is not to be ranked among sentient beings, but among things--obtains an undoubted law in all of these [the slave] states." The law of South Carolina says, "Slaves shall be deemed, held, taken, reputed, and adjudged in law to be chattels personal in the hands of their owners and possessors, and their executors, administrators, and assigns, to ALL INTENTS, CONSTRUCTIONS, AND PURPOSES WHATSOEVER." Brev. Dig., 229. In Louisiana, "A slave is one who is in the power of a master to whom he belongs; the master may sell him, dispose of his person, his industry, and his labor; he can do nothing, possess nothing, nor acquire any thing, but what must belong to his master." Civ. Code, Art. 35.

This is American slavery. The eternal distinction between a person and a thing, trampled under foot--the crowning distinction of all others--alike the source, the test, and the measure of their value--the rational, immortal principle, consecrated by God to universal homage in a baptism of glory and honor, by the gift of his Son, his Spirit, his word, his presence, providence, and power; his shield, and staff, and sheltering wing; his opening heavens, and angels ministering, and chariots of fire, and songs of morning stars, and a great voice in heaven proclaiming eternal sanctions, and confirming the word with signs following.

Having stated the principle of American slavery, we ask, DOES THE BIBLE SANCTION SUCH A PRINCIPLE?" "To the law and the testimony!"

The Moral Law against Slavery

Just after the Israelites were emancipated from their bondage in Egypt, while they stood before Sinai to receive the law, as the trumpet waxed louder, and the mount quaked and blazed, God spake the ten commandments from the midst of clouds and thunderings. Two of those commandments deal death to slavery. "THOU SHALT NOT STEAL," or, "thou shalt not take from another what belongs to him." All man's powers are God's gift to HIM. Each of them is a part of himself, and all of them together constitute himself. All else that belongs to him, because the principal does; the product is his, because he is the producer. Ownership of any thing, is ownership of its use. The right to use according to will, is itself ownership. The eighth commandment presupposes and assumes the right of every man to his powers, and their product. Slavery robs of both. A man's right to himself, is the only right absolutely original and intrinsic--his right to anything else is merely relative to this, is derived from it, and held only by virtue of it. SELF-RIGHT is the foundation right--the post in the middle, to which all other rights are fastened. Slaveholders, when talking about their RIGHT to their slaves, always assume their own right to themselves. What slave-holder ever undertook to prove his right to himself? He knows it to be a self-evident proposition, that a man belongs to himself--

that the right is intrinsic and absolute. In making out his own title, he makes out the title of every human being. As the fact of being a man is itself the title, the whole human family have one common title deed. If one man's title is valid, all are valid. If one is worthless, all are. To deny the validity of the slave's title is to deny the validity of his own; and yet in the act of making a man a slave, the slaveholder asserts the validity of his own title, while he seizes him as his property who has the same title. Further, in making him a slave, he does not merely disfranchise of humanity one individual, but UNIVERSAL MAN. He destroys the foundations. He annihilates all rights. He attacks not only the human race, but universal being, and rushes upon JEHOVAH. For rights are rights; God's are no more--man's are no less.

The eighth commandment forbids the taking of any part of that which belongs to another. Slavery takes the whole. Does the same Bible which prohibits the taking of any thing from him, sanction the taking of every thing? Does it thunder wrath against the man who robs his neighbor of a cent, yet commission him to rob his neighbor of himself? Slaveholding is the highest possible violation of the eighth commandment. To take from a man his earnings, is theft. But to take the earner, is a compound, life-long theft-- supreme robbery that vaults up the climax at leap--the dread, terrific, giant robbery, that towers among other robberies a solitary horror. The eighth commandment forbids the taking away, and the tenth adds, "Thou shalt not covet any thing that is thy neighbor's;" thus guarding every man's right to himself and property, by making not only the actual taking away a sin, but even that state of mind which would tempt to it. Who ever made human beings slaves, without coveting them? Why take from them their time, labor, liberty, right of self-preservation and improvement, their right to acquire property, to worship according to conscience, to search the Scriptures, to live with their families, and their right to their own bodies, if they do not desire them? They COVET them for purposes of gain, convenience, lust of dominion, of sensual gratification, of pride and ostentation. THEY BREAK THE TENTH COMMANDMENT, and pluck down upon their heads the plagues that are written in the book. Ten commandments constitute the brief compound of human duty. Two of these brand slavery as sin.

Six Sermons on the Nature, Occasions, Signs...of Intemperance

LYMAN BEECHER

Lyman Beecher (1775-1863) was graduated from Yale College in 1797. He was converted during the Second Awakening by Yale president Timothy Dwight, who turned him to the ministry and thoroughly shaped his theological mind. It was Beecher more than anyone else who helped distinguish the evangelical resurgence of the first half of the nineteenth century for its close association of evangelicalism with moral reform and social activism. His reform activity was especially noteworthy in the temperance movement. He was the author of a great number of published sermons and addresses. Among them were his Six Sermons on the Nature, Occasions, Signs, Evils, and Remedy of Intemperance printed by the American Tract Society in 1843. What did Beecher believe could be done by society at large to retard the spread of intemperance? What did he believe the churches could do to aid in this reformation? According to Beecher, what could magistrates, physicians, and government officials do to assist the church in reducing the impact of ardent spirits?

Let us now take an inventory of the things which can be done to resist the progress of intemperance. I shall set down nothing which is chimerical, nothing which will not commend itself to every man's judgment, as entirely practicable.

1. It is entirely practicable to extend universal information on the subject of intemperance. Its nature, causes, evils, and remedy--may be universally made known. Every pulpit and every newspaper in the land may be put in requisition to give line upon line, on this subject, until it is done. The National Tract Society may, with great propriety, volunteer in this glorious work, and send out its warning voice by winged messengers all over the land. And would all this accomplish nothing? It would prevent the formation of intemperate habits in millions of instances, and it would reclaim thousands in the early stages of this sin.

2. It is practicable to form an association for the special purpose of superintending this great subject, and whose untiring energies shall be exerted in sending out agents to pass through the land, and collect information, to confer with influential individuals, and bodies of men, to deliver addresses at popular meetings, and form societies auxiliary to the parent institution. This not only may be done, but I am persuaded will be done before another year shall have passed away. Too long have we slept. From every part of the land we hear of the doings of the destroyer, and yet the one half is not told. But when the facts are collected and published, will not the nation be moved? It will be moved. All the laws of the human mind must cease, if such disclosures as may be made, do not produce a great effect.

3. Something has been done, and more may be done, by agricultural, commercial, and manufacturing establishments, in the exclusion of ardent spirits as an auxiliary to labor. Every experiment which has been made by capitalists to exclude ardent spirits and intemperance, has succeeded, and greatly to the profit and satisfaction, both of the laborer and his employer. And what is more natural and easy than the extension of such examples by capitalists, and by voluntary associations, in cities, towns, and parishes, of mechanics and farmers, whose resolutions and success may from time to time be published, to raise the flagging tone of hope, and assure the land of her own self-preserving powers? Most assuredly it is not too late to achieve a reformation; our hands are not bound, our feet are not put in fetters--and the nation is not so fully set upon destruction, as that warning and exertion will be in vain. It is not too much to be hoped, that the entire business of the nation, by land and by sea, shall yet move on without the aid of ardent

spirits, and by the impulse alone of temperate freemen. This would cut off one of the most fruitful occasions of intemperance, and give to our morals and to our liberties an earthly immortality.

The young men of our land may set glorious examples of voluntary abstinence from ardent spirits, and, by associations for that purpose, may array a phalanx of opposition against the incroachments of the destroyer; while men of high official standing and influence, may cheer us by sending down the good example of their firmness and independence, in the abolition of long-established, but corrupting habits.

All the professions too may volunteer in this holy cause, and each lift up its warning voice, and each concentrate the power of its own blessed example. Already from all clerical meetings the use of ardent spirits is excluded; and the medical profession has also commenced a reform in this respect which, no doubt, will prevail. Nor is it to be expected that the bar, or the agricultural interest as represented in agricultural societies, will be deficient in magnanimity and patriotic zeal, in purifying the morals, and perpetuating the liberties of the nation. A host may be enlisted against intemperance which no man can number, and a moral power be arrayed against it, which nothing can resist.

All denominations of Christians in the nation may with great ease be united in the effort to exclude the use and the commerce in ardent spirits. They alike feel and deplore the evil, and, united, have it in their power to put a stop to it. This union may be accomplished through the medium of a national society. There is no object for which a national society is more imperiously demanded, or for which it can be reared under happier auspices. God grant that three years may not pass away, before the entire land shall be marshalled, and the evils of intemperance be seen like a dark cloud passing off, and leaving behind a cloudless day.

The churches of our Lord Jesus Christ, of every name, can do much to aid in this reformation. They are organized to shine as lights in the world, and to avoid the very appearance of evil. A vigilant discipline is doubtless demanded in the cases of members who are of a lax and doubtful morality in respect to intemperance. It is not enough to cut all those who are past reformation, and to keep those who, by close watching, can be preserved in the use of their feet and tongue. Men who are mighty to consume strong drink, are unfit members of that kingdom which consisteth not in "meat and drink," but in "righteousness and peace." The time, we trust, is not distant, when the use of ardent spirits will be proscribed by a vote of all the churches in our land, and when the commerce in that article shall, equally with the slave trade, be regarded as inconsistent with a credible profession of Christianity. All this, I have no doubt, can be accomplished with far less trouble than is now constantly occasioned by the maintenance, or the neglect of discipline, in respect to cases of intemperance.

The Friends, in excluding ardent spirits from the list of lawful articles of commerce, have done themselves immortal honor, and in the temperance of their families, and their thrift in business, have set an example which is worthy the admiration and imitation of all the churches in our land.

When the preceding measures have been carried, something may be done by legislation, to discourage the distillation and importation of ardent spirits, and to discountenance improper modes of vending them. Then, the suffrage of the community may be expected to put in requisition men of talents and integrity, who, sustained by their constituents, will not hesitate to frame the requisite laws, and to give to them their salutary power. Even now there may be an amount of suffrage, could it be concentrated and expressed, to sustain laws which might go to limit the evil; but it is scattered, it is a dispersed, unorganized influence, and any effort to suppress intemperance by legislation, now, before the public is prepared for an efficient cooperation, could terminate only in defeat. Republics must be prepared by moral sentiment for efficient legislation.

Much may be accomplished to discountenance the commerce in ardent spirits by a silent, judicious distribution of patronage in trade.

Let that portion of the community, who would exile from society the traffick in ardent spirits, bestow their custom upon those who will agree to abandon it; and a regard to interest will soon produce a competition in well doing. The temperate population of a city or town are the best customers, and have it in their power to render the commerce in ardent spirits disadvantageous to those who engage in it. This would throw an irresistible argument upon the side of reformation. There are many now who would gladly be released from the necessity of dealing in spirituous liquors, but they think that their customers would not bear it. Let their sober customers, then, take off their fears on this hand, and array them on the other, and a glorious reformation is achieved. When the temperate part of the community shall not only declaim against mercantile establishments which thrive by the dissemination of moral contagion, but shall begin to act with a silent but determined discrimination, the work is done;--and can any conscientious man fail to make the experiment? "To him who knoweth to do good and doeth it not, to him it is sin." If we countenance establishments in extending and perpetuating a national calamity, are we not partakers in other men's sins? How many thousands may be saved from entering into temptation, and how many thousands rescued who have entered, if temperate families will give their custom to those who have abandoned the traffick in ardent spirits! And to how much crime, and suffering, and blood, shall we be necessary, if we fail to do our duty in this respect! Let every man, then, bestow his custom in the fear of the Lord, and as he expects to give an account with joy or grief, of the improvement or neglect of that powerful means of effecting moral good.

When all these preliminary steps have been taken, petitions may be addressed to the Legislatures of the States and to Congress, by all denominations, each under their own proper name, praying for legislative interference to protect the health and morals of the nation. This will call to the subject the attention of the ablest men in the nation, and enable them to touch some of the springs of general action with compendious energy. They can reach the causes of disastrous action, when the public sentiment will bear them out in it, and can introduce principles which, like the great laws of nature, will, with silent simplicity, reform and purify the land.

And now, could my voice be extended through the land, to all orders and descriptions of men, I would "cry aloud and spare not." To the watchmen upon Zion's walls--appointed to announce the approach of danger, and to say unto the wicked

man, "thou shalt surely die"--I would say--can we hold our
peace, or withhold the influence of our example in such an
emergency as this, and be guiltless blood? Are we not
called upon to set examples of entire abstinence? How
otherwise shall we be able to preach against intemperance,
and reprove, rebuke, and exhort? Talk not of "habit," and
of "prudent use," and a little for the "stomach's sake."
This is the way in which men become drunkards. Our security
and our influence demand immediate and entire abstinence.
If nature would receive a shock by such a reformation, it
proves that it has already been too long delayed, and can
safely be deferred no longer.

To the churches of our Lord Jesus Christ,--whom he hath purchased with his blood, that he might redeem them from all
iniquity, and purify them to himself, a peculiar people--I
would say--Beloved in the Lord, the world hath need of your
purified example;--for who will make a stand against the encroachments of intemperance, if professors of religion will
not? Will you not, then, abstain from the use of it entirely, and exile it from your families? Will you not watch
over one another with keener vigilance--and lift an earlier
note of admonition--and draw tighter the bands of brotherly
discipline--and with a more determined fidelity, cut off
those whom admonition cannot reclaim? Separate, brethren,
between the precious and the vile, the living and the dead,
and burn incense between them, that the plague may be stayed.

To the physicians of the land I would cry for help, in this
attempt to stay the march of ruin. Beloved men--possessing
our confidence by your skill, and our hearts by your assiduities in seasons of alarm and distress--combine, I beseech
you, and exert, systematically and vigorously, the mighty
power you possess on this subject, over the national understanding and will. Beware of planting the seeds of intemperance in the course of your professional labors, but become our guardian angels to conduct us in the paths of
health and of virtue. Fear not the consequences of fidelity
in admonishing your patients, when diseased by intemperance,
of the cause, and the remedy of their malady: and whenever
one of you shall be rejected for your faithfulness, and
another be called in to prophesy smooth things, let all the
intemperate, and all the land know, that in the whole nation
there are no false prophets among physicians, who, for filthy
lucre, will cry peace to their intemperate patients, when

there is no peace to them, but in reformation. Will you not speak out on this subject in all your medical societies, and provide tracts sanctioned by your high professional authority, to be spread over the land?

Ye magistrates, to whom the law has confided the discretionary power of giving license for the vending of ardent spirits, and the sword for the punishment of the violations of law--though you alone could not resist the burning tide, yet, when the nation is moved with fear, and is putting in requisition her energies to strengthen your hands--will you not stand up to your duty, and do it fearlessly and firmly? No class of men in the community possess as much direct power as you possess, and, when sustained by public sentiment, your official influence and authority may be made irresistible. Remember, then, your designation by Heaven to office for this self-same thing;--and, as you would maintain a conscience void of offence, and give up to God a joyful account--be faithful. Through you, let the violated law speak out--and righteousness and peace become the stability of our times.

To the governments of the states and of the nation, appointed to see to it, "that the commonwealth receives no detriment," while they facilitate and guide the energies of a free people, and protect the boundless results of industry --I would say--Beloved men and highly honored, how ample and how enviable are your opportunities of doing good--and how trivial, and contemptible, and momentary, are the results of civil policy merely, while moral principle, that mainspring of the soul, is impaired and destroyed by crime. Under the auspices of the national and state governments, science, commerce, agriculture and the arts flourish, and our wealth flows in like the waves of the sea. But where is the wisdom of filling up by a thousand streams the reservoir of national wealth, to be poured out again by as many channels of profusion and crime? Colleges are reared and multiplied by public munificence, while academies and common schools enlighten the land. But to what purpose-- when a single crime sends up exhalations enough to eclipse half the stars and suns destined to enlighten our moral hemisphere, before they have reached their meridian.

The medical profession is patronized, and ought to be, and the standard of medical attainment is rising. But a single crime, unresisted, throws into the distance all the achievements of art, and multiplies disease and death much faster than the improvements in medical science can multiply the means of preventing them.

The improvements by steam and by canals augment the facilities and the motives to national industry. But, while intemperance rages and increases, it is only to pour the tide of wealth into one mighty vortex which swallows it up, and, with a voice of thunder, and the insatiable desire of the grave, cries, Give, give; and saith not, It is enough.

Republican institutions are guaranteed to the states, and the whole nation watches with sleepless vigilance the altar of liberty. But a mighty despot, whose army is legion, has invaded the land--carrying in his course taxation, and chains, and fire, and the rack--insomuch that the whole land bleeds and groans at every step of his iron foot--at every movement of his massy sceptre--at every pulsation of his relentless heart. And yet in daylight and midnight he stalks unmolested--while his myrmidons with infernal joy are preparing an ocean of blood in which our sun may set never to rise.

The friends of the Lord and his Christ, with laudable enterprise, are rearing temples to Jehovah, and extending his word and ordinances through the land, while the irreligious influence of a single crime balances, or nearly balances, the entire account.

And now, ye venerable and honorable men, raised to seats of legislation in a nation which is the freest, and is destined to become the greatest, and may become the happiest upon earth--can you, will you behold unmoved the march of this mighty evil? Shall it mine in darkness, and lift fearlessly its giant form in daylight--and deliberately dig the grave of our liberties--and entomb the last hope of enslaved nations--and nothing be done by the national government to stop the destroyer? With the concurrent aid of an enlightened public sentiment, you possess the power of a most efficacious legislation; and, by your example and influence, you of all men possess the best opportunities of forming a correct and irresistible public sentiment on the side of temperance. Much power to you is given to check and extirpate this evil, and to roll down to distant ages, broader, and deeper, and purer, the streams of national prosperity. Save us by your wisdom and firmness, save us by your own example, and, "as in duty bound, we will ever pray." . . .

MANIFEST DESTINY   7

Justification by Scripture

JOHN QUINCY ADAMS

John Quincy Adams (1767-1848), son of President John Adams, served as secretary of state in the Monroe administration. While occupying that office, he was responsible for the Adams-Onis Treaty of 1819 by which the United States acquired the Floridas and Spanish claims to the Oregon region. In 1823 he was the guiding force behind the presidential statements that became known as the Monroe Doctrine. Following his term as president from 1825 to 1829, he was elected to the House of Representatives in 1831, where he served until his death in 1848. While serving in the House, his vision of a United States spanning the North American continent, with a sphere of influence extending throughout South America, drew him into the congressional debate over the American claim to Oregon. On February 9, 1846, in his well known address before the House, Adams insisted the American claim to Oregon was superior to the British claim in that the former nation would utilize the land in ways more excellent than the latter nation. How did Adams use Scripture to support his ideas in regard to American expansionism? How did Adams use history to support those same ideas? How did Adams' sentiments reflect the attitudes of a nation "on the move"?

. . . Sir, there has been so much said on the question of title in this case, that I believe it would be a waste of time for me to say anything more about it, unless I refer to a little book you have there upon your table, which you sometimes employ to administer a solemn oath to every member of this House to support the Constitution of the United States. If you have it, be so good to pass it to the Clerk, and I will ask him to read what I conceive to be the foundation of our title.

If the Clerk will be so good as to read the 26th, 27th, and 28th verses of the 1st chapter of Genesis, the committee will see what I consider to be the foundation of the title of the United States.

The Clerk read accordingly as follows:

"26. And God said, Let us make man in our image, after our likeness; and let them have dominion over the fish of the sea, and over the fowl of the air, and over the cattle, and over all the earth, and over every creeping thing that creepeth upon the earth.

"27. So God created man in his own image, in the image of God created he him: male and female created he them.

"28. And God blessed them, and God said unto them. Be fruitful and multiply, and replenish the earth, and subdue it; and have dominion over the fish of the sea, and over the fowl of the air, and over every living thing that moveth upon the earth."

That, sir, (continued Mr. A) in my judgment, is the foundation not only of our title to the territory of Oregon, but the foundation of all human title to all human possessions. It is the foundation of the title by which you occupy that chair; it is the territory of Oregon; and we cannot do it without putting a close to any agreement which we have made with Great Britain that we will not occupy it.

And here I beg leave to repeat an idea that I have already expressed before, and that is, that there is a very great misapprehension of the real merits of this case founded on the misnomer which declares that convention to be a convention of joint occupation. Sir, it is not a convention of joint occupation. It is a convention of non-occupation -- a promise on the part of both parties that neither of the parties will occupy the territory for an indefinite space; first for ten years, then until the notice shall be given from one party to the other that the convention shall be terminated--that is to say, that the restriction, the fetter upon our hands shall be thrown off, which prevents occupation, and prevents the carrying into execution the law of God, which the Clerk has read from the Holy Scriptures. How, if this controversy in relation to the territory of Oregon was with any other than a Christian nation, I could not cite that book. With the Chinese, and all nations who do not admit the canon of Scripture, it would be quite a different question. It would be a different question between us and the Indian savages, who occupy that country as far as there is any right of occupation, for they do not believe this book. I suppose the mass of this House believe this book. I see them go up and take their oath of office upon it; and many of the southern members kiss the book in token, I suppose, of their respect for it. It is between Christian nations that the foundation of title to land is laid in the first chapter of Genesis, and it is in this book that the title to jurisdiction, to eminent domain, to individual property, had its foundation--all of which flow from other sources subsequent to that which the Clerk read.

Now I will ask the Clerk to read another passage of that book; and that is, I think the 8th verse of the 2nd Psalm.

The Clerk read:

"8. Ask of me, and I shall give thee the heathen for thine inheritance, and the uttermost parts of the earth for thy possession."

If the Clerk will read a verse or two before that which he has just read it will be seen to whom it is said He will give them.

The Clerk read:

"6. Yet have I set my king upon my holy hill of Zion.

"7. I will declare the decree: the Lord hath said unto me, Thou art my son; this day have I begotten thee.

"8. Ask of me, and I shall give thee the heathen for thine inheritance, and the uttermost parts of the earth for thy possession."

That (continued Mr. A) is the Personage to whom the promise was made of giving the heathen for his inheritance, and the uttermost parts of the earth for his possession. Now, the promise contained in that verse was understood by all commentators upon the Bible, and by the Christian nations of all denominations, certainly before the reformation of Luther, to apply to the Lord Jesus Christ. Then, sir, without entering into any long historical detail, by the Christians and Christian nations, (for he spoke now of international law,) the Pope, or the Bishop of Rome, was considered as the representative of Christ upon earth; and this verse from the Psalm promising the heathen for his inheritance and the uttermost parts of the earth for his possession, together with another verse at the close of one of the gospels, (which he would not detain the committee by asking the Clerk to read at the desk,) in which the Lord Jesus Christ, after rising from the dead, said to his disciples, (in substance,) "Go forth and preach to all nations my Gospel; and I will be with you to the end of the world." From these three several passages of the Scriptures, the Pope of Rome asserted, and for many ages it was admitted he had, the power of giving to any king or sovereign to whom he pleased, the power of going and subduing all barbarous nations, and subduing and conquering all territory, either not subdued at all, or subdued by barbarous nations, for the purpose of converting them to Christianity. At the time of the discovery of the continents of North and South America by Christopher Columbus, this was the law of nations between Christians, recognized, acknowledged, admitted; and when Christopher Columbus came, under a commission from Ferdinand and Isabella, King and Queen of Castile, Leon, and Aragon--when he came and made his discovery, which he did in October, 1492, in the next year, some time in the month of March or April, 1493, the Pope of Rome--at that time authorized, according to all international law between Christians to do it--gave to Ferdinand and Isabella the whole continents of North and South America. He authorized the drawing of a line from pole to pole, to Ferdinand and Isabella, King and

Queen of Castile, Leon, and Aragon. Now, do I intend to say that that is one of our titles? I must say it, although I think, perhaps, as little of it as any member of this House. But it was a good title when it was given. It was the understanding, the faith, the belief of all the Christian nations of Europe, that the Pope had his power; and it was acquiesced in by them all for a time. That same Pope at that time was in the custom of giving away not only barbarous nations, but civilized nations. He dethroned sovereigns, put them under interdict, and excommunicated them from intercourse with all other Christians; and it was submitted to. And now, sir, the Government of Great Britain--the nation of Great Britain--holds the island of Ireland on no other title. Three hundred years before that time, Pope Adrian of Rome gave, by that same power, to Henry I of England the island of Ireland, and England has held it from that day to this under that title, and no other. That is, no other, unless by conquest; (for it has been in a continued state of rebellion ever since, and now the question is, whether Ireland shall ever become an independent kingdom. If we come to a war with Great Britain, she will find enough to do to maintain that island.) I do not think it of very great value; though I think it does not go for nothing. Now, that general authority given to man to increase, multiply, and replenish the earth, and subdue it, was a grant from the Creator to man as man; it was a grant to every individual of the human race in his individual capacity. But, then, the portion that belongs to the individual, and was given thereby, was a matter for the whole human race to accommodate amoung themselves. That is to say, in communities, communities were to agree together what should be the metes and bounds of that portion of the earth given them by the general grant from the Creator. When communities were formed, it became a matter of legislation amoung them to whom any particular property-- e.g. a lot of land on which to build a house--should belong. Any territorial right whatever, as between individuals, was to be regulated by legislation; as between nations it was to be regulated by consent, by convention; and in that way the laws of nations, as they are called, (which are nothing more than the customs of nations,) and the treaties and conventions of nations, have regulated how every spot, every inch of land, shall be occupied. And among the rest, it is by these laws and regulations--internal among communities and international among nations--that you hold that seat, (referring to the Speaker's seat,) and I do not, because you have it, elevated to it by the laws of the country, and no other man can take, except by permission, so long as your right continues.

Well, sir, our title to Oregon stands on the same foundation. When this discovery of Columbus came to be a matter of great importance among the nations of the earth, other nations took into their heads to plant colonies on this continent, and then came the question of controversy between them, which never has been settled to this day. Our question now with Great Britain is one of the consequences of that state of things. There never has been any agreement between the nations of the earth how these points shall be settled.

There have been titles derived from treaty, from agreement, from conquest; there have been sources from which they have derived title to territory. We have been told here that our title to Columbia river and all the territory that is drained by it, is in consequence of discovery and exploration. Well, sir, that has been partially an agreement between the nations that they will say they consider that where a nation discovers the mouth of a river, and explores that river to its source, then that nation is entitled, and has been generally allowed, to maintain their authority. But that is not the foundation of any of our titles. . . .

Coming down to this pretended principle, that the discovery of the mouth of a river gives title to all the land watered by that river and its tributaries--and this is the ground on which we contend that the Mississippi valley, among the rest, belongs to us--that title is a parcel of the rights by which you hold that seat, and by which all property is held. This charter of Charles I, to the colony of Massachusetts Bay, gives from 40 to 48 degrees of latitude, without reference to any rivers. The kings of England, following the example of the Pope of Rome, undertook to grant lands all over this continent, and upon such terms as they thought proper. When they found the mouth of a river, and it was for their interest to claim the territory watered by that river, they claimed it. Louis XIV gave to Crozart-- and that is the title by which we still hold that country-- he gave him no land, but gave him merely the power to trade with the Mississippi river and all its tributaries, because that river had been discovered by French subjects many years before coming from Canada.

All these titles are imperfect. Discovery is, therefore, no title of itself. The discovery of a river and of land is no title of itself. Exploration comes next. That gives something more of a title. Continuity and contiguity both concur to give a title. They are none of them perfect in themselves. There is nothing complete in the way of title, but actual possession; and that is the only thing we now want, to have a perfect, clear, indisputable, and undoubted right to the territory of Oregon. It is possession; it is occupation, if you please. . . .

. . . She herself [Great Britain] admits that she has no title there; she pretends that she has none. But what does she say? She says that it is an open country; that it is one of those countries occupied, as far as it is occupied at all, only by barbarous nations--that it is a country which is open to all parties. She does not claim exclusive jurisdiction. I promise you she will, if you suffer her to do it, before she has done, not only to what you choose to give her, but to the whole territory. But at this day she claims no exclusive jurisdiction over the whole country. She claims, and by virtue of this convention, to have the country free and open--that is, to keep it in a savage and barbarous state for her hunters--for the benefit of the Hudson Bay Company for hunting. Now, she knows that it would have no value to her at all from the day that it is settled by tillers of the ground. It is abolished from that time by the nature of things. And therein consists the difference between her claims and our claims. We claim that country--for what? To make the wilderness blossom as the rose, to establish laws, to increase, multiply, and subdue the earth, which we are commanded to do by the first behest of God Almighty. That is what we claim it for. She claims to keep it open for navigation, for her hunters to hunt wild beasts; and of course she claims for the benefit of the wild beasts, as well as of the savage nations. There is the difference between our claims.

Letter to Rev. L. P. Judson

MARCUS WHITMAN

    Marcus Whitman (1802-47), a medical doctor, and Rev. Henry Spalding were appointed by the American Board of Commissioners for Foreign Missions in 1836 as the board's first missionaries to Oregon. Along with their wives, who were the first white women to cross the Rocky Mountains, Whitman and Spalding carried on religious, medical, agricultural, and educational efforts among the Cayuse Indians for over a decade. Whitman's letter to his brother-in-law which follows indicates his interest in the development of civilization in Oregon and the role of the missionary in that development. He was troubled by some of the contemporary religious developments which he believed detracted from the work of spreading Protestantism and allowed Catholicism to infiltrate the Northwest. About a year after he wrote the letter, Whitman, his wife, their two adopted children, and ten others were massacred by the Cayuses, who believed Whitman was responsible for a series of epidemics among them. How does the letter suggest some new opportunities for Christianity that were produced by westward expansion? What religious ideas and practices by Judson does Whitman oppose? What negative factor stimulated Whitman in his move to the West to carry on mission work?

Waiilatpu, Nov. 5th, 1846.

Rev. L. P. Judson, My Dear Brother:--

I have a last moment to spare in writing, and I have resolved to write to you, inasmuch as you have given me the hint by the note you appended to a family letter from Mrs. Whitman's friends. I am going to write plainly to you, for we love you and do not like to see your influence and usefulness abridged. I have known you long and well--better perhaps than you me. I esteem you for your warm affections and ardent temperament, but although these are amiable qualities, they are like the health of an infant, of so high and excitable a nature that it is but a step between them and derangement or disease. Mental disease is not suspected by the person who is the subject of it. But do not be surprised at what I am intimating. There are but few who are possessed of perfectly balanced minds. I have felt and acted with you on points to which the public mind was not awake, nor ready for action. It is well to be awake on all important points of duty and truth, but it can do no good to be ultra on any of these points. Why part friends for an opinion only, and that, too, when nothing is to be gained for truth and principle, and much lost of confidence, love, usefulness, enjoyment, and interest.

Why trouble those you cannot convince with any peculiarity of your own sentiment, especially if it is likely to debar you from the opportunity of usefulness to them. By one part of your own confession let me confute your ultra perfectionism; that is, you complain of not being perfect and pray for more sanctification. Now, brother, let that suffice that as long as you have to pray for sanctification you are not perfect, and that as long as you live you will pray for it and then conclude you will be perfect when "this mortal shall put on incorruption," and not till then; and then let us cry, grace; grace unto it. Do not think of being an ultra perfectionist until you could bear to hear a man say, I have already attained and am already perfect, and to use only thanksgiving to God for his having attained to and being perfect, instead [of] praying for more sanctification. If you could arrive at the point where you felt you were perfect, of course you would no longer pray for sanctification,

143

and what would be your prayer after that? Let the thought
awe you, for such cannot be the prayer of mortals in the
flesh. Prayer becomes us, and we shall not be fitted in this
life to join in the song of praise triumphant, of Moses and
the Lamb.

And now for Millerism. I was in Boston when the famous time
came for the end of the world, but I did not conclude that
as the time was so short I would not concern myself to return to my family. But I did conclude that inasmuch as you
had adopted such sentiments, you were not prepared for any
work calling for time in its execution, and thinking the work
of time so short with you that it would be in vain to call
forth any principle to your mind that would involve length
of time for its execution, I was contented to pass you in
silence. For to my mind all my work and plans involved time
and distance, and required confidence in the stability of
God's government and purpose to give the heathen to his Son
for an inheritance, and among them those uttermost parts of
the earth for his possession.

I had adopted Oregon as my country, as well as the Indians
for my field of labour, so that I must superintend the immigration of that year, which was to lay the foundation for the
speedy settlement of the country if prosperously conducted
and safely carried through; but if it failed and became disastrous, the reflex influence would be to discourage for a
long time any further attempt to settle the country across
the mountains, which would be to see it abandoned altogether.
Now, mark the difference between the sentiments of you and
me. Since that time you have allowed yourself to be laid
aside from the ministry, and have parted with tried friends
for an opinion only, and that opinion has done you nor no
one else any good. Within the same time, I have returned
to my field of labour, and in my return brought a large
immigration of about one thousand individuals safely through
the long and the last part of it an untried route to the
western shores of the continent. Now that they were once
safely conducted through, three successive immigrations have
followed after them, and two routes for wagons are now open
into the Willamette valley. Mark; had I been of your mind
I should have slept, and now the Jesuit Papists would have
been in quiet possession of this the only spot in the western
horizon of America not before their own. They were fast

fixing themselves here, and had we missionaries had no American population to come in to hold on and give stability, it would have been but a small work for them and the friends of English interests, which they had also fully avowed, to have routed us, and then the country might have slept in their hands forever.

Time is not so short yet but it is quite important that such a country as Oregon should not on the one hand fall into the exclusive hands of the Jesuits, nor on the other under the English government. In all the business of this world we require time. And now let us redeem it, and then we shall be ready, and our Lord will not come upon us unawares. Come, then, to Oregon, resume your former motto, which seemed to be onward and upward--that is in principle, action, duty and attainments, and in holiness. Dismiss all ultraism, and then you will be cooperative and happy in the society of acting and active Christians. I say again, come to Oregon; but do not bring principles of discord with you.

This is a country requiring devoted, pious labourers in the service of our Lord. There are many and great advantages offered to those who select and that of the best of land, and in a near proximity to a vast ocean and in a mild climate where stock feed out all winter, is not a small boon. Nor should men of piety and principle leave it all to be taken by worldlings and worldly men.

A man of your stamp can do much by coming to this country, if you adopt correct principles and action. Should you come, the best way is to take a raft at Olean, if you are near Cuba at the time of starting. You will need to bring bedding with you for the journey, so that you can come on a raft, and also take a deck passage on the steamboat if you wish to be saving of money. A piece of cloth painted suitable to spread under a bed will be most useful. Do not bring feathers, but let your bed be made of blankets, quilts, etc. If you want any goods after you get into the country, be sure and have them come around by water, if you do not like to trust the shippers in the country. A train of oxen will be the best with a light wagon; no loading except provisions. Good sheep are excellent stock to drive, and travel well. Some sheep we imported from the Sandwich Islands in 1838, have increased one hundred and twenty-five per cent in eight years. Think of what a few good men could do to come together into the country. On the way they could make a party of their own and so rest on the Sabbath. With 640 acres of land as bounty, they could, by mutual consent, set apart a portion for the maintenance of the gospel and for schools and learning in such form as they felt disposed.

A large country to the south as far as the California line is now open by the new wagon route made this fall. You have a good faculty to be a pioneer and lead out a colony; that is to start people to come. But when once on the way do not overpersuade the mind but remember that the best of men and women when fatigued and anxious by the way will be very jealous of all their rights and privileges and must be left to take their own way if possible. Restraint will not be borne under such circumstances.

As I do not know where to send to reach you, I will direct this to the care of Father Prentiss [the father of Judson's wife], who will forward it to you, after reading it himself.

The Indians are doing very well we think in their way and their habits of civilization. A good attention is paid to religious instruction. Morning and evening worship is quite general in their lodges, and a blessing is strictly regarded as being a duty to be asked upon taking food.

I do not think you can be ignorant of the advantages of this country, nor of its disadvantages. I wrote a letter of Father Hotchkin, which I hope was copied and sent to Father Prentiss, which you may have seen. That applies to this section and climate. The country best suited for settlement are the Willamette valley and the coast west. Then the valley of the Umpqua on the south, and still south the Klamath which takes you south to the California line.

North of the Columbia, you know, is in dispute between the British and the States; you may early learn the result. The greatest objection to the country west of the Cascade range is the rains of winter. But that is more than overbalanced by the exemption from the care and labour of feeding stock. It is not that so much rain falls, but that it rains a great many days from November to April or May. People that are settled do not find it so rainy as to be much of an objection. It is a climate much like England in that respect.

I hope you will excuse the freedom with which I have written.
If we shall see each other, we can better bring our thoughts
to harmonize.

Narcissa's health is on the gain, and is now pretty good.
She joins me in love to yourself and wife, hoping to see you
both in due time.

In the best of bonds,

         Yours truly,

         MARCUS WHITMAN

Redeem Mexico from Misrule and Civil Strife

ROBERT F. STOCKTON

    Robert F. Stockton (1795-1866), who served in the U.S. Navy for nearly forty years, was well known in the 1840's for his military exploits against the Mexicans in the gaining of California for the United States. In a speech he delivered at a dinner held in his honor in Philadelphia on December 30, 1847, Stockton boasted of America's unlimited military success in Mexico and called upon American officials to extend further the blessings of American civilization. It was Stockton's opinion that the United States' great mission to humanity was to be enhanced by "redeeming Mexico from misrule and civil strife." His speech which follows was published in Niles' National Register, LXXIII (January 22, 1848). Why did Stockton support the cause of the U.S. in the war with Mexico? What evidence is there that Stockton was acting upon racist sentiments? To what extent does Stockton believe the U.S. was fulfilling its divine mission by suppressing the Mexicans in the war?

No thoughtful observer of the progress of the U. States, can fail to be impressed with the conviction that we enjoy a degree of happiness and prosperity never heretofore vouchsafed to the nations of mankind. With an unexampled measure of political liberty; unbroken social order; extraordinary growth of the arts and sciences--philanthropic and benevolent institutions, the fair offspring of the Christian faith, extending their blessed agency, in all directions--unbounded religious toleration, heaven's best gift; for which our fathers risked and suffered most--with all these rich endowments, do we not indeed present an example of the beneficient care of Providence for which we can find no parallel in the history of man? And now when engaged in war, find ourselves, followed by the same blessed influences. Wherever our soldiers have carried our arms, victory has awaited them. We see them rushing against walls, bristling with bayonets and artillery, and lined with legions of armed men--we see our youthful heroes precipitating themselves from parapet to parapet, and charging from bastion to bastion--we hear the crash of grape and canister, and amid the smoke and thunder of the battle we behold the flag of our country, waiving-- [the remainder of the sentence was lost in the tremendous cheering which here burst forth from the assemblage.] We behold the flag of civil and religious freedom waiving over what had been regarded as unpregnable fortresses and the remains of armies fleeing to the mountains.

Gentlemen, how has all this been accomplished? Whence those achievements? I speak to intellectual men. All in the hearing of my voice entertain, I doubt not, a just and abiding sense of their deep responsibility not only on this earth, but in time hereafter. I ask you, then, how has all this happened? Is it to be attributed exclusively to the wisdom of our cabinet and the powers of our armies? These are all well--admittably well. But our successes have overleaped the bounds of all human calculating and the most sanguine hope. Therefore we must look beyond all this for the secret of our successes and the source of our remarkable prosperity. It is because the spirit of our pilgrim fathers is with us. --It is because of the God of armies and Lord of hosts is with us. [Tremendous applause.] And how is it with poor, unfortunate, wretched Mexico? Ever since the day of the last of the Montezumas, intestine broils have disturbed her peace. Her whole territory has been drenched with the blood of her own children. Within the last quarter of a century revolution has succeeded revolution. Now in the encounter with us she has been beaten in every field. She has been driven from fortress to fortress--from town to town, until the scattered remnants of her broken armies are fleeing to the mountains and calling upon the rocks to hide them. [Applause.] Is it not, therefore, in this disposition of public affairs, proper to rise superior to the consideration of party influence, and in true philosophical spirit and patriotic fidelity, take an honest view of our condition, in the sight of God and beneath the scrutiny of the christian and civilized world?

What you may think of it, I know not; and you must permit me to add, I care not; but for myself I speak not to you as a party man. Remember, gentlemen, that I go for my country. I cannot be bound, I cannot be kept within the restraints of party discipline when my country calls me forth. [Tremendous cheering, which lasted several minutes.] I go for my country--my whole country and nothing but my country. I desire to address you now in the spirit of the father of a large family, desirous to transmit to his latest posterity the blessings of civil and religious liberty. I speak to you as a Christian man--as a son, perhaps an unworthy son of this great republic, but one whose heart burns with an ardent desire to transmit, not only to his own immediate descendants, the blessings of which I speak, but to extend them to our neighbors on this continent. [Great applause.]

But do not mistake me. Do not misunderstand me. I am no propagandist in the common reception of the term. In my judgment, principles depend much upon relations and circumstances, and that which in the abstract may be well enough, often wastes itself in fanaticism. All things must bide their time.

I have no respect for the man or set of men who will recklessly disturb the social order of my community and produce civil war for the purpose of hastening such a result, no matter how beneficial in the abstract it may seem to be. [Cheers.] And I am bound to say farther, that I have quite as little respect for the man or set of men, who have in the Providence of God been placed in stations, when the great questions of civil and religious liberty are to be determined, who will shrink from the responsibilities of that station. [Cheers.] In

the application of these principles to the future policy of
this country, let it not be supposed for a moment that I
would presume to censure the great men of this nation.
--Nor would I attempt to instruct the most humble of my
countrymen. I present these views merely for the purpose
of rendering more distinct and clear the remarks which I
have offered, and which I may not have stated with sufficient explicitness.

I suppose the war with Mexico was caused by the repeated
insults which time after time had been heaped upon this nation. [Great applause.] I regard this much talked of indemnity as merely collateral or incidental, arising out of
the circumstances of the war. In my opinion, that question
will be set aside, if not wholly lost sight of in the pressure of the great considerations which are to grow out of
the high responsibilities and delicate duties crowding upon
us, and the unexampled victories which have attended our
arms. [Cheer.] In pursuing a legitimate object of war--in
the providence of God we are placed, or are likely to be
placed, in a position where by a fair and legitimate construction of the law of nations, the fate of Mexico and the
peace of this continent, to a greater or less extent, will
devolve upon the virtue, the wisdom, and the humanity of
our rulers. [Applause.] In these rulers I have the greatest confidence, and for them I entertain the most profound
respect. [Applause.]

I tell you again gentlemen, this matter of indemnity, in
money or any thing else, will be secondary, altogether secondary, in comparison with the considerations which I have
no doubt will be presented to this nation in the farther prosecution of this war. The insults have been resented--
nobly resented--they have been wiped out--they have been
washed out with blood. [Enthusiastic applause.] If, then
indemnity, mean money, any financier will tell you that if
that is what you seek as the only object of the war, you had
better withdraw your troops as soon as possible, and you
will save money. [A laugh.]

But indemnity is not the object of the war. No man here or
elsewhere will consent to weigh blood against money. [Great
applause.] I do not care who presents the proposition--when
it is presented; or to whom it is presented, whig or demo-
crat, no man will weigh blood for money. [Loud applause.]

But this is not, I repeat, our condition. Higher and nobler objects present themselves for the attainment of which you must increase your armies in Mexico, cost what it may. [Great applause.] Let me then state the objects for the attainment of which, in my judgment, this augmentation of our force in Mexico is required.

Mexico is poor and wretched. Why? Misgovernment--insatiable avarice--unintermitted wrong unsparing cruelty and unbending insolence--these have inflicted their curse on the unhappy country, and made her what she is. But as the darkest hour is that which just precedes the advent of the morning sun, so let us hope that a better and happier day is now about to dawn upon fortunate Mexico. Be it ours, now to forgive her all her trespasses, and returning good for evil, make her free and happy!--

If I were now the sovereign authority as I was once the viceroy--[laughter]--I would prosecute this war for the express purpose of redeeming Mexico from misrule and civil strife. If, however, such a treaty were offered me as that offered to the government of the United States, before God, I would consider it my bounden duty to reject it. [Loud applause.] --I would say to them, we can pay the indemnity ourselves. But we have a duty before God which we cannot--we must not evade. The priceless bond of civil and religious liberty has been confided to us as trustees--[cheers]--I would insist, if the war were to be prolonged for fifty years, and cost money enough to demand from us each year the half of all that we possess, I would still insist that the inestimable blessings of civil and religious liberty should be guaranteed to Mexico. We must not shrink from it. We cannot lose sight of the great truth that nations are accountable as well as individuals, and that they too must meet the stern responsibilities of their moral character--they too must encounter the penalty of violated law in the more extended sphere adapted to their physical condition.

Let the solemn question come home to the bosom and business of every citizen of this great republic: "What have I done--what has this generation done for the advancement of civil and religious liberty!--[Applause.]

It is in view of this responsibility--of our obligations to the infinite source of all our peace, prosperity and happiness--of our duty to fulfil the great mission of liberty committed to our hands, that I would insist, cost what it may, on the establishment of a permanent, independent republic in Mexico.-- [Cheers.] I would insist that the great principle of religious toleration should be secured to all-- that the Protestant in Mexico should be guaranteed the enjoyment of all the immunities and privileges enjoyed by Mexicans in the United States: [Loud cheers.] These great and benevolent objects I would accomplish by sending into Mexico a force adequate to maintain all the posts which we now occupy, to defend them against any assaults that might be made against them, and to keep open our communications. I would seize upon Paredes, Arista, and other military chieftains, and send them to St. Helena, if you please. [Laughter and applause.] I would declare an armistice; and the executive should be called upon to issue a proclamation, and send six or more commissioners to meet Mexico in a liberal and generous spirit.

We have vanquished Mexico. She is prostrate at our feet-- we can afford to be magnaminous. Let us act so that we need not fear the strictest scrutiny of the Christian and civilized world. I would with a magnaminous and kindly hand gather these wretched people within the fold of republicanism. [Loud applause.] This I would accomplish at any cost. --"Oh!" but it is said, this will bring us to direct taxation." Well, let it come. We must not shrink from our responsibility. We have ample means. --Throwing aside long financial reports which nobody understands, [Laughter] let us in a manly, upright and philanthropic spirit meet every emergency which we may be called upon to encounter in the discharge of duty. . . .

RELIGION AND THE CIVIL WAR 8

An Address to Christians throughout the World

During the heat of Civil War battles, churches and denominations continued their debates and discussions in regard to slavery and states' rights, much like they had done during ante-bellum years. But now during the war the wearers of blue and gray would also challenge each other on the rightfulness and wrongfulness of the internecine struggle. Again, the religious community participated in the verbal barrages that tore apart numerous religious institutions. The address which follows was delivered at a convention of Confederate ministers assembled at Richmond, Virginia in April 1863. The tone of the speech, however, was reflective of similar sentiments to be found within Union borders. How does the address suggest that those gathered at Richmond believed the Civil War was a "holy war?" What was the convention's attitude toward Abraham Lincoln? Why did the convention of ministers believe the South would win the war?

Christian Brethren: --In the name of our holy Christianity we address you in this form, respecting matters of great interest to us, which we believe deeply concern the cause of our Blessed Master, and to which we invoke your serious attention.

We speak not in the spirit of controversy, not by political inspiration, but as servants of the Most High God, we speak the "truth in love," concerning things which make for peace.

In the midst of war--surrounded by scenes that pain the souls of all good men--deploring the evils which are inseparable from national contention--we feel most deeply impressed by the conviction that, for our own sake, for the sake of our posterity, for the sake of humanity, for the sake of the truth, above all for the sake of our Redeemer's kingdom, it behooves us to testify of certain things in our beloved land which seem neither to be understood nor appreciated by our enemies, nor yet clearly appreciated by Christians of other nations.

We put forth this address, after much prayer, solemnly invoking the blessing of Almighty God, and committing what we say to that Providence by which we trust we are directed, and by whose authority and power the governments of the earth stand or fall. If we were moved to make this address by any fears of the final issue of the war in which our country is now engaged, by any inclination to meddle with political questions, by any desire to resume controversy in respect to matters which have been referred to the arbitration of the sword; if, indeed, anything that compromised the simplicity, dignity and purity of Christian duty moved us to issue this address, we should deserve to have it despised by you, and could hope for no blessing of God to rest upon it. But for all we say in the following declarations, we are willing to be judged by succeeding generations, and to answer in that day when the secrets of all hearts shall be made known.

We do not propose to discuss the causes of the war. They are matters of recent history, easily known and read of all men. To discuss them would obviously involve much more than, as Christian ministers, we feel it our province to argue. We submit for your consideration, as the first point of our testimony and ground of protest:

<u>That the war waged against our people, in principle and in fact, proposes to achieve that which, in the nature of the case, it is impossible to accomplish by violence.</u>

The war proposes the restoration of the Union. We can rationally suppose a war for conquest, or to expel an invader, or to compel respect for stipulations of peace and international intercourse which have been violated; but how measures of violence can reunite independent States, restore their broken fellowship, reestablish equality of representative rights, or coerce a people to brotherly kindness, unity and devotion to each other, is utterly beyond our conception.

But if our enemies be disingenuous in their professions; if they fight not to recover seceded States, but to subjugate them, what promise do men find in the numbers, intelligence, courage, resources and moral energies of the millions who inhabit the Confederate States, that such a people can ever become profitable or happy, as subordinate to mere military force? If subjugation, therefore, were possible, is it desirable? Would the United States gain anything? Would Christian civilization gain anything? Said a great British statesman, in 1775, when arguing in favor of adopting conciliatory measures in respect to the revolted colonies of America--colonies, not seceding States--that were in actual rebellion against their sovereign: "The use of force is but temporary. It may subdue for a moment, but it does not remove the necessity for subduing again; and a nation is not governed which is perpetually to be conquered. My next objection is its uncertainty. Terror is not always the effect of force, and an armament is not a victory. . . . A farther objection is that you impair the object by your very endeavors to preserve it. The thing you fought for is not the thing you recover." Christian brethren, could the hand of violence win you to desire fellowship with a people while it destroyed your peace, polluted your sanctuaries, invaded the sacred precincts of your homes, robbed you of your property, slaughtered your noble sons, clothed your daughters in grief, filled your land with sorrow, and employed its utmost strength to reduce your country to the degradation of a subjugated province? Would it not rather animate you to prefer death--honorable--the patriot's alternative, the Christian's martyrdom?

As an excuse for violence, our enemies charge that the Confederate States have attempted to overthrow "<u>the best government on earth</u>," and call us "traitors," "rebels." We deny the charge, and as to the epithets, if they defined our position, under the circumstances we should glory in them as do the people of God persecuted for truth and conscience' sake. But we regard such terms as gratuitously assuming the very point at issue. If employed sincerely, we will not complain; but we are persuaded that many have uttered these expressions, under the influence of resentful feelings, who would not otherwise assert the political doctrines they imply. We are not disposed to engage in angry retort, and only mention these things to show that we appreciate them. It will appear singular, when men reflect upon it, that so many intelligent and Christian people should desire to withdraw from "the best government on earth." And we need not discuss the kindness of those who so generously propose to confer on us, by force of arms, "the best government." No attempt has been made to overthrow the government of the United States, unless by the fanatical party which now administers its affairs. The South never entertained such an idea. If that government fall for lack of Southern support, let men discriminate between the downfall of an oppression when the oppressed have escaped, and a wanton effort to break up a good government. So Pharaoh fell, but not by the hand of Israel. The dismemberment of the Union by secession was not a blow at the government. It was for our own deliverance. It was an election of the people, only hastened, and rendered in some cases imperative, by the violent movements of the Executive of the United States. Virginia may be referred to as an illustration. The State was not willing to secede hastily: but the demand of President Lincoln that she furnish troops to fight her sister States ended all hesitation. At once she took position with the Confederacy, preferring to battle in defence of liberty rather than, in opposition to all her principles, to invade or suffer the invasion of the South. So far, therefore, from desiring to destroy the United States government, the great object of those States which first seceded was to secure their own rights and their tranquillity; while the immediate object of the States which last seceded was to place themselves as barriers in the way of a fanatical administration, and if possible, stay the bloody effort to coerce independent States to remain in the Union, when their constitutional rights would not be respected, and when the very purpose to coerce them showed a readiness to sacrifice the loves of citizens to the demands of sectional hostility. The South would never vote in favor of annexing or retaining a Northern State by force of arms. Instead, therefore, of waging war for the overthrow of the United States, the Confederate States simply defend themselves.

The war is forced upon us. We have always desired peace. After a conflict of opinions between the North and the South, in Church and State, of more than thirty years, growing more bitter and painful daily, we withdraw from them to secure peace--they send troops to compel us into reunion! Our proposition was peaceable separation, saying, "we are <u>actually</u> divided, our <u>nominal</u> union is only a platform in strife." The answer is a call for <u>seventy-five thousand</u> troops to force submission to a government whose character, in the judgment of the South, had been sacrificed to sectionalism. From the speech of Mr. Burke, already referred to, the following language may be quoted as not inappropriate to our position in respect to peace: "The proposition is peace. Not peace through the medium of war; not peace to be hunted through the labyrinth of intricate and endless negotiation; not peace to arise out of universal discord, fomented from principle, in all parts of the empire, not peace to depend on the judicial determination of perplexing questions, or the precise marking of the shadowy boundaries of a complex government. It is simple peace, sought in the spirit of peace and laid in principles purely pacific." Such a proposition of peace was clearly the appropriate duty of a Christian people. The South can point out on the pages of history the names, and refer to the earnest and repeated efforts of her commissioners of peace. But our foes preferred war--violence--and by violence the end they aimed at was unattainable, as the purpose was unworthy of a Christian nation. <u>Against this violence</u>, upon principle, and in the light of all the facts of the case, we, as servants of God and ministers of peace, testify and solemnly protest. The second general point which we submit for your Christian consideration is:

<u>The separation of the Southern States is universally regarded by our people as final, and the formation of the Confederate States government as a fixed fact, promising in no respect a restoration of the former Union.</u>

Politically and ecclesiastically the line has been drawn between North and South. It has been done distinctly, deliberately, finally, and in most solemn form. The Confederacy claims to possess all the conditions and essential characteristics of an independent government. Our institutions, habits, tastes, pursuits and religion suggest no wish for reconstruction of the Union. We regard the Confederacy, in the wise providence of the Almighty, as the result of causes which render its independent existence a moral and political necessity, and its final and future independence of the United States not a matter that admits of the slightest doubt.

Among all the indefensible acts growing out of the inexcusable war waged against us, we will refer to one especially, in regard to which, for obvious reasons, we would speak, and as becometh us, plainly and earnestly:

The recent proclamation of the President of the United States, seeking the emancipation of the slaves of the South, is in our judgment, a suitable occasion for solemn protest on the part of the people of God throughout the world.

First, upon the hypothesis that the proclamation could be carried out in its design, we have no language to describe the bloody tragedy that would appall humanity. Christian sensibilities recoil from the vision of a struggle that would inevitably lead to the slaughter of tens of thousands of poor deluded insurrectionists! Suppose their owners suffered; in the nature of things the slaves would suffer infinitely more. Make it absolutely necessary for the public safety that the slaves be slaughtered, and he who would write the history of that event would record the darkest chapter of human woe yet written.

But, secondly, suppose the proclamation--as indeed we esteem it in the South--a mere political document, devised to win favor among the most fanatical of the Northern people, uttering nothing that has not already been attempted practically, but in vain, by the United States; suppose it to be worth no more than the paper on which its bold iniquity is traced, nevertheless, it is an avowal of a principle, the declaration of a wish, the deliberate attempt of the chief magistrate of a nation to do that which, as a measure of war, must be repugnant to civilization, and which we calmly denounce as worthy of universal reprobation, and against which Christians in the name of humanity and religion ought to protest. What shall sound Christianity say to that one idea philanthropy which, in the name of an imaginary good, in blind fury rushes upon a thousand unquestionable evils? If it were the time for such an argument, we should not fear the issue of a full discussion of this whole question of slavery.

We fear no investigation, we decline no debate; but we would not, at an hour like this and in an address which is chiefly a protest, invoke the spirit of controversy. We content ourselves with what we regard as infinitely more solemn; we stand before the world, while war silences the voices of disputants, and men in deadly contention wrestle in fields of blood, protesting against the crimes that, in the name of liberty and philanthropy, are attempted. Let it go forth from our lips while we live; let it be recorded of us when we are dead, that we--ministers of our Lord Jesus Christ, and members of his holy Church, with our hands upon the Bible, at once the sacred chart of our liberties and the foundation of our faith, call heaven and earth to record that, in the name of Him whose we are and whom we serve, we protest! No description we can give of this measure of the Executive of the United States, even though indignation alone inspired us to utter it, would exaggerate what we regard as an unholy infatuation, a ruthless persecution, a cruel and shameful device, adding severity and bitterness to a wicked and reckless war.

When it is remembered that, in the name of a "military necessity," this new measure was adopted, we may pass by the concession of weakness implied in this fact, and contest ourselves with calling attention to the immorality of a necessity created by a needless war of invasion. "Military necessity" an excuse not for self-defence--not for self-preservation--but for violating the rules of civilized warfare, and attempting a barbarity. If "military necessity" be the inspiration to attempt emancipation, how shall men praise it as philanthropy? Are other nations uninterested in such conduct? Proclaim the right first to invade and subjugate independent States, exhaust all resources, and then avow the principle of "military necessity" as an excuse to add severity to a wrong, as a plea upon which to project a scheme violative of every manly, honorable and Christian sentiment! Suppose an invader happens to be too weak to conquer upon any other plan, has he therefore the right to proclaim that poison and the indiscriminate slaughter of women and children shall be his legal method? The common cause of humanity and the common hope of Christian civilization, as they appeal to every nation, cry out against this wretched subterfuge. If the "military necessity" of weakness may righteously adopt any measure that an invader's ingenuity can invest, or his malice suggest, what laws, what principles of justice and equity shall nations at war respect? At one time the world is told that "the rebellion is weak and will be crushed out in sixty days;" at another, "Union men abound in the South, and will welcome the United States troops as deliverers;" and now the invader is so hopeless of his task that it is a "military necessity" that he obtain the help of slaves!

May it not pertinently be asked what that is creditable to this invasion, ought men to believe, and to what end is this deceitful war waged?

When this last resort, like all the enemy's preceding schemes shall signally fail, as it certainly will, to achieve the ruin of the South, what is promised? Nothing but war, cruel, relentless, desperate war! Because the President, by his scheme, violates the Constitution, we might condemn him; though the constitutionality of his acts be less important to us than to the people over whom he presides: because he has violated his word, his special promise, and even his solemn oath of office, we might abhor his act; though that is a matter which may chiefly concern his conscientiousness, and illustrate the character of that officer whom Southerners refused to salute as their President: because of the diabolical mischief intended we might, in the name of heaven, indignantly denounce his proclamation; though no weapon formed against us be, practically, more harmless. But these are not the considerations which move us to protest; we solemnly protest because, under the guise of philanthropy and the pretext of doing good, he would seek the approbation of mankind upon a war that promises to humanity only evil and that continually. Let philanthropists observe, even according to its own terms, this measure is in no proper sense an act of mercy to the slave, but of malice toward the master. It provides for freeing only the slaves of those who fight against the United States. The effort is not to relieve that government of slavery, where the philanthropy has full opportunity for displaying its generosity, and the power to exercise it in respect to slavery, if it exist at all, can be indulged; but the effort is simply to invoke slavery as an agent against the South, reckless of the consequences to the slaves themselves. Shall a pretext at once so weak and so base mislead intelligent men, and make them imagine that Abraham Lincoln is a philanthropist? His position ought to be offensive to every sincere abolitionist, as well as disgusting to every sincere friend of the slave, of every shade of opinion on the question of slavery. How does it affect the cause of the Confederacy? If to awaken a deeper resentment than ever inflamed the people of the South before; if to quench the last sentiment of respect that lingered in their breasts for the United States government; if to unite them more resolutely than ever, and to make it to the individual interest of every person in the bounds of the Confederacy to sustain and strengthen it with every dollar and every arm, and every prayer, and every energy of manly virtue and Christian encouragement--be to advance the invader's interest and give him hope of success, then has the proclamation furnished him opportunity of congratulating himself.

We submit further: That the war against the Confederate States has achieved no good result, and we find nothing in the present state of the struggle that gives promise of the United States accomplishing any good by its continuance. Though hundreds of thousands of lives have been lost, and many millions of treasure spent: though a vast amount of valuable property has been destroyed, and numbers of once happy homes made desolate: though cities and towns have been temporarily captured, and aged men and helpless women and children have suffered such things as it were even a shame to speak of plainly: though sanctuaries have been desecrated, and ministers of God been dragged from sacred altars to loathsome prisons: though slaves have been instigated to insurrection, and every measure has been adopted that the ingenuity of the enemy could devise or his ample resources afford by sea and by land: yet we aver, without fear of contradiction, that the only possession which the United States holds in the Confederate States is the ground on which United States troops pitch their tents; and that whenever those troops withdraw from a given locality in our territory, the people resident therein testify a warmer devotion to the Confederate cause than even before their soil was invaded. Nothing is therefore conquered--no part of the country is subdued; the civil jurisdiction of the United States, the real test of their success, has not been established by any force of arms. Where such civil jurisdiction exists at all along the border, it has existed all the while, was not obtained by force, and is not the fruit of conquest. This fact is submitted by our enemies themselves.

It is worthy of special notice, that notwithstanding the gigantic exertions of the United States, they have not been able to secure the return of a single county, or section of a county, much less a single State that has seceded. No civil order and peace spring up in the track of their armies. All in front of them is resolute resistance, and behind them when they have entered our territory, is a deep, uncompromising opposition, over which only military force can for a moment be trusted. Thus the civilized world is called upon to observe an invasion which has lasted for nearly two years, and achieved nothing but cruelty. Before it a people ready to die, but neither ready to submit, nor weak enough to be conquered; and for its gloomy prospect an interminable war, growing more bitter and unfeeling every day, because more hopeless to them that by it have sought things impossible as well as unrighteous. In the name of the great Prince of Peace, has Christianity, has civilization, nothing to say to such an awful tragedy? Such is the war for the <u>Union</u>! Yet every day our foes are deepening and widening that river of blood which divides us from them forever!

The only change of opinion among our people since the beginning of the war, that is of material importance to the final issue, has been the change from all lingering attachment to the former Union to a more sacred and reliable devotion to the Confederate government. The sentiments of the people are not alterable in any other respects by force of arms. If the whole country were occupied by United States troops, it would merely exhibit a military despotism, against which the people would struggle in perpetual revolutionary effort while any Southrons remained alive. Extermination of the inhabitants could alone realize civil possession of their soil. Subjugation is therefore clearly impossible. Is extermination desired by Christians?

<u>The moral and religious interests of the South ought to be appreciated by Christians of all nations.</u>

These interests have realized certainly no benefit from the war. We are aware that in respect to the moral aspects of the question of slavery, we differ from those who conceive of emancipation as a measure of benevolence, and on that account we suffer much reproach which we are conscious of not deserving. With all the facts of the system of slavery in its practical operations before us, "as eye-witnesses and ministers of the word, having had perfect understanding of all things" on this subject of which we speak, we may surely claim respect for our opinions and statements. Most of us have grown up from childhood among the slaves; all of us have preached to and taught them the word of life; have administered to them the ordinances of the Christian Church; sincerely love them as souls for whom Christ died; we go among them freely and know them in health and sickness, in labor and rest, from infancy to old age. We are familiar with physical and moral condition, and alive to all their interests; and we testify in the sight of God, that the relation of master and slave among us, however we may deplore abuses in this, as in other relations of mankind, is not incompatible with our holy Christianity, and that the presence of the Africans in our land is an occasion of gratitude on their behalf, before God; seeing that thereby Divine Providence has brought them where missionaries of the cross may freely proclaim to them the word of salvation, and the work is not interrupted by agitating fanaticism. The South has done more than any people on earth for the Christianization of the African race. The condition of the slave here is not wretched, as Northern fictions would have men believe, but prosperous and happy, and would have been yet more so but for the mistaken zeal of the abolitionists. Can emancipation obtain for them a better portion? The practicable plan for benefiting the African race must be the Providential plan--the Scriptural plan. We adapt that plan in the South, and while the States would seek by wholesome legislation to regard the interest of master and slave, we, as ministers would preach the word to both as we are commanded of God. This war has not benefited the slaves. Those that have been encouraged or compelled by the enemy to leave their masters, have gone, and we aver can go, to no state of society that offers them any better things than they have at home, either in respect to their temporal or eternal welfare. We regard abolitionism as an interference with the plans of Divine Providence. It has not the signs of the Lord's blessing. It is a fanaticism which puts forth no good fruit; instead of blessing, it has brought forth cursing; instead of love, hatred; instead of life, death; bitterness and sorrow, and pain, and infidelity, and moral degeneracy follow its labors. We remember how the apostle has taught the minister of Jesus upon this subject, saying: "Let as many servants as are under the yoke, count their own masters worthy of all honor that the name of God and his doctrine be not blasphemed. And they that have believing masters, let them not despise them because they are brethren; but rather do them service because they are faithful and beloved, partakers of the benefit. <u>These things teach and exhort.</u> If any man teach otherwise, and consent not to wholesome words, even the words of our Lord Jesus Christ, and to the doctrine which is according to godliness, he is proud, knowing nothing, but doting about questions and strifes of words, whereof cometh envy, strife, railings, evil surmisings, perverse disputings of men of corrupt minds, and destitute of the truth, supposing that gain is godliness: from such withdraw thyself."

This is what we teach, and obedient to the last verse of the text, from men that "teach otherwise"--hoping for peace-- we "withdraw" ourselves.

The Christians of the South, we claim, are pious, intelligent and liberal. Their pastoral and missionary works have points of peculiar interest. There are hundreds of thousands here, both white and colored, who are not strangers to the blood that bought them. We rejoice that the great Head of the Church has not despised us. We desire, as much as in us lieth, to live peaceably with all men, and though reviled, to revile not again.

Much harm has been done to the religious enterprises of the Church by the war; we will not tire you by enumerating particulars. We thank God for the patient faith and fortitude of our people during these days of trial.

Our soldiers were before the war our fellow citizens, and many of them are of the household of faith, who have carried to the camp so much of the leaven of Christianity, that amid all the demoralizing influence of army life, the good work of salvation has gone forward there.

Our President, some of our most influential statesmen, our commanding General, and an unusual proportion of the principal Generals, as well as scores of other officers, are prominent and we believe consistent members of the Church. Thousands of our soldiers are men of prayer. We regard our success in the war as due to divine mercy, and our government and people have recognized the hand of God in the formal and humble celebration of his goodness. We have no

fear in regard to the future. If the war continues for
years, we believe God's grace sufficient for us.

In conclusion, we ask for ourselves, our churches, our
country, the devout prayers of all God's people--"the will
of the Lord be done."

Christian brethern, think on these things and let your
answer to our address be the voice of an enlightened Christian sentiment going forth from you against war, against
persecution for conscience' sake, against the ravaging of
the Church of God by fanatical invasion. But if we speak
to you in vain, nevertheless we have not spoken in vain in
the sight of God: for we have proclaimed the truth--we
have testified in behalf of Christian civilization--we have
invoked charity--we have filed our solemn protest against a
cruel and useless war. And our children shall read it and
honor our spirit, though in much feebleness we may have
borne our testimony.

"Charity beareth all things, believeth all things, hopeth
all things, endureth all things." We desire to "follow
after charity;" and "as many as walk according to this
rule, peace be on them and mercy, and upon the Israel of
God."

Second Inaugural Address

ABRAHAM LINCOLN

President Abraham Lincoln (1809-65) gave his Second Inaugural Address on Saturday, March 4, 1865. This was six weeks before his death and less than five weeks before the end of the war. His short speech of 701 words, 505 of which are of one syllable, did not include any battle cries or predictions of triumph. The first paragraph, which is devoid of celebration or self-congratulation, sets the tone for the total document. The distinctive feature of the second paragraph is its balanced treatment of the two sides, as is seen with the words <u>all</u> and <u>both</u>. Lincoln did have an interpretation, however, of the cause of the war, which he states in the third paragraph. The final paragraph, which consists of only one sentence, contains his call for and anticipation of the war's end. How did Lincoln interpret the war as within God's purpose for the North and South? How does the last paragraph of the address express a strain of American idealism?

Fellow Countrymen:

At this second appearing to take the oath of the presidential office, there is less occasion for an extended address than there was at the first. Then a statement, somewhat in detail, of a course to be pursued, seemed fitting and proper. Now, at the expiration of four years, during which public declarations have been constantly called forth on every point and phase of the great contest which still absorbs the attention, and engrosses the energies of the nation, little that is new could be presented. The progress of our arms, upon which all else chiefly depends, is as well known to the public as to myself; and it is, I trust, reasonably satisfactory and encouraging to all. With high hope for the future, no prediction in regard to it is ventured.

On the occasion corresponding to this four years ago, all thoughts were anxiously directed to an impending civil-war. All dreaded it--all sought to avert it. While the inaugural address was being delivered from this place, devoted altogether to <u>saving</u> the Union without war, insurgent agents were in the city seeking to <u>destroy</u> it without war--seeking to dissolve the Union, and divide effects, by negotiation. Both parties deprecated war; but one of them would <u>make</u> war rather than let the nation survive; and the other would <u>accept</u> war rather than let it perish. And the war came.

One eighth of the whole population were colored slaves, not distributed generally over the Union, but localized in the Southern part of it. These slaves constituted a peculiar and powerful interest. All knew that this interest was, somehow, the cause of the war. To strengthen, perpetuate, and extend this interest was the object for which the insurgents would rend the Union, even by war; while the government claimed no right to do more than to restrict the territorial enlargement of it. Neither party expected for the war, the magnitude, or the duration, which it has already attained. Neither anticipated that the <u>cause</u> of the conflict might cease with, or even before, the conflict itself should cease. Each looked for an easier triumph, and a result less fundamental and astounding. Both read the same Bible, and pray to the same God; and each invokes His aid against the other. It may seem strange that any men should dare to ask a just God's assistance in wringing their bread from the sweat of other men's faces; but let us judge not that we be not judged. The prayers of both could not be answered; that of neither has been answered fully. The Almighty has His own purposes. "Woe unto the world because of offences! for it must needs be that offences come; but woe to that man by whom the offence cometh!" If we shall suppose that American Slavery is one of those offences which, in the providence of God, must needs come, but which, having continued through His appointed time, He now wills to remove, and that He gives to both North and South, this terrible war, as the woe due to those by whom the offence came, shall we discern therein any departure from those divine attributes which the believers in a Living God always ascribe to Him, Fondly do we hope--fervently do we pray--that this mighty scourge of war may speedily pass away. Yet, if God wills that it continue, until all the wealth piled by the bond-men's two hundred and fifty years of unrequited toil shall be sunk, and until every drop of blood drawn with the lash, shall be paid by another drawn with the sword, as was said three thousand years ago, so still it must be said "the judgments of the Lord, are true and righteous altogether."

With malice toward none; with charity for all; with firmness in the right, as God gives us to see the right, let us strive on to finish the work we are in; to bind up the nation's wounds; to care for him who shall have borne the battle, and for his widow, and his orphan--·to do all which may achieve and cherish a just, and a lasting peace, among ourselves, and with all nations.

Address at the Raising of the Union Flag over Fort Sumter

HENRY WARD BEECHER

Henry Ward Beecher (1813-87), son of Lyman Beecher and brother of Harriet Beecher Stowe, was one of America's most influential preachers during the nineteenth century. His unconventional preaching style was characterized by showmanship and punctuated with humor because he believed it was necessary to appeal to his audience emotionally. Prior to the Civil War he expressed consistently his opposition to slavery, which he contended would eventually die out as an institution if it were limited to the South. At the conclusion of the war he was invited by the Union government to deliver an address at Charleston, South Carolina on the anniversary of the fall of Fort Sumter. It was later published in Patriotic Addresses in America and England, from 1850 to 1885 (New York: Ford, Howard, and Hulbert, 1891), pp. 676-97. As a clergyman, how does Beecher assess the war which had just ended? What was his opinion of the South and those of its people who had "caused" the war? What benefits did Beecher believe the war had brought to the South?

Ladies and Gentlemen:--

On this solemn and joyful day, we again lift to the breeze our fathers' flag, now again the banner of the United States, with the fervent prayer that God would crown it with honor, protect it from treason, and send it down to our children, with all the blessings of civilization, liberty, and religion. Terrible in battle, may it be beneficient in peace. Happily, no bird or beast of prey has been inscribed upon it. The stars that redeem the night from darkness, and the beams of red light that beautify the morning, have been united upon its folds. As long as the sun endures, or the stars, may it wave over a nation neither enslaved or enslaving. Once, and but once, has treason dishonored it. In that insane hour, when the guiltiest and bloodiest rebellion of time hurled their fires upon this fort, you, Sir [turning to General Anderson], and a small heroic band, stood within these now crumbled walls, and did gallant and just battle for the honor and defense of the nation's banner. . . .

Hail to the flag of our fathers, and our flag! Glory to the banner that has gone through four years black with tempests of war, to pilot the nation back to peace without dismemberment! And glory be to God, who, above all hosts and banners, hath ordained victory, and shall ordain peace!

Wherefore have we come hither, pilgrims from distant places? Are we come to exult that Northern hands are stronger than Southern? No, but to rejoice that the hands of those who defend a just and beneficent government are mightier than the hands assaulted it! Do we exult over fallen cities? We exult that a nation has not fallen. We sorrow with the sorrowful. We sympathize with the desolate. We look upon this shattered fort, and yonder dilapidated city, with sad eyes, grieved that men should have committed such treason, and glad that God hath set such a mark upon treason that all ages shall dread and abhor it.

We exult, not for a passion gratified, but for a sentiment victorious; not for temper, but for conscience; not as we devoutly believe that our will is done, but that God's will hath been done. We should be unworthy of that liberty entrusted to our care, if, on such a day as this, we sullied our hearts by feelings of aimless vengeance; and equally unworthy, if we did not devoutly thank Him who hath said,

<u>Vengeance</u> <u>is</u> <u>mine</u>, <u>I</u> <u>will</u> <u>repay</u>, <u>saith</u> <u>the</u> <u>Lord</u>, that he hath set a mark upon arrogant Rebellion, ineffaceable while time lasts! . . .

We raise our fathers' banner that it may bring back better blessings than those of old; that it may cast out the devil of discord; that it may restore lawful government, and a prosperity purer and more enduring than that which it protected before; that it may win parted friends from their alienation; that it may inspire hope, and inaugurate universal liberty; that it may say to the sword, "Return to thy sheath," and to the plow and sickle, "Go forth;" that it may heal all jealousies, unite all policies, inspire a new national life, compact our strength, purify our principles, ennoble our national ambitions, and make this people great and strong, not for aggression and quarrelsomeness, but for the peace of the world, giving to us the glorious prerogative of leading all nations to juster laws, to more humane policies, to sincerer friendship, to rational, instituted civil liberty, and to universal Christian brotherhood.

Reverently, piously, in hopeful patriotism, we spread this banner on the sky, as of old the bow was planted on the cloud; and, with solemn fervor, beseech God to look upon it, and make it the memorial of an everlasting covenant and decree that never again on this fair land shall a deluge of blood prevail. . . .

When God would prepare Moses for Emancipation, he overthrew his first steps, and drove him for forty years to brood in the wilderness. When our flag came down, four years it lay brooding in darkness. It cried to the Lord, "Wherefore am I deposed?" Then arose before it a vision of its sin. It had strengthened the strong, and forgotten the weak. It proclaimed liberty, but trod upon slaves.

In that seclusion it dedicated itself to liberty. Behold, to-day it fulfills its vows! When it went down, four million people had no flag. To-day it rises, and four million people cry out, "Behold <u>our</u> banner!" Hark! they murmur. It is the Gospel that they recite in sacred words: "It is a Gospel to the poor, it heals our broken hearts, it preaches deliverance to captives, it gives sight to the blind, it sets at liberty them that are bruised." Rise up, then, glorious Gospel Banner, and roll out these messages of God. Tell the air that not a spot now sullies thy whiteness. The red is not the blush of shame, but the flush of joy. Tell the dews that wash thee that thou art as pure as they. Say to the night, that thy stars lead toward the morning; and to the morning, that brighter day arises with healing in its wings. And then, O glorious flag, bid the sun pour light on all thy folds with double brightness, whilst thou art bearing around and round the world the solemn joy-- a race set free, a nation redeemed!

The mighty hand of Government, made strong in war by the favor of the God of Battles, spreads wide to-day the banner of liberty that went down in darkness, that rose in light; and there it streams, like the sun above it, neither parceled out nor monopolized, but flooding the air with light for all mankind. Ye scattered and broken, ye wounded and dying, bitten by the fiery serpents of oppression, everywhere, in all the world, look upon this sign lifted up, and live! And ye homeless and houseless slaves, look, and ye are free! At length you, too, have part and lot in this glorious ensign, that broods with impartial love over small and great, the poor and the strong, the bond and the free! In this solemn hour, let us pray for the quick coming of reconciliation and happiness, under this common flag!

But we must build again, from the foundations, in all these now free Southern States. No cheap exhortation "to forgetfulness of the past, to restore all things as they were," will do. God does not stretch out his hand, as he has for four dreadful years, that men may easily forget the might of his terrible acts. Restore things as they were? What, the alienations and jealousies? The discords and contentions, and the causes of them? No. In that solemn sacrifice on which a nation has offered up for its sins so many precious victims, loved and lamented, let our sins and mistakes be consumed utterly and forever.

No, never again shall things be restored as before the war. It is written in God's decree of events fulfilled, "Old things are passed away." That new earth, in which dwelleth righteousness, draws near. . . .

I charge the whole guilt of this war upon the ambitious, educated, plotting, political leaders of the South. They have shed this ocean of blood. They have desolated the

South. They have poured poverty through all her towns and cities. They have bewildered the imagination of the people with phantasms, and led them to believe that they were fighting for their homes and liberty, whose homes were unthreatened, and whose liberty was in no jeopardy.

These arrogant instigators of civil war have renewed the plagues of Egypt, not that the oppressed might go free, but that the free might be oppressed. A day will come when God will reveal judgment, and arraign at his bar these mighty miscreants; and then every orphan that their bloody game has made, and every widow that sits sorrowing, and every maimed and wounded sufferer, and every bereaved heart in all the wide regions of this land, will rise up and come before the Lord to lay upon these chief culprits of modern history their awful testimony. And from a thousand battle-fields shall rise up armies of airy witnesses, who, with the memory of their awful sufferings, shall confront these miscreants with shrieks of fierce accusation, and every pale and starved prisoner shall raise his skinny hand in judgment. Blood shall call out for vengeance, and tears shall plead for justice, and grief shall silently beckon, and love, heart-smitten, shall wail for justice. Good men and angels will cry out, "How long, O Lord, how long, wilt thou not avenge!"

And, then, these guiltiest and most remorseless traitors, these high and cultured men with might and wisdom, used for the destruction of their country; these most accursed and detested of all criminals, that have drenched a continent in needless blood, and moved the foundations of their times with hideous crimes and cruelty, caught up in black clouds full of voices of vengeance and lurid with punishment, shall be whirled aloft and plunged downward forever and forever in an endless retribution; while God shall say, "Thus shall it be to all who betray their country;" and all in heaven and upon the earth will say, "Amen!" . . .

I now pass to the considerations of benefits that accrue to the South in distinction from the rest of the nation. At present the South reaps only suffering, but good seed lies buried under the furrows of war, that peace will bring to harvest.

1. Deadly doctrines have been purged away in blood. The

subtle poison of secession was a perpetual threat of revolution. The sword has ended that danger. That which reason had affirmed as a philosophy, the people have settled as a fact. Theory pronounces, "There can be no permanent government where each integral particle has liberty to fly, off." Who would venture upon a voyage on a ship, each plank and timber of which might withdraw at its pleasure? But the people have reasoned by the logic of the sword and of the ballot, and they have declared that States are inseparable parts of national government. They are not sovereign. State <u>rights</u> remain; but <u>sovereignty</u> is a right higher than all others; and that has been made into a common stock for the benefit of all. All further agitation is ended. This element must be cast out of our political problems. Henceforth that poison will not rankle in the blood.

2. Another thing has been learned: the rights and duties of minorities. The people of the whole nation are of more authority than the people of any section. These United States are supreme over Northern, Eastern, Western, and Southern States. It ought not to have required the awful chastisement of this war to teach that a minority must submit the control of the nation's government to a majority. The army and the navy have been good political schoolmasters. The lesson is learned. Not for many generations will it require further illustration.

3. No other lesson will be more fruitful of peace than the dispersion of those conceits of vanity, which, on either side, have clouded the recognition of the manly courage of all Americans. If it be a sign of manhood to be able to fight, then Americans are men. The North certainly are in no doubt whatever of the soldierly qualities of Southern men. Southern soldiers have learned that all latitudes breed courage on this continent. Courage is a passport to respect. The people of all the regions of this nation are likely hereafter to cherish generous admiration of each other's prowess. The war has bred respect, and respect will breed affection, and affection peace and unity.

4. No other event of the war can fill an intelligent Southern man of candid nature with more surprise than the revelation of the capacity, moral and military, of the black race. It is a revelation, indeed. No people were ever less understood by those most familiar with them. They

were said to be lazy, lying, impudent, and cowardly wretches, driven by the whip alone to the tasks needful to their own support, and the functions of civilization. They were said to be dangerous, blood-thirsty, liable to insurrection; but four years of tumultuous distress and war have rolled across the area inhabited by them, and I have yet to hear of one authentic instance of the misconduct of a colored man. They have been patient and gentle and docile in the land, while the men of the South were away in the army, they have been full of faith and hope and piety; and when summoned to freedom they have emerged with all the signs and tokens that freedom will be to them what it was to be--the swaddling band that shall bring them to manhood. And after the Government, honoring them as men, summoned them to the field, when once they were disciplined and had learned the art of war, they proved themselves to be not second to their white brethren in arms. And when the roll of men that have shed their blood is called in the other land, many and many dusky face will rise, dark no more, when the light of eternal glory shall shine upon it from the throne of God.

5. The industry of the Southern States is regenerated and now rests upon a basis that never fails to bring prosperity. Just now industry is collapsed; but it is not dead. It sleepeth. It is vital yet. It will spring like mown grass from the roots, that need but showers and heat and time to bring them forth. Though in many districts not a generation will see wanton wastes of self-invoked war repaired, and many portions may lapse again to wilderness; yet, in our life-time we shall see States, as a whole, raised to a prosperity, vital, wholesome and immovable.

6. The destruction of class interests, working with a religion which tends towards true democracy in proportion as it is pure and free, will create a new era of prosperity for the common laboring people of the South. Upon them has come the labor, the toil, and the loss of this war. They have fought for a class that sought their degradation, while they were made to believe that it was for their own homes and altars. Their leaders meant a supremacy which would not long have left them political liberty, save in name. But their leaders are swept away. The sword has been hungry for the ruling classes. It has sought them out with remorseless zeal. New men are to rise up; new ideas are to bud and blossom; and there will be men with different ambition and altered policy.

7. Meanwhile, the South, no longer a land of plantations, but of farms; no longer tilled by slaves, but by freemen, will find no hindrance to the spread of education. Schools will multiply. Books and papers will spread. Churches will bless every hamlet. There is a good day coming for the South. Through darkness and tears, and blood she has sought it. It has been an unconscious Via Dolorosa. But, in the end, it will be worth all it has cost. Her institutions before were deadly. She nourished death in her bosom. The greater her secular prosperity, the more sure was her ruin. Every year of delay but made the change more terrible. Now, by an earthquake, the evil is shaken down. Her own historians, in a better day, shall write that from the day the sword cut off the cancer she began to find her health.

What, then, shall hinder the rebuilding of this republic? The evil spirit is cast out: why should not this nation cease to wander among tombs, cutting itself? Why should it not come, clothed in its right mind, to "sit at the feet of Jesus"? Is it feared that the Government will oppress the conquered States? What possible motive has the Government to narrow the base of that pyramid on which its own permanence stands? . . .

From this pulpit of broken stone we speak forth our earnest greeting to all our land.

We offer to the President of these United States our solemn congratulations that God has sustained his life and health under the unparalleled burdens and sufferings of four bloody years, and permitted him to behold this auspicious consummation of that national unity for which he has waited with so much patience and fortitude, and for which he has labored with such disinterested wisdom.

To the members of the Government associated with him in the administration of perilous affairs in critical times: to the Senators and Representatives of the United States who have eagerly fashioned the instruments by which the popular will might express and enforce itself, we tender our grateful thanks.

To the officers and men of the army and navy, who have so faithfully, skillfully, and gloriously upheld their country's authority, by suffering, labor, and sublime courage, we offer here a tribute beyond the compass of words.

Upon those true and faithful citizens, men and women, who have borne up with unflinching hope in the darkest hour, and covered the land with the labors of love and charity, we invoke the divinest blessing of Him whom they have so truly imitated.

But chiefly to Thee, God of our fathers, we render thanksgiving and praise for that wondrous providence that has brought forth, from such a harvest of war, the seed of so much liberty and peace.

We invoke peace upon the North. Peace be to the West. Peace be upon the South!

In the name of God, we lift up our banner, and dedicate it to Peace, Union, and Liberty, now and forevermore. Amen.

PART 3   ENERGIZING AMERICA
1865-1920

The energy unleashed with the rise of industrial capitalism, mechanization, and urbanization between 1865 and 1920 brought many social and economic changes to America. But the intellectual and cultural transformations produced by the scientific thought of evolutionary naturalism were of a different kind, which cannot be measured in dollars or percentages. The very presuppositions of traditional Christianity upon which the American society rested in 1865 were undermined by the doctrine of the evolution of species popularized by Charles Darwin in his 1859 publication of <u>The Origin of Species</u>.

It was during this time of transition when religion became less an independent variable, and in turn, became more a dependent variable. After 1865 leaders in science, education, industry, and other areas replaced religious leaders as dominant spokesmen in American society. Although the secularization of America was moving gradually across the social and intellectual landscape long before 1865, from 1865 to 1920 the process was accelerated at an unprecedented rate. In the words of historian Paul A. Carter, America experienced a "spiritual crisis" during the last third of the nineteenth century. In part this is what Arthur M. Schlesinger had in mind when he referred to this period as "a critical period in American religion."

Within organized religion evolution raised issues and problems that threatened the traditional beliefs as well as practices of most Americans. The emerging conflict within Protestantism between liberals and fundamentalists was paralleled by equally significant power struggles within Catholicism and Judaism. Little did Darwin know in 1859 that his ideas would have such far-reaching religious influence, but by the 1870's the battle lines were drawn between the scientific and religious supporters of the evolutionary naturalism tenets and its opponents. Works by scientist Asa Gray and theologians Charles Hodge and Henry Ward Beecher suggest how some thinkers responded to Darwin's ideas, while the writings of clergymen Theodore T. Munger, Washington Gladden, and Walter Rauschenbusch explain the new theology of liberalism.

The implications of naturalistic evolution went far beyond the biological and theological realms. If the evolutionary process expounded by Darwin were to be applied to socio-economic relationships, might not an inevitable progress automatically follow there also? Many businessmen like Andrew Carnegie believed and behaved as though it were so, for reasons he explained in his 1889 essay, "Wealth." Churchmen William Lawrence and Russell H. Conwell concurred and then added their own religious perspectives to Carnegie's secular ideals.

Not all naturalists agreed, however, that inevitable progress was a function of evolutionary forces. The reformer evolutionists asserted that man's ability to think must be used to direct the evolutionary process into socially desirable channels. Among the reformers were the social gospelers Washington Gladden and Richard T. Ely, who believed it was essential for man to remold society into something better.

During the late nineteenth century the energy and ambition of America were loosened in a mighty expansionist thrust abroad, a result in part of the adherence to evolutionary precepts. Josiah Strong, Albert J. Beveridge, and William Jennings Bryan discuss the rise of the United States to world power stature as the nation entered the twentieth century.

SCIENCE AND RELIGION

What is Darwinism?

CHARLES HODGE

Charles Hodge (1797-1878), a foremost Presbyterian theologian of the nineteenth century, taught at Princeton Seminary for more than a half century. In the 1870's he emerged as a staunch conservative opponent of Darwinism. While some antagonists of the evolutionary doctrines used ridicule in their efforts to laugh evolutionary theories out of serious consideration, Hodge engaged a much more reasoned approach in his analysis of Darwin's propositions. In his orthodox repudiation, What is Darwinism?, he appropriately identified natural selection as the essential factor and promptly pronounced it to be a contradiction of the doctrine of an omnipotent, omniscient Creator. The excerpted essay which follows was taken from What is Darwinism? (New York: Scribner, Armstrong and Company, 1874), passim. According to Hodge, how does Darwin account for the origin of matter? Did Darwin believe in the theory of spontaneous generation? What were the four natural laws which Darwin used to explain how all living things descended from one primordial germ? What are the implications of Darwin's theory of natural selection for the Biblical account of the fall of man? Is Darwinism atheistic?

This is a question which needs an answer. Great confusion and diversity of opinion prevail as to the real views of the man whose writings have agitated the whole world, scientific and religious. If a man says he is a Darwinian, many understand him to avow himself virtually an atheist; while another understands him as saying that he adopts some harmless form of the doctrine of evolution. This is a great evil.

It is obviously useless to discuss any theory until we are agreed as to what that theory is. The question, therefore, What is Darwinism? must take precedence of all discussion of its merits.

The great fact of experience is that the universe exists. The great problem which has ever pressed upon the human mind is to account for its existence. What was its origin? To what causes are the changes we witness around us to be referred? As we are a part of the universe, these questions concern ourselves. What are the origin, nature, and destiny of man? . . . Mr. Darwin undertakes to answer these questions. He proposes a solution of the problem which thus deeply concerns every living man. Darwinism is, therefore, a theory of the universe, at least so far as the living organisms on earth are concerned. . . .

The Scriptural solution of the problem of the universe is stated in words equally simple and sublime: "In the beginning God created the heavens and the earth." We have here, first, the idea of God. The word God has in the Bible a definite meaning. It does not stand for an abstraction, for mere force, for law or ordered sequence. God is a spirit, and as we are spirits, we know from consciousness that God is, (1.) A Substance; (2.) That He is a person; and, therefore, a self-conscious, intelligent, voluntary agent. He can say I; we can address Him as thou; we can speak of Him as He or Him. This idea of God pervades the Scriptures. It lies at the foundation of natural religion. It is involved in our religious consciousness. It enters essentially into our sense of moral obligation. It is inscribed ineffaceably, in letters more or less legible, on the heart of every human being. The man who is trying to be an atheist is trying to free himself from the laws of his being. He might as well try to free himself from liability to hunger or thirst.

The God of the Bible, then, is a Spirit, infinite, eternal, and unchangeable in his being, wisdom, power, holiness, goodness, and truth. As every theory must begin with some postulate, this is the grand postulate with which the Bible begins. This is the first point.

The second point concerns the origin of the universe. It is not eternal either as to matter or form. It is not independent of God It is not an evolution of his being, or his existence form. He is extramundane as well as antemundane. The universe owes its existence to his will.

Thirdly, as to the nature of the universe; it is not a mere phenomenon. It is an entity, having real objective existence, or actuality. This implies that matter is a substance endowed with certain properties, in virtue of which it is capable of acting and of being acted upon. These properties being uniform and constant, are physical laws to which, as their proximate causes, all the phenomena of nature are to be referred.

Fourthly, although God is extramundane, He is nevertheless everywhere present. That presence is not only a presence of essence, but also of knowledge and power. He upholds all things. He controls all physical causes, working through them, with them, and without them, as He sees fit. As we, in our limited spheres, can use physical causes to accomplish our purposes, so God everywhere and always cooperates with them to accomplish his infinitely wise and merciful designs.

Fifthly, man a part of the universe, is, according to the Scriptures, as concerns his body, of the earth. So far, he belongs to the animal kingdom. As to his soul, he is a child of God, who is declared to be the Father of the spirit of all men. God is a spirit, and we are spirits. We are, therefore, of the same nature with God. We are God-like; so that in knowing ourselves we know God. No man conscious of his manhood can be ignorant of his relationship to God as his Father.

The truth of the theory of the universe rests, in the first place, so far as it has been correctly stated, on the infallible authority of the word of God. In the second place, it is a satisfactory solution of the problem to be solved:

(1.) It accounts for the origin of the universe. (2.) It accounts for all the universe contains, and gives a satisfactory explanation of the marvellous contrivances which abound in living organisms, of the adaptations of these organisms to conditions external to themselves, and for those provisions for the future, which on any other assumption are utterly inexplicable. (3.) It is in conflict with no truth of reason and with no fact of experience. (4.) The Scriptural doctrine accounts for the spiritual nature of man, and meets all his spiritual necessities. It gives him an object of adoration, love, and confidence. It reveals the Being on whom his indestructible sense of responsibility terminates. The truth of this doctrine, therefore, rests not only on the authority of the Scriptures, but on the very constitution of our nature. The Bible has little charity for those who reject it. It pronounces them to be either derationalized or demoralized, or both. . . .

We have not forgotten Mr. Darwin. It seemed desirable, in order to understand his theory, to see its relation to other theories of the universe and its phenomena, with which it is more or less connected. His work on the "Origin of Species" does not purport to be philosophical. . . . Darwin does not speculate on the origin of the universe, on the nature of matter, or of force. He is simply a naturalist, a careful and laborious observer; skillful in his descriptions, and singularly candid in dealing with the difficulties in the way of his peculiar doctrine. He set before himself a single problem, namely, How are the fauna and flora of our earth to be accounted for? In the solution of this problem, he assumes: (1.) The existence of matter, although he says little on the subject. Its existence however, as a real entity, is everywhere taken for granted. (2.) He assumes the efficiency of physical causes, showing no disposition to resolve them into mind-force, or into the efficiency of the First Cause. (3.) He assumes also the existence of life in the form of one or more primordial germs. He does not adopt the theory of spontaneous generation. What life is he does not attempt to explain. . . . (4.) To account for the existence of matter and life, Mr. Darwin admits a Creator. This is done explicitly and repeatedly. Nothing, however, is said of the nature of the Creator and of his relation to the world, further than is implied in the meaning of the word. (5.) From the primordial germ or germs (Mr. Darwin seems to have settled down to the assumption of only one primordial germ), all living organisms, vegetable and animal, including man, on our globe, through all the stages of its history, have descended. (6.) As growth, organization, and reproduction are the functions of physical life, as soon as the primordial germ began to live, it began to grow, to fashion organs, however simple, for its nourishment and increase, and for the reproduction, in some way, of living forms like itself. How all living things on earth, including the endless variety of plants, and all the diversity of animals--insects, fishes, birds, the ichthyosaurus, the mastodon, the mammoth, and man--have descended from the primordial animalcule, he thinks, may be accounted for by the operation of the following natural laws:

First, the law of Heredity, or that by which like begets like. The offspring are like the parent.

Second, the law of Variation, that is, while the offspring are, in all essential characteristics, like their immediate progenitor, they nevertheless vary more or less within narrow limits, from their parent and from each other. Some of these variations are indifferent, some deteriorations, some improvements, that is, they are such as enable the plant or animal to exercise its functions to greater advantage.

Third, the law of Over Production. All plants and animals tend to increase in a geometrical ratio; and therefore tend to overrun enormously the means of support. . . . Hence of necessity arises a struggle for life. Only a few of the myriads born can possible live.

Fourth, here comes in the law of Natural Selection, or the Survival of the Fittest. That is, if any individual of a given species of plant or animal happens to have a slight deviation from the normal type, favorable to its success in the struggle for life, it will survive. This variation, by the law of heredity, will be transmitted to its offspring, and by them again to theirs. Soon these favored ones gain the ascendency, and the less favored perish; and the modification becomes established in the species. After a time another and another of such favorable variations occur, with like results. Thus very gradually, great changes of structure are introduced, and not only species, but genera, families, and orders in the vegetable and animal world, are produced. Mr. Darwin says he can set no limit to the changes of structure, habits, instincts, and milliards or milliards of centuries may bring into existence. He says, "we cannot comprehend what the figures 60,000,000 really imply, and during this, or perhaps a longer roll of years, the land and waters have everywhere teemed with living creatures, all exposed to the struggle for life, and undergoing change." . . . Years in this connection have no meaning. We might as well try to give the distance of the fixed stars in inches. As astronomers are obliged to take the diameter of the earth's orbit as the unit of space, so Darwinians are obliged to take a geological cycle as their unit of duration. . . .

We have not reached the heart of Mr. Darwin's theory. The main idea of his system lies in the word "natural." He uses that word in two senses: first, as antithetical to the word artificial. Men can produce very marked varieties as to structure and habits of animals. This is exemplified in the production of the different breeds of horses, cattle, sheep, and dogs; and specially, as Mr. Darwin seems to think, in the case of pigeons. . . . If, then he argues, man, in a comparatively short time, has by artificial selection produced all these varieties, what might be accomplished on the boundless scale of nature, during the measureless ages of the geologic periods?

Secondly, he uses the word natural as antithetical to supernatural. Natural selection is a selection made by natural laws, working without intention and design. It is, therefore, opposed not only to artificial selection, which is made by the wisdom and skill of man to accomplish a given purpose, but also to supernatural selection, which means either a selection originally intended by a power higher than nature; or which is carried out by such power. In using the expression Natural Selection, Mr. Darwin intends to exclude design, or final causes. All the changes in structure, instinct, or intelligence, in the plants or animals, including man, descended from the primordial germ, or animalcule, have been brought about by unintelligent physical causes. On this point he leaves us in no doubt. It is affirmed that natural selection is the operation of natural laws, analogous to the action of gravitation and of chemical affinities. It is denied that it is a process originally designed, or guided by intelligence, such as the activity which foresees an end and consciously selects and controls the means of its accomplishment. Artificial

selection, then, is an intelligent process; natural selection
is not.

There are in the animal and vegetable worlds innumerable instances of at least apparent contrivance, which have excited
the admiration of men in all ages. There are three ways of
accounting for them. The first is the Scriptural doctrine,
namely, that God is a Spirit, a personal, self-conscious,
intelligent agent; that He is infinite, eternal, and unchangeable in his being and perfections; that He is ever
present; that this presence is a presence of knowledge and
power. In the external world there is always and everywhere
indisputable evidence of the activity of two kinds of force:
the one physical, the other mental. The physical belongs to
matter, and is due to the properties with which it has been
endowed; the other is the everywhere present and ever acting
mind of God. To the latter are to be referred all the manifestations of design in nature, and the ordering of events
in Providence. This doctrine does not ignore the efficiency
of second causes; it simply asserts that God overrules and
controls them. Thus the Psalmist says, "I am fearfully and
wonderfully made. . . . My substance was not hid from thee,
when I was made in secret, and curiously wrought. . . in the
lower parts of the earth. Thine eyes did see my substance
yet being imperfect; and in they book all my members were
written, which in continuance were fashioned, when as yet
there were none of them." . . . He sends rain, frost, and
snow. He controls the winds and the waves. He determines
the casting of the lots, the flight of an arrow, and the
falling of a sparrow. This universal and constant control
of God is not only one of the most patent and pervading
doctrines of the Bible, but it is one of the fundamental
principles of even natural religion.

The second method of accounting for contrivances in nature
admits that they were foreseen and purposed by God, and that
He endowed matter with forces which He foresaw and intended
should produce such results. But here his agency stops. He
never interferes to guide the operation of physical causes.
He does nothing to control the course of nature, or the
events of history. . . . Paley indeed says, that if the
construction of a watch be an undeniable evidence of design
it would be a still more wonderful manifestation of skill,
if a watch could be made to produce other watches; and, it
may be added, not only other watches, but all kinds of time

pieces in endless variety. So it has been asked, if man can make a telescope, why cannot God make a teleschope which produces others like itself? This is simply asking, whether matter can be made to do the work of mind? The idea involves a contradiction. For a telescope to make a telescope, supposes it to select copper and zinc in due proportions and fuse them into brass; to fashion that brass into interentering tubes; to collect and combine the requisite materials for the different kinds of glass needed; to melt them, grind, fashion, and polish them, adjust their densities and focal distances, etc., etc. A man who can believe that brass can do all this, might as well believe in God. . . .

This banishing God from the world is simply intolerable, and, blessed be his name, impossible. An absent God who does nothing is, to us, no God. Christ brings God constantly near to us. . . . It may be said that Christ did not teach science. True, but He taught the truth; and science, so called, when it comes in conflict with truth, is what man is when he comes in conflict with God.

The advocates of these extreme opinions protest against being considered irreligious. Herbert Spencer says, that his doctrine of an inscrutable, unintelligent, unknown force, as the cause of all things, is a much more religious doctrine than that of a personal intelligent, and voluntary Being of infinite power and goodness. Matthew Arnold holds that an unconscious "power which makes for right," is a higher idea of God than the Jehovah of the Bible. Christ says, God is a Spirit. . . .

The third method of accounting for the contrivances manifested in the organs of plants and animals, is that which refers them to the blind operation of natural causes. They are not due to the continued cooperation and control of the divine mind, nor to the original purpose of God in the constitution of the universe. This is the doctrine of the Materialists, and to this doctrine, we are sorry to say, Mr. Darwin, although himself a theist, has given in his adhesion. It is on this account the Materialists almost deify him.

From what has been said, it appears that Darwinism includes three distinct elements. First evolution, or the assumption that all organic forms, vegetable and animal, have been evolved or developed from one, or a few, primordial living germs; second, that this evolution has been effected by natural selection, or the survival of the fittest; and third, and by far the most important and only distinctive element of his theory, that this natural selection is without design, being conducted by unintelligent physical causes. . . .

It is however neither evolution nor natural selection, which give Darwinism its peculiar character and importance. It is that Darwin rejects all teleology, or the doctrine of final causes. He denies design in any of the organisms in the vegetable or animal world. He teaches that the eye was formed without any purpose of producing an organ of vision. . . . It is the distinctive doctrine of Mr. Darwin, that species owe their origin, not to the original intention of the divine mind; not to special acts of creation calling new forms into existence at certain epochs; not to the constant and everywhere operative efficiency of God, guiding physical causes in the production of intended effects; but to the gradual accumulation of unintended variations of structure and instinct, securing some advantage to their subjects. . . .

All the innumerable varieties of plants, all the countless forms of animals, with all their instincts and faculties, all the varieties of men with their intellectual endowments, and their moral and religious nature, have, according to Darwin, been evolved by the agency of the blind, unconscious laws of nature. . . . The grand and fatal objection to Darwinism is this exclusion of design in the origin of species, or the production of living organisms. . . .

The conclusion of the whole matter is, that the denial of design in nature is virtually the denial of God. Mr. Darwin's theory is virtually atheistical; his theory, not he himself. He believes in a Creator. But when that Creator, millions on millions of ages ago, did something,--called matter and a living germ into existence,--and then abandoned the universe to itself to be controlled by chance and necessity, without any purpose on his part as to the result, or any intervention or guidance, then He is virtually consigned, so far as we are concerned, to nonexistence. . . . This is the vital point. The denial of final causes is the formative idea of Darwin's theory, and therefore no teleologist can be a Darwinian. . . .

We have thus arrived at the answer to our question, What is Darwinism? It is Atheism.

Natural Science and Religion

ASA GRAY

Asa Gray (1810-88) was distinguished botanist and amateur thologian who taught natural history at Harvard for many years. Even before Darwin's The Origin of Species appeared in 1859, Gray had openly stated his belief in a single origin of plant and animal species. In 1860 he appeared in a series of debates with his colleague at Harvard, zoologist Louis Agassiz. In contrast to Agassiz' antagonism to Darwinism, Gray made a public commitment to Darwinian ideas and to their compatibility with theism. The following is from Gray's Natural Science and Religion (New York: Charles Scribner's Sons, 1880), pp. 44-52, 55-56, 62-68. According to Gray, how does natural selection take place? How did he come to the conclusion that evolution (mediate creation) and the Christian faith were compatible?

All animals vary more or less: agriculturalists improve domesticated animals by selection. What is thus done by art is done with equal efficacy, though more slowly, by Nature, in the formation of varieties of mankind, fitted for the country which they inhabit, and in this way: Negroes and mulattoes enjoy immunity from certain tropical diseases, and white men a comparative immunity from those of cold climates. Under the variation common to all animals, some of the darker would be better adapted than the rest to bear the diseases of a warm country,--say, of tropical Africa. This race would consequently multiply, while the others would decrease, directly, because the prevalent diseases would be more fatal to them, and indirectly, by inability to contend with their more vigorous neighbors. Through the continued operation of the same causes, darker and darker races would prevail over the less dark, and in time would monopolize the region where they originated or into which they had advanced. Similarly would white races, to the exclusion of dark, be developed and prevail in cooler regions.

Now, this simple principle,--extended from races to species; from the present to geological ages; from man and domesticated animals to all animals and plants; from struggle with disease to struggle for food, for room, and against the diverse hardships which at times beset all living things, and which are intensified by the Malthusian Law of the pressure of the population on subsistence,--population tending to multiple in geometrical progression, while food can increase only in a much lower ratio, and room may not be increasable at all, so that out of curcumstances in each generation can possibly survive and propagate,--this is Darwinism; that is, Darwinism pure and simple, free from all speculative accretions.

Here, it may be remarked that natural selection by itself is not an hypothesis, nor even a theory. It is a truth,--a catena of facts and direct inferences from facts. As has been happily said, it is a truth of the same kind as that which we enunciate in saying that round stones will roll down a hill further than flat ones. There is no doubt that natural selection operates; the open question is, what do its operations amount to. The hypothesis based on this principle is, that the struggle for life and survival of only the fittest among individuals, all disposed to vary and no two alike, will account for the diversification of the species and forms of vegetable and animal life,--will even account for the rise, in the course of countless ages, from simpler and lower to higher and more specialized living beings.

We need not here enter into any further explanation of this now familiar but not always well understood hypothesis; nor need I here pronounce any judgment of my own upon it. No doubt it may account for much which has not received other scientific explanation; and Mr. Darwin is not the man to claim that it will account for every thing. But before we can judge at all of its capabilities, we need clearly to understand what is contained in the hypothesis; for what can be got out of it, in the way of explanation, depends upon what has gone into it. So certain discriminations should here be attended to.

Natural selection we understand to be a sort of personification or generalized expression for the processes and the results of the whole interplay of living things on the earth with their inorganic surroundings and with each other. The hypothesis asserts that these may account, not for the introduction of life, but for its diversification into the forms and kinds which we now behold. This, I suppose, is tantamount to asserting that the differences between one species and another now existing, and between these and their predecessors, has come to pass in the course of Nature; that is, without miracle. In these days, all agree that a scientific inquiry whether this may be so--that is, whether there are probable grounds for believing it (no thoughtful person expects to prove it)--is perfectly legitimate; and, so far as it becomes probable, I imagine that you might safely accept it. For the hypothesis, in its normal and simplest form,-- when kept close to the facts, and free from extraneous assumptions--is merely this:--

Given the observed capacity for variation as an inexhaustible factor, assuming that what has varied is still prone to vary (and there are grounds for the assumption), and natural selection will--so to say--lead on and diversify them, and by continual elimination of the less fit, segregate the survivors into distinct species. This, you see, assumes, and does not account for, the impulse to variation, assumes that variation is an inherent and universal capacity, and is the efficient cause of all the diversity; while natural selection is the proximate cause of it. So it is the selection, not the creation of forms that is accounted for. Darwinism does not so much explain why we have the actual forms, as it does why we have only these and not all intermediate forms,--in short, why we have <u>species</u>. There is of course a cause for the variation. Nobody supposes that any thing changes without a cause; and there is no reason for thinking that proximate causes of variation may not come to be known; but we hardly know the conditions, still less the causes now. The point I wish to make here is that natural selection--however you expand its meaning--cannot be invoked as the cause of that upon which it operates, <u>i.e.</u>, variation. Otherwise, if by natural selection is meant the totality of all the known and unknown causes of whatever comes to pass in organic nature, then the term is no longer an allowable personification, but a sheer abstraction, which meaning every thing, can explain nothing. It is like saying that whatever happens is the cause of whatever comes to pass.

We may conclude, therefore, that natural selection, in the sense of the originator of the term, and in the only congruous sense, stands for the influence of inorganic nature upon living things, along with the influence of these upon each other; and that what it purports to account for is the picking out, from the multitude of incipient variations, of the few which are to survive, and which thereby acquire distinctness.

There is a further assumption in the hypothesis which must not be overlooked; namely, that the variation of plants and animals, out of which so much comes, is indefinite or all-directioned and accidental. This, I would insist, is no fundamental part of the hypothesis of the derivation of species, and is clearly no part of the principle of natural selection. But it is an assumption which Mr. Darwin judges to be warranted by the facts, and in some of its elements it is unavoidable. Evidently if the innate tendency to vary upon which physical circumstances operate is indefinite, then the variations which the circumstances elicit, and which could not otherwise amount to any thing, must be accidental in the same sense as are the circumstances themselves. Out of this would immediately rise the question as to what can be the foundation and beginning of this long and wonderful chapter of accidents which has produced and maintained, not only for this time but through all biological periods, an ever varying yet ever well-adapted cosmos.

But the facts, so far as I can judge, do not support the assumption of every-sided and indifferent variation. Variation is somehow and somewhere introduced in the transit from parent to offspring. The actual variations displayed by the progeny of a particular plant or animal may differ much in grade, and tend in more than one direction, but in fact they do not appear to tend in many directions. It is generally agreed that the variation is from within, is an internal response to external impressions. All that we can possibly know of the nature of the inherent tendency to vary must be gathered from the facts of the response. And these, I judge, are not such as to require or support the assumption of a tendency to wholly vague and all-directioned variation.

Let us here correct a common impression that Darwinian evolution predicates actual or necessary variation of all existing species, and counts that the variation must be in some definite ratio of the time. That is not the idea, nor the fact. "Evolution is not a course of haphazard and incessant change, but a continuing re-adjustment, which may or may not, according to circumstances, involve considerable changes in a given time." Every form is in a relatively stable equilibrium, else it would not exist. Forms adjusted to their surroundings ought by the hypothesis to remain unchanged until the circumstances change. Only those of their variations could come to any thing which happened to be equally well adapted to the unchanged circumstances; and inhabit similiar stations in the same area. . . .

As has just been intimated, the characteristic of that particular theory of evolution which is now in the ascendant is that, by taking advantage of "every creature's best" for bettering conditions, it has made strife work for good, throughout an immensely long line of adjustments and readjustments, in a series ascending as it advanced; that it supposes a process, not from discord to harmony, but from simpler to fuller and richer harmonies, conserving throughout the best adaptations to the then existing conditions. So while its advocates nowhere contemplate a state

"When Nature underneath a heap,
Of jarring atoms lay,
And could not heave her head,"
they may appropriate Dryden's closing lines,--
"From harmony, from heavenly harmony,
This universal frame began,
From harmony to harmony
Through all the compass of the notes it ran,

The diapason closing full in man."

I have now indicated, at more than sufficient length for one discourse, some of the principal recent changes and present tendencies in scientific belief, especially in biology. Even the most advanced of the views here presented are held by very many scientific men,--some as established truths, some as probable opinions. There is a class, moreover, by whom all these scientific theories, and more, are held as ascertained facts, and as the basis of philosophical inferences which strike at the root of theistic beliefs.

It remains to consider what attitude thoughtful men and Christian believers should take respecting them, and how they stand related to beliefs of another order. . . .

How the more exact physical sciences are becoming more reconditely hypothetical, especially in the imagination of entities of which there can be no possible proof beyond their serviceability in explaining phenomena, we must not stop to consider. Only this may be said, that the adage, "Where faith begins science ends" is now well nigh inverted. For faith, in a just sense of the word, assumes as prominent a place in science as in religion. It is indispensable to both.

Let it be noted, moreover, that the case we have to consider does not come before the tribunal of reason with antecedent presumptions all on one side, as theologians generally suppose. They say to the naturalists, not improperly, we will think about adopting your conclusions, contrary as they are to all our prepossessions, when they are thoroughly and irrevocably substantiated, and not till then. Your theory may prove true, but it seems vastly improbable. Here the naturalist is ready with a rejoinder: In this world of law you cannot expect us to adopt your assumption of specific creation by miraculous intervention with the course of Nature, not once for all at a beginning, but over and over in time. We will accept intervention only when and where you can convincingly establish it, and where we are unable to explain it away, as in the case of absolute beginning. If the naturalist starts with the presumption against him when he broaches the theory of the descent of later from preceding forms in the course of Nature, so no less does the theologian when in a world governed by law he asserts a break in the continuity of natural cause and effect.

But indeed, you are not so much concerned to know whether evolutionary theories are actually well-founded or ill-founded, as you are to know whether if true, or if received as true, they would impair the foundations of religion. And, surely, if views of Nature which are incompatible with theism and with Christianity can be established, or can be made as tenable as the contrary, it is quite time that we knew it. If, on the other hand, all real facts and necessary inferences from them can be adjusted to our grounded religious convictions, as well as other ascertained facts have been adjusted, it may relieve many to be assured of it.

The best contribution that I can offer towards the settlement of these mooted questions may be the statement and explanation of my own attitude in this regard, and of the reasons which determine it.

I accept substantially, as facts, or as apparently well grounded inferences, or as fairly probable opinions,--according to their nature and degree,--the principal series of changed views which I brought before you in the preceding lecture. I have no particular predilection for any of them; and I have no particular dread of any of the consequences which legitimately flow from them, beyond the general awe and sense of total insufficiency with which a mortal man contemplates the mysteries which shut him in on every side. I claim, moreover, not merely allowance, but the right to hold these opinions along with the doctrines of natural religion and the verities of the Christian faith. There are perplexities enough to bewilder our souls whenever and wherever we look for the causes and reasons of things; but I am unable to perceive that the idea of the evolution of one species from another, and of all from an initial form of life, adds any new perplexity to theism.

In unfolding my thought upon the subject, I wish to keep close "to the solid ground of Nature" as I possibly can, even where the discourse must rise from the ground of science into the finer air of philosophy. Specially I must heed the injunction: "If thou has any tidings, prithee, deliver them like a man of this world," the objective reality and substantiality of what we see and deal with, though I am told it cannot be proved; and I assume,--although demonstration is impossible,—that what I and my fellow men cannot help believing we ought to believe, or at least must rest content with. I suppose you will agree with me that it is not science, at least not natural science, which raises the most formidable difficulties to Christian theism, but philosophy, and that it is for philosophy to surmount them.

The question which science asks of all it meets is, What is the system and course of things, and how is this or that a part of it in the fixed sequence of cause and effect? Philosphy asks whence the system itself, and what are causes and effects. Theology is partly historical science, and partly philosophy. Now I, as a scientific man, might rest in the probability of evolution as a general inference from the facts or a good hypothesis, and relegate the questions you would ask to the philosophers and theologians. But I am not one of those who think that scientific men should not concern themselves with such matters; and having gone so far as to say that the evolution which I accept does not seem to me to add any new perplexity to theism, and well knowing that others are of a contrary opinion, I am bound to further explanation and argument.

But I have not the presumption to suppose that I can make any new contribution to this discussion; and what I may suggest must not be expected to cover the ground widely nor penetrate it deeply. I am sure that you will not look to me for the rehandling of insoluble problems and inevitable contradictions, into which the philosophical consideration of the relations of Nature and man to God ultimately lands us. Certainly they are not peculiar to evolution. So, in so far as we may fairly refer any of its perplexities to old antinomies, which can neither be reconciled nor evaded, the burden will be off our shoulders. It might suffice to show that evolution need raise no other nor greater religious or philosophical difficulties than the views which have already been accepted, and held to be not inimical to religion.

But, indeed, our universal concession that __Nature is__, and that it is a system of fixed laws and uniformities, under which every thing we see and know in the inorganic universe, and very much in the organic world, have come to be as they are, in unbroken sequence, implicitly gives away the principle of all ordinary objection to the evolution of living as well as lifeless forms, of species as well as of individuals. It leaves the matter simply as one of fact and evidence. Indeed, mediate creation is just what the thoughtful and thorough observer of the ways of God in Nature would expect, and is what some of the most illustrious of the philosophic saints and fathers of the church have more or less believed in.

In saying that the doctrine of the evolution of species has taken its place among scientific beliefs, I do not mean it is accepted by all living naturalists; for there are some who wholly reject it. Nor that it is held with equal conviction and in the same way by all who receive it; for some teach it dogmatically, along with assumptions, both scientific and philosophical, which are to us both unwarranted and unwelcome; more accept it, with various confidence, and in a tentative way, for its purely scientific uses, and without any obvious reference to its ultimate outcome; and some, looking to its probable prevalence, are adjusting their conditional belief in it to cherished beliefs of another order. One thing is clear, that the current is all running one way, and seems unlikely to run dry; and that evolutionary doctrines are profoundly affecting all natural science.

Evolution and Religion

HENRY WARD BEECHER

Henry Ward Beecher (1813-87), minister at Brooklyn's Plymouth Church for many years, provided a significant boost to the acceptance of evolution among Protestants with his efforts to accommodate theism with Darwinism. In 1885 he delivered a series of sermons on evolution in which he discussed the bearing of evolution on the fundamental doctrines of orthodox Christianity. Beecher insisted he had no problem with divine design in the light of evolution, stating that he hailed the "evolutionary philosophy with joy." The following excerpt taken from his <u>Evolution</u> and <u>Religion</u> (New York: Ford, Howard, and Hulbert, 1886), pp. 112-17, illustrates why he could identify himself as a Christian evolutionist. How does Beecher accommodate the teachings of evolution with traditional Biblical teaching? Discuss the two illustrations Beecher used to argue that evolution lifted the evidence of divine design to a higher plane than was contended by previous advocates of design.

The law of cause and effect is fundamental to the every existence of science, and, I had almost said, to the very operation of the human mind. So, then, we gain nothing by excluding divine intelligence, and to include it smooths the way to investigation, and is agreeable to the nature of the human mind. It is easier to conceive of the personal divine being with intelligence, will and power, than it is to conceive of a world of such vast and varied substance as this, performing all the functions of intelligence and will and power. That would be giving to miscellaneous matter the attributes which we denied to a personal God.

The doctrine of Evolution, at first sight, seems to destroy the theory of intelligent design in creation, and in its earlier stages left those who investigated it very doubtful whether there was anything in creation but matter, or whether there was a knowable God.

So sprang up the Agnostic school, which includes in it some of the noblest spirits of our day. "God may exist, but we do not know it." That is what the Bible says from beginning to end; that is what philosophy is now beginning to explain. We cannot understand the divine nature, so exalted above everything that has yet been developed in human consciousness, except it dawns upon us when we are ourselves unfolding and rising to such a higher operation of our minds as does not belong to the great mass of the human race. God is to be seen only by those faculties that verge upon the divine nature, and to them only when they are in a state of exaltation. Moral intuitions are not absolute revelations, but they are as sure of higher truths as the physical senses are of material truths.

But the question of design in creation, which has been a stable argument for the proof of the existence of God and his attributes, seems to have been shaken from its former basis. It is being restored in a larger and grander way, which only places the fact upon a wider space, and makes the outcome more wonderful. Special creation, and the adaptation in consequence of it, of structure to uses in animals, and in the vegetable kingdom to their surroundings, has always been an element of God's work regarded as most remarkable. How things fit to their places; how regular all the subordinations and developments that are going on; how fit they are to succeed one another! Now the old theory conceived God as creating things for special uses. When the idea of the lily dawned on him, he smiled and said: "I will make it;" and he made it to be just as beautiful as it is. And when the rose was to be added, like an artist God thought just how it should be all the way through. That is the old view that some plants were made to do without water and could live in parched sands; and that some could live only in the tropics; and thus God adapted all his creation to the climate and the soil and the circumstances, and it was a beautiful thing to see how things did fit, by the divine wisdom, the places where they were found.

Then comes Evolution and teaches that God created through the mediation of natural laws; that creation, in whole or detail, was a process of slow growth, and not an instantaneous process; that plants and animals alike were affected by their surrounding circumstances favorably or unfavorably; and that, in the long run, those which were best adapted to their environment survived, and those perished which could not adapt themselves to the conditions of soil, climate, moisture, cold or heat which in the immeasurable periods of creation befell them. The adaptation then of plants to their condition did not arise from the direct command of the Great Gardener; but from the fact that, among these infinite gradations of plants, only those survived and propagated themselves which were able to bear the climate and soil in which they found themselves; all others dwindled and perished. Of course there would be a fine adjustment of the plant to its condition; it came to this by a long preparation of ancestral influences.

How beautiful it is to see a plant growing right under the cheek of a precipice or a snow bed, or by the edges of winter through the year! Men say how beautiful the thought was that God should create in vegetables and flowers right alongside the snow, as it were, to cheer the bosom of winter: whereas it turned out that everything that could live there died; and, by and by, there were some plants so tough that they could live there, and they did; and the adaptation was the remainder after a long series of perishings. Men say, What a remarkable instance of divine design that the cactus can live on arid deserts, where water scarcely falls more than once or twice a year; and what a special creation and adaptation it was on the part of God that he should make such plants as that! But the Evolutionist says that all the plants were killed in succession until it came about, in the endless variations of the vegetable kingdom, that a plant developed whose structure was covered, as it were, with an india rubber skin, and whose leaves were substantially little cisterns, which drank up all the water they wanted to use through the summer, and so continued to live in spite of their dry surroundings, when others could not live because they could not adapt themselves. So the argument for special design, as we used to hold it, fails there.

Through long periods all things tended to vary more or less from their original forms, and adapted themselves to their necessary conditions; and what could not do this perished; for the theory of Evolution is as much a theory of destruction and degradation as of development and building up. As the carpenter has numberless shavings, and a vast amount of wastage of every log which he would shape to some use, so creation has been an enormous waste, such as seems like squandering, on the scale of human life, but not to Him that dwells in Eternity. In bringing the world to its present conditions, vast amounts of things have lived for a time and were unable to hold on, and let go and perished. We behold the onflowing, through immeasurable ages of creation, of this peculiar tendency to vary, and in some cases to improve. The improvement is transmitted; and in the battle of life, one thing conflicting with another, the strong or the best adapted crowd out the weak, and these continue to transmit their qualities until something better yet shall supplant them.

Vast waste and the perishing of unfit things is one of the most striking facts in the existence of this world; for while life is the consummation, death seems to be the instrument by which life itself is supplied with improvement and advancement. Death prepares the way for life. Things are adapted thus to their condition, to their climate, to their food; or by their power of escape from their adversaries, or their power of establishing themselves and of defending their position, they make it secure. The vast universe, looked at largely, is moving onward and upward in determinate lines and directions, while on the way the weak are perishing. Yet, there is an unfolding process that is carrying creation up to higher planes and upon higher lines, reaching more complicated conditions in structure, in function, in adaptation, with systematic and harmonious results, so that the whole physical creation is organizing itself for a sublime march toward perfectness.

If single acts would evince design, how much more a vast universe, that by inherent laws gradually built itself, and then created its own plants and animals, a universe so adjusted that it left by the way the poorest things, and steadily wrought toward more complex, ingenious, and beautiful results! Who designed this mighty machine, created matter, gave to it its laws, and impressed upon it that tendency which has brought forth the almost infinite results on the globe, and wrought them into a perfect system? Design by wholesome is grander than design by retail.

You are familiar with the famous illustration of Dr. Paley, where a man finds a watch, and infers irresistibly that that watch was made by some skillful, thoughtful watchmaker. Suppose that a man, having found a watch, should say to himself, "Somebody thought this out, somebody created this; it is evidently constructed and adapted exactly to the end in view the keeping of time." Suppose, then, that some one should take him to Waltham, and introduce him into that vast watch factory, where watches are created in hundreds of thousands by machinery; and suppose the question should be put to him, "What do you think, then, about the man who created this machinery, which of itself goes on cutting out wheels, and springs, and pinions, and everything that belongs to making a watch? If it be an argument of design that there is a man existing who could create a manufactory turning out millions of watches, and machinery too, so that the human hand has little to do but to adjust the parts already created by machines?" If it be evidence of design in creation that God adapted one single flower to its place and functions, is it not greater evidence if there is a system of such adaptations going on from eternity to eternity? Is not the Creator of the system a more sublime designer than the creator of any single act?

Or, let me put down before you an oriental rug, which we all know has been woven by women squatting upon the ground, each one putting in the color that was wanted to form the figure, carrying out the whole with oriental harmony of color. Looking upon that, you could not help saying, "Well, that is a beautiful design, and these are skillful women that made it, there can be no question about that." But now behold the power loom where not simply a rug with long, drudging work by hand is being created, but where the machine is creating carpets in endless lengths, with birds, and insects, and flowers, and scrolls, and every element of beauty. It is all being done without a hand touching it. Once start the engine, and put the perforated papers above the loom, and that machine turns out a carpet that puts to shame the beauty of these oriental rugs. Now the question is this: Is it an evidence of design in these women that they turn out such work, and is it not evidence of a higher design in the man who turned out that machine--that loom--which could carry on this work a thousandfold more magnificently than human fingers did?

It may be safely said, then, that Evolution, instead of obliterating the evidence of divine Design, has lifted it to a higher plane, and made it more sublime than it ever was contemplated to be under the old reasonings.

THE GOSPEL OF WEALTH AND BIG BUSINESS   10

Wealth

ANDREW CARNEGIE

Andrew Carnegie (1835-1919) was the son of a poor Scottish weaver who emigrated to America with his family in 1848. During his early years in America, Andrew worked as a bobbin boy in a cotton mill and then as an engine tender. In 1853 he gained a job with the Pennsylvania Railroad, where he stayed until 1865. After the Civil War he entered business for himself, and in 1868 founded Union Iron Mills. Over the course of the next thirty years he became so successful that his company was turning out the bulk of American steel. Along with the amassing of a large personal fortune, Carnegie was concerned with the ethical responsibilities of the person of wealth, whom he believed must see to it that his private fortune was used for the public welfare. Before he died he disposed of 90 percent of his wealth by endowing more than 2500 libraries, donating organs and public buildings, and creating numerous foundations. The following selection, "Wealth," North American Review, 148 (June, 1889), 653-64, presents his personal viewpoints concerning wealth. What positive and negative consequences of the law of competition does Carnegie discuss, and which set of consequences does Carnegie believe outweighs the other? Which of the three modes for the disposing of wealth does Carnegie favor? What is the duty of the man of wealth?

The problem of our age is the proper administration of wealth, so that the ties of brotherhood may still bind together the rich and poor in harmonious relationship. The conditions of human life have not only been changed, but revolutionized, within the past few hundred years. In former days there was little difference between the dwelling, dress, food, and environment of the chief and those of his retainers. The Indians are today where civilized man then was. When visiting the Sioux, I was led to the wigwam of the chief. It was just like the others in external appearance, and even within the difference was trifling between it and those of the poorest of his braves. The contrast between the palace of the millionaire and the cottage of the laborer with us to-day measures the change which has come with civilization.

This change, however, is not to be deplored, but welcomed as highly beneficial. It is well, nay, essential for the progress of the race, that the houses of some should be homes for all that is highest and best in literature and the arts, and for all the refinements of civilization, rather than that none should be so. Much better this great irregularity than universal squalor. Without wealth there can be no Maecenas. The "good old times" were not good old times. Neither master nor servant was as well situated then as today. A relapse to old conditions would be disastrous to both--not the least so to him who serves and would sweep away civilization with it. But whether the change be for good or ill, it is upon us, beyond our power to alter, and therefore to be accepted and made the best of. It is a waste of time to criticize the inevitable. . . .

The price we pay for this salutary change is, no doubt, great. We assemble thousands of operatives in the factory, in the mine, and in the counting-house, of whom the employer can know little of nothing, and to whom the employer is little better than a myth. All intercourse between them is at an end. Rigid Castes are formed, and, as usual, mutual ignorance breeds mutual distrust. Each Caste is without sympathy for the other, and ready to credit anything disparaging in regard to it. Under the law of competition, the employer of thousands is forced into the strictest economies, among which the rates paid to labor figure prominently, and often there is friction between the employer and the employed, between capital and labor, between rich and poor. Human society loses homogeneity.

The price which society pays for the law of competition, like the price it pays for cheap comforts and luxuries, is also great; but the advantages of this law are also greater still, for it is to this law that we owe our wonderful material development, which brings improved conditions in its train. But, whether the law be benign or not, we must say of it, as we say of the change in the conditions of men to which we have referred: It is here; we cannot evade it; no substitutes for it have been found; and while the law may be sometimes hard for the individual, it is best for the race, because it insures the survival of the fittest in every department. We accept and welcome, therefore, as conditions to which we must accommodate ourselves, great inequality of environment, the concentration of business, industrial and commercial, in the hands of a few, and the law of competition between these, as being not only beneficial, but essential for the future progress of the race. Having accepted these, it follows that there must be great scope for the exercise of special ability in the merchant and in the manufacturer who has to conduct affairs upon a great scale. That this talent for organization and management is rare among men is proved by the fact that it invariably secures for its possessor enormous rewards, no matter where or under what laws or conditions. The experienced in affairs always rate the MAN whose services can be obtained as a partner as not only the first consideration, but such as to render the question of his capital scarcely worth considering, for such men soon create capital; while, without the special talent required, capital soon takes wings. Such men become interested in firms or corporations using millions; and estimating only simple interest to be made upon the capital invested, it is inevitable that their income must exceed their expenditures, and that they must accumulate wealth. Nor is there any middle ground which such men can occupy, because the great manufacturing or commercial concern which does not earn at least interest upon its capital soon becomes bankrupt. It must either go forward or fall behind: to stand still is impossible. It is a condition essential for its successful operation that it should be thus far profitable, and even that, in addition to interest on capital, it should make profit. It is a law, as certain as any of the others named, that men possessed of this peculiar talent of affairs, under the free play of economic forces, must, of necessity, soon be in receipt of more revenue than can be judiciously expended upon themselves; and this law is as beneficial for the race as the others.

Objections to the foundations upon which society is based are not in order, because the condition of the race is better with these than it has been with any others which have been tried. Of the effect of any new substitutes proposed we cannot be sure. The Socialist or Anarchist who seeks to overturn present conditions is to be regarded as attacking the foundation upon which civilization itself rests, for civilization took its start from the day that the capable, industrious workman said to his incompetent and lazy fellow, "If thou dost not sow, thou shalt not reap," and thus ended primitive Communism by separating the drones from the bees. One who studies this subject will soon be brought face to face with the conclusion that upon the sacredness of property civilization itself depends--the right of the laborer to his hundred dollars in the savings bank, and equally the legal right of the millionaire to his millions. To those who propose to substitute Communism for this Individualism the answer, therefore is: The race has tried that. All progress from that barbarous day to the present time has resulted from its displacement. Not evil, but good, has come to the race from the accumulation of wealth by those who have the ability and energy that produce it. But even if we admit for a moment that it might be better for the race to discard its present foundation, Individualism,--that it is a nobler ideal that man should labor, not for himself alone, but in and for a brotherhood of his fellows, and share with them all in common, realizing Swedenborg's idea of Heaven, where as he says, the angels derive their happiness, not from laboring for self, but for each other,--even admit all this, and a sufficient answer is, This is not evolution, but revolution. It necessetates the changing of human nature itself--a work of aeons, even if it were good to change it, which we cannot know. It is not practicable theoretically, it belongs to another and

long-succeeding sociological stratum. Our duty is with what
is practicable now; with the next step possible in our day
and generation. It is a criminal act to waste our energies
in endeavoring to uproot, when all we can profitably or possibly accomplish is to bend the universal tree of humanity
a little in the direction most favorable to the production
of good fruit under existing circumstances. We might as well
urge the destruction of the highest existing type of man because he failed to reach our ideal as to favor the destruction of Individualism, Private Property, the Law of Accumulation of Wealth, and the Law of Competition; for these are
the highest results of human experience, the soil in which
society so far has produced the best fruit. Unequally or
unjustly perhaps, as the laws sometimes operate, and imperfect as they appear to the Idealist, they are, nevertheless,
like the highest type of man, the best and most valuable of
all that humanity has yet accomplished.

We start, then, with a condition of affairs under which the
best interests of the race are promoted, but which inevitably gives wealth to the few. Thus far, accepting conditions
as they exist, the situation can be surveyed and pronounced
good. The question then arises,--and, if the foregoing be
correct, it is the only question with which we have to deal--
What is the proper mode of administering wealth after the
laws upon which civilization is founded have thrown it into
the hands of the few? And it is of this great question that
I believe I offer the true solution. It will be understood
that _fortunes_ are here spoken of, not moderate sums saved
by many years of effort, the returns from which are required
for the comfortable maintenance and the education of families. This is not _wealth_, but only _competence_, which it
should be the aim of all to acquire.

There are but three modes in which surplus wealth can be
disposed of. It can be left to the families of the descendents; or it can be bequeathed for public purposes; or, finally, it can be administered during their lives by its
possessors. Under the first and second modes most of the
wealth of the world that has reached the few has hitherto
been applied. Let us in turn consider each of these modes.
The first is the most injudicious. In monarchical countries,
the estates and the greatest portion of the wealth are left
to the first son, that the vanity of the parent may be gratified by the thought that his name and title are to descend

to succeeding generations unimpaired. The condition of this class in Europe to-day teaches the futility of such hopes or ambitions. The successors have become impoverished through their follies or from the fall in the value of land. Even in Great Britain the strict law of entail has been found inadequate to maintain the status of an hereditary class. Its soil is rapidly passing into the hands of the stranger. Under republican institutions the division of property among the children is much fairer, but the question which forces itself upon thoughtful men in all lands is: Why should men leave great fortunes to their children? If this is done from affection, is it not misguided affection? Observation teaches that, generally speaking, it is not well for the children that they should be so burdened. Neither is it well for the state. Beyond providing for the wife and daughters moderate sources of income, and very moderate allowances indeed, if any, for the sons, men may well hesitate, for it is no longer questionable that great sums bequeathed oftener work more for the injury than for the good of the recipients. Wise men will soon conclude that, for the best interests of the members of their families and of the state, such bequests are an improper use of their means. . . .

As to the second mode, that of leaving wealth at death for public uses, it may be said that this is only a means for the disposal of wealth, provided a man is content to wait until he is dead before it becomes of much good in the world. Knowledge of the results of legacies bequeathed is not calculated to inspire the brightest hopes of much posthumous good being accomplished. The cases are not few in which the real object sought by the testator is not attained, nor are they few in which his real wishes are thwarted. In many cases the bequests are so used as to become only monuments of his folly. It is well to remember that it requires the exercise of not less ability than that which acquired the wealth to use it so as to be really beneficial to the community. Besides this, it may fairly be said that no man is to be extolled for doing what he cannot help doing, nor is he to be thanked by the community to which he leaves wealth at death. Men who leave vast sums in this way may fairly be thought men who would not have left it at all, had they been able to take it with them. The memories of such cannot be held in grateful remembrance, for there is no grace in their gifts. It is not to be wondered at that such bequests seem so generally to lack the blessing. . . .

There remains, then, only one mode of using great fortunes; but in this we have the true antidote for the temporary unequal distribution of wealth, the reconciliation of the rich and the poor--a reign of harmony--another ideal, differing, indeed, from that of the Communist in requiring only the further evolution of existing conditions, not the total overthrow of our civilization. It is founded upon the present most intense individualism, and the race is prepared to put it in practice by degrees whenever it pleases. Under its sway we shall have an ideal state, in which the surplus wealth of the few will become, in the best sense, the property of the many, because administered for the common good, and this wealth, passing through the hands of the few, can be made a much more potent force for the elevation of our race than if it had been distributed in small sums to the people themselves. Even the poorest can be made to see this, and to agree that great sums gathered by some of their fellow citizens and spent for public purposes, from which the masses reap the principal benefit, are more valuable to them than if scattered among them through the course of many years in trifling amounts. . . .

Poor and restricted are our opportunities in this life; narrow our horizon; our best work most imperfect; but rich men should be thankful for one inestimable boon. They have it in their power during their lives to busy themselves in organizing benefactions from which the masses of their fellows will derive lasting advantage, and thus dignify their own lives. The highest life is probably to be reached, not by such imitation of the life of Christ as Count Tolstoi gives us, but, while animated by Christ's spirit, by recognizing the changed conditions of this age, and adopting modes of expressing this spirit suitable to the changed conditions under which we live; still laboring for the good of our fellows, which was the essence of his life and teaching, but laboring in a different manner.

This, then, is held to be the duty of the man of Wealth: First, to set an example of modest, unostentatious living, shunning display or extravagance; to provide moderately for the legitimate wants of those dependent upon him; and after doing so to consider all surplus revenues which come to him simply as trust funds, which he is called upon to administer, and strictly bound as a manner which, in his judgment, is best calculated to produce the most beneficial results for the community--the man of wealth thus becoming the mere agent and trustee for his poorer brethren, bringing to their service his superior wisdom, experience, and ability to administer, doing for them better than they would or could do for themselves.

We are met here with the difficulty of determining what are moderate sums to leave to members of the family; what is modest, unostentatious living; what is the test of extravagance. There must be different standards for different conditions. The answer is that it is as impossible to name exact amounts or actions as it is to define good manners, good taste, or the rules of propriety; but, nevertheless, these are verities, well known although undefinable. Public sentiment is quick to know and to feel what offends these. So in the case of wealth. The rule in regard to good taste in the dress of men or women applies here. Whatever makes one conspicuous offends the canon. If any family be chiefly known for display, for extravagance in home, table, equipage, for enormous sums ostentatiously spent in any form upon itself,--if these be its chief distinctions, we have no difficulty in estimating its nature or culture. So likewise in regard to the use or abuse of its surplus wealth, or to generous, freehanded cooperation in good public uses, or to unabated efforts to accumulate and hoard to the last, whether they administer or bequeath. The verdict rests with the best and most enlightened public sentiment. The community will surely judge, and its judgments will not often be wrong.

The best uses to which surplus wealth can be put have already been indicated. Those who would administer wisely must, indeed, be wise, for one of the serious obstacles to the improvement of our race is indiscriminate charity. It were better for mankind that the millions of the rich were thrown into the sea than so spent as to encourage the slothful, the drunken, the unworthy. Of every thousand dollars spent in so called charity today, it is probable that $950 is unwisely spent; so spent, indeed, as to produce the very evils which it proposes to mitigate or cure. A well-known writer of philosophic books admitted the other day that he had given a quarter of a dollar to a man who approached him as he was coming to visit the house of his friend. He know nothing of the habits of this beggar; knew not the use that would be made of this money, although he had every reason to suspect that it would be spent improperly. This man professed to be a disciple of Herbert Spencer; yet the quarter-dollar given that night will probably work more injury than all the money which its thoughtless donor will be able to give in true charity will do good. He only gratified his own feelings, saved himself from annoyance,--and this was probably one of the most selfish and very worst actions of his life, for in all respects he is most worthy.

In bestowing charity, the main consideration should be to help those who will help themselves; to provide part of the means by which those who desire to improve may do so; to give those who desire to rise the aids by which they may rise; to assist, but rarely or never to do all. Neither the individual nor the race is improved by alms-giving. Those worthy of assistance, except in rare cases, seldom require assistance. The really valuable men of the race never do, except in cases of accident or sudden change. Every one has, of course, cases of individuals brought to his own knowledge where temporary assistance can do genuine good, and these he will not overlook. But the amount which can be wisely given by the individual for individuals is necessarily limited by his lack of knowledge of the circumstances connected with each. He is the only true reformer who is as careful and as anxious not to aid the unworthy as he is to aid the worthy, and, perhaps, even more so, for in alms-giving more injury is probably done by rewarding vice than by relieving virtue.

The rich man is thus almost restricted to following the examples of Peter Cooper, Enoch Pratt of Baltimore, Mr. Pratt of Brooklyn, Senator Stanford, and others, who know that the best means of benefiting the community is to place within its reach the ladders upon which the aspiring can rise--parks, and means of recreation, by which men are helped in body and mind; works of art, certain to give pleasure and improve the public taste, and public institutions of various kinds, which will improve the general condition of the people;--in this manner returning their surplus wealth to the mass of their fellows in the forms best calculated to do them lasting good.

Thus is the problem of Rich and Poor to be solved. The laws of accumulation will be left free; the laws of distribution free. Individualism will continue, but the millionaire will be but a trustee for the poor; intrusted for a season with a great part of the increased wealth of the community, but administering it for the community far better than it could or would have done for itself. The best minds will thus have reached a stage in the development of the race in which it is clearly seen that there is no mode of disposing of surplus wealth creditable to thoughtful and earnest men into whose hands it flows save by using it year by year for the general good. This day already dawns. But a little while, and although, without incurring the pity of their fellows, men may die sharers in great business enterprises from which their capital cannot be or has not been withdrawn, and is left chiefly at death for public uses, yet the man who dies leaving behind him millions of available wealth, which was his to administer during life, will pass away "unwept, unhonored, and unsung," no matter to what uses he leaves the dross which he cannot take with him. Of such as these the public verdict will then be: "The man who dies thus rich dies disgraced."

Such, in my opinion, is the true Gospel concerning Wealth, obedience to which is destined some day to solve the problem of the Rich and the Poor, and to bring "Peace on earth, among men Good-Will."

The Relation of Wealth to Morals

WILLIAM LAWRENCE

William Lawrence (1850-1941) was born into a family whose roots went back to the early Puritans. After graduation from Harvard in 1871, he received his theological degree from an Episcopalian school, where he later served as professor and dean. In 1893 he was named Episcopal Bishop of

Massachusetts, a position he held until 1926. Lawrence was highly successful in raising money for his church and for Harvard, and often spoke out on the contemporary problem of wealth and morality. Denying any conflict necessarily existed between the two, he supported the Protestant ethic with its theory of the stewardship of wealth. The selection which follows, "The Relation of Wealth to Morals," World's Week, I (January, 1901), was first delivered as an address to the New York City Chamber of Commerce. What relationship did Lawrence say there is between morality and wealth? How does he respond to the objection presented to him that some wealthy people are immoral?

There is a certain distrust on the part of our people as to the effect of material prosperity on their morality. We shrink with some foreboding at the great increase of riches, and question whether in the long run material prosperity does not tend toward the disintegration of character.

History seems to support us in our distrust. Visions arise of their fall from splendor of Tyre and Sidon, Babylon, Rome, and Venice, and of great nations too. The question is started whether England is not to-day, in the pride of her wealth and power, sowing the wind from which time she will reap the whirlwind.

Experience seems to add its support. Is it not from the ranks of the poor that the leaders of the people have always risen? Recall Abraham Lincoln and patriots of every generation.

The Bible has sustained the same note. Were ever stronger words of warning uttered against the deceitfulness of riches than those spoken by the peasant Jesus, who Himself had no place to lay His head? And the Church has through the centuries upheld poverty as one of the surest paths to Heaven: it has been a mark to the saint.

To be sure, in spite of history, experience, and the Bible, men have gone on their way making money and hailing with joy each age of material prosperity. The answer is: "This only proves the case; men are of the world, riches are deceitful, and the Bible is true; the world is given over to Mammon. In the increase of material wealth and the accumulation of riches the man who seeks the higher life has no part."

In the face of this comes the statement of the chief statistician of our census--from one, therefore, who speaks with authority: "The present census, when completed, will unquestionably show that the visible material wealth in this country now has a value of ninety billion dollars. This is an addition since 1890 of twenty-five billion dollars. This is a saving greater than all the people of the Western Continent had been able to make from the discovery of Columbus to the breaking out of the Civil War."

If our reasoning from history, experience, and the Bible is correct, we, a Christian people, have rubbed a sponge over the pages of the Bible and are in for orgies and a downfall to which the fall of Rome is a very tame incident.

May it not be well, however, to revise our inferences from history, experience and the Bible? History tells us that, while riches have been an item and an indirect cause of national decay, innumerable other conditions entered in. Therefore, while wealth has been a source of danger, it has not necessarily led to demoralization.

That leaders have sprung from the ranks of the poor is true and always will be true, so long as force of character exists in every class. But there are other conditions than a lack of wealth at the source of their uprising.

And as to the Bible:--while every word that can be quoted against the rich is as true as any other word, other words and deeds are as true; and the parables of our Lord on the stewardship of wealth, His association with the wealthy, strike another and complementary note. Both notes are essential to the harmony of His life and teachings. His thought was not of the conditions, rich or poor, but of a higher life, the character rising out of the conditions--fortunately, for we are released from that subtle hypocrisy which has beset the Christian through the ages, bemoaning the deceitfulness of riches and, at the same time, working with all his might to earn a competence, and a fortune if he can.

Now we are in a position to affirm that neither history, experience, nor the Bible necessarily sustains the common distrust of the effect of material wealth on morality. Our path of study is made more clear. Two positive principles lead us on our path.

The first is that man, when he is strong, will conquer Nature, open up her resources, and harness them to his service. This is his play, his exercise, his divine mission.

"Man," says Emerson, "is born to be rich. He is thoroughly related, and is tempted out by his appetites and fancies to the conquest of this and that piece of Nature, until he finds his well being in the use of the planet, and of more planets than his own. Wealth requires, besides the crust of bread and roof, the freedom of the city, the freedom of the earth." "The strong race is strong on these terms."

Man draws to himself material wealth as surely, as naturally, and as necessarily as the oak tree draws the elements into itself from the earth.

The other principle is that, in the long run, it is only to the man of morality that wealth comes. We believe in the harmony of God's Universe. We know that it is only by working along His laws natural and spiritual that we can work with efficiency. Only by working along the lines of right thinking and right living can the secrets and wealth of Nature be revealed. We, like the Psalmist, occasionally see the wicked prosper, but only occasionally.

Put two men in adjoining fields, one man strong and normal, the other weak and listless. One picks up his spade, turns over the earth, and works till sunset. The other turns over a few clods, gets a drink from the spring, takes a nap, and loafs back to his work. In a few years one will be rich for his needs, and the other a pauper dependent on the first, and growling at his prosperity.

Put ten thousand immoral men to live and work in one fertile valley and ten thousand moral men to live and work in the next valley, and the question is soon answered as to who wins the material wealth. Godliness is in league with riches.

Now we return with an easier mind and clearer conscience to the problem of our twenty-five billion dollars in a decade.

My question is: Is the material prosperity of this Nation favorable or unfavorable to the morality of the people?

The first thought is, Who has prospered? Who has got the money?

I take it that the loudest answer would be, "The millionaires, the capitalists, and the incompetent but luxurious rich"; and, as we think of that twenty-five billion, our thoughts run over the yachts, the palaces, and the luxuries that flaunt themselves before the public. . . .

When, then, the question is asked, "Is the material prosperity of this nation favorable or unfavorable to the morality of the people?" I say with all emphasis, "In the long run, and by all means, favorable!"

In other words, to seek for and earn wealth is a sign of a natural, vigorous, and strong character. Wherever strong men are, there they will turn into the activities of life. In the ages of chivalry you will find them on the crusades or seeking the Golden Fleece; in college life you will find them high in rank, in the boat, or on the athletic field; in an industrial age you will find them eager, straining every nerve in the development of the great industries. The race is to the strong. The search for material wealth is therefore as natural and necessary to the man as is the pushing out of its roots for more moisture and food to the oak. This is man's play, his personality. You can no more suppress it than you can suppress the tide of the ocean. For one man who seeks money for its own sake there are ten who seek it for the satisfaction of the seeking, the power there is in it, and the use they can make of it. There is the exhilaration of feeling one's self grow in one's surroundings; the man reaches out, lays hold of this, that, and the other interest, scheme, and problem. He is building up a fortune? Yes, but his job is also that he is building up a stronger, abler, and more powerful man. There are two men that have none of this ambition: the gilded, listless youth and the ragged listless pauper to whom he tosses a dime; they are in the same class. . . .

One other dark shadow, and I am done. The persistent companion of riches,--luxury and an ability to have what you want. That vice and license are rampant in certain quarters is clear; that vulgar wealth flaunts itself in the face of the people is beyond question; and that the people are rather amused at the spectacle must be confessed. The theatre syndicate will turn on to the boards whatever the people want; and the general tone of the plays speaks not well for the taste and morality of the people. The strain of temptation overwhelms a fraction of our youth. But one has no more right to test the result of prosperity by the small class of the lazy and luxurious than he has to test the result of poverty by the lazy tramp.

With all this said, the great mass of the people are self-restrained and simple. Material prosperity has come apace, and on the whole it uplifts. Responsibility sobers men and nations. We have learned how to win wealth; we are learning how to use and spend it. Every year marks a long step in advance in material prosperity, and character must march in step. Without wealth, character is liable to narrow and harden. Without character, wealth will destroy. Wealth is upon us, increasing wealth. The call of today is, then, for the uplift of character,--the support of industry, education, art, and every means of culture; the encouragement of the higher life; and, above all, the deepening of the religious faith of the people; the rekindling of the spirit, that, clothed with her material forces, the great personality of this Nation may fulfill her divine destiny.

I have been clear, I trust, in my opinion that material prosperity is in the long run favorable to morality. Let me be as clear in the statement of that eternal truth, that neither a man's nor a nation's life consists in the abundance of things he possesseth.

In the investment of wealth in honest enterprise and business, lies our path of character. In the investment of wealth in all that goes towards the uplift of the people in education, art, and religion is another path of character. Above all, and first of all, stands the personal life. The immoral rich man is a traitor to himself, to his material as well as spiritual interests. Material prosperity is upon us;

it is marching with us. Character must keep step, ay, character must lead. We want great riches; we want also great men.

Acres of Diamonds

RUSSELL H. CONWELL

Russell H. Conwell (1843-1925) was brought up the son of a poor farmer in the hills of western Massachusetts, where his father had known John Brown and Frederick Douglass. While attending school, Russell earned money by selling a biography of Brown. Following his service in the Civil War, Conwell invested in real estate, practiced law, and ran a large Bible class in Boston. He moved to Philadelphia where he used his fund-raising talent to erect a large Baptist temple and establish a night school that later became Temple University. Conwell insisted it was the duty of each person to make money and become rich, the key sentiment in his speech "Acres of Diamonds," which he delivered over 6000 times between 1868 and 1925. The following excerpt from the speech was taken from <u>Acres of Diamonds</u> (New York: Harper and Brothers, 1915), pp. 17-22. Upon what basis did Conwell insist it is the duty of all people to get rich? Why did he believe some people were poor?

Now then, I say again that the opportunity to get rich, to attain unto great wealth, is here in Philadelphia now, within the reach of almost every man and woman who hears me speak tonight, and I mean just what I say. I have not come to this platform even under these circumstances to recite something to you. I have come to tell you what in God's sight I believe to be the truth, and if the years of life have been of any value to me in the attainment of common sense, I know I am right; that the men and women sitting here, who found it difficult perhaps to buy a ticket to this lecture or gathering to-night, have within their reach "acres of diamonds," opportunities to get largely wealthy. There never was a place on earth more adapted than the city of Philadelphia to-day, and never in the history of the world did a poor man without capital have such an opportunity to get rich quickly and honestly as he has now in our city. I say it is the truth, and I want you to accept it as such; for if you think I have come to simply recite something, then I would better not be here. I have no time to waste in any such talk, but to say the things I believe, and unless some of you get richer for what I am saying to-night my time is wasted.

I say that you ought to get rich, and it is your duty to get rich. How many of my pious brothers say to me, "Do you, a Christian minister, spend your time going up and down the country advising young people to get rich, to get money?" "Yes, of course I do." They say, "Isn't that awful! Why don't you preach the gospel instead of preaching about man's making money?" "Because to make money honestly is to preach the gospel." That is the reason. The men who get rich may be the most honest men you find in the community.

"Oh," but says some young man here to-night, "I have been told all my life that if a person has money he is very dishonest and dishonorable and mean and contemptible." My friend, that is the reason why you have none, because you have that idea of people. The foundation of your faith is altogether false. Let me say here clearly, and say it briefly though subject to discussion which I have not time for here, ninety-eight out of one hundred of the rich men of America are honest. That is why they are rich. That is why they are trusted with money. That is why they carry on great enterprises and find plenty of people to work with them. It is because they are honest men.

Says another young man, "I hear sometimes of men that get millions of dollars dishonestly." Yes, of course you do, and so do I. But they are so rare a thing in fact that the newspapers talk about them all the time as a matter of news until you get the idea that all the other rich men got rich dishonestly.

My friend, you take and drive--if you furnish the auto--out into the suburbs of Philadelphia, and introduce me to the people who own their homes around this great city, those beautiful homes with gardens and flowers, these magnificent homes so lovely in their art, and I will introduce you to the very best people in character as well as in enterprise in our city, and you know I will. A man is not really a true man until he owns his own home, and they that own their homes are made more honorable and honest and pure, and true and economical and careful, by owning the home.

For a man to have money, even in large sums is not an inconsistent thing. We preach against covetousness, and you know we do, in the pulpit, and often times preach against it so long and use the terms about "filthy lucre" so extremely that Christians get the idea that when we stand in the pulpit we believe it is wicked for any man to have money until the collection basket goes around, and then we almost swear at the people because they don't give more money. Oh, the inconsistency of such doctrines as that!

Money is power, and you ought to be reasonably ambitious to have it. You ought because you can do more good with it than you could without it. Money printed your Bible, money builds your churches, money sends your missionaries, and money pays your preachers, and you would not have many of them, either, if you did not pay them. I am always willing that my church should raise my salary, because the church that pays the largest salary always raises it the easiest. You never knew an exception to it in your life. The man who gets the largest salary can do the most good with the power that is furnished to him. Of course he can if his spirit be right to use it for what it is given to him.

I say, then, you ought to have money. If you can honestly attain unto riches in Philadelphia, it is your Christian and godly duty to do so. It is an awful mistake of these pious people to think you must be awfully poor in order to be pious.

Some men say, "Don't you sympathize with the poor people?" Of course I do, or else I would not have been lecturing these years. I won't give in but what I sympathize with the poor, but the number of poor who are to be sympathized with is very small. To sympathize with a man whom God has punished for his sins, thus to help him when God would still continue a just punishment, is wrong, no doubt about it, and we do that more than we help those who are deserving. While we should sympathize with God's poor--that is, those who cannot help themselves--let us remember there is not a poor person in the United States who was not made poor by his own shortcomings, or by the shortcomings of some one else. It is all wrong to be poor, anyhow. Let us give in to that argument and pass that to one side.

A gentleman gets up back there, and says, "Don't you think there are some things in this world that are better than money?" Of course I do, but I am talking about money now. Of course there are some things higher than money. Oh yes, I know by the grave that has left me standing alone that there are higher and sweeter and purer than money. Well do I know there are some things higher and grander than gold. Love is the grandest thing on God's earth, but fortunate the lover who has plenty of money. Money is power, money is force, money will do good as well as harm. In the hands of good men and women it could accomplish, and it has accomplished, good.

I hate to leave that behind me. I heard a man get up in a prayer-meeting in our city and thank the Lord he was "one of God's poor." Well, I wonder what his wife thinks about that? She earns the money that comes into that house, and he smokes a part of that on the veranda. I don't want to see any more of the Lord's poor of that kind, and I don't believe the Lord does. And yet there are some people who think in order to be pious you must be awfully poor and awfully dirty. That does not follow at all. While we sympathize with the poor, let us not teach a doctrine like that.

THE SOCIAL GOSPEL   11

Applied Christianity

WASHINGTON GLADDEN

Washington Gladden (1836-1918) was a major awakener of the American Protestant social conscience during the Gilded Age of the late nineteenth century. From the time he entered the Congregational ministry in 1860, he was identified as a theological liberal. His popular exposition of the New Theology was consistently linked with the social concern of the social gospel movement's liberal wing. In 1875 he began a seven-year ministry in the industrial city of Springfield, Massachusetts, where he gained first-hand knowledge of the problems of unemployed workers. During his ministry at the First Congregational Church of Columbus, Ohio from 1882 to 1914, he added thirty books to the six he had already written and became one of the nation's most influential clergymen. Though he never became a socialist, he was a severe critic of the free enterprise system who insisted from pen and pulpit that the churches must do more to bring America's economic life in line with the laws of God's kingdom. The following selection appears in Gladden's <u>Applied Christianity: Moral Aspects of Social Christianity</u> (Boston: Houghton Mifflin and Company, 1886), pp. 146-59, 162-69. How does Gladden account for the lack of church attendance on the part of wage-workers living in cities? On

what grounds does he argue that the preaching of
the gospel in itself is not sufficient to meet the
needs of workers living in the cities? What does
Gladden suggest as the solution for the problems of
the urban workers?

We often say that Christianity is the cure of the evils that
threaten modern civilization, but the troublesome fact that
rises up to confound us whenever we express this confidence
is the fact that a large section of the population is wholly
outside our churches, and apparently beyond the reach of
their direct influence. It is true that Christian ideas and
sentiments do, to a certain extent, pervade all our society;
the social atmosphere contains more or less of its vital elements,
and no man can breathe in this Christian land without
unconsciously assimilating some of its truth. But the complete
separation of large numbers of our people from the
institutions of religion, their utter ignorance of us and
of all that we are trying to do, is a discouraging fact.
This was brought home to me a few years ago in a manner that
ought to have humbled my conceit, whether it did or not. I
had been working pretty busily for almost eight years in a
city of New England where neighbors generally know one another,
and where the church-going population is exceptionally
large, and I had tried to bear my part in the social
and political life of the city as well as in its religious
life. One Sunday a friend of mine, unfamiliar with the city,
was walking down the principal street looking for my church,
and three of my fellow-citizens of whom he inquired, in succession,
did not know where the church was, and did not appear
to have ever heard of its pastor. I suspect we should
all be somewhat surprised if we could know just how many
people there are within hearing of our church bells who do
not know the name of the churches or of their ministers, to
whose thought all our interests are foreign, to whose ear
our familiar speech is an unknown tongue. Many others there
are who know something of us, but do not love us; who listen
with indifference, if not with resentment, when our church
bells ring; who regard our assemblies with suspicious criticism;
who are not so accessible to our influence as those
who know less about us.

I do not mean to be understood as affirming that the majority of our population is thus wholly outside of all church relations. This class of entire neglecters is, as yet, a minority in most of our cities, but it is a minority large enough to cause us anxiety and to furnish us one of our hardest problems. Certain it is that Christianity can never cure the social ills under which we are suffering while so large a class remains practically untouched by its healing influences.

Our perplexity increases when we discover that this neglect is greatest in that class to be specially interested, to which it has always made its most gracious promises and its most successful appeals, with which its Founder himself was identified while He was on the earth--the wage-workers and the poor. The strongest of the evidences of Christianity has always been that one to which our Lord himself pointed the disciples of John: "The Gospel is preaching to the poor." It must be confessed that this proof of Christ's divine mission is losing its cogency.

I do not think that church neglect is increasing, as a rule, in other classes of the population. There are exceptional cities in which this neglect pervades all orders to an alarming degree, and seems to be steadily growing. But, generally, in our cities and large towns, I am inclined to think that the proportion of the people who attend the church or the Sunday-school--who are present in the house of God during some part of the Lord's day--is as large as ever it was. The merchants, the clerks, the professional people, the teachers, are not deserting the churches. Of course there are multitudes of these persons who do not come to church now, and such multitudes have always been with us; but neglect does not <u>increase</u> among them, and it does increase among the wage-workers. The <u>proportion</u> of wage-workers in our churches is diminishing.

Proof of this proportion is not easily furnished, and I would much rather those who listen to me would search out the facts for themselves, than take my word for them. I suppose that there are localities in which the statements just made would not hold good, but a pretty careful study convinces me that they do hold good of the country at large, and especially of the cities. My analysis of the census makes it probable to me that the mechanics, the shop hands, and the common laborers--the wage-workers employed in manual labor of one kind or another, with their families, constitute fully one-fourth of the population. Is it true that one-fourth of the membership of our city churches belongs to this class? That is a question that every pastor can easily answer for himself, so far as his own church is concerned. It is true that in our Roman Catholic churches the proportion of wage-laborers will be found to be much larger than one-fourth; the average in our Protestant churches should, therefore, be somewhat less than one-fourth. It would be well for every pastor to satisfy himself what the proportion is in his congregation. Of course the reckoning must be made by families, rather than by individuals. In my own congregation, which worships in a very plain church, the seats of which are free, in a neighborhood easily accessible to the working classes, and which has been known always as an extremely democratic congregation, I find only about one-tenth of the families on my list belonging to this class. The proportion would be slightly increased if I added the families which are represented in our Sunday-school, but which send no adults to any of our services. This is the result of repeated special efforts made in the interest of the working classes, with several courses of lectures on Sunday evenings for their benefit. Goodly numbers of them have attended these lectures, and there is, I think, a kindly feeling among them toward our church--certainly toward its pastor; but the number of those who identify themselves with us is still very small.

It is true that there are missions in all our cities into which larger numbers of these people are drawn; all these must be taken into account in our estimates, for although the arrangement whereby the rich are separated from the poor in their worship is not the ideal of Christianity, and although it may be a question whether in the long run church neglect may not be caused rather than cured by this arrangement; yet the question we are now considering respects the actual church attendance of the working classes--it is the question whether the proportion of wage-workers in our churches and missions is as large as it is in our population.

To get at the workingmen's ideas respecting this question, whether the people of their class are drawing away from the churches, and, if so, why, I sent out circulars, a few months ago, to workingmen connected with the various manufacturing industries of my own city, and obtained from them a large number of replies. From establishments employing in the aggregate between three and four thousand men, I had letters, and out of these, as nearly as I can estimate, from the figures given me, not more than one-third attend church; and of those who do go, a good share are Roman Catholics.

How is it with the other extreme of society? In this same city I asked one of the best informed citizens to make me out a list of fifty of the leaders of business. He did not know my reason for wishing such a list, but after it was put into my hands, I found that fifty-five percent of these men were communicants in the churches, and that seventy-seven percent of them were regular attendants upon the churches. A large proportion of the capitalists are more or less closely identified, and the number tends to decrease rather than to increase.

This statement is sometimes disputed, but I am quite sure that it cannot be successfully controverted. Some of those who have expressed a contrary opinion have counted clerks, book-keepers, teachers, and office-boys into the "working class," but the question we are considering has nothing to do with these. We are talking now about the manual wage-workers--the mechanics, the operatives, and the day laborers; as to what may be the degree of neglect among those other classes, I am not prepared to express an opinion.

If the tendency of the class with which we are now dealing is what I have represented it to be, the fact is one of grave significance. If the churches are losing their hold on these working people, not only are they exhibiting a most alarming sign of their own degeneracy, but they are permitting the growth of elements and forces which will prove fatal to the peace, and even to the existence, of society. There is no other cement that can hold society together but that genuine good-will which is the heart of Christianity. The weakening of this bond is an ominous sign. I do not think that it is the part of wisdom to ignore it. If it is true, we cannot too speedily discover it, nor too frankly confess it, nor too earnestly seek to know what it means.

What is the cause of this tendency? Why is it that the working people are slowly and sullenly drawing apart from the churches?

Many reasons are given. First, and most conclusive to the minds of some philosophers, is the comprehensive fact of total depravity. The working people stay away from church because their hearts are set against God and divine things; because they prefer to spend the day in idleness and pleasuring. Undoubtedly the working people have their full share of this universal moral disability; but I am not prepared to admit that they have any more than their share. Total depravity will account for just as much church neglect among working people as it will account for among traders, and lawyers, and teachers, and no more; and what we are now considering is the exceptional degree of church neglect existing among working people. The cause assigned will not account for this unless we assume that their depravity is considerably more than total.

Another explanation finds the reason of this fact in the infidelity prevalent among the working classes. It then becomes necessary to show that infidelity is more prevalent in these classes than in the mercantile and professional classes. I am not sure that this can be shown. Admit, for the sake of the argument, that there is more skepticism among wage-workers than among the other classes of society. The next question is, how came this to be so? What has made skeptics of these workingmen? Infidelity is not what Dr. Emmons said Romanism was, "an ultimate fact." It needs to be explained, quite as much as church neglect needs to be explained. Perhaps the same cause that drove these people out of the churches robbed them also of their faith in the doctrines on which the churches are founded. Perhaps when we have learned the reason of their church neglect we shall know the reason of their doubt.

When we ask the working people themselves to tell us why they are not in the churches, they give us various responses. I have a large bundle of letters at home in which this question is answered in many different ways. Some of these reasons are manifestly pretexts, destitute of serious meaning. One says that it costs too much to support the churches; but this objection was made respecting a church which it costs no man a cent to attend; where he can contribute as much or as little as he chooses, and the amount of his contribution will be known to nobody. Another says that some ministers preach politics; but he is perfectly aware, of course, that some ministers do not. Another urges that workingmen need the day for rest; but he can hardly be ignorant of the fact that the Sabbath rest is not prevented, but most effectually promoted by the quiet and refreshing service of the sanctuary. All these are pleas that the advocates do not expect us to take very seriously.

The real reasons for the absence of the working people from church, as they reveal themselves in this correspondence of mine, resolve themselves into two: first, their inability to dress well enough to appear in a place as stylish and fashionable as the average church; secondly, their sense of the injustice that workingmen, as a class, are receiving at the hands of capitalist employers, as a class. These two reasons are often combined. It is because the workingman is not receiving a fair compensation for his labor, that he cannot dress his wife and children well enough to go to church. The plain or shabby raiment is the badge of his poverty, the evidence of the wrong that he is suffering.

> One reason [writes one of my correspondents] for not attending the larger churches, which have wealthy congregations and good ministers, is that they are composed of the class who hire men to work for them, and, of course, dress themselves and their families better than the mere wage-worker can afford to do. When we see our employers going to church in broadcloth, and silk, and satin, and furs, and laces, and ribbons, it is natural for the man with a faded and patched coat, and the woman with a calico dress, to feel rather uncomfortable in the midst of such finery.

> One reason of their absence [writes another] is their inability to clothe themselves in a manner to make a respectable appearance in church, owing to the starva-wages paid to them.

> You want to know what the workingmen think about capitalists? [writes another] We think [he answers compendiously] that they are thieves and robbers.

> Of course [writes another] the manufacturers can and should dress better than the laborer; but when we see them so full of religion on Sunday, and then grinding the faces of the poor on the other six days, we are apt to think they are insincere. They say to us, "We are not making as much as we would like; we will have to reduce cost of our goods by cutting down your wages

a little." We say, "Hard work gives us a good appetite, and we can't set a substantial table." They say, "Corn is cheap; your table ought not cost too much." This creates an ill-feeling between capital and labor. When the capitalist prays for us one day in the week, and preys on us the other six, it can't be expected that we will have much respect for his Christianity.

This letter fairly expresses the sentiment that runs through a good share of my correspondence. The assumption of most of the letters is that the churches are chiefly attended and controlled by the capitalist and the employing classes; they make it evident that there is but little sympathy between these classes and the laboring class; and they show that the laborers have no desire to attend the churches in which their employers worship. The social barrier between them is high and strong on week days; they are not inclined to lower it on Sundays. Beyond a doubt, a great many conversations of the same nature as that reported by the workingman above do take place between masters and men; and when, after all this talk about reduced wages, and consequent corn cake and calico for the workman's family, the workman sees his employer's family faring sumptuously, and walking or riding abroad in the most gorgeous array, he is not, naturally, in the proper mood to sing the same hymns and pray the same prayers.

Nothing is more certain than that the wage-workers of this country feel that they are falling behind in the race for life. They know that the nation's wealth is increasing with almost miraculous rapidity, the figures of the census tell them so, and the fact thrusts itself upon their senses on every side. They know, moreover, if they have memories reaching back twenty or thirty years, that their condition is not greatly improved; that the _real_ wages of labor are but little increased; and that, relatively to the rest of the community, they are worse off than they were thirty years ago. The annual expenditure for living purposes of the average employer has enormously increased, the annual expenditure of the average mechanic or operative has not greatly increased.

The workman feels that this tendency is due to the pitiless action of natural forces which the employing classes do not try to restrain. If he does reason much about it, he has a pretty strong notion that the fates are against him, and that his employer is on the side of fate. He knows that money, when it is massed in great corporations or companies, or heaped up in accumulations, is power, . . .

It is evident that the wage-workers, as a class, are discontented. They feel that they are not getting their fair share of the gains of advancing civilization.

It is evident that they are becoming more and more widely separated from their employers in the social scale.

It is evident that the old relations of friendliness between the two classes are giving place to alienation and enmity.

It is evident that the working people have the impression that the churches are mainly under the control of the capitalists and of those in sympathy with them.

If all these things are so, the reasons why the working people are inclined to withdraw from the churches ought also to be plain.

The fact of a great and growing discontent among the working classes, the fact of the increasing separation and alienation between wage-workers and their employers, are facts that cannot be disputed by any intelligent person. It may be doubted whether existing circumstances are bearing as severely upon the laborers as he imagines; it may be that he is better off than he thinks he is. But the question with which we are now concerned is: What does he think about it? He may be wrong in cherishing such unfriendly and resentful feelings toward his employer; but does he cherish them? He may be in error in thinking that the capitalist classes exercise a preponderating influence in the churches; but does he think so? If his state of mind is what it is assumed to be in this discussion, you have reason for church neglect which is widespread and deep-seated; you have a disorder to cure which is constitutional and obstinate, and which will never be removed by the sprinkling of rosewater; you have a problem on your hands which calls for clear thinking and heroic endeavor.

The "masses" of our cities that we are trying to reach are composed, to a large extent, of these wage-workers, and we shall never reach them over this barrier. The sooner the churches recognize this fact and adjust their theories and their methods to it, the sooner they will begin to see daylight shine through this dark problem of church neglect. So long as we ignore this fundamental difficulty, all our efforts to allure these neglecters will be in vain. A few of them will come in now and then in response to our urgent invitations; some of them, less thoughtful, or more hopeful, or more long-suffering than the rest, will continue to worship with us, finding in the promise of the life to come some help to bear the hardships of the life that now is; but the great multitude will turn upon us suspiciously or resentfully when they hear our invitations, saying; We want none of your free seats, we can do without your fine music and your pious commonplaces, we do not greatly care for your hand-shaking in the house of God and the perfunctory calls of your visitors at our houses. All we ask is justice. We want a chance to earn a decent living. We want a fair share of the wealth that our labor is helping to produce. We do not want to be left far behind when our neighbors, the employers, the traders, the professional people, are pushing on to plenty and prosperity. In the midst of all this overflowing bounty, we want something more than meagre subsistence. We are not quite sure whether you people of the churches want us to have it or not. Many of you, as we are bitterly aware, act as though you did not greatly care what became of us; and we hear from many of you hard and heartless comments on every effort we make to fight the fates that are bearing us down. It looks to us as though your sympathies were chiefly given to the people who are getting rich at our expense. Until our minds are clearer on this score, we shall never be drawn to your churches, charm you never so wisely.

What are you going to do with people who talk in this way? That is the one tremendous question which the Church of God is called to answer to-day.

Suppose you say that these people are all wrong in these theories, and all astray in their censure. Suppose you insist that they are getting their full share of the gains of this advancing civilization, or, if they are failing to do so, that it is wholly their own fault. Then it is your business to convince them of this by patient and thorough discussion. You cannot remove their misconceptions by denouncing them, or contemptuously ignoring them. You cannot disabuse them by abusing them. If they are wholly in error with respect to this matter, their error is most deplorable and hurtful to them, and to society at large; and the Church has no more urgent duty than that of convincing them that they are wrong.

Suppose that they are all wrong in their impression that the sympathies of the churches are on the side of the classes with which they are in conflict. The impression is there, and no headway can be made in bringing them into the churches until it is somehow eradicated.

"The only cure of all this trouble," some one will confidently answer, "is the gospel. Preach the gospel faithfully, and it will make an end of all this strife." This answer assumes that the fault all lies with the people now in the churches. What effect can the faithful preaching of the gospel have upon those who do not and will not hear it? If the gospel thus preached reaches these neglecting multitudes, it can only be through those who now listen to it. And the very trouble we are considering is that those who now frequent the churches find it difficult, and almost impossible, to put themselves into friendly relations with the neglecting multitudes.

What is meant by those who use this language is simply this: That the strife between labor and capital arises from the natural depravity of the human heart; and that, if men were soundly converted, all these grounds of contention would be removed. Unfortunately, this reasoning overlooks some important facts. The gospel, considered simply as an evangelistic or converting agency, will never put an end to this trouble. There are plenty of people in our churches to-day, who give every evidence of having been soundly converted, but who are conducting themselves continually in such a manner as to cause this trouble, instead of curing it. When a man is converted, he has a purpose to do right; and if you choose to go a little farther and say that he has the disposition to do right, I will not stop to dispute you. But he may have very crude ideas as to what right is; his heart may be regenerated, but his head may still be sadly muddled. And there are thousands of people in all our churches who mean to do right by their working people, but those ideas have been so perverted by a false political economy that they are continually doing them grievous wrong. If a man has been taught the wage-fund theory, or if he has got into his head the idea that <u>laissez faire</u> is the chief duty of man, the gospel, in the ordinary acceptation of that term, will not correct the defects in his conduct towards his work people. He may believe that he is a sinner, that he cannot save himself, that he must be saved from his sins by faith in Christ; and he may humbly confess his conscious faults, and trust in Christ for forgiveness and salvation. But his habit of taking the law of supply and demand as his sole guide in dealing with his working people is not a conscious fault. He has been diligently taught that labor is simply a commodity; that what Carlyle calls the "cash-nexus" is the only bond between himself and his employees. As Toynbee puts it, Political Economy has steadily said to him, whenever he has thought of governing himself, in his relations with his work people, by Christian principles, "You are doing a very foolish thing. You might as well try to make iron swim as to alter the rate of wages by your individual will. The rate of wages, like the succession of night and day, is independent of the will of either employer or employed. Neither workmen nor employers can change the rate determined by competition at any particular time." Fortified by this philosophy, the converted employer feels that any attempt to give his men a larger share of his gains would be superfluous, if not mischievous; that the fates will have it all their own way in spite of him; that all he can do is to buy his labor in the cheapest market, and sell his wares in the dearest. In other words, he has been taught, and he believes, that the industrial world is a world in which the Christian laws of conduct have no sway; in which sympathy is fallacious, and good-will foolishness. What can preaching the gospel, in the ordinary sense of the word, do for such a man? His purpose is right, his heart is right, but his theories are all wrong. Some people say that it makes no difference what a man believes if his heart is right. It makes a tremendous difference!

The gospel, then, as the simple evangel, will not cure this evil. But Christianity will cure it. Christianity is something more than a gospel. Christianity is a law, as well as a gospel. And the Christian law, faithfully preached, as the foundation of the gospel, will put an end to all this trouble. We sometimes hear it said that the pulpit of the present day is derelict, because there is not enough preaching of the law. It is true. What the Church needs is a great deal more enforcement of law--not necessarily more threatening of penalty, but more preaching of law--of the law of Christ, in its application to the relations of men in their every-day life. By the law is the knowledge of sin. Many of the Christian people in our churches have not been convicted of their sins, because the law has not been laid down to them. . . .

Social Aspects of Christianity

RICHARD T. ELY

Richard T. Ely (1854-1943) influenced the social gospel movement through his theological liberalism and expertise in economics. Following his college education at Dartmouth and Columbia, he went to Germany for advanced study in philosophy and economics. There his thinking was shaped by economic theorists who rejected the alleged laws of classical economics and revealed the unethical implications of absolutist theories. Upon his return to the United States, Ely published numerous books in which he brought his intense moral concern of ethical economics to bear upon America's severe social problems. With his writing of Social Aspects of Christianity in which he detailed his understanding of social questions in the light of Christian ethics, he did much to link the interests of the social gospel and the discipline of economics. The excerpt which follows was taken from Social Aspects of Christianity (New York: T. Y. Crowell and Co., 1889), pp. 1-9, 39-48. What does Ely say is the relationship between the two great commandments of Christ? What were the reasons he cited for the alienation of the wage-workers from the Church? On what bases does Ely contend that church-goers do not love the laborers, and in what ways does he suggest that Christians could show their concern for the masses?

Statement of Fundamental Principles

"But when the Pharisees had heard that He had put the Sadducees to silence, they were gathered together.

"Then one of them which was a lawyer, asked Him a question, tempting Him, and saying,

"Master, which is the great commandment in the Law?

"Jesus said unto him, Thou shalt love the Lord thy God with all thy heart, and with all thy soul, and with all thy mind.

"This is the first and great commandment.

"And the second is like unto it, Thou shalt love thy neighbor as thyself.

"On these two commandments hang all the law and the prophets."

(Matthew 22: 34-40)

This is a most remarkable, and at the same time a most daring, summary of the whole duty of man. A human teacher would never have ventured to reduce all God's commandments to two simple statements; nor would such a teacher have presumed to exalt man's obligation to love and serve his fellows to an equal plane with his obligations to love his Creator. All other religious systems will be searched in vain for such a classification of human duties. The first and great commandment, "Thou shalt love the Lord thy God with all thy heart, and with all thy soul, and with all thy mind," does not strike us as strange. It is natural that the Supreme Being of the universe should require of us, His creatures, an unconditional and unlimited homage; but--listen!--The second commandment is like unto it--is like unto it--of the same nature: Thou shalt love thy neighbor as thyself--and--on these two commandments, on these two equally--hang all the law and the prophets.

But John, the beloved apostle, the apostle of love, and, as

God is love, we may suppose that he understood better than others the nature of Christ, is very bold in his exposition of our duty to love our fellows, making that a test of one's love to God. "If a man say, I love God, and hateth his brother, he is a liar: for he that loveth not his brother whom he hath seen, how can he love God whom he hath not seen?" And in another verse in the same chapter of his Epistle, John says, "We know that we have passed from death unto life, because we love the brethren." St. Paul, indeed, goes so far as to say, "For all the law is fulfilled, even in this: Thou shalt love thy neighbor as thy self" (Galatians 5: 14). St. Paul evidently felt that love to neighbor carried with it love to God.

Christ, himself, has told us the method by which he will at the last Judgment separate the sheep from the goats. Listen to his words, which must be quoted in full, and every word should receive careful attention:

"When the Son of man shall come in his glory and all the holy angels with Him, then shall He sit upon the throne of His glory:

"And before Him shall be gathered all nations; and He shall separate them one from another, as a shepherd divideth his sheep from his goats:

"And He shall set the sheep on His right hand, but goats on His left.

"Then shall the King say unto them on His right hand, Come, ye blessed of my Father, inherit the Kingdom prepared for you from the foundation of the world:

"For I was an hungered, and ye gave me meat: I was thirsty, and ye gave me drink: I was a stranger, and ye took me in;

"Naked, and ye clothed me: I was sick, and ye visited me; I was in prison, and ye came unto me.

"Then shall the righteous answer Him, saying, Lord, when saw we Thee an hungered, and fed Thee or thirsty, and gave Thee drink?

"When saw we Thee a stranger, and took Thee in, naked, and clothed Thee?

"Or, when saw we Thee sick, or in prison, and came unto Thee?

"And the King shall answer and say unto them, Verily, I say unto you, Inasmuch as ye have done it unto one of the least of these my brethren, ye have done it unto me.

"Then shall He say also unto them on His left hand, Depart from me, ye cursed, into everlasting fire, prepared for the devil and his angels;

"For I was an hungered, and ye gave me no meat; I was thirsty, and ye gave me no drink;

"I was a stranger, and ye took me not in, naked and ye clothed me not; sick, and in prison, and he visited me not.

"Then shall they also answer Him, saying, Lord, when saw we Thee an hungered, or athirst, or a stranger, or naked, or sick, or in prison, and did not minister unto Thee?

"Then shall He answer to them, saying, Verily, I say unto you, inasmuch as you did it not unto one of the least of these, ye did it not to me.

"And those shall go away into everlasting punishment: but the righteous into life eternal."

(Matthew 25: 31-46)

The minds of readers have been so generally absorbed by the awful punishment meted out to the wicked, that terror has not allowed them to notice what is the most marked feature in the narrative; namely, the exquisite beauty of the humanitarianism which it breathes. It is the Gospel of Humanity, because it is the gospel of the Son of man.

The marks of distinction are perceived. They are not regular attendance at church--not sound notions in regard to the form of baptism or methods of ordination, or apostolic succession, or the nature of the Lord's Supper, or Church organization--not any notions, whatever, as regards the future life--not any subjective feelings in regard to God. These are all, doubtless, important; but these are not the distinctive things by which Christ separates the good from the bad. The performance or non-performance of social duties in the gospel narrative separates the doomed from the blessed: "I was in prison, and ye visited me," etc.

I say this is something new in religious systems. All false systems of religion exalt the love of God above the love due our fellow-men, and tell us that we may serve God by injuring our fellows. How many millions of human beings have thought that they did God service by human sacrifices! Not only is this true, but it is furthermore true that, in proportion as believers in the true religion depart from the mind which was in Jesus Christ, they neglect the second commandment.

Thus, when Christ dwelt on earth, He found men excusing themselves from duty to their fellows on the plea of higher obligation to Deity. The reader will recall at once one instance. Moses commanded men to honor their fathers and mothers, and included, as a matter of course, the maintenance of father or mother in case of need; but the Hebrew theologians said a man could exempt himself from his duty to support his parent by consecrating his goods to the Lord. "But, ye say"--thus Christ addressed the scribes and Pharisees--"If a man shall say to his father or mother, It is corban, that is to say a gift (devoted to God), by whatsoever thou mightest be profited by me (by which I might support thee), he shall be free."

"And ye suffer him no more to do aught for his mother or father." But Christ added, "Ye have made the commandment of God of none effect by your tradition," and He upbraided them by addressing them as "Ye hypocrites."

Nothing is more difficult, nothing more requires divine grace, than the constant manifestation of love to our fellows in all our daily acts, in our buying, selling, getting gain. People still want to substitute all sorts of beliefs and observances in the place of this, for it implies a totally different purpose from that which animates this world. It is when men attempt to regulate their lives seven days in the week by the Golden Rule that they begin to perceive that they cannot serve God and mammon; for the ruling motive of the one service--egotism, selfishness--is the opposite of the ruling motive of the other--altruism, devotion to others, consecration of heart, soul, and intellect to the service of others. Men are still quite willing to make long prayers on Sunday, if on week days they may devour widows' houses; or as Rev. Mark Guy Pearse said two summers since at Chautauqua, they are ready to offer their prayers and their praise on Sunday, if on Monday they may go into the market place and skin their fellows and sell their hides.

The second commandment, which is like the first, means that in every act and thought and purpose, in our laws and in their administration, in all public as well as private affairs, we--if indeed we profess to be Christians--should seek to confer true benefits upon our fellow men. It means that the man who professes to love God and who attempts to deceive others in regard to the real value of railway stock, or, for that matter any other property, that he may coax their money into his pockets, is a hypocrite and a liar. It means that the man who oppresses the hireling in his wages is no Christian, but a pagan, whatever may be his declarations to the contrary notwithstanding. What does God say of such an one? He says: "I will be a swift witness against those that oppress the hireling in his wages." What does His second commandment mean for those rich men who keep back the hire of their laborers? It means that they "must" weep and howl "for the miseries that shall come upon them." And what does this message mean for monopolists who use their superior advantages of wealth or intellect, or bodily strength or other resources, to crowd out and grind down their fellows according to the methods of modern commercial competition? The prophet Isaiah shall tell us: "Woe unto them that join house to house, that lay field to field, till there be no place, that they may be placed alone in the midst of the earth."

It is needless to enlarge upon this. It must be seen that the arrangements of this world are not in accord with the commandment given to love our neighbor as ourselves. These words may be found in writings previous to Christ, but never before His time has there been a serious attempt to carry this teaching into all the relations of life with all men. Thus it was a true word when Christ said to His disciples: "A _new_ commandment I give unto you, That ye love one another; as _I_ have loved you, that ye love one another."

It is indeed a strange conception that some people have of the gospel of Christ. That gospel which in its highest unity is Love is divided into two parts: the first is theology, the second is sociology--the science of society.

"Theology treats of God and His relations to His creatures, and of the existance, character, and attributes of God, His laws and government, the doctrines we are to believe and the duties we are to practice." Such is the definition of theology found in Webster's dictionary. The first words are sufficient. Theology "is the science of God and His relations to His creatures." But the whole science is simply an elaboration of the first of the two great commandments on which hang all the law and the prophets. It is a proper study for man; especially is it fitting study for those who are called to serve as ministers in God's church. We all know with what assiduity the study of theology has been pursued. Men of great intellect have by the thousands devoted their entire lives to it, and every clergyman is expected to prepare himself for his sacred office by a training in a theological seminary for several years. This is well so far as it goes. This ought not to be left undone, but this is not enough. What has the Church done with the second commandment, which in its elaboration, becomes social science or sociology? . . .

The Alienation of Wage Workers from the Church

There are those who deny that wage-workers are alienated from the Church, and I have carefully considered their arguments; but after years of observation and reflection I have been forced to the conclusion that there is a clear alienation of thinking wage-workers from the Church which, on the whole, is growing. I do not say this with any other feeling than one of profound regret; but as it appears to me a fact which can be denied only by those who are ignorant of the actual situation, I hold it to be well that it should be known.

I could give evidence which would fill pages of this book; but as there are other things to be said, I can only leave my readers to look carefully into the matter, and by a perusal of the labor press, and by conversation with representative wage-workers, to form an opinion for themselves. I think, however, I can safely say that I have had unusually favorable opportunities for getting at the facts, as I have followed the labor movement with interest, and have enjoyed the confidence of representative workingmen to a great extent.

This alienation sometimes amounts to positive hostility, as I think is quite generally the case in New York and Chicago. In other places, as in Baltimore, there is little aggressive opposition, but simply widespread indifference. I will quote a few sentences from a labor paper, published in Chicago, by men who are inclined to be comparatively conservative, and who resist all proposals of violence and anarchy as stoutly as any so-called "capitalistic" newspaper. These words, I think, represent fairly the honest opinion of a large class of our best wage-workers:--

> On Thursday evening the Rev. C. F. Goss addressed a meeting called under the auspices of the Brotherhood

of Carpenters. . . . In order to get an expression of opinion from his audience, he asked those who had ceased to sympathize with the churches to hold up their hand. It is needless to say the number of hands that were uplifted caused a pang of regret to the speaker.

A question that we would like to propound to the ministers of Chicago is: Have the working classes fallen away from the churches, or have churches fallen away from the working classes? We know hundreds and thousands of workingmen who have the utmost respect, admiration, and even love for the pure and simple teachings of the gospel, and the beneficient and exalted character of Jesus Christ, and yet they scarcely ever put their feet inside the church that "is called" His. Not because they love the Church less, but because they love their self-respect more. They realize that there is no place in the average Chicago church for the poor man unless it is in the position of janitor, certainly not in the cushioned pews surrounded by individuals who not only regard poverty as a disgrace, but by their vulgar display endeavor to perpetually remind the poor man of his poverty. . . . While there are noble and notable exceptions, it must be confessed that but few of the average Chicago preachers go out of their way to "preach the gospel to the poor"--of course "good" people who are "rich" establish mission schools for "bad" people who are "poor", and they occasionally succeed in bringing within the fold a few women and children who are not sufficiently intelligent to realize that a mission school is a sort of a religious souphouse, where the gospel is distributed as charity.

One reason why wage-workers do not love the Church is not peculiar. The wickedness of men's hearts leads them to resist the gospel. Workingmen are like others in this respect, although certain temptations, as pride, and arrogance, and absorption by concerns of this world, are not so powerful in their case. We must remember that Christ said it was hard for a rich man to enter the kingdom of heaven, and never alluded to any special difficulties in the way of the poor as a class. We are also told that time was when the common people heard Christ gladly. These, however, are general considerations. What is now desired is to know the peculiar cause which alienates wageworkers as a class of industrial society from the Church, and this may be stated in a single sentence.

The leaders of the Church, the representative men and women in the Church, profess to love the working classes, but as a matter of fact, they do not love them, and this wide divergence between profession and practice is keenly felt. I here state a grave charge, but who among my readers will deny it? Before any one does, let him examine his own conscience.

How do I know that church-goers do not love the day laborer? How do I know that my wife loves me? There is a conduct suitable to love; a conduct not prescribed by law, but which is the natural, spontaneous outcome of love. Now the consequences which would inevitably follow--did the representative men and women of the Church love the bread winners of the United States--are sadly missing. I will give a few specifications.

First, these church leaders are so far away from the toiling masses that they fail to understand their desires, and the motives of their action. I meet few clergymen who, even when they want to be friendly, can give an intelligent statement of the side of labor in any of its many controversies with capital. They rarely converse with leaders of the workingmen, and perhaps more rarely read any labor paper. If they loved the masses, they would instinctively draw near enough to know their aims and motives. Christ moved among the masses and understood them, and to-day the poorest laborer and the most obstinate trades unionists, yes, even the despised walking delegate, will feel a strange attraction for that wonderful Being who spoke words which go straight to the heart. Did not an assembly of workingmen in these United States not long ago greet the name of Christ with applause, and the mention of the Church with hisses?

Second, the failure to rebuke wickedness in high places is noticed. When you go into a church on Fifth Avenue in New York, rarely, if ever, do you hear the corrupt methods by which the masses have been robbed, and prominent people made millionnaires, described and denounced with righteous indignation. When not a workingman is present, the wicked labor agitators are lashed with fury. Why this? Is there any danger that a wealthy congregation in one of our cities will be carried away by the pleadings of the agitator? None at all. Those who sit in the pews have a sufficient appreciation of the wickedness of Knights of Labor and socialists. If the aim were to draw men together, those who minister to congregations made up of employers would so put the case of their employes that it could be understood, and would say everything favorable which could be said in their behalf.

More ought to be said about the duties of property, for we Americans have a sufficiently keen appreciation of the rights of property. Could the idea be conveyed to the supporters of our churches that property exists for the sake of man, and not man for the sake of property, incalculable good would follow.

Third, the negative attitude of the Church with respect to every proposed reform discourages, disgusts, and even angers, workingmen. The religious press is concerned with the "errors of any one who proposes anything positive." "The errors of socialism!" Why talk about them? Are they living issues? Is there the slightest danger that they will not be sufficiently discussed? There is about as much prospect of a realization of the socialist's dream, in our day, as there is that New Hampshire farmers will harvest grain in January. If we could hear something about the "truths of socialism" and "the truths of Henry George," it would be far more to the point.

Workingmen--I am talking all the time about the thinking workingmen--instinctively feel that if the Church were animated by love, she would be more anxious to discover truths than errors in the plans of those who are working for the elevation of the masses.

Nothing so disheartens one as the failure of Christians to engage in positive work for the masses. One would at least suppose that such a question as freedom from toil on Sunday would concern the clergy. Yet it does not seem to. Scarcely a question is more alive to-day among all labor organizations than compulsory Sunday work. All over the country, when laboring men meet, they pass resolutions on this subject, and appeal to the public to help them to secure one day in seven for rest. Yet the pulpit is silent. The bakers in New York recently sent petitions to the clergymen of New York and Brooklyn to preach on the subject, and to help them to abolish Sunday work. What came of it? I wrote to the secretary of their national organization to tell me, and here are extracts from his letter: "The Sunday law was not even presented to that Legislature. . . . Relying on what the clergy will ever do to assist in enforcing Sabbath laws is equal to relying on a rain of manna that may make labor superfluous. . . . These gentlemen are more interested in the movement of boodle than in the movement of labor. . . . I consented to convince our men that I was right. They are convinced to-day. Out of 500 circulars sent to the clergy of New York and Brooklyn, half a dozen answered. You will have a hard time, Professor, to convince the toilers of this country that the clergy will ever do anything for them. There is no money in it, you know."

When the clergy of one denomination in Pittsburg, Pa., learned that a gentleman had given money for public conservatories, on condition that they should be kept open on Sunday, they denounced the man, and passed formal resolutions against the acceptance of the gift. What kind of effect must that produce on the workingmen of Pittsburg, who never received aid from these clergymen in attempts to abolish Sunday work? A prominent Presbyterian clergyman of Baltimore called on me recently, and wanted to know why the Church failed to get hold on the workingmen of our city. Had he gone with me to listen to one of his eloquent friends the following Sunday, he would have heard some sound doctrine on Sabbath-keeping, and some courageous utterances on the subject of Sunday festivities in homes of the wealthy of Baltimore. A workingman would have reflected that not a word was said about those who must toil seven days a week. The bakers in Baltimore might have been favorably impressed by something on that topic. And a word to stockholders in street railways would not have been out of place, for shortly after the sermon one of the conductors remarked to me, incidentally, that he had had only one Sunday "off" in twenty-two months.

Anarchistic workingmen contribute, from their scanty earnings, money to disseminate their pernicious doctrines, and wage-workers can at least ask the question, Why do not Christians who profess to love us manifest the same zeal for the dissemination of true doctrines on social and economic topics, if these things which we hear are so bad? The Economic Association published a monograph, by Dr. Albert Shaw of the Minneapolis Tribune, on Co-operation, which was most instructive and wholesome in tone. It did not advocate any rash measures, but told the story of some successful enterprises in Minneapolis. Many workingmen are engaged in like enterprises, and it is safe to say so practical a treatise would save them $100,000 a year. Five hundred dollars would be ample to print 10,000 copies to advertise them, and to sell them for a small sum, say ten cents, whereas the monograph in its original form cost seventy-five cents. The New York Tribune reviewed it favorably, and expressed the hope that a cheap reprint might appear for wide circulation. Hon. Andrew D. White wrote to me, and urged that it be reprinted for workingmen. Rev. Dr. Thwing of Minneapolis wrote a similar letter. I tried to raise the money, but my appeals to Christians of means were of no avail. I might as well have addressed the ocean. How can men full of love be so careless and indifferent?

Then there is the question of the rights of the masses. What safety is there for the property of the masses, for public property, in the fact that our cities are full of churches? I visited Montreal last summer, and when I saw the many churches I asked myself this question: Are the rights of the people better protected here than elsewhere? Afterwards I learned that the franchise for street railways had been extended for twenty-one years without any compensation to the public. This was public robbery; for had the franchise been put up at auction, it would have brought a large sum to the relief of the taxpayers; or lower fares might have been established, a blessing to workingmen and workingwomen. In Baltimore I fear public property is about to be sacrificed similarly. Many churches exist, but the forgotten millions are still the forgotten, plundered millions.

This is not exhaustive, but my essay is too long. I trust that it may start useful trains of thought in my readers, and arouse more than one conscience to a keener sense of duty. It is not pleasant to write a paper like this, but I believe it is time some one should speak plainly. Some say the condition of the Church is hopeless. This I do not believe.

There is in the Church a conscience which can be pricked, and it is probably as sensitive to-day as it has been in centuries gone by. There is power back of the Church, in her divine Master, which makes for righteousness, and which urges her on to a higher life. What is needed is to go back to Christ and learn of Him.

THEOLOGY

The New Theology

THEODORE T. MUNGER

Theodore T. Munger (1830-1910) was graduated from Yale in 1851 and from Yale Divinity School in 1855. From 1856 to 1875 he pastored several New England Congregational churches before going to San Jose, California where he stayed long enough to establish a church in 1876. From that time until 1885 he pastored in North Adams, Massachusetts, at which church he authored The Freedom of Faith. This was a pioneer work in developing the New Theology, a theology which resulted in a fundamental reorientation of American Protestantism. Munger merged the latest ideas of science, evolution, and historical criticism with his theistic, though undogmatic, faith, thereby resulting in a theology for the social gospel which implied that Christian duty meant the application of Christianity to society itself. The following selection from The Freedom of Faith (Boston: Houghton Mifflin and Co., 1883), is Munger's attempt to define the basic elements of the New Theology. What does Munger say the new theology is not, and on what bases does he contend this is true? On the other hand, what does he say are the features of the new theology, and how do these features compare with the old theology?

In attempting to give some expression of the New Theology, I wish to state with the utmost emphasis that I do not speak for any party, but only describe things as I see them. And especially would I disclaim any <u>ex-cathedra</u> tone that may seem to issue from any form of words. I speak from the standpoint of the sharpest and even most isolated individuality,-- for myself alone.

I will first refer to certain negative features, indicating what it is <u>not</u>; and then more fully to its positive character.

1. It does not propose to do without a theology.

It seeks no such transformation of method or form that it can no longer claim the name of a science. It does not resolve belief into sentiment, nor etherealize it into mysticism, nor lower it into mere altruism; yet it does not deny an element of sentiment, it acknowledges an element of mysticism, and it insists on a firm basis in ethics. It is the determined foe of agnosticism, yet it recognizes a limitation of human knowledge. While it insists that theology is a science, and that therefore its parts should be coordinate and mutually supporting, and an induction from all the facts known to it, it realizes that it deals with eternal realities that cannot be wholly compassed, and also with the mysteries and contradictions of a world involved in mystery and beset by contradictory forces. If it finds itself driven into impenetrable mystery, as it inevitably must, it prefers to take counsel of the higher sentiments and better hopes of our nature, rather than project into it the frame-work of a formal logic, and insist on its conclusion. It does not abjure logic, but it refuses to be held by what is often deemed logic. While it believes in a harmony of doctrines, it regards with suspicion what have been known as systems of theology, on the ground that it rejects the methods by which they are constructed. It will not shape a doctrine in order that it may fit another which has been shaped in the same fashion,--a merely mechanical interplay, and seeking a mechanical harmony. Instead, it regards theology as an induction from the revelations of God--in the Bible, in history, in the nation, in the family, in the material creation, and in the whole length and breadth of human life. It will have, therefore, all the definiteness and harmony it can find in these revelations under a process still enacting, and not as under a finality. . . .

2. The New Theology does not part with the historic faith of the Church, but rather seeks to put itself in its line while recognizing a process of development. It does not propose to commit "retrospective suicide" at every fresh stage of advance. It holds to progress by slow and cosmic growth rather than the later theologies, and finds in the early Greek theology conceptions more harmonious with itself than those in the theology shaped by Augustine.

3. It does not reject the specific doctrines of the church of the past. It holds to the Trinity, though indifferent to the use of the word, but not to a formal and psychologically impossible Trinity; to the divine sovereignty, but it does not make it the corner-stone of its system, preferring for that place the divine righteousness, i.e., a moral rather than a dynamic basis; to the Incarnation, not as a mere physical event, for that has entered into many religions, but as the entrance into the world through a person of a moulding and redeeming force in humanity,--the central and broadest fact of theology; to the Atonement as a divine act and process of ethical and practical import--not as a mystery of the distant heavens and isolated from the struggle of the world, but a comprehensible force in the actual redemption of the world from its evil; to the Resurrection as covering the whole essential nature of man; to Judgment as involved in the development of a moral nature; to the eternal awards of conduct considered as laws and principles of character, but not necessarily set in time-relations; to human sinfulness under a conception of moral freedom; to Justification by faith in the sense of a faith that, by its law, induces an actual righteousness--a simple, rational process realized in human experience; to Regeneration and Sanctification by the Spirit as most imperative operations based on the utmost need, and on the actual presence and power of the Spirit in the life of humanity. It does not explain away from these doctrines their substance, nor minimize them, nor aim to do else than present them as revealed in the Scriptures and as developed in history and in the life of the church and of the world.

4. It is not iconoclastic in its temper; it is not pervaded by a spirit of denial, but is constructive--taking away nothing without supplying its place; it does not, indeed, find so much occasion to take away and replace as to uncover and bring to light. Believing that revelation is not so much

from God as of God, its logical attitude is that of seeing and interpreting.

5. It is not disposed to find a field and organization outside of existing churches, conscious that it is building on the Eternal Foundation which alone has given strength to the church in every age. It claims only that liberty whereunto all are called in the church of Christ. It asserts that the real ground of membership in the church is fidelity to the faith, and that this ground is not forfeited because it refuses to assent to human and formal conditions that the church has taken on, and which are not of the substance of the faith. Emphasizing as it does the headship of Christ in the visible as well as invisible church, it would retain its place in the church on the basis of its loyalty to Christ and as its all-sufficient warrant, paying small heed to a narrow, ecclesiastical logic that now confounds, and now distinguishes between the bounds of the visible body and the breadth and freedom of Christ's church.

I pass now to the positive features of the New Theology.

1. It claims for itself a somewhat larger and broader use of the reason than has been accorded to theology. . . .

There are indeed limits to reason, and it has in it an element of faith, but so far as it goes, it goes surely and firmly; it is not a rotten foundation, it is not a broken reed, it is not false light. It may be so sure that it can justly protest in the face of Heaven, "Shall not the Judge of all the earth do right?" It will be humble and docile and trustful, but these qualities are not abrogations of itself. It does not claim for itself the ability to measure the whole breadth and reach of truth; it does not say, I will not believe what I cannot understand, for it knows full well that human reason is not commensurate with eternal truth. . . .

2. The New Theology seeks to interpret the Scriptures in what may be called a more natural way, and in opposition to a hard, formal, unsympathetic, and unimaginative way.

Its strongest denial and its widest divergence from the Old Theology lie here. It holds profoundly to inspiration, but it also holds that the Scriptures were written by living men, whose life entered into their writings; it finds the color

and temper of the writer's mind in his work; it finds also
the temper and habit of the age; it penetrates the forms of
Oriental speech; it seeks to read out of the mind and conception and custom of the writer instead of reading present
conceptions into his words. In brief, it reads the Scriptures as literature, yet with no derogation from their inspiration. It refuses to regard the writers as automatic
organs of the Spirit,--"moved", indeed, but not carried outside of themselves nor separated from their own ways and conceptions. It is thus that it regards the Bible as a <u>living</u>
book; it is warm and vital with the life of a divine humanity, and thus it speaks to humanity. . . .

3. The New Theology seeks to replace an excessive individuality by a truer view of the solidarity of the race.

It does not deny a real individuality, it does not predicate
an absolute solidarity, but simply removes the emphasis from
one to the other. It holds that every man must live a life
of his own, build himself up into a full personality, and
give an account of himself to God: but it also recognizes
the blurred truth that man's life lies in its relations; that
it is a derived and shared life; that it is carried on and
perfected under laws of heredity and of the family and the
nation; that while he is "himself alone" he is also a son, a
parent, a citizen, and an inseparable part of the human race;
that in origin and character and destiny he cannot be regarded as standing in a sharp and utter individuality. It differs from the Old Theology in a more thorough and consistent
application of this distinction. That holds to an absolute
solidarity in evil, relieved by a doctrine of election of individuals; this holds to a solidarity running throughout the
whole life of humanity in the world,--not an absolute solidarity, but one modified by freedom. . . .

Still, it does not submerge the individual in the common life,
nor free him from personal ill desert, nor take from him the
crown of personal achievement and victory. It simply strives
to recognize the duality of truth, and hold it well poised.
It turns our attention to the corporate life of man here in
the world,--an individual life, indeed, but springing from
common roots, fed by a common life, watched over by one
Father, inspired by one Spirit, and growing to one end; no
man, no generation, being "made perfect" by itself. Hence
its ethical emphasis; hence its recognition of the nation,

and of the family, and of social and commercial life, as
fields of the manifestation of God and of the operation of
the Spirit; hence its readiness to ally itself with all
movements for bettering the condition of mankind,--holding
that human society itself is to be redeemed, and that the
world itself, in its corporate capacity, is being reconciled
to God; hence also an apparently secular tone, which is,
however, but a widening of the field of the divine and
spiritual.

4. This theology recognizes a new relation to natural science; but only in the respect that it ignores the long apparent antagonism between the kingdom of faith and of natural law,--an antagonism that cannot, from the nature of things, have a bias in reality. But while it looks on the external world as a revelation of God and values the truth it may reveal; while even it recognizes in it analogies to the spiritual world and a typical similarity of method, it does not merge itself in natural science. It is not yet ready, and it shows no signs that it ever will be ready, to gather up its beliefs, and go over into the camp of natural science, and sit down under the manipulations of a doctrine of evolution, with its one category of matter and one invariable force. It is not ready to commit itself to a finite system, a merely phenomenal section of the universe and of time, with no <u>whence</u>, or <u>whither</u>, or <u>why</u>,--a system that simply supplies man with a certain kind of knowledge, but solves no problem that weighs on his heart, answers no question that he much cares to ask, and throws not one glimmer of additional light on his origin, his nature, or his destiny. It accepts gratefully the knowledge it discloses of the naterial universe, its laws and its processes; it admits that science has anticipated theology in formulating the method of creation known as evolution, that it has corrected modern theology by suggesting a closer and more vital relation between God and creation, and so has helped it throw off a mechanical theory and regain its forgotten theory of the divine immanence in creation. . . .

5. The New Theology offers a contrast to the Old in claiming for itself a wider study of man.

It chooses for its field the actual life of men in the world in all their varying conditions, rather than as masses in a few ideal conditions. It finds its methods in the every-day processes of humanity, rather then in a formal logic. It deals with human life as do the poets and dramatists: it views humanity by a direct light, looks straight at it, and into it, and across its whole breadth. A recognition of human nature and life,--this is a first principle with the New Theology. . . .

6. The New Theology recognizes the necessity of a restatement of belief in Eschatology, or the doctrine of Last Things. . . .

But the New Theology does not plant its entire conception of the subject upon the word. It seeks rather to enlighten itself by the general light of the entire revelation of God; and thus it finds itself driven to such conclusions as these: namely, that every human being will have the fullest opportunity for attaining to the end of his creation as a child of God; that every human being will receive from the Spirit of God all the influence impelling to salvation that his nature can endure and retain its moral integrity; that no human being will be given over to perish while there is a possibility of his salvation. These are the very truisms of the faith, its trend, its drift, its logic, its spirit, and its letter, when the letter is interpreted under the spirit; and they are equally the demand of the human reason. . . .

Such are some of the features of this fresh movement in the realm of theology, for it can scarcely be called more than a movement, an advance to meet the unfolding revelation of God. It is not an organization, it is little aggressive, it does not herald itself with any Lo here or Lo there, it does not crowd itself upon the thought of the age, it is not keyed to such methods. It has no word of contempt for those who linger in ways it has ceased to walk in; it has no synpathy with those who have forsaken the one way. It does not reduce the proportions of evil nor dim the glory of righteousness; it does not chill the enthusiasm of faith, nor hold it back from its mightiest effort of sacrifice. It seeks no conquest represented in outward form, but is content to add its thought to the growing thought of the world, and if it speaks, content to speak to those who have ears to hear. It makes no haste, it seeks no revolution, but simply holds itself open and receptive under the breathing of the Spirit that has come, and is ever coming, into the world; passive, yet quick to respond to the heavenly visions that do not cease to break upon the darkened eyes of humanity.

Present Day Theology

WASHINGTON GLADDEN

Washington Gladden (1836-1918) was a giant among the social gospelers of the late nineteenth century, as well as an early formulator of the New Theology which supported it. The following excerpt appears in his Present Day Theology (Cleveland: McClelland and Co., 1913), pp. 69-81, passim. How does Gladden define sin, and upon what grounds does he build his definition? What does he say is the penalty for sin, and what are its consequences?

What, now, is the nature of sin?

It is well to dispose at once of some of the traditional theories, which have played a great part in the history of Christian thought.

The theology on which most of us older folks were brought up divided sin into two categories--original and actual sin. Actual sin was the conscious and intentional transgressions of the moral law, the evil deeds or the culpable omissions of which we in our own persons and by our choices are guilty. This is the kind of sin of which we have been talking. Concerning this the new theology, as I understand it, raises no question. It is a phenomenon too sadly familiar to be disputed.

But the other kind of sin--what the theologians call original sin--the new theology does not believe in. The old theology held that on account of the sin of Adam all the descendants of Adam were made sinners. It was not only that we inherited from our first ancestor weakened or impaired moral natures, tendencies to evil. That might well have been true. The doctrine was that we had inherited his guilt; that God held us blameworthy on account of his sin and punishable because of it. Adam, as the theory figured it, was the federal head of the race. God had a covenant with him, that if he was obedient all his descendants should be virtuous and blessed; while if he disobeyed and as the old catechism says, we "all have sinned in him and fell with him in his first transgression,"--or as the New England pioneer more tersely put it:

>"In Adam's fall
>We sinned all."

In consequence of this sin of our first parent we all come into the world "under the wrath and curse" of God, "and (are) so made liable to all the miseries of this life and the pains of hell forever." Thus, for nothing that we had done, or consented to, the old theology told us that God held us all deserving of eternal punishment in hell.

The doctrine of election came in here, however, and assured us that God, out of his mere good pleasure, has chosen some of these doomed and lost ones upon whom he would bestow his grace; and the sins of these were remitted through the expiation made by Christ upon the cross. Among infants who died in infancy, before they were capable of actual transgression some were elect and some non-elect; the elect infants were saved by the blood of Christ; the non-elect infants were consigned to eternal misery on account of original sin,--their implication in the sin of Adam. . . .

It is amazing that a notion, so horribly unethical, should linger in the minds of human beings in the twentieth century. It is strange that any one who has known anything about the God and Father of our Lord Jesus Christ should deem it possible that he could count all the children of Adam guilty of

Adam's sin, and worthy of eternal death because of something
that happened thousands of years before they were born.

But is it not true, you ask, that we suffer the consequences
of sin of our ancestors? Yes, we are so linked together that
the evil that parents do entails upon their children weakness
and disability and suffering; but sin is not entailed; sin is
not inherited. The children are not to blame for what their
parents did, nor are they to blame for being in this weak and
disabled condition; they are not to blame for anything which
they inherit; every just man pities them for that evil inheritance;
how much more does our heavenly Father regard them
with compassion, and seek to rescue them from their infirmities!
If they come into the world with blunted sensibilities,
and abnormal cravings, and tendencies to evil, he takes all
that into consideration, in judging their conduct. You and
I would do that, and if we, being evil, can make such allowances,
how much more will our heavenly Father deal mercifully
with children!

So then, the new theology puts aside, as essentially pagan,
the old doctrine of original sin by which most of the old
theology was shaped. Sin cannot be inherited. God is just.
Do I call this the new theology? It is not really so very
new. Listen to the prophet Ezekiel:

> "The soul that sinneth, it shall die; the son shall not
> bear the iniquity of the father, neither shall the
> father bear the iniquity of the son; the righteousness
> of the wicked shall be upon him."

How the framers of that old dogma managed to interpret this
eighteenth chapter of Ezekiel I have never been able to understand.
There is no such thing as inherited sin. Sin, as
old Dr. Emmons insisted, consists in sinnings. All sin is
actual sin. And now what is the nature of actual sin?

It is sometimes supposed to be simple animalism-- the predominance
of the bodily appetites. But the bodily appetites
are not necessarily sinful. Under normal control they are
elements of wholesome life. It is true that the progress of
man is from animalism to spirituality, and that many of his
worst temptations are due to the imperfect subjugation of the
lower nature to the higher, yet as one says, "the sin does
not dwell in the fact that man still retains a nature akin to

that of the animals below him, but in this, that the nature that is akin to God yields to the nature that is common to man and beasts." Yet it still remains true that the worst sins of man have nothing to do with the flesh; the perversion of the higher nature is deadlier than the indulgence of the lower.

We still may say that sin is simply abnormal action. It is the violation by the soul, of its own law of life. Whatever tends to the perfection of my soul of my manhood in its physical, intellectual and moral elements, is right; whatever interferes with that tendency and prevents me from realizing my manhood is wrong.

Does some one say that sin is an offense against God? Well, that is true. But what Matthew Arnold says is also profoundly true, that the stream of tendency by which all things strive to fulfill the law of their being is only another name for God. Any action of my will which hinders me from fulfilling the law of my being is therefore a sin against God. God is working in me, to perfect my manhood. Whatever I do to obstruct that working, to impair manhood is a sin against him.

But we have not yet reached the heart of the matter. And here we will let Professor Clarke help us once more:

> "Sin may be viewed with reference to its motive and inner moral quality; we observe the evil, whether in act or in character and estimate it in the light of the principles from which it springs. Thus sin is the placing of self-will and selfishness above the claims of love and duty" . . . .

If this is the essential nature of sin,--if it is essentially a kind of self-love which makes us indifferent to the welfare of others,--it is rather absurd to deny its existence or its prevalence. The new theology, at any rate, is not disposed to ignore it. It is a stubborn fact of portentous dimensions. We do not need to go back to Adam, or to resort to any theories of imputation; the evidence confronts us whenever we open our eyes.

To prove that a man is a sinner is not necessary, then, to show that he is a murderer or a liar or a thief or a counterfeiter or a forger or a burglar; he may even be a man who never drinks nor smokes nor dances nor plays cards nor goes to the theatre; the only question is whether he is chargeable with putting selfishness or self-will above love and duty. That sin is enough to shut any man out of heaven. There cannot be any heaven where that spirit is. That spirit brings hell wherever it goes, in this world and every other world.

If this is the nature of sin, what is the penalty of sin? The old theology made this penalty to consist of suffering inflicted upon the sinner by a judicial process in the future life. Hell was a place of eternal punishment, provided by the divine justice, to which were consigned after death and the judgment all unforgiven sinners. Of the meaning of heaven and hell I shall speak in the next lecture. The penalty of sin will also be more fully considered at that time. It is sufficient to say that the new theology regards those conceptions of judicial punishment as based on analogies which convey much less than the whole truth, and teaches that the reality of punishment is something much closer to our experience and more verifiable than those old theories made it.

The penalty of sin, as the new theology teaches, consists in the natural consequences of sin. Sin is selfishness; what, then are the natural consequences of selfishness? If a man freely indulges this disposition to place his own interest and pleasure above the claims of love and duty what will be the natural effect upon the character of that man? You do not need to go to the creeds or to the Bible or to the theologians to find out; just read the newspapers and the novels, and keep your eyes open to what is going on about you. The new theology doesn't refer you to authorities on this subject--it goes straight to human life for its facts.

In the first place the man who indulges this selfish disposition will find it strengthening its hold upon him; that is a law of mind, and it works itself out in his experience. The habit of preferring his own happiness to other peoples' grows on him; he has less and less compunction about prospering at the expense of other people; he has less and less compassion for those less fortunate; he is more and more inclined to say that those whom he pushes from his path in his progress are themselves to blame for their misfortunes; he becomes more and more self-centered and intolerant and unsocial. This is the natural penalty of selfishness.

Other sins grow out of this by a logical necessity. The man who makes his own interest supreme is apt to think that those who interfere with his interests have no right to the truth, and deception or falsehood is the natural consequences. When he begins to lie it is easy to keep on; every lie he tells is a seed from which other lies spring and multiply, thirty, sixty, an hundred fold. His love of the truth is weakened and gradually disappears.

Perhaps the animal propensities in him clamor for indulgence, and as it is always the self to which they minister they easily get their own way. These indulgences, also, grow into habits which strengthen as time goes on; the man comes more and more under the domain of his fleshly nature; his finer sensibilities are dulled; his imagination is filled with pictures of sensual delights; he loses his relish for cleanliness and manliness and purity; he becomes false and foul in thought and life.

It is needless to protract this analysis. These are facts which every one of you can verify in your daily observation. These are the natural penalties of sin, as they are working themselves out in the characters of men before your eyes every day. Perhaps some of you have even clearer evidence of them within your own consciousness, in your own experiences. The penalty of sin is sin. Whatever a man soweth that that shall he also reap. If you sow selfishness you will reap selfishness. If you sow falsehood you will reap falsehood. If you sow to the flesh you will reap corruption. These are natural consequences. They are immediate. They are inevitable. They are cumulative.

There are also social consequences, of vast importance, on which I cannot dwell. Such a life affects other lives continually; it entails suffering and loss upon the victims of its selfishness; it communicates contagion; it kindles resentments and antagonisms; it tends to produce enmity and strife and malevolence. What kind of a society would it be in which every man freely indulged his selfish tendencies, and permitted them to produce their natural fruits in his character?

It is generally assumed that pain and suffering of some kind

is the penalty of sin. It often does bring suffering as its
consequence, but that is not always true, and it is by no
means the worst consequence of sin. The wages of sin is always death, not always suffering, for spiritual death is often a painless process. It may be accompanied by numbness,--
by insensibility. Deterioration, degradation, is the penalty
of sin. He that sows to the flesh reaps not always suffering,
but always corruption.

There is, indeed, one natural consequence of sin, of which
most of us have some knowledge. That is remorse, the rank-
ling memory of wrong committed, which is now, perhaps, reme-
diless; the bitter scourgings of conscience for faithless-
ness or disloyalty or cruelty or neglect for which it is now
beyond our power to atone.

Such then is sin, and such is the penalty of sin. . . .

A Theology for the Social Gospel

WALTER RAUSCHENBUSCH

Walter Rauschenbusch (1861-1918) was raised
in Rochester, New York, where he gained both his
university and seminary educations. He was ordained a Baptist minister and served as a pastor of a
New York City church for eleven years, during which
time he saw firsthand the hardships of the industrial depression that began in 1893. His extensive reading in socialist and reform literature
led him to renovate orthodox theology. In the
process he became the foremost American philosopher

of the social gospel, advocating a form of revisionist socialism whereby a new society could be created with the application of the concept of the Kingdom of God to the social organism. Though he held out hope for a better world to come, he did not believe the Kingdom could be fully realized on earth. The selection which follows is from his most important work, A Theology for the Social Gospel (New York: Macmillan, 1917), pp. 23-26, 131-37. What historical basis for the social gospel does Rauschenbusch suggest? What does he mean by the "Kingdom of God," and how does the social gospel relate to it according to him? What did he say were some of the theological consequences of a shriveled doctrine of the Kingdom of God?

In these introductory chapters my aim is to win the benevolent and serious attention of conservative readers for the discussions that are to follow. I have thus far tried to show that the spread of the social gospel will inevitably react on theology, and that this influence is likely to be constructive and salutary. Let us add the important fact that the social gospel imports into theology nothing that is new or alien.

Frequent attempts have been made in the history of our religion to blend alien elements with it. The early Gnostics and mediaeval Albigenses, for instance, tried to combine historical Christianity with dualistic conceptions of the universe and strict asceticism. Modern Mormonism, Theosophy, and Christian Science represent syncretistic formation, minglings of genuine Christianity with new and alien elements.

The belief in the universal reign of law, the doctrine of evolution, the control of nature by man, and the value of education and liberty as independent goods,--these are among the most influential convictions of modern life and have deeply modified our religious thought. But they are novel elements of theology. They are not alien, but certainly they held no such controlling position in the theology of the past as they do with us. We may discover prophetic forecasts of them in the Bible, but we have to look for them.

On the other hand the idea of the redemption of the social organism is nothing alien. It is simply a proper part of the Christian faith in redemption from sin and evil. As soon as the desire for salvation becomes strong and intelligent enough to look beyond the personal sins of the individual, and to discern how our personality in its intake and output is connected with the social groups to which we belong, the problem of social redemption is before us and we can never again forget it. It lies like a larger concentric circle around a smaller one. It is related to our intimate personal salvation like astronomy to physics. Only spiritual and intellectual immaturity have kept us from seeing it clearly before. The social gospel is not an alien element in theology.

Neither is it novel. The social gospel is, in fact, the oldest gospel of all. It is "built on the foundation of the apostles and prophets." Its substance is the Hebrew faith which Jesus himself held. If the prophets ever talked about the "plan of redemption," they meant the social redemption of the gospel, the Kingdom of God was its central word, and the ethical teaching of both, which was their practical commentary and definition of the Kingdom idea, looked toward a higher social order in which new ethical standards would become practicable. To the first generation of disciples the hope of the Lord's return meant the hope of a Christian social order on earth under the personal rule of Jesus Christ, and they would have been amazed if they had learned that this hope was to be motioned out of theology and other ideas substituted.

The social gospel is nothing alien or novel. When it comes to a question of pedigree and birth-right, it may well turn on the dogmas on which the Catholic and Protestant theologies are based and inquire for their birth certificate. They are neither dominant in the New Testament nor clearly defined in it. The more our historical investigations are laying bare the roots of Catholic dogma, the more we see them running back into alien Greek thought, and not into the substance of Christ's message nor into the Hebrew faith. We shall not get away again from the central proposition of Harnack's History of Dogma, that the development of Catholic dogma was the process of the Hellenization of Christianity; in other words, that alien influences streamed into the religion of Jesus Christ and created a theology which he never taught nor intended. What would Jesus have said to the symbol of

Chalcedon or the Athanasian Creed if they had been read to him?

The doctrine of the Kingdom of God was left undeveloped by individualistic theology and finally mislaid by it almost completely, because it did not support nor fit in with that scheme of doctrine. In the older handbooks of theology it is scarcely mentioned, except in the chapters on eschatology; in none of them does it dominate the table of contents. What a spectacle, that the original teaching of our Lord has become an incongruous element in so-called evangelical theology, like a stranger with whom the other doctrines would not associate, and who was finally ejected because he had no wedding garment! In the same way the distinctive ethics of Jesus, which is part and parcel of his Kingdom doctrine, was long the hidden treasure of suppressed democratic sects. Now, as soon as the social gospel began once more to be preached in our own time, the doctrine of the Kingdom was immediately loved and proclaimed afresh, and the ethical principles of Jesus are once more taught without reservation as the only alternative for the greedy ethics of capitalism and militarism. These antipathies and affinities are a strong proof that the social gospel is neither alien nor novel, but is a revival of the earliest doctrines of Christianity, of its radical ethical spirit, and of its revolutionary consciousness. . . .

If theology is to offer an adequate doctrinal basis for the social gospel, it must not only make room for the doctrine of the Kingdom of God, but give it a central place and revise all other doctrines so that they will articulate organically with it.

This doctrine is itself the social gospel. Without it, the idea of redeeming the social order will be but an annex to the orthodox conception of the scheme of salvation. It will live like a negro servant family in a detached cabin back of the white man's house in the South. If this doctrine gets the place which has always been legitimate right, the practical proclamation and application of social morality will have a firm footing.

To those whose minds live in the social gospel, the Kingdom of God is a dear truth, the marrow of the gospel, just as the incarnation was to Athanasius, justification by faith alone to Luther and the sovereignty of God to Jonathan Edwards. It was just as dear to Jesus. He too lived in it, and from it looked out on the world and the work he had to do.

Jesus always spoke of the Kingdom of God. Only two of his reported sayings contain the word "Church," and both passages are of questioned authenticity. It is safe to say that he never thought of founding the kind of institution which afterward claimed to be acting for him.

Yet immediately after his death, groups of disciples joined and consolidated by inward necessity. Each local group knew that it was part of a divinely founded fellowship mysteriously spreading through humanity, and awaiting the return of the Lord and the establishing of his Kingdom. This universal Church was loved with the same religious faith and reverence with which Jesus had loved the Kingdom of God. It was the partial and earthly realization of the divine Society, and at the Parousia the Church and The Kingdom would merge.

But the Kingdom was merely a hope, the Church a present reality. The chief interest and affection flowed toward the Church. Soon, through a combination of causes, the name and idea of "the kingdom" began to be displaced by the name and idea of "the church" in the preaching, literature, and theological thought of the Church. Augustine completed this process in his <u>De Civitate Dei</u>. The Kingdom of God which has, throughout human history, opposed the Kingdom of Sin, is today embodied in the Church. The millennium began when the Church was founded. This practically substituted the actual, not the ideal Church for the Kingdom of God. The beloved ideal of Jesus became a vague phrase which kept intruding from the New Testament. Like Cinderella in the kitchen, it saw the other great dogmas furbished up for the ball, but no prince of theology restored it to its rightful place. The reformation, too, brought no renascence of the doctrine of the Kingdom; it had only eschatological value, or was defined in blurred phrases borrowed from the Church. The present revival of the Kingdom idea is due to the combined influence of the historical study of the Bible and of the social gospel.

When the doctrine of the Kingdom of God shriveled to an undeveloped and pathetic remnant in Christian thought, this loss was bound to have far-reaching consequences. We are told that the loss of single tooth from the arch of the mouth in childhood may spoil the symmetrical development of the skull and produce malformations affecting the mind and character. The atrophy of that idea which had occupied the chief place in the mind of Jesus, necessarily affected the humanity, and the structure of theology. I shall briefly enumerate some of the consequences affecting theology. This list, however, is by no means complete.

1. Theology lost its contact with the synoptic thought of Jesus. Its problems were not at all the same which had occupied his mind. It lost his point of view and became to some extent incapable of understanding him. His ideas had to be rediscovered in our time. . . .

2. The distinctive ethical principles of Jesus were the direct outgrowth of his conception of the Kingdom of God. When the latter disappeared from theology, the former disappeared from ethics. Only persons having the substance of the Kingdom ideal in their minds, seem to be able to get relish out of the ethics of Jesus. Only those church bodies which have been in opposition to organized society have looked for a better city with its foundation in heaven, have taken the Sermon on the Mount seriously.

3. The Church is primarily a fellowship for worship; the Kingdom is a fellowship of righteousness. When the latter was neglected in theology, the ethical force of Christianity was weakened; when the former was emphasized in theology, the importance of worship was exaggerated. The prophets and Jesus had cried down sacrifices and ceremonial performances, and cried up righteousness, mercy, solidarity. . . .

4. When the Kingdom ceased to be the dominating religious reality, the Church moved up into the position of the supreme good. To promote the power of the Church and its control over all rival political forces was equivalent to promoting the supreme ends of Christianity. This increased the arrogance of churchmen and took the moral check off their policies. For the Kingdom of God can never be promoted by lies, draft, crime or war, but the wealth and power of the Church have often been promoted by these means. The medieval ideal of the supremacy of the Church over the State was the logical consequences of making the church the highest good with no superior ethical standard by which to test it. . . .

5. The Kingdom ideal is the test and corrective of the influence of the Church. When the Kingdom ideal disappeared, the conscience of the Church was muffled. It became possible for the missionary expansion of Christianity to halt for centuries without creating any sense of shortcoming. It became possible for the most unjust social conditions to fasten themselves on Christian nations without awakening any consciousness that the purpose of Christ was being defied and beaten back. . . .

6. The Kingdom ideal contains the revolutionary force of Christianity. When this ideal faded out of the systematic thought of the Church, it became a conservative social influence and increased the weight of the other stationary forces in society. If the kingdom of God had remained part of the theological and Christian consciousness, the Church could not, down to our times have been salaried by autocratic class governments to keep the democratic and economic impulses of the people under check.

7. Reversely, the movements for democracy and social justice were left without a religious backing for lack of the Kingdom idea. The Kingdom of God as the fellowship of righteousness, would be advanced by the abolition of industrial slavery and the disappearance of slums of civilization; the Church would only indirectly gain through such social changes. Even today many Christians cannot see any religious importance in social justice and fraternity because it does not increase the number of conversions nor fill the churches. . . .

8. Secular life is belittled as compared with church life. Services rendered to the Church get higher religious rating than services rendered to the community. Thus the religious value is taken out of the activities of the common man and the prophetic services to society. Wherever the Kingdom of God is a living reality in Christian thought, any advance of social righteousness is seen as a part of redemption and arouses inward joy and the triumphant sense of salvation. When the Church absorbs interest a subtle asceticism creeps back into our theology and the world looks different.

9. When the doctrine of the Kingdom of God is lacking in theology, the salvation of the individual is seen in its relation to the Church and to the future life, but not in its relation to the task of saving the social order. Theology

had left this important point in a condition so hazy and muddled that it has taken us almost a generation to see that the salvation of the individual and the redemption of the social order are closely related, and how.

10. Finally, theology has been deprived of the inspiration of great ideas contained in the idea of the Kingdom and in labor for it. The Kingdom of God breeds prophets; the Church breeds priests and theologians. The Church runs to tradition and dogma; the Kingdom of God rejoices in forecasts and boundless horizons. The men who have contributed the most fruitful impulses to Christian thought have been men of prophetic vision, and their theology has been most concerned with past history, with present social problems and with the future of human society.

RELIGION AND INTERNATIONAL RELATIONS   13

Our Country

JOSIAH STRONG

Josiah Strong (1847-1916) was raised in an orthodox Protestant home, but became an admirer of the New Theology during the late nineteenth century. As a central figure in the social gospel movement, he believed the movement was the solution to not only America's domestic perils, which he discussed in great detail in his writings, but also to the outstanding problems of the world. In 1885, while serving as minister of the Central Congregational Church in Cincinnati, he expounded his ideas in one of the most influential books of the nineteenth century, Our Country: Its Possible Future and Its Present Crisis. In it Strong combined the social gospel with Anglo-Saxonism, the social Darwinian principle of the "survival of the fittest," and the doctrine of God's providence--a combination which posited the argument that Anglo-Saxons were destined to transmit their superior civilization to inferior races abroad. This was dynamite in the pulpits of churchmen who used it in support of America's openly expansionist policies in the late nineteenth century. The following excerpt was taken from Our Country, rev. ed. (New York: Baker and

Taylor Co., 1891), pp. 200-18, passim. Upon what
bases does Strong argue the supremacy of the Anglo-
Saxon nationalities? What evidence is there in this
selection that Strong has adopted much of Darwin's
thought and applied it to his own thought? How has
Strong blended nationalism and Christianity into
his own expression of imperialism?

The Anglo-Saxon and the World's Future--

Every race which has deeply impressed itself on the human
family has been representative of some great idea--one or
more--which has given direction to the nation's life and form
to its civilization. Among the Egyptians this seminal idea
was life, among the Persians it was light, among the Hebrews
it was purity, among the Greeks it was beauty, among the Romans it was law. The Anglo-Saxon is the representative of
two great ideas, which are closely related. One of them is
that of civil liberty. Nearly all of the civil liberty of
the world is enjoyed by Anglo-Saxons: the English, the British colonists, and the people of the United States. To some,
like the Swiss, it is permitted by the sufferance of their
neighbors; others, like the French, have experimented with it;
but, in modern times, the peoples whose love of liberty has
won it, and whose genius for self-government has preserved
it, have been Anglo-Saxons. The noblest races have always
been lovers of liberty. The love ran strong in early German
blood, and has profoundly influenced the institutions of all
the branches of the great German family; but it was left for
the Anglo-Saxon branch fully to recognize the right of the
individual to himself, and formally to declare it the foundation stone of government.

The other great idea of which the Anglo-Saxon is the exponent
is that of a pure spiritual Christianity. It was no accident
that the great reformation of the sixteenth century originated
among a Teutonic, rather than a Latin people. It was the fire
of liberty burning in the Saxon heart that flamed up against
the absolutism of the Pope. Speaking roughly, the peoples of
Europe which are Celtic are Roman Catholic, and those which
are Teutonic are Protestant; and where the Teutonic race was
purest, there Protestantism spread with the greatest rapidity. But, with beautiful exceptions, Protestantism on the

continent has degenerated into mere formalism. By confirmation at a certain age, the state churches are filled with members who generally know nothing of a personal spiritual experience. In obedience to a military order, a regiment of German soldiers files into church and partakes of the sacrament, just as it would shoulder arms or obey any other word of command. It is said that, in Berlin and Leipsic, only a little over one percent of the Protestant population are found in church. Protestantism on the continent seems to be about as poor in spiritual life and power as Romanism. That means that most of the spiritual Christianity in the world is found among Anglo-Saxons and their converts; for this is the great missionary race. If we take all of the German missionary societies together, we find that, in the number of workers and amount of contributions, they do not equal the smallest of the three great English missionary societies. The year that the Congregationalists in the United States gave one dollar and thirty-seven cents per caput to foreign missions, the members of the great German State Church gave only three quarters of a cent per caput to the same cause. Evidently it is chiefly to the English and American peoples that we must look for the evangelization of the world.

It is not necessary to argue to those for whom I write that the two great needs of mankind, that all men may be lifted up into the light of the highest Christian civilization, are, first a pure, spiritual Christianity, and second, civil liberty. Without controversy, these are the forces which, in the past, have contributed most to the elevation of the human race, and they must continue to be, in the future, the most efficient ministers to its progress. It follows, then, that the Anglo-Saxon, as the great representative of these two ideas, the depositary of these two greatest blessings, sustains peculiar relations to the world's future, is divinely commissioned to be, in a peculiar sense, his brother's keeper. Add to this the fact of his rapidly increasing strength in modern times, and we have well nigh a demonstration of his destiny. . . .

And it is possible that, by the close of the next century, the Anglo-Saxons will outnumber all the other civilized races of the world. Does it not look as if God were not only preparing in our Anglo-Saxon civilization the die with which to stamp the peoples of the earth, but as if he were also massing behind that die the mighty power with which to press it? My confidence that this race is eventually to give its civilization to mankind is not base on mere numbers--China forbid! I look forward to what the world has never yet seen united in the some race; viz., the greatest numbers, and the highest civilization.

There can be no reasonable doubt that North America is to be the great home of the Anglo-Saxon, the principal of his power, the center of his life and influence. . . .

America is to have the great preponderance of numbers and of wealth, and by the logic of events will follow the scepter of controlling influence. This will be but the consummation of a movement as old as civilization--a result to which men have looked forward for centuries. . . .

Mr. Darwin is not only disposed to see, in the superior vigor of our people, an illustration of his favorite theory of natural selection, but even intimates that the world's history thus far has been simply preparatory for our future, and tributary to it. He says: "There is apparently much truth in the belief that the wonderful progress of the United States, as well as the character of the people, are the results of natural selection; for the more energetic, restless, and courageous men from all parts of Europe have emigrated during the last ten or twelve generations to that great country, and have there succeeded best. Looking at the distant future, I do not think that the Rev. Mr. Zincke takes an exaggerated view when he says: 'All other series of events--as that which resulted in the Empire of Rome--only appear to have purpose and value when viewed in connection with, or rather as subsidiary to, the great stream of Anglo-Saxon emigration to the West!'"

There is abundant reason to believe that the Anglo-Saxon race is to be, is, indeed, already becoming, more effective here than in the mother country. The marked superiority of this race is due in large measure, to its highly mixed origin. . . .

It seems to me that God, with infinite wisdom and skill, is training the Anglo-Saxon race for an hour sure to come in the world's future. Heretofore there has always been in the history of the world a comparatively unoccupied land westward, into which the crowded countries of the East have poured their surplus populations. But the widening waves of migration, which millenniums ago rolled east and west from the valley of the Euphrates, meet today on our Pacific coast. There are no more new worlds. The unoccupied arable lands of the earth are limited, and will soon be taken. The time is coming when the pressure of population on the means of subsistence will be felt here as it is now felt in Europe and Asia. Then will the world enter upon a new stage of its history--the final competition of races, for which the Anglo-Saxon is being schooled. Long before the thousand millions are here, the mighty centrifugal tendency, inherent in this stock and strengthened in the United States, will assert itself. Then this race of unequaled energy, with all the majesty of numbers and the might of wealth behind it--the representative, let us hope, of the largest liberty, the purest Christianity, the highest civilization--having developed peculiarly aggressive traits calculated to impress its institutions upon mankind, will spread itself over the earth. If I read not amiss, this powerful race will move down upon Mexico, down upon Central and South America, out upon the islands of the sea, over upon Africa and beyond. And can any one doubt that the result of this competition of races will be the "survival of the fittest?" "Any people," says Dr. Bushnell, "that is physiologically advanced in culture, though it be only in a degree beyond another which is mingled with it on strictly equal terms, is sure to live down and finally live out its inferior. Nothing can save the inferior race but a ready and pliant assimilation. Whether the feebler and more abject races are going to be regenerated and raised up, is already very much of a question. What if it should be God's plan to people the world with better and finer material?"

"Certain it is, whatever expectations we may indulge, that there is a tremendous overbearing surge of power in the Christian nations, which, if the other are not speedily raised to some vastly higher capacity, will inevitably submerge and bury them forever. These great populations of Christendom--what are they doing, but throwing out their colonies on every side, and populating themselves, if I may so speak, into the possession of all countries and climes?" To this result no war of extermination is needful; the contest is not one of arms, but of vitality and of civilization. "At the present day," says Mr. Darwin, "civilized nations are everywhere supplanting barbarous nations, excepting where the climate opposes a deadly barrier; and they succeed mainly, though not exclusively, through their arts, which are the products of the intellect." Thus the Finns were supplanted by the Aryan races in Europe and Asia, the Tartars by the Russians, and thus the aborigines of North America, Australia, and New Zealand are now disappearing before the all-conquering Anglo-Saxons. It seems as if these inferior tribes were only precursors of a superior race, voices in the wilderness crying: "Prepare ye the way of the Lord!"

Some of the stronger races, doubtless, may be able to preserve their integrity; but, in order to compete with the Anglo-Saxons, they will probably be forced to adopt his methods and instruments, his civilization and his religion. Significant movements are now in progress among them. While the Christian religion was never more vital, or its hold upon the Anglo-Saxon mind stronger, there is taking place among the nations a widespread intellectual revolt against traditional beliefs. "In every corner of the world," says Mr. Froude, "there is the same phenomenon of the decay of established religions. . . . Among the Mohammedans, Jews. Buddhists, Brahmins, traditionary creeds are losing their hold. An intellectual revolution is sweeping over the world, breaking down established opinions, dissolving foundations on which historical faiths have been built up." The contact of Christian with heathern nations is awakening the latter to new life. Old superstitions are loosening their grasp. The dead crust of fossil faiths is being shattered by the movements of life underneath. In Catholic countries, Catholicism is losing its influence over educated minds, and in some cases the masses have already lost all faith in it. Thus, while on this continent God is training the Anglo-Saxon race for its mission, a complemental work has been in progress in the great world beyond. God has two hands. Not only is he preparing in our civilization the die with which to stamp the nations, but, by what Southey called the "timing of Providence," he is preparing mankind to receive the impress.

Is there room for reasonable doubt that this race, unless devitalized by alcohol and tobacco, is destined to dispossess many weaker races, assimilate others, and mold the remainder, until, in a very true and important sense, it has Anglo-Saxonized mankind? Already "the English language, saturated with Christian ideas, gathering up into itself the best thought of all the ages, is the great agent of Christian civilization throughout the world; at this moment affecting the destinies and molding the character of half the human race." Jacob Grimm, the German philologist, said of this language: "It

seems chosen, like its people, to rule in future times in a
still greater degree in all the corners of the earth." He
predicted, indeed, that the language of Shakespeare would
eventually become the language of mankind. Is not Tennyson's
noble prophecy to find its fulfillment in Anglo-Saxondom's
extending its dominion and influence--

> "Till the war-drum throb no longer, and the battle-
> flags are furl'd, In the Parliament of man, the
> Federation of the world."

In my mind, there is no doubt that the Anglo-Saxon is to exercise the commanding influence in the world's future; but the exact nature of that influence is, as yet, undetermined. How far his civilization will be materialistic and atheistic, and how long it will take thoroughly to Christianize and sweeten it, how rapidly he will hasten the coming of the kingdom wherein dwelleth righteousness, or how many ages he may retard it, is still undertain; but _is now being swiftly determined_. Let us weld together in a chain the various links of our logic which we have endeavored to forge. Is it manifest that the Anglo-Saxon holds in his hands the destinies of mankind for ages to come? Is it evident that the United States is to be the home of this race, the principal seat of his power, the great center of his influence? Is it true that the great West is to dominate the nation's future? Has it been shown that this generation is to determine the character, and hence the destiny of the West? Then may God open the eyes of this generation! When Napoleon drew up his troops before the Mamelukes, under the shadow of the Pyramids, pointing to the latter, he said to his soldiers: "Remember that from yonder heights forty centuries look down on you." Men of this generation, from the pyramid top of opportunity on which God has set us, _we look down on forty_ centuries! We stretch our hand into the future with power to mold the destinies of unborn millions.

> "We are living, we are dwelling,
> In a grand and awful time,
> In an age on ages telling--
> To be living is sublime!"

Notwithstanding the great perils which threaten it, I cannot think our civilization will perish; but I believe it is fully in the hands of the Christians of the United States, during the next ten or fifteen years, to hasten or retard the coming of Christ's kingdom in the world by hundreds, and perhaps thousands, of years. We of this generation and nation occupy the Gibraltar of the ages which commands the world's future.

The March of the Flag

ALBERT J. BEVERIDGE

Albert J. Beveridge (1862-1927) served as United States senator from Indiana from 1899 to 1911. As one of the leading imperialist senators at the turn of the century, he declared himself for "America first! Not only America first, but America only!" He was a pronounced nationalist who was suspicious of foreign countries, and therefore it was natural that he should support American expansionism abroad during his term in office. The selection below appears in Thomas B. Reed, ed., Modern Eloquence, Vol. 2 (Philadelphia: John D. Morris and Co., 1903), pp. 224-43, passim. In what ways do Strong and Beveridge agree? How does Beveridge join profit and providence into a single argument?

It is a noble land that God has given us; a land that can feed and clothe the world; a land whose coast lines would inclose half the countries of Europe; a land set like a sentinel between the two imperial oceans of the globe; a greater England and a nobler destiny. It is a mighty people that He has planted on this soil; a people sprung from the most masterful blood of history; a people perpetually revitalized by the virile workingfolk of all the earth; a people imperial by virtue of their power, by right of their institutions, by authority of their heaven-directed purposes, the propagandists and not the misers of liberty. It is a glorious history our God has bestowed upon His chosen people; a history whose keynote was struck by the Liberty Bell; a history heroic with faith in our mission and our future; a history of statesmen, who flung the boundaries of the Republic out into unexplored lands and savage wildernesses; a history of soldiers, who carried the flag across blazing deserts and through the ranks of hostile mountains, even to the gates of sunset; a history of a multiplying people, who overran a continent in half a century; a history divinely logical, in the process of whose tremendous reasoning we find ourselves to-day.

Therefore, in this campaign the question is larger than a party question. It is an American question. It is a world question. Shall the American people continue their restless march toward the commercial supremacy of the world? Shall free institutions broaden their blessed reign as the children of liberty wax in strength until the empire of our principles is established over the hearts of all mankind? Have we no mission to perform--no duty to discharge to our fellow man? Has the Almighty endowed us with gifts beyond our deserts, and marked us as the people of His peculiar favor, merely to rot in our own selfishness, as men and nations must who take cowardice for their companion and self for their deity as China has, as India has, as Egypt has? Shall we be as the man who had one talent and hid it, or as he who had ten talents and used them until they grew to riches? And shall we reap the reward that waits on the discharge of our high duty as the sovereign power on earth; shall we occupy new markets for what our farmers raise, new markets for what our factories make, new markets for what our merchants sell, aye, and please God, new markets for what our ships will carry? Shall we avail ourselves of new sources of supply of what we do not raise or make, so that what are luxuries today shall be necessities tomorrow? Shall we conduct the mightiest commerce of history with the best money known to man or shall we use the pauper money of Mexico, China, and the Chicago platform? Shall we be worthy of our mighty past of progress, brushing aside, as we have always done, the spider webs of technicality, and march ever onward upon the highway of development, to the doing of real deeds, the achievement of real things, and the winning of real victories?

In a sentence, shall the American people endorse at the polls the American administration of William McKinley, which, under the guidance of Divine Providence, has started the Republic on its noblest career of prosperity, duty and glory, or shall the American people rebuke that administration, reverse the wheels of history, halt the career of the flag. . . ?

William McKinley is continuing the policy that Jefferson began, Monroe continued, Seward advanced, Grant promoted, Harrison championed. Hawaii is ours; Puerto Rico is to be ours; at the prayer of its people Cuba will finally be ours; in the islands of the East, even to the gates of Asia, coaling stations are to be ours; at the very least the flag of a liberal government is to float over the Philippines, and it will be the stars and stripes of glory. And the burning question of this campaign is whether the American people will accept the gifts of events; whether they will rise, as lifts their soaring destiny; whether they will proceed along the lines of national development surveyed by the statesmen of our past, or whether, for the first time, the American people doubt their mission, question their fate, prove apostate to the spirit of their race, and halt the ceaseless march of free institutions?

The opposition tells us that we ought not to govern a people without their consent. I answer, the rule of liberty that all just government derives its authority from the consent of the governed, applies only to those who are capable of self-government. We govern the Indians without their consent; we govern our Territories without their consent; we govern our children without their consent. I answer, would not the natives of the Philippines prefer the just, humane, civilizing government of this Republic to the savage, bloody rule of pillage and extortion from which we have rescued them? Do not the blazing fires of joy and the ringing bells of gladness in Puerto Rico prove the welcome of our flag? And regardless of this formula of words made only for enlightened, self-governing peoples, do we owe no duty to the world? Shall we turn these peoples back to the reeking hands from which we have taken them? Shall we save them from those nations, to give

them to a self rule of tragedy? It would be like giving a
razor to a babe and telling it to shave itself. It would be
like giving a typewriter to an Esquimau and telling him to
publish one of the great dailies of the world. . . .

Today, we are making more than we can use. Therefore, we must
find new markets for our produce, new occupation for our capital, new work for our labor. And so, while we did not need
the territory taken during the past century at the time it was
acquired, we do need what we have taken in 1898, and we need
it now. Think of the thousands of Americans who will pour
into Hawaii and Puerto Rico when the Republic's laws cover
those islands with justice and safety. Think of the tens of
thousands of Americans who will invade the Philippines when a
liberal government shall establish order and equity there.
Think of the hundreds of thousands of Americans who will build
a soap and water, common school civilization of energy and industry in Cuba, when a government of law replaces the double
reign of anarchy and tyranny. . . .

The resources of the Philippines have hardly been touched by
the finger tips of modern methods. And they produce what we
cannot, and they consume what we produce--the very predesti-
nation of reciprocity. And William McKinley intends that
their trade shall be ours. It means an opportunity for the
rich man to do something with his money, besides hoarding it
or lending it. It means occupation for every workingman in
the country at wages which the development of new resources,
the launching of new enterprises, the monopoly of new markets always brings. . . .

Why mumble the meaningless phrases of a tale that is told
when the golden future is before us, the world calls us, its
wealth awaits us and God's command is on us? . . .

Fellow-Americans, we are God's chosen people. Yonder at
Bunker Hill and Yorktown His providence was above us. At New
Orleans and on ensanguined seas His hand sustained us. Abraham Lincoln was His minister, and His altar of freedom the
boys in blue set up on a hundred battlefields. His power
directed Dewey in the east, and He delivered the Spanish fleet
into our hands on Liberty's natal day as He delivered the
elder Armada into the hands of our English sires two centuries ago. His great purposes are revealed in the progress
of the flag, which surpasses the intentions of Congresses and

Cabinets, and leads us, like a holier pillar of cloud by day and pillar of fire by night, into situations unforeseen by finite wisdom and duties unexpected by the unprophetic heart of selfishness. The American people cannot use a dishonest medium of exchange; it is ours to set the world its example of right and honor. We cannot fly from our world duties; it is ours to execute the purposes of a fate that has driven us to be greater than our small intentions. We cannot retreat from any soil where Providence has unfurled our banner; it is ours to save that soil for liberty and civilization. For liberty and civilization and God's promises fulfilled, the flag must henceforth be the symbol and the sign of all mankind.

America's Mission

WILLIAM JENNINGS BRYAN

William Jennings Bryan (1860-1925), who was twice elected to Congress (1890 and 1892), was a three-time Democratic presidential nominee, as well as secretary of state in the Wilson administration. Among the major issues of his second bid for the presidency was the imperialistic policy of the Republican administration of William McKinley. Though Bryan had volunteered for military service in Cuba during the Spanish-American War, he spoke against American expansionism in the 1900 presidential campaign. No doubt his position on the issue contributed to his defeat in the election, as some voters doubted his sincerity, while many others had been thoroughly convinced by the expansionists that they opposed Bryan without questioning his sincerity.

The following excerpt, which was part of a 1900 campaign speech, was taken from his Speeches, Newspaper Articles, and Interviews (Chicago: Bentley and Co., 1900), pp. 20-24. On what basis does Bryan argue that "destiny is not a matter of chance, it is a matter of choice?" Why does he argue that conquest of other nations by the United States is not proper nor necessary?

When the advocates of imperialism find it impossible to reconcile a colonial policy with the principles of our government or with the cannons of morality; when they are unable to defend it upon the ground of religious duty or pecuniary profit, they fall back in helpless despair upon the assertion that it is destiny. "Suppose it does violate the constitution," they say; "suppose it does break all the commandments; suppose it does entail upon the nation an incalculable expenditure of blood and money; it is destiny and we must submit."

The people have not voted for imperialism; no national convention has declared for it; no Congress has passed upon it. To whom then, has the future been revealed? Whence this voice of authority? We can all prophesy, but our prophesies are merely guesses, colored by our hopes and our surroundings. Man's opinion of what is to be is half wish and half environment. Avarice paints destiny with a dollar mark before it, militarism equips it with a sword.

He is the best prophet who, recognizing the omnipotence of truth, comprehends most clearly the great forces which are working out the progress, not of one party, not of one nation, but of the human race.

History is replete with predictions which once wore the hue of destiny, but which failed of fulfillment because those who uttered them saw too small an arc of the circle of events. When Pharaoh pursued the fleeing Israelites to the edge of the Red Sea he was confident that their bondage would be renewed and that they would again make bricks without straw, but destiny was not revealed until Moses and his followers

reached the farther shore dry shod and the waves rolled over
the horses and chariots of the Egyptians. When Belshazzar,
on the last night of his reign, led his thousand lords into
the Babylonian banquet hall and sat down to a table glitter-
ing with vessels of silver and gold he felt sure of his kingdom for many years to come, but destiny was not revealed
until the hand wrote upon the wall those awe-inspiring words,
"Mene, Mene, Tekel Upharsin." When Abderrahman swept north-
ward with his conquering hosts his imagination saw the Cres-
cent triumphant throughout the world, but destiny was not
revealed until Charles Martel raised the cross above the
battlefield of Tours and saved Europe from the sword of Mo-
hammendanism. When Napoleon emerged victorious from Marengo,
from Ulm and from Austerlitz he thought himself the child of
destiny, but destiny was not revealed until Blucher's forces
joined the army of Wellington and the vanquished Corsican
began his melancholy march toward St. Helena. When the red-
coats of George the Third routed the New Englanders at Lex-
ington and Bunker Hill there arose before the British sovereign visions of wealth by foreign made laws, but destiny
was not revealed until the surrender of Cornwallis completed
the work begun at Independence Hall and ushered into existence a government deriving its just powers from the consent
of the governed.

We have reached another crisis. The ancient doctrine of imperialism, banished from our land more than a century ago,
has recrossed the Atlantic and challenged democracy to mortal
combat upon American soil.

Whether the Spanish war shall be known in history as a war for
liberty or as a war of conquest; whether the principles of
self-government shall be strengthened or abandoned; whether
this nation shall remain a homogeneous republic or become a
heterogeneous empire--these questions must be answered by the
American people--when they speak, and not until then will,
destiny be revealed.

Destiny is not a matter of chance, it is a matter of choice;
it is not a thing to be waited for, it is a thing to be
achieved.

No one can see the end from the beginning, but every one can
make his course an honorable one from beginning to end, by
adhering to the right under all circumstances. Whether a man

steals much or little may depend upon his opportunities, but whether he steals at all depends upon his own volition.

So with our nation. If we embark upon a career of conquest no one can tell how many islands we may be able to seize, or how many races we may be able to subjugate; neither can any one estimate the cost, immediate and remote, to the nation's character, but whether we shall enter upon such a career is a question which the people have a right to decide for themselves.

Unexpected events may retard or advance the nation's growth but the nation's purpose determines its destiny.

What is the nation's purpose?

The main purpose of the founders of our government was to secure for themselves and for posterity the blessings of liberty, and that purpose has been faithfully followed up to this time. Our statesmen have opposed each other upon economic questions, but they have agreed in defending self-government as the controlling national idea. They have quarreled among themselves over tariff and finance, but they have been united in their opposition to an entangling alliance with any European power.

Under this policy our nation has grown in numbers and in strength. Under this policy its beneficent influence has encircled the globe. Under this policy the taxpayers have been spared the burden and the menace of a large military establishment and the young men have taught the arts of peace rather than the science of war. On each returning Fourth of July our people have met to celebrate the signing of the Declaration of Independence; their hearts have renewed their vows to free institutions and their voices have praised the forefathers whose wisdom and courage and patriotism made it possible for each succeeding generation to repeat the words, "My country, 'tis of thee, Sweet land of liberty, Of thee I sing."

This sentiment was well-nigh universal until a year ago. It was to this sentiment that the Cuban insurgents appealed; it was this sentiment that impelled our people to enter into the war with Spain. Have the people so changed within a few short months that they are now willing to apologize for the War of the Revolution and force upon the Filipinos the same system of government against which the colonists protested with fire and sword?

The hour of temptation has come, but temptations do not destroy, they merely test the strength of individuals and nations; they are stumbling blocks or stepping stones; they lead to infamy or fame, according to the use made of them.

Benedict Arnold and Ethan Allen served together in the Continental army and both were offered British gold. Arnold yielded to the temptation and made his name a synonym for treason; Allen resisted and lives in the affections of his countrymen.

Our nation is tempted to depart from its "standard of morality" and adopt a policy of "criminal aggression." But will it yield?

If I mistake not the sentiment of the American people they will spurn the bride of imperialism, and, by resisting temptation, win such a victory as has not been won since the battle of Yorktown. Let it be written of the United States: Behold a republic that took up arms to aid a neighboring people, struggling to be free; a republic that, in the progress of the war, helped distant races whose wrongs were not in contemplation when hostilities began; a republic that, when peace was restored, turned a deaf ear to the clamorous voice of greed and to those borne down by the weight of a foreign yoke, spoke the welcome words, Stand up; be free--let this be the record made on history's page and the silent example of this republic, true to its principles in the hour of trial, will do more to extend the area of self-government and civilization than could be done by all the wars of conquest that we could wage in a generation.

The forcible annexation of the Philippine islands is not necessarily to make the United States a world power. For over ten decades our nation has been a world power. During its brief existence it has exerted upon the human race an influence more potent for good than all the other nations of the earth combined, and it has exerted upon the human race that influence without the use of sword or Gatling gun. Mexico and the republics of Central and South America testify to the benign influence of our institutions, while Europe and Asia give evidence of the working of the leaven of self-government. In the growth of democracy we observe the triumphant march of an idea--an idea that would be weighted down rather than aided by the armor and weapons proffered by imperialism.

Much has been said of late about Anglo-Saxon civilization. Far be it for me to detract from the service rendered to the world by the sturdy race whose language we speak. The union of the Angle and the Saxon formed a new and valuable type, but the process of race evolution was not completed when the Angle and the Saxon met. A still later type appeared which is superior to any which has existed heretofore; and with this new type will come a higher civilization than any which has preceded it. Great has been the Greek, the Latin, the Slav, the Celt, the Teuton and the Anglo-Saxon, but greater than any of these is the American, in whom are blended the virtues of them all.

Civil and religious liberty, universal education and the right to participate, directly or through representatives chosen by himself, in all the affairs of government--these give to the American citizen an opportunity and an inspiration which can be found nowhere else.

Standing upon the vantage ground already gained the American people can aspire to a grander destiny than has opened before any other race.

Anglo-Saxon civilization has taught the individual to protect his own rights, American civilization will teach him to respect the rights of others.

Anglo-Saxon civilization has taught the individual to take care to himself, American civilization proclaiming the equality of all before the law, will teach him that his own highest good requires the observance of the commandment: "Thou shalt love they neighbor as thyself."

Anglo-Saxon civilization has carried its flag to every clime and defended it with forts and garrisons. American civilization will imprint its flag upon the hearts of all who long for freedom.

To American civilization, all hail!

PART 4   EVALUATING AMERICA SINCE 1920

Changes brought about in America due to industrialization, urbanization, and the spread of technology, along with crucial events on the world scene in the twentieth century--the World Wars, the Great Depression, the struggles of the League of Nations and United Nations--have forced Americans to evaluate often the state of the nation since 1920. The search for national meaning has led some to repudiate supernaturalistic religion, only to return to lives of faith. In the course of the search, uncertainty has characterized the people's evaluation of the individual and collective conscience.

The armistice which brought World War I to an end did not remove this distant conflict from the minds of Americans who engaged in a conscious attempt to "return to normalcy." Idealism and reform were dismissed, while materialism nurtured by laissez-faire was welcomed enthusiastically. Calvin Coolidge's declaration that "the business of America is business" captured the spirit of the age not only for the captains of industry, but also for many in the religious community who fashioned their churches in accord with the latest business practices and values. Bruce Barton's redesigned image of Jesus illustrated the impact of business upon religion. The evaluation of America was sparked, too, by intellectual currents inherited from the late nineteenth century. One of these currents, Darwin's theory of evolution, produced a showdown at Dayton, Tennessee, when fundamentalists challenged the teaching of the theory in the public schools. Some of these same religious conservatives were responsible in part for the defeat of presidential candidate Alfred E. Smith, whose Catholicism troubled many in the predominately Protestant nation.

The growth of religious liberalism fostered in the 1920's by the good times of economic prosperity was rebuffed by the onslaughts of the depression in the 1930's. Edwin Lewis was only one of the new breed of neo-orthodox religionists whose evaluation of liberalism resulted in a new synthesis of biblical ideals and forces in the modern world. Some religious figures like Gerald L. K. Smith, Gerald Winrod, and Charles Coughlin were in the vanguard of protesters who proclaimed the hopelessness of American capitalism and democracy, and called for solutions ranging from the far left, such as communism, to the extreme right, which included fascism.

As the nation braced for the impending Second World War it resurrected some of the threadbare arguments concerning the issues of majority rule and minority rights, separation of church and state, and civil liberties. Inevitably the courts became involved in the related tension between education and religion as new questions arose over the rights of religious minorities, the use of school time for religious instruction, and the recitation of a state-composed prayer in the public schools.

World War I had left a bad taste in the mouths of Americans, and a new course had to be charted for the future. During the twenties and most of the thirties, the church lent its collective voice to the national pursuit of peace-at-all-costs. Ray Abrams traced the steps of the church as it moved from neutrality in the late thirties to belligerency in the early forties. Arthur H. Darken continued with the postbellum story of how the National Council of Churches helped support the activist cold war foreign policy of containment.

The selections by Billy James Hargis, Robert Bellah, and Ronald Enroth examine facets of the turbulent 1960's and demonstrate the interaction of religion with American society. That the religious community has not only affected the shaping of society, but also has been shaped by that society is illustrated by their writings which evaluate the condition of America during the past two decades. This is the same reciprocal relationship experienced by the colonists in the seventeenth century.

AMERICA AND RELIGION IN THE UNCERTAIN TWENTIES

The Man Nobody Knows

BRUCE BARTON

Bruce Barton (1886-1967), the son of a preacher, and a partner in the high-powered advertising company of Batten, Barton, Durstine, and Osborn, did much during the 1920's to make religion relevant to modern America. Written in a vain compatible with Russell Conwell's "Acres of Diamonds," Barton's first book, The Man Nobody Knows, was the fourth best-selling work of nonfiction in 1925 and the top seller in 1926. It redesigned the image of Christ from a meek and lowly man into a man of strength and drive who knew how to gain success through the use of love and charisma. The following is taken from The Man Nobody Knows (New York: Grosset and Dunlap, 1925). In what ways does Barton suggest that Jesus demonstrated the skills of an executive? What are some of the examples Barton uses to illustrate that Jesus implemented some of the methods of a businessman? On what bases does he conclude that Jesus was "the founder of modern business?"

The little boy's body sat bolt upright in the rough wooden chair, but his mind was very busy.

This was his weekly hour of revolt.

The kindly lady who could never seem to find her glasses would have been terribly shocked if she had known what was going on inside the little boy's mind.

"You must love Jesus," she said every Sunday, "and God."

The little boy did not say anything. He was afraid to say anything; he was almost afraid that something would happen to him because of the things he thought.

Love God! Who was always picking on people for have a good time, and sending little boys to hell because they couldn't do better in a world which he had made so hard! Why didn't God take some one his own size?

Love Jesus! The little boy looked up at the picture which hung on the Sunday-school wall. It showed a pale young man with flabby forearms and a sad expression. The young man had red whiskers.

Then the little boy looked across to the other wall. There was Daniel, good old Daniel, standing off the lions. The little boy liked Daniel. He liked David, too, with the trusty sling that landed a stone square on the forehead of Goliath. And Moses, with his rod and his big brass snake. They were winners--those three. He wondered if David could whip Jeffries. Samson could! Say, that would have been a fight!

But Jesus! Jesus was the "lamb of God." The little boy did not know what that meant, but it sounded like Mary's little lamb. Something for girls--sissified. Jesus was also "meek and lowly," a "man of sorrows and acquainted with grief." He went around for three years telling people not to do things.

Sunday was Jesus' day; it was wrong to feel comfortable or laugh on Sunday.

The little boy was glad when the superintendent thumped the bell and announced: "We will now sing the closing." One more bad hour was over. For one more week the little boy had got rid of Jesus.

Years went by and the boy grew up and became a business man.

He began to wonder about Jesus.

He said to himself: "Only strong magnetic men inspire great enthusiasm and build great organizations. Yet Jesus built the greatest organization of all. It is extraordinary."

The more sermons the man heard and the more books he read the more mystified he became.

One day he decided to wipe his mind clean of books and sermons.

He said, "I will read what the men who knew Jesus personally said about him. I will read about him as though he were a new historical character, about whom I had never heard anything at all."

The man was amazed.

A physical weakling! Where did they get that idea? Jesus pushed a plane and swung an adze; he was a successful carpenter. He slept outdoors and spent his days walking around his favorite lake. His muscles were so strong that when he drove the money-changers out, nobody dared to oppose him!

A kill-joy! He was the most popular dinner guest in Jerusalem! The criticism which proper people made was that he spent too much time with republicans and sinners (very good fellows, on the whole, the man thought) and enjoyed society too much. They called him a "wine bibber and a gluttonous man."

A failure! He picked up men from the bottom ranks of business and forged them into an organization that conquered the world.

When the man had finished his reading he exclaimed, "This is a man nobody knows."

"Some day," said he, "some one will write a book about Jesus. Every business man will read it and send it to his partners and his salesmen. For it will tell the story of the founder of modern business."

So the man waited for some one to write the book, but no one did. Instead, more books were published about the "lamb of God" who was weak and unhappy and glad to die.

The man became impatient. One day he said, "I believe I will try to write that book, myself."

And he did. . . .

HIS METHOD

Many leaders have dared to lay out ambitious programs, but this is the most daring of all:

"Go ye into all the world," Jesus said, "and preach the gospel to the whole creation."

Consider the sublime audacity of that command. To carry Roman civilization across the then known world had cost millions of lives and billions in treasure. To create any sort of reception for a new idea or product to-day involves a vast machinery of propaganda and expense. His organization was a tiny group of uneducated men, one of whom had already abandoned the cause as hopeless, deserting to the enemy. He had come proclaiming a Kingdom and was to end upon a cross; yet he dared to talk of conquering all creation. What was the source of his faith in that handful of followers? By what methods had he trained them? What had they learned from him of the secrets of influencing men?

We speak of the law of "supply and demand," but the words have got turned around. With anything which is not a basic necessity the supply always precedes the demand. Elias Howe invented the sewing machine, but it nearly rusted away before American women could be persuaded to use it. With their sewing finished so quickly what would they ever do with their spare time? Howe had vision, and had made his vision come true; but he could not sell! So his biographer paints a tragic picture--the man who had done more than any other in his generation to lighten the labor of women is forced to attend the funeral of the woman he loved in a borrowed suit of clothes! . . .

Surely no one will consider us lacking in reverence if we say that every one of the "principles of modern salesmanship" on

which businessmen so much pride themselves, are brilliantly
exemplified in Jesus' talk and work. The first of these and
perhaps the most important is the necessity for "putting yourself in step with your prospect." A great sales manager used
to illustrate it in this way:

> "When you want to get aboard a street car which is al-
> ready in motion, you don't run at it from right angles
> and try to make the platform in one wild leap," he
> would say. "If you do, you are likely to find your-
> self on the floor. No. You run along beside the car,
> increasing your pace until you are moving just as
> rapidly as it is moving and in the same direction.
> Then you step aboard easily, without danger or jolt.
>
> "The minds of busy men are in motion," he would con-
> tinue. "They are engaged with something very differ-
> ent from the thought you have to present. You can't
> jump directly at them and expect to make an effective
> landing. You must put yourself in the other man's
> place; try to imagine what he is thinking; let your
> first remark be in line with his thoughts; follow it
> by another with which you know he will easily agree.
> Thus, gradually, your two minds reach a point where
> they can join without conflict. You encourage him to
> say 'yes' and 'yes' and 'that's right' and 'I've
> noticed that myself,' until he says the final 'yes'
> which is your favorable decision."

Jesus taught all this without ever teaching it. Every one
of his conversations, every contact between his mind and
others, is worthy of the attentive study of any sales manager.
Passing along the shores of a lake one day, he saw two of the
men whom he wanted as disciples. *Their* minds were in motion;
their hands were busy with their nets; their conversation was
about conditions in the fishing trade, and the prospects of a
good market for the day's catch. To have broken in on such
thinking with the offer of employment as preachers of a new
religion would have been to confuse them and invite a certain
rebuff. What was Jesus' approach?

"Come with me," he said, "and I will make you fishers of men."

Fishers . . . that was a word they could understand . . . fishers of men . . . that was a new idea . . . what was he

driving at . . . fishers of men . . . it sounded interesting . . . well, what is it, anyway?

He sat on a hillside overlooking a fertile country. Many of the crowd who gathered around him were farmers, with their wives and sons and daughters. He wanted their interest and attention; it was important to make them understand, at the very outset, that what he had to say was nothing vague or theoretical but of direct and immediate application to their daily lives.

"A sower went forth to sow," he began, "and when he sowed some seeds fell by the wayside and the fowls came and devoured them up. . . ." Were they interested . . . <u>were</u> they? Every man of them had gone through that experience . . . the thievish crows . . . many a good day's work <u>they</u> had spoiled. . . . So this Teacher knew something about the troubles that farmers had to put up with, did he? Fair enough . . . let's hear what he has to say. . . .

I propose in this chapter to speak of the advertisements of Jesus which have survived for twenty centuries and are still the most potent influence in the world.

Let us begin by asking why he was so successful in mastering public attention and why, in contrast, his churches are less so? The answer is twofold. In the first place he recognized the basic principle that all good advertising is news. He was never trite or commonplace; he had no routine. If there had been newspapers in those days, no city editor could have said, "No need to visit him to-day; he will be doing just what he did last Sunday." Reporters would have followed him every single hour, for it was impossible to predict what he would say or do; every action and word were news.

The activity begins at sunrise. Jesus was an early riser; he knew that the simplest way to live <u>more</u> than an average life is to add an hour to the fresh end of the day. At sunrise, therefore, we discover a little boat pushing out from the shore of the lake. It makes its steady way across and deposits Jesus and his disciples in Capernaum, his favorite city. He proceeds at once to the house of a friend, but not without being discovered. The report spreads instantly that he is in town, and before he can finish breakfast a crowd has collected outside the gate--a poor palsied chap among them.

The day's work is at hand.

Having slept soundly in the open air he meets the call with quiet nerves. The smile that carried confidence into even the most hopeless heart spreads over his features; he stoops down toward the sufferer.

"Be of good cheer, my son," he cries, "your sins are all forgiven."

Sins forgiven! Indeed! The respectable members of the audience draw back with sharp disapproval. "What a blasphemous phrase," they exclaim. "Who authorized him to exercise the functions of God? What right has he to decide whose sins shall be forgiven?"

Jesus sensed rather than heard their protest. He never courted controversy but he never dodged it; and much of his fame arose out of the reports of his verbal victories. Men have been elected to office--even such high office as the Presidency-- by being so good-natured that they never made an enemy. But the leaders who are remembered are those who had plenty of critics and dealt with them vigorously.

"What's the objection?" he exclaimed, turning on the dissenters. "Why do you stand there and criticize? Is it easier to say, 'Thy sins be forgiven thee,' or to say, 'Arise, take up thy bed and walk?' The results are the same." Bending over the sick man again he said: "Arise, take up thy bed and go unto thine house."

The man stirred and was amazed to find that his muscles responded. Slowly, doubtingly he struggled to his feet, and with one great shout of happiness started off, surrounded by his jubilant friends. The critics had received their answer, but they refused to give up. For an hour or more they persisted in angry argument, until the meeting ended in a tumult.

Can you imagine the next day's issue of the Capernaum News, if there had been one?

PALSIED MAN HEALED
JESUS OF NAZARETH CLAIMS RIGHT TO FORGIVE SINS
PROMINENT SCRIBES OBJECT
"BLASPHEMOUS," SAYS LEADING CITIZEN.

"BUT ANYWAY I CAN WALK," HEALED MAN RETORTS.

Front page story number one and the day is still young.

One of those who had been attracted by the excitement was a taxcollector named Matthew. Being a man of business he could not stay through the argument, but slipped away early and was hard at work when Jesus passed by a few minutes before noon.

"Matthew, I want you," said Jesus.

That was all. No argument; no offer of inducements; no promise of rewards. Merely "I want you"; and the prosperous taxcollector closed his office, made a feast for the brilliant young teacher and forthwith announced himself a disciple. . . .

He was advertised by his service, not by his sermons; this is the second noteworthy fact. Nowhere in the Gospels do you find it announced that:

> Jesus of Nazareth Will Denounce
> The Scribes and Pharisees in the
> Central Synagogue
> To-night at Eight O'Clock
> Special Music

His preaching was almost incidental. On only one occasion did he deliver a long discourse, and that probably interrupted often by questions and debates. He did not come to establish a theology but to lead a life. Living more healthfully than any of his contemporaries he spread health wherever he went. Thinking more daringly, more divinely, he expressed himself in thoughts of surpassing beauty, as naturally as a plant bursts into bloom. His sermons, if they may be called sermons, were chiefly explanatory of his service. He healed a lame man, gave sight to a blind man, fed the hungry, cheered the poor; and by these works he was advertised much more than by his words. . . .

These are Jesus' works, done in Jesus' name. If he were to live again, in these modern days, he would find a way to make them known--to be advertised by his service, not merely by his sermons. One thing is certain: he would not neglect the market-place. . . .

The present day market-place is the newspaper and the magazine. Printed columns are the modern thoroughfares; published advertisements are the cross-roads where the sellers and the buyers meet. Any issue of a national magazine is a world's fair, a bazaar filled with the products of the world's work. Clothes and clocks and candle-sticks; soup and soap and cigarettes; lingerie and limousines--the best of all of them are there, proclaimed by their makers in persuasive tones. That every other voice should be raised in such great market-places, and the voice of Jesus of Nazareth be still--this is a vital omission which he would find a way to correct. He would be a national advertiser today, I am sure, as he was the great advertiser of his own day. . . .

THE FOUNDER OF MODERN BUSINESS

When Jesus was twelve years old his father and mother took him to the Feast at Jerusalem.

It was the big national vacation; even peasant families saved their pennies and looked forward to it through the year. Towns like Nazareth were emptied of their inhabitants except for the few old folks who were left behind to look after the very young ones. Crowds of cheerful pilgrims filled the highways, laughing their way across the hills and under the stars at night.

In such a mass of folk it was not surprising that a boy of twelve should be lost. When Mary and Joseph missed him on the homeward trip, they took it calmly and began a search among the relatives.

The inquiry produced no result. Some remembered having seen him in the Temple, but no one had seen him since. Mary grew frightened: Where could he be? Back there in the city alone? Wandering hungry and tired through the friendless streets? Carried away by other travelers into a distant country? She pictured a hundred calamities. Nervously she and Joseph hurried back over the hot roads, through the suburbs, up through the narrow city streets, up to the courts of the Temple itself.

And there he was.

Not lost; not a bit worried. Apparently unconscious that the Feast was over, he sat in the midst of a group of old men, who were tossing questions at him and applauding the shrewd common sense of his replies. Involuntarily his parents halted--they were simple folk, uneasy among strangers and disheveled by their haste. But after all they were his parents, and a very human feeling of irritation quickly overcame their diffidence. Mary stepped forward and grasped his arm.

"Son, why hast thou thus dealt with us?" she demanded. "Behold they father and I have sought thee sorrowing."

I wonder what answer she expected to receive. Did she ever know exactly what he was going to say: did any one in Nazareth quite understand this keen, eager lad, who had such curious moments of abstraction and was forever breaking out with remarks that seemed so far beyond his years?

He spoke to her now with deference, as always, but in words that did not dispel but rather added to her uncertainty.

"How is it that ye sought me?" he asked. "Wist ye not that I must be about my father's business? . . .

What interests us most in this one recorded incident of his boyhood is the fact that for the first time he defined the purpose of his career. He did not say, "Wist ye not that I must get ready to meet the arguments of men like these?" The language was quite different, and well worth remembering. "Wist ye not that I must be about my father's business?" he said. He thought of his life as business. What did he mean by business? To what extent are the principles by which he conducted his business applicable to ours? And if he were among us again, in our highly competitive world, would his business philosophy work?

One on occasion, you recall, he stated his recipe for success. It was on the afternoon when James and John came to ask him what promotion they might expect. They were two of the most energetic of the lot called "Sons of Thunder," by the rest, being noisy and always in the midst of some sort of a storm. They had joined the ranks because they liked him, but with no very definite idea of what it was all about; and now they wanted to know where the enterprise was heading, and just what there would be in it for them.

"Master," they said, "we want to ask what plans you have in

mind for us. You're going to need big men around you when
you establish your kingdom; our ambition is to sit on either
side of you, one on your right and the other on your left."

Who can object to that attitude? If a man fails to look after
himself, certainly no one will look after him. If you want a
big place, go ask for it. That's the way to get ahead.

Jesus answered with a sentence which sounds poetically absurd.

"Whosoever will be great among you, shall be your minister,"
he said, "and whosoever of you will be the chiefest, shall be
the servant of all."

A fine piece of rhetoric, now isn't it? Be a good servant
and you will be great; be the best possible servant and you
will occupy the highest possible place. Nice idealistic talk
but utterly impractical; nothing to take seriously in a common
sense world. That is just what men thought for some hundreds
of years; and then, quite suddenly, Business woke up to a
great discovery. You will hear that discovery proclaimed in
every sales convention as something distinctly modern and up
to date. It is emblazoned in the advertising pages of every
magazine. . . .

The World's Most Famous Court Trial: Tennessee Evolution Case

More commonly known as the "monkey trial" the Scopes trial in 1925 was a test case that involved the public school teaching of evolution. When first-year high school teacher John Scopes was indicted for teaching evolution in violation of Tennessee's Butler Act, the case gained national publicity when the famous trial lawyer Clarence Darrow and the American Civil Liberties Union represented Scopes. Across the court aisle providing special counsel to the prosecution was William Jennings Bryan, who was making his last public appearance before his death which came a few days after the completion of the trial. The court found Scopes guilty of the charges, but the State Supreme Court of Tennessee rejected its findings on a technicality. The following transcript excerpt is found in The World's Most Famous Court Trial: Tennessee Evolution Case (Cincinnati: National Book Company, 1925). Why did Mr. Darrow and his associates want to get Mr. Bryan to say that the world was created before 4004 B.C.? Why did Darrow seek to have Bryan concede that the says of creation were not twenty-four-hour days? How would you characterize the level of the dialogue between Darrow and Bryan?

    Q--You have given considerable study to the Bible, haven't you, Mr. Bryan?
    A--Yes, sir, I have tried to.
    Q--Well, we all know you have, we are not going to dispute that at all. But you have written and published articles almost weekly, and sometimes made interpretations of various things.
    A--I would not say interpretations, Mr. Darrow, but comments on the lesson.
    Q--If you comment to any extent these comments have been interpretations.
    A--I presume that my discussion might be to some extent interpretations, but they have not been primarily intended as interpretations.
    Q--But you have studied that question, of course?
    A--Of what?
    Q--Interpretation of the Bible.
    A--On this particular question?
    Q--Yes, sir.
    A--Yes, sir.

Q--Then you have made a general study of it.

A--Yes, I have: I have studied the Bible for about fifty years, or sometime more than that, but, of course, I have studied it more as I have become older than when I was but a boy.

Q--Do you claim that everything in the Bible should be literally interpreted?

A--I believe everything in the Bible should be accepted as it is given there; some of the Bible is given illustratively. For instance: "Ye are the salt of the earth." I would not insist that man was actually salt, or that he had flesh of salt, but it is used in the sense of salt as saving God's people. . . .

The Witness--These gentlemen have not had much chance--they did not come here to try this case. They came here to try revealed religion. I am here to defend it, and they can ask me any question they please.

The Court--All right.

(Applause from the court yard.)

Mr. Darrow--Great applause from the bleachers.

The Witness--From those whom you call "yokels."

Mr. Darrow--I have never called them yokels.

The Witness--That is the ignorance of Tennessee, the bigotry.

Mr. Darrow--You mean who are applauding you?

The Witness--Those are the people whom you insult.

Mr. Darrow--You insult every man of science and learning in the world because he does not believe in your fool religion.

The Court--I will not stand for that.

Mr. Darrow--For what he is doing?

The Court--I am talking to both of you.

Gen. Stewart--This has gone beyond the pale of a lawsuit, your honor. I have a public duty to perform, under my oath and I ask the court to stop it. Mr. Darrow is making an effort to insult the gentleman on the witness stand, and I ask that it be stopped, for it has gone beyond the pale of a lawsuit. . . .

Q--But when you read that Jonah swallowed the whale--or that the whale swallowed Jonah--how do you literally interpret that?

A--When I read that a big fish swallowed Jonah--it does not say whale.

Q--Doesn't it? Are you sure?

A—That is my recollection of it. A big fish, and I believe it, and I believe in a God who can make a whale and can make a man and make both to do what He pleases.

Q—Mr. Bryan, doesn't the New Testament say whale?
A—I am not sure. My impression is that it says fish; but it does not make so much difference; I merely called your attention to where it says fish—it does not say whale.
Q—But in the New Testament it says whale, doesn't it?
A—That may be true; I cannot remember in my own mind what I read about it.
Q—Now, you say, the big fish swallowed Jonah, and he there remained how long—three days—and then he spewed him upon the land. You believe that the big fish was made to swallow Jonah?
A—I am not prepared to say that; the Bible merely says it was done.
Q—You don't know whether it was the ordinary run of fish, or made for that purpose?
A—You may guess; you evolutionists guess.
Q—But when we do guess, we have a sense to guess right.
A—But do not do it often.
Q—You are not prepared to say whether that fish was made especially to swallow a man or not?
A—The Bible doesn't say, so I am not prepared to say.
Q—You don't know whether that was fixed up especially for the purpose.
A—No, the Bible doesn't say.
Q—But do you believe He made them—that He made such a fish and that it was big enough to swallow Jonah?
A—Yes, sir. Let me add: One miracle is just as easy to believe as another.
Q—It is for me.
A—It is for me.
Q—Just as hard?
A—It is hard to believe for you, but easy for me. A miracle is a thing performed beyond what man can perform. When you get within the realm of miracles; and it is just as easy to believe the miracle of Jonah as any other miracle in the Bible.
Q—Perfectly easy to believe that Jonah swallowed the whale?
A—If the Bible said so; the Bible doesn't make as extreme statements as evolutionists do.
Mr. Darrow—That may be a question, Mr. Bryan, about

some of those you have known?

A—The only thing is, you have a definition of fact that includes imagination.

Q—And you have a definition that excludes everything but imagination, everything but imagination?

Gen. Stewart—I object to that as argumentative.

The Witness—You. . . .

Mr. Darrow—The Witness must not argue with me, either.

Q—Do you consider the story of Jonah and the whale a miracle?

A—I think it is. . . .

Q—What do you think?

A—I do not think about things I don't think about.

Q—Do you think about things you do think about?

A—Well, sometimes.

(Laughter in the courtyard.)

The Policeman—Let us have order. . . .

Q—Do you think the earth was made in six days?

A—Not six days of twenty-four days.

Q—Doesn't it say so?

Gen. Stewart—I want to interpose another objection. What is the purpose of this examination?

Mr. Bryan—The purpose is to cast ridicule on everybody who believes in the Bible, and I am perfectly willing that the world shall know that these gentlemen have no other purpose than ridiculing every Christian who believes in the Bible.

Mr. Darrow—We have the purpose of preventing bigots and ignoramuses from controlling the education of the United States and you know it, and that is all.

Mr. Bryan—I am glad to bring out that statement. I want the world to know that this evidence is not for the view Mr. Darrow and his associates have filed affidavits here stating, the purposes of which I understand it, is to show that the Bible story is not true.

Mr. Malone—Mr. Bryan seems anxious to get some evidence in the record that would tend to show that those affidavits are not true.

Mr. Bryan—I am not trying to get anything into the record. I am simply trying to protect the word of God against the greatest atheist or agnostic in the United States. (Prolonged applause.) I want the papers to know I am not afraid to get on the stand in front of him and let him do his worst. I want the world to know. (Prolonged applause.)

Mr. Darrow—I wish I could get a picture of these clackers.

Gen. Stewart—I am not afraid of Mr. Bryan being perfectly able to take care of himself, but this examination cannot be a legal examination and it cannot be worth a thing in the world, and, your honor, I respectfully except to it, and call on your honor, in the name of all that it legal, to stop this examination and stop it here.

Mr. Hays—I rather sympathize with the general, but Mr. Bryan is produced as a witness because he is a student of the Bible and he presumably understands what the Bible means. He is one of the foremost students in the United States, and we hope to show Mr. Bryan, who is a student of the Bible, what the Bible really means in connection with evolution. Mr. Bryan has already stated that the world is not merely 6,000 years old and that is very helpful to us, and where your evidence is coming from, this Bible which goes to the jury, is that the world started in 4004 B.C.

Mr. Bryan—You think the Bible says that?

Mr. Hays—The one you have taken in evidence says that.

Mr. Bryan—I don't concede that it does.

Mr. Hays—You know that that chronology is made up by adding together the ages of the people in the Bible, counting their ages; and now then, let us show the next stage from a Bible student, that these things are not to be taken literally, but each man is entitled to his own interpretation.

Gen. Stewart—The court makes the interpretation.

Mr. Hays—But the court is entitled to information on what is the interpretation of an expert Bible student.

Gen. Stewart—This is resulting in a harangue and nothing else.

Mr. Darrow—I didn't do any of the haranging; Mr. Bryan has been doing that.

Gen. Stewart—You know absolutely you have done it.

Mr. Darrow—Oh, all right.

Mr. Malone—Mr. Bryan doesn't need any support.

Gen. Stewart—Certainly he doesn't need any support, but I am doing what I conceive my duty to be, and I don't need any advice, if you please, sir. (Applause.)

The Court—That would be irrelevant testimony if it was going to the jury. Of course, it is excluded from the jury on the point it is not competent testimony, on the same ground as the affidaviting.

Mr. Hicks—Your honor, let me say a word right there. It is in the discretion of the court how long you will allow them to question witnesses for the purpose of taking testimony to the supreme court. Now, we as taxpayers of this county, feel that this has gone beyond reason.

The Court--Well, now, that taxpayers' concern doesn't appeal to me so much, when it is only fifteen or twenty minutes time.

Mr. Darrow--I would have been through in a half-hour if Mr. Bryan had answered my questions.

Gen. Stewart--They want to put in affidavits as what other witnesses would swear, why not let them put in affidavits as to what Mr. Bryan would swear?

Mr. Bryan--God forbid.

Mr. Malone--I will just make this suggestion. . .

Gen. Stewart--It is not worth anything to them, if your honor please, even for the record in the supreme court.

Mr. Hays--Is not it worth anything to us if Mr. Bryan will accept the story of creation in detail, and if Mr. Bryan, as a Bible student states you cannot take the Bible necessarily as literally true?

Mr. Stewart--The Bible speaks for itself.

Mr. Hays--You mean to say the Bible itself tells whether these are parables? Does it?

Gen. Stewart--We have left all annals of procedure behind. This is an harangue between Col. Darrow and his witness. He makes so many statements that he is forced to defend himself.

Mr. Darrow--I do not do that.

Gen. Stewart--I except to that as not pertinent to this lawsuit.

The Court--Of course, it is not pertinent, or it would be before the jury.

Gen. Stewart--It is not worth anything before a jury.

The Court--Are you about through, Mr. Darrow?

Mr. Darrow--I want to ask a few more questions about the creation.

The Court--I know. We are going to adjourn when Mr. Bryan comes off the stand for the day. Be very brief, Mr. Darrow. Of course, I believe I will make myself clearer. Of course, it is incompetent testimony before the jury. The only reason I am allowing this to go in at all is that they may have it in the appellate courts, as showing what the affidavit would be.

Mr. Bryan--The reason I am answering is not for the benefit of the superior court. It is to keep these gentlemen from saying I was afraid to meet them and let them question me, and I want the Christian world to know that any atheist, agnostic, unbeliever, can question me any time as to my belief in God, and I will answer him.

Mr. Darrow--I want to take an exception to this conduct of this witness. He may be very popular down here in the hills. I do not need his explanation for his answer.

The Court--Yes.

Mr. Bryan--If I had not, I would not have answered the question.

Mr. Hays--May I be heard? I do not want your honor to think we are asking questions of Mr. Bryan with the expectation that the higher court will not say that those questions are proper testimony. The reason I state that is this, your law speaks for the Bible. Your law does not say the literal interpretation of the Bible. If Mr. Bryan, who is a student of the Bible, will state that everything in the Bible need not be interpreted literally, that each man must judge for himself; if he will state that, of course, then your honor would charge the jury. We are not bound by a literal interpretation of the Bible. If I have made my argument clear enough for the attorney-general to understand, I will retire.

Gen. Stewart--I will admit you have frequently been difficult of comprehension, and I think you are as much to blame as I am.

Mr. Hays--I know I am. . . .

Q--Mr. Bryan, do you believe that the first woman was Eve?
A--Yes.
Q--Do you believe she was literally made out of Adam's rib?
A--I do.
Q--Did you ever discover where Cain got his wife?
A--No sir; I leave the agnostics to hunt for her.
Q--You have never found out?
A--I have never tried to find.
Q--You have never tried to find?
A--No.
Q--The Bible says he got one, doesn't it? Were there other people on the earth at that time?
A--I cannot say.
Q--You cannot say. Did that ever enter your consideration?
A--Never bothered me.
Q--There are no others recorded, but Cain got a wife.
A--That is what the Bible says.
Q--Where she came from you do not know. All right. Does

the statement, "The morning and the evening were the first day," and "The morning and the evening were the second day," mean anything to you?

A--I do not think it necessarily means a twenty-four-hour day.

Q--You do not?

A--No.

Q--What do you consider it to be?

A--I have not attempted to explain it. If you will take the second chapter--let me have the book. (Examining Bible.) The fourth verse of the second chapter says: "These are the generation of the heavens and of the earth, when they were created in the day that the Lord God made the earth and the heavens," the word "day" there in the very next chapter is used to describe a period. I do not see that there is any necessity for construing the words, "the evening and the morning," as meaning necessarily a twenty-four-hour day, "in the day when the Lord made the heaven and the earth."

Q--Then, when the Bible said, for instance, "and God called the firmament heaven. And the evening and the morning were the second day," that does not necessarily mean twenty-four hours?

A--I do not think it necessarily does.

Q--Do you think it does or does not?

A--I know a great many think so.

Q--What do you think?

A--I do not think it does.

Q--You think those were not literal days?

A--I do not think they were twenty-four-hour days.

Q--What do you think about it?

A--That is my opinion--I do not know that my opinion is better on that subject than those who think it does.

Q--You do not think that?

A--No. But I think it would be just as easy for the kind of God we believe in to make the earth in six days as in six years or in 6,000,000 years or in 600,000,000 years. I do not think it important whether we believe one or the other.

Q--Do you think those were literal days?

A--My impression is they were periods, but I would not attempt to argue as against anybody who wanted to believe in literal days.

Q--Have you any idea of the length of the periods?

A--No; I don't.

Q--Do you think the sun was made on the fourth day?

A--Yes.

Q—And they had evening and morning without the sun?
A—I am simply saying it is a period.
Q—They had evening and morning for four periods without the sun, do you think?
A—I believe in creation as there told, and if I am not able to explain it I will accept it. Then you can explain it to suit yourself.
Q—Mr. Bryan, what I want to know is, do you believe the sun was made on the fourth day?
A—I believe just as it says there. . . .

Up to Now

ALFRED E. SMITH

Alfred E. Smith (1873-1944), a native of New York City, began his political career in 1903 with his election to the state assembly. In 1918 he was elected governor of New York. After his defeat for the same office in 1920, he was re-elected in 1922, 1924, and 1926. His terms as governor were notable for progressive social legislation in the areas of education, hospitals, and workmen's compensation. His opposition to prohibition, along with his distinction as the first Catholic ever nominated for the United States presidency, contributed significantly to his overwhelming defeat by Herbert Hoover in the 1928 election. As the following selection illustrates, his Catholicism was the subject of much debate during the 1928 campaign. The excerpt reprinted here by permission of Viking Penguin Inc. is from pages 366-69 of

Up to Now, copyrighted in 1928 by Alfred E. Smith, and renewed in 1957 by Walter J. Smith. Apparently what was the concern of the Marshall letter, and how did Smith answer the charges contained in the letter?

Immediately following the election of 1926 it was apparent at Albany that a nation-wide interest in me was developing. This was evidenced by personal visitors from other states and by the enormous volune of letters, printed circulars and inquiries that poured into Albany. By 1927 correspondence and requests for interviews had grown to such volume that I did not believe that the state employees should be taxed with the care and consideration of them. Accordingly, I permitted the organization of an unofficial volunteer committee of personal friends in New York City to assort and answer as best they could the great volume of correspondence that came in day after day.

The trend of public thought in America began to take shape in May of 1927 when the Atlantic Monthly published an open letter from Charles C. Marshall, who to my way of thinking challenged the fundamental declaration contained in the United States constitution guaranteeing the right of citizens of the United States to freedom of religious belief. The appearance in the public prints of the Marshall letter was a warning of what would have to be met later and what would unquestionably become a campaign issue in the event of my nomination for the presidency. My reply printed in the same publication a month later brought a new volume of mail to the Albany post office that taxed it to the utmost of its capacity.

My correspondence indicated to me that the Marshall letter came as something of a shock to thoughtful people throughout the country. Here was the first time in our history that the qualifications of a man for public office were openly challenged because of his adherence to a particular religious belief. During our national existence we have prided ourselves upon our accepted declaration of political faith that no man was to be questioned because of the church he attended in the worship of God. Small-fry politicians may have used such tactics and they undoubtedly did under cover, and conducted "whispering campaigns." But the Marshall letter brought the religious question into the open, printed as it was in one of the most reputable magazines published in this country.

I saw a copy of this letter in galley from before the publication of the magazine, and after consultation with a number of advisers I promptly determined to make open answer to it and to publish my reply in the same magazine. I gave the reply no title, but the publishers of the magazine entitled it "Alfred E. Smith, Catholic and Patriot, Replies."

The Marshall letter raised questions of theology. At no time in my life have I ever pretended any fundamental knowledge of this subject and in the preparation of my reply I was assisted by Father Francis J. Duffy, chaplain of the 69th Regiment and at one time professor of theology. I was also most ably assisted by Justice Joseph M. Proskauer. So far as the fundamental principles contained in the reply had to do with the relationship of the Church and the State I had but my own experience to draw upon and I was reasonably sure that I was on solid ground. Nothing that has happened since has refuted a single line contained in that reply. Nothing in it has ever been successfully challenged and that observation does not come to me from people of my own faith alone. It comes generally from fair-minded, reasonable, liberal and intelligent people. The last section of my reply to Mr. Marshall summarizes the whole contents. It says:

> I summarize my creed as an American Catholic. I believe in the worship of God according to the faith and practice of the Roman Catholic Church. I recognize no power in the institution of my Church to interfere with the operations of the Constitution of the United States or the enforcement of the law of the land. I believe in absolute freedom of conscience for all men and in equality of all churches, all sects, and all beliefs before the law as a matter or right and not as a matter of favor. I believe in the absolute separation of Church and State and in the strict enforcement of the provisions of the Constitution that Congress shall make no law respecting an establishment of religion or prohibiting the free exercise thereof. I believe that no tribunal of any church has any power to make any decree of any

force in the law of the land, other than to establish the status of its own communicants within its own church. I believe in the support of the public school as one of the corner-stones of American liberty. I believe in the right of every parent to choose whether his child shall be educated in the public school or in a religious school supported by those of his own faith. I believe in the principle of non-interference by this country in the internal affairs of other nations and that we should stand steadfastly against any such interference by whomsoever it may be urged. And I believe in the common brotherhood of man under the common fatherhood of God.

In this spirit I join with fellow Americans of all creeds in a fervent prayer that never again in this land will any public servant be challenged because of the faith in which he has tried to walk humbly with his God.

The year 1928 bid fair to be historical in my lifetime. I clung steadfastly to my determination not to let any future happening no matter of how much moment interfere with the duties of the position to which I had been elected. I began anew on the first Wednesday of January my last battle for the progressive reforms for which I had worked throughout. When I penned my annual message to the legislature of 1928 I fully realized that it would be the last document of its kind to be signed by me, because whether I was nominated for president or not I had definitely determined to retire from the office of governor.

RELIGION IN THE AGE OF DEPRESSION

15

A Christian Manifesto

EDWIN LEWIS

Edwin Lewis (1881-1959) was born in England and educated in Canada, Scotland, and the United States. From 1918 to 1951 he was professor of systematic theology and philosophy of religion at Drew Theological Seminary in Madison, New Jersey. Upon his retirement from Drew, he taught for a time at Temple University in Philadelphia. In the late 1920's while he was editing the Abingdon Bible Commentary, Lewis changed his own understanding of the Christian faith. He moved from modern liberalism to neo-orthodoxy, and in the process acknowledged the extensive influence of Karl Barth. In his best known book, A Christian Manifesto, he describes his rejection of his former liberalism and criticizes the church, especially his own Methodist Episcopal Church, for abandoning the heart of the gospel and becoming too involved in the world. Like other spokesmen of neo-orthodoxy, however, he did not reject the social gospel or modern science. The following excerpt is taken from A Christian Manifesto (New York: Abingdon Press, 1934), pp. 9-10, 196-204. Copyright renewal in 1961 by Olin A. Lewis. Used by permission of the publisher, Abingdon Press. Why does Lewis warn church leaders concerning their tendency to adopt "business methods" in conducting the affairs of the churches? What wrong directions did he believe the church had taken in the previous twenty years? Writing in 1934, what did Lewis see in the church that he believed needed to be corrected?

Foreward

In the fall number, 1933, of <u>Religion in Life</u>, I published an article entitled "The Fatal Apostasy of the Modern Church." The article attracted a good deal of attention, if I may judge by the correspondence arising from it. Most of the letters I received expressed gratitude for the position I took in the article. A considerable number, however, were definitely hostile (the word is not too strong). I was told that I had evidently "gone Barthian," that I had "sold out to the Fundamentalists," that I had "abandoned my own cause," that clearly I had "passed my creative period and was becoming senile and conservative," and so on. I was reminded of certain books I had written, and of the theological position which those books were generally supposed to represent, and I was asked if I desired to be regarded as a man who had "slipped back into orthodoxy."

Nobody enjoys criticism of this kind, especially when it comes, as much of it did, from loyal friends whose affection one would wish to keep. But some things cannot but be as they are, and some steps are taken not of choice but of necessity. Consistency is always a consideration, but consistency may come too high. The intellectual record is far less important than the moral record, and it may be that the first must be marred to keep the second intact.

Many who read the article referred to above urged me to elaborate it into a book. I was loath to do so, partly because I was conscious of the ferment in my own mind, and partly because I realized how sharply the implications of the article cut across much of the accepted thinking of the time. The hesitation, however, had the curious result of clarifying my own mind at the very points where I had been most uncertain, and when that had taken place, the natural shrinking from what I know is inevitable criticism largely disappeared, and I wrote the book. Because the book is intended primarily as "A Christian Manifesto," I have tried to keep it free from the usual paraphernalia of mere scholarship. In the first half of the book, however, it seemed impossible to avoid some discussion of certain rather technical questions raised by modern criticism. I have tried to keep the discussion of them as simple as possible.

Just as I was finishing the book, one day, after a class in which I had been saying some of the things here written, a student came to me and said, "Professor, I think that something has happened lately deep down inside of you." I did not deny it. The real question is as to the _meaning_ of what "happened."

Chapter IX: The Great Tribulation

Our age prides itself on being pragmatic. It burns its incense at the shrine of the great god "Results." It has surrendered to the guidance of the efficiency expert, and the basic principle of the efficiency expert seems to be that nothing is justifiable which cannot show a definite, tangible, measurable result. Action for the joy of the action, emotion for the sake of the emotion, belief for the satisfaction it yields, life as an end in itself—in many quarters these are all tabooed. Apparently, the only reason for your existence is that you might "bring things to pass." You must count that day wasted on which you have not "done things," and the "things" to be "done" are such as can be put down in black and white, entered in a ledger, where they may be seen by the eyes of all. The measuring rod could well enough be chosen for the symbol of the age in which we live: perhaps it will be done for us by some future historian. State policies, educational practice, economic readjustments, social schemes of all sorts, are to be judged exclusively by how well they conform to a neatly turned pragmatic yardstick. The whole of life is to be regimented. The individual is to be as "totalitarianized" as the state. The goose step is to be universalized—and the race will then be a flock of geese! Somebody is to say "Go!" and we are all to move in a prearranged way to a prearranged position, having reached which we are again to move when the same somebody is once more moved to say "Go!" Spontaneity is to be abolished. Individuality is to be penalized. Qualities just as these interfere with the precision of the social machine. A straight line is the shortest distance between two points, and the most efficient man is the man who can travel that shortest distance in the least time. It matters not that he is so intent on reaching his goal that he has never a moment on the way for beautiful sights and melodious sounds. Even our homes, we are told, are to be built on the straight-line principle, architecturally and every other way. Slough off the superfluous! Do away with unnecessary movements! It never seems to occur to the reformers that since the time and energy that are "saved" by their devices are only saved so that still other "things" may be "done," more bridge may be played, more radio buttons may be turned, the alleged "gains" may prove in the end to be of very doubtful advantage. A man does to-day in two hours what called yesterday for four hours--and we name that "progress." It may be that or it may not. What does he do with the two hours he has "saved?" If he uses them for "increased productivity" of what nobody wants or can buy, or if he adds them to his "leisure" which he does not know how to use, of what advantage is the saving? It is infinitely more important that a man should be enabled to find joy of his work than it is that he should ever be seeking to lessen the amount of it. It is infinitely more important that ways should be devised whereby the conditions under which work is done should be agreeable than it is that ways should be devised in the name of "efficiency" for getting out of a man every last bit of productivity of which he is capable. In a word, it is infinitely more important that life should be judged by the satisfactions that accompany it and that these satisfactions be of the kind that are lasting, than it is that life should be judge by its "measurable output"--measurable because of the value it has in the exchange markets of the world.

Under the leadership of "practical" men, this utilitarian and efficiency philosophy has laid hold upon the modern church. Anyone who knows what has been going on in American Protestantism during the last twenty years or so knows that too many of its leaders have conceived the church as exclusively an "organization" to be "run" according to the most approved "business methods." I am far from suggesting that the conducting of the affairs of the church does not call for common sense. Where property and funds and social obligations of various sorts are involved, it goes without saying that there should be the most scrupulous care in their use and administration! Carelessness is none the less blamable because it is connected with the corporate aspects of religion: If anything, it is the more blamable. Nevertheless, when it is supposed--as it has been--that the cultivation and propagation of religious faith calls for the same methods that are employed by "men of the world" as they seek their ends, then religion is given an almost fatal blow. If there is one thing more than another that religion needs to do in our time, it is to bear witness to another side of life and to another form of reality than that side of life and that form of reality which is present to men at almost every moment of their secular pursuits. Yet what have we seen happening but the attempt of religion to "talk the language of the street?" Without question, religion should make every possible effort to win the hearing of men, but when "a religious talk" (an impossible phrase!) is couched in the same language as "a sales talk," it is only natural that the audience should suppose that the speaker is trying to "sell something." Indeed, of all the abominations that have entered the vocabulary of modern religious propaganda, incomparably the worst is the expression that "the church is in the business of selling religion." Religion--at least, Christianity--ought to be the one thing in all the world which should be kept free from the suggestion of the market place: which, by the way, is very far from saying that religion is to be kept out of business. Only, you do not necessarily get religion into business simply by teaching religion to talk business jargon. Do you "sell" the music of the spheres, or "buy" the beauties of "rosy-fingered dawn"? It is true that you may need to be taught how to appreciate these great free gifts of God to his creatures, but to "buy" them or to "sell" them--no! The church is confronted with a task incredibly great in bringing the appeal of religion to bear upon an age such as ours; but if the church thinks that because the age is "business-minded" and "pragmatic," the message of religion must be couched in business terms and its appeal be based on pragmatic considerations, and that the success of the church is to be judged by an auditing committee, then the church is surely sounding its own death-knell.

I would not presume to be critical of the church in general as respects matters such as these, but I may perhaps be conceded the right to speak frankly of the particular church to which I belong. Concerning that church at least, I am sure

I am not wrong when I say that we have too generally abandoned the passion which was once our glory and which had no great difficulty in finding appropriate avenues of expression: we have abandoned the passion for carefully worked-out programs which had "efficiency" written all over them, but which have been strangely futile in deeping the fires burning on the altars of the church and in bringing the gospel to bear in an overwhelming way on the life of the world. I have what I believe is a justly grounded pride in the history and achievements of Methodism, the church in which I was cradled and to which I have given my life. It has written a great chapter in the story of Christian conquest. It has done a work for Jesus Christ second to none done by any other branch of Protestantism. In the Old World and in the New, and in the lands beyond the seas, it has borne a valiant and successful testimony of the power of the Evangel in the transformation of human lives and in the creation of social institutions which seek the good of men. It can be only a question of time before the Methodist Church as such must cease to exist as a separate entity and be gathered up into a reunited Protestantism--dare one say even a reunited Christendom? But its contribution when that day comes will be of value in proportion to its continued loyalty to the spirit and the faith and the purpose in which it had its origin. And what we have seen in recent years all along the line has been a weakening of that loyalty because we have fallen victim to the lure of grandiose schemes whose counterparts in the secular world are the hundred story skyscraper, the vast corporation whose energies head up at the cash register, the advertising "drive" aimed to reach "the last man" by whatever means may be. Anyone who knows the life of our church for the last twenty years or so knows that under the goading of the "experts" we have adopted scheme after scheme, participated in drive after drive, set ourselves even the impossible task of making America "dry" by legislation, and the total result of the prodigious efforts--what is it? That there is some gain in the total need not be denied, but there has certainly been much more of loss. We have created in the minds of many a totally false conception of nature and the function of the Christian Church. We have laid financial and property burdens on the backs of our people that either altogether discourage them or demand so much of their time and energy that little is left for active and aggressive and constructive Christian work. We have built churches that we can neither pay for nor adequately man. We have thrown out a missionary

line so long that it lacks depth and striking power, and so
detached from sacrificial support at home that its chief
occupation in recent years has been conducting strategic re-
treats. We have incurred the distrust, even the antagonism,
of great numbers of people in America because we have suffered
the machinery of the church to be operated for ends which,
while moral in themselves, were foolishly made contingent on
political action. It is questionable whether even yet we have
learned our lesson, for if it was an error to commit the
church to legislative Prohibition, it is equally an error to
commit it to legislative Socialism. "A bigger and better
Church" had been our slogan, but let those who know the truth
tell, if they dare, what we meant by "bigger" and what we
meant by "better." We borrowed our criteria of evaluation
from the world about us--a world gone mad in its worship of
mere size, a world that had set itself to create bigger ships,
bigger aeroplanes, bigger locomotives, bigger buildings, big-
ger universities, bigger corporations, bigger banks, bigger
everything--except men! It will be well if the monstrous
Frankenstein does not yet turn and rend us. And we were
guilty of the incredible folly of supposing that "Christ's
church was of this world," to be judged by the world's standards, to be modeled on the world's ways, to walk in the
world's procession, and to keep step to the crashing discord
of its brazen shawms. The result could not be but what it
has been. We have seen the bursting of the inflated bubble
into which a mad world poured its lungs. The huge thing was
mostly air--and the church may be grateful if it has escaped
going so completely flat as the world it sought to imitate.

You will say that this is nothing but rhetorical pessimism.
Nevertheless look about you. In a time like this, the church
which ought to be as a lion rampant is as a lion supine--
supine because an enemy has it by the throat. The enemy is
naturalism, or if you prefer the more recent term, secularism,
which is but a new name for an ancient foe. Not once nor
twice in the long history of the church has that enemy threatened it, but it is to be questioned if ever before the threat
was so menacing, the peril so deadly. What makes the peril
so deadly is the fact that the supineness of the church today
comes rather of a weakening from within than because of an
overpowering force from without. The church can never be
overthrown save as it abandons its own natural defense, which
is the faith once received. Let it keep that, and the gates
of hell cannot prevail against it. Let it surrender that,

and it puts itself in competition with a secular spirit before which it is as impotent as a new-born babe before a pack of wolves. Are there not signs that to a very considerable extent the church has made that surrender? There has been a chiseling of the ancient faith; wherefore the defenses of the church are weakening, and wild beasts beginning to trample over the erstwhile pleasant vineyard of the Lord.

Why the surrender? Because as a church we listened too readily to those who assured us that unless we spoke a new language the world would not heed our message. We were told that we had come into a new age--a fact which nobody would want to deny. We were told that therefore we must cut our garment according to the cloth, which turns out to have been only another way of saying that before we delivered our message we were to be sure that our message had the approval of the censors. To their everlasting honor be it said that there were those among us as there have always been, who would not so easily be deprived their convictions. They were willing to be counted as refuse that so they might gain Christ and proclaim Him and His gospel to others. Not of these do I speak now, save to express the hope that their tribe may increase. I am speaking, rather, of that vast body in the church who followed the lead of those who saw in the church nothing whatever but a social institution, whose test of its worth was a purely external test, and who would eliminate from its faith, and therefore from its message, everything that savored of "other-worldiness." I am not questioning their <u>motive</u>. I am quite sure that they "meant all right." Nevertheless, they were blind, and we were as blind who followed them. They wanted the church to be a great and glorious reality in the nation's life--and who of us would not? They saw visions and they dreamed dreams--and may the vision never pass nor the dreams vanish! But what they saw could never come by the means which they advocated.

Five Years of the New Deal

CHARLES COUGHLIN

Charles Coughlin (1891-1979), better known as the "radio priest," rose to fame during the 1930's. The Great Depression spawned many fiery preachers who played upon the emotions of the American populace, but none was more revered by his followers and loathed by his opponents than Father Coughlin. As the poverty and unrest of the depression beset America in 1930, Coughlin used the radio broadcasts from his perish in Royal Oak, Michigan, the Shrine of the Little Flower, to spread his political opinions. In 1932 he climbed on the Roosevelt bandwagon, but by 1934 he had moved away from the New Deal and spoke in favor of isolationism and anti-unionism. Due to the controversies which surrounded his broadcasts, in 1936 CBS dropped his program, but Coughlin continued the broadcasts on his own network of stations. That same year he formed his own Union Party and was rebuked by his Catholic Church superiors for attacking labor and the New Deal, as well as for his friendly references to Hitler and Mussolini. The selection which follows is from his <u>Sixteen Radio Lectures</u>, 1938 Series (Royal Oak, Mich.: Rev. Chas. E. Coughlin, 1938), pp. 79-88. Used by permission of the Shrine of the Little Flower. Why did Coughlin support the New Deal before 1934, but then begin to oppose Roosevelt and his programs thereafter? What factors did he cite to give support to his contention that the New Deal did not help the poor but only helped the rich get richer?

Motivated by a spirit of helpfulness and construction, I am impelled to offer you an explanation of my attitude towards the New Deal both prior to November, 1936 and following that date.

For more than ten years I was acutely conscious of the failure on the part of the government to act for the common welfare of the people. I was aware that politics in America had so degenerated that Congress became the protector and abettor of the social crimes committed by capitalism in the name of law and good government. The party leaders of both Democrats and Republicans, to my mind, were nothing more than supine servants of the financial classes. Plutocracy, the wolf which devoured the substance of the laboring and agricultural classes, reigned supreme in the sheep's clothing of democracy.

Thus, as early as 1928 I was happy to cast my lot with those whom capitalism and so-called democracy were exploiting in the name of sound economics and of sound government.

By 1932 I became a public sponsor of the New Deal because it pledged to drive the money changers and their servants from the temple. Like millions of Americans, I was convinced that the greedy individualism of capitalism had run its course; that living annual wages would be substituted for insufficient hourly wages; that the gospel of plenty would supplant the gospel of scarcity; and that the private control of money and, through it, of government, of prosperity and of human lives, would cease forthwith.

By 1934 I began to suffer the pangs of disillusionment. I suspected that the policy of the New Dealers was unsound when I discovered that the commercial gold of the United States had been confiscated for the private use of the privately owned Federal Reserve Banking System and was not nationalized for the common use of the American public. Gradually this suspicion gave way to moral certainty when the new Banking Act of 1935 made it plain to every informed person that this government had no intention of destroying the monopoly of money; that it still persisted in permitting a small group of citizens to issue and control, on a scarcity level, 95 percent of the life-blood of our nation—its money—and thereby curtail the productivity of factories and farms and the purchasing power of our people.

Planned want in the midst of plenty, although not advertised, was still the order of the day.

It is true that the hungry were fed, that the naked were clothed and the homeless sheltered. It is true that certain public works were undertaken to alleviate unemployment, but it was still true that these things were accomplished through manufactured credit borrowed by our Government from privately owned banks to whom the very recipients of the crust of bread and the rag of clothing were obligated, through the process of taxation, to restore wealth-money for the debt-money which had been borrowed.

The fundamental economic error which had characterized the administration of Hoover, of Coolidge and their predecessors in office, was accepted by the New Deal. Accidentally the New Deal differed from the Old Deal. Substantially, one was the left wing and the other the right wing of the same bird of prey.

If similar causes produced similar effects, it was a foregone conclusion that a similar depression was just around the corner for America.

Deliberately, therefore, in 1936 I chose to stand on the unpopular side at a moment when the majority of my fellow citizens still believed that the policies of the New Deal were remedial.

Although the laboring class and many of the agricultural class were not conscious of the deception practiced upon them, nevertheless, my conscience would not permit me to sustain them in their error lest, at a later and inevitable date, when this bad tree would produce only the bad fruit of another depression, I should be blamed as being partly responsible for the disaster about to follow.

Permit me, therefore, to present to you official facts and figures to sustain the statement that the New Deal is still wedded to a policy of wealth concentration and scarcity.

Surrounding us are 14-million able-bodied citizens unemployed through no fault of their own. The vast majority of them are under forty years of age.

Never before was Government relief so necessary as at the moment. Local governments at Detroit, Philadelphia, Buffalo, Minneapolis, Cleveland, Seattle and elsewhere are endeavoring to feed and clothe their starving populations after all their funds have been exhausted.

"We planned it that way and don't let anybody tell you to the contrary," are the unfortunate words of our Chief Executive, who was responsible for spending 10-billion dollars on relief that failed to relieve, and for piling up a national debt of 38-billion dollars.

Confronted with this crisis, Mr. Morgenthau, the Secretary of the Treasury, in an official statement recently said:

> This situation is most acute. I consider it a very serious emergency. For the unemployed it could not be worse.
>
> Whether we have reached the bottom of this downturn or not, I do not know and I do not think anybody else knows.

These are bitter words for the millions who, a few years ago, thought they did know; humiliating words for those who, with pontifical certitude, maintained that the back of the depression had been broken.

In his statement, the Secretary of the Treasury inadvertently admitted the point long since maintained that this Administration does not know where it is going and has sustained the argument that the more bankers' credit money the nation borrows, the darker is the prospect for all its citizens.

What has resulted from the insane taxation which this kind of borrowing necessitated? Last year the sum of 375-million dollars was collected as the undistributed corporation surplus tax.

Stocks and bonds depreciated 30-billion dollars in 1937.

A shrinkage of 7-billion dollars in the surplus funds of business concerns is recorded on the books of our nation since 1933--7-billion dollars less with which to operate factories, hire laborers and pay wages.

Only an untutored child could applaud such a tax policy, thinking that such huge levies against industry pointed towards the redistribution of wealth. Every thoughtful person knows the present tax policy is concentrating wealth in the hands of Federal Reserve bankers for whom labor and industry and agriculture and commerce are all working.

And many analytic minds go a step beyond this thought to a more pertinent conclusion. They are conscious that this is the beginning of state socialism; for after the Federal Reserve Banks and the bondholders will have gained ownership or control over the nation, then it will be possible for a government, that confessedly admits it does not know how far this thing is going, to seize the Federal Reserve Banks and gain control of the wealth of the state.

"How could this Administration have done otherwise?" questions the innocent critic.

The answer is brief. By constitutional authority Congress has the right to coin and issue and regulate the value of money. Against the billions of dollars of idle gold buried in the vaults of Kentucky, Congress could have issued its own credit, tax-free; Congress could have issued an adequate amount of currency to raise the price levels to a proper standard.

This appears to be recognized by every informed person except the officials at Washington.

Even the <u>Wall Street Journal</u>, on February 16, 1938, states:

> The essential thing involved in the issue of more currency is that it increases the supply of price-measured money. . . .
>
> The sole function of bank credit is the making of exchanges. . . the volume of substantial bank credit does not act upon prices at all.

Thus, even the bankers' economists indirectly inveigh against this Administration for keeping a scarcity of money in circulation with its consequent scarcity of production, scarcity of employment and scarcity of bread and butter, or clothing and shelter in the midst of plenty.

Time after time you have heard spokesmen for this Administration decry the poverty which surrounds us and castigate the economic royalists who are exploiting our people. For five years the airways have been thundering with denunciations of the princes of privilege. But after five years of this wordy war, after the smoke of the sham battle has cleared away, behold, the princes of privilege are more secure in their privileges following five years of the New Deal than they were before it.

Here is the official picture of "before and after," painted by New Deal Government statisticians: In 1929, 93 per cent of our people received incomes under $5,000. This represented 60 per cent of the total wealth produced in that year. Seven per cent of our population obtained 40 per cent of the national income and they represented people receiving more than $5,000 a year.

That was back in 1929. Those official figures certainly gave us something to complain about relative to the uneconomic distribution of wealth--93 per cent of our population with 60 per cent of its wealth, representing incomes under $5,000 a year; and 7 per cent of our population with 40 per cent of the income, representing persons with incomes over $5,000 a year. But what are the latest available figures after five years of New Deal activity and rhetoric?

From the Federal Reserve Bulletin we find that 96.7 per cent of all deposits, according to number and not according to amount, in member banks of the Federal Reserve, were $2,500 or less. In other words, 33-million depositors--96.7 per cent of all depositors--were in the $2,500 class or less, with deposits amounting in their total to 5-billion 800-million dollars or 22 per cent of the total deposits of the nation.

Keep that figure clearly in mind: 96.7 per cent of our population hold only 22 per cent of the total deposits.

The same chart shows that 49,000 depositors own 12-billion 800-million dollars or 42.8 per cent of all deposits; that a little more than one-tenth of one per cent of our depositors had in the banks more than twice as much as 96.7 per cent of all the depositors. And almost 90-million people have no deposits at all in the Federal Reserve Banks and their affiliates.

There is a picture for you. Under the New Deal wealth has become more concentrated and poverty more widespread than they were under the Old Deal.

To bear out this statement with another proof, I invite you to read Volume One, page 32 of Senate Document No. 415 of the Sixty-Fourth Congress in its first session.

In that year, 1916, the United States Commission on Industrial Relations, in its final report and testimony says:

> The ownership of wealth in the United States has become concentrated to a degree which is difficult to grasp.
>
> The rich 2 per cent of the people own 60 per cent of the wealth; the middle class, 33 per cent of the people, own 35 per cent of the wealth; the poor, 65 per cent of the people, own 5 per cent of the wealth.

Contrast that condition of wealth concentration and mass poverty with 1937. In 1937, 35 per cent of our people owned scarcely any wealth. Sixty-four per cent of our people owned outright only 10 per cent of our wealth. One and seven-tenths per cent of our people owned and controlled 90 per cent of the wealth.

Ladies and gentlemen, let us be honest even though we are critical. Whose chief responsibility is this chaotic condition of affairs? We maintain that the party system of government, broadly speaking, and the Congress of the United States, specifically speaking, must share the major portion of blame for these outrageous conditions.

Congress is the law-making body. It has failed to pass equitable laws, and in doing so it has not only left Congressmen open to attack but it has called into question the advisability of continuing with a Congress of the United States.

In no sense am I even intimating a return to the Old Deal with its abject disregard of human rights even though I cannot support the present policies of the New Deal which have produced the record which I have exposed to you.

It is the New Deal record, it is not mine.

In no sense am I suggesting the adoption either of state socialism which is identified with Communism or of parliamentary socialism which, under the guise of democracy, seizes industry, enslaves labor, regiments agriculture and protects the private coinage and regulation of money for the international bankers.

I am appealing for a restoration of American democracy divorced from party-ism and pledged to the service of all people independent of party, of race and of creed. I am appealing to all classes, rich and poor alike, to sacrifice, if necessary, the ephemeral value of debt bonds in order to save our institutions and our people from being converted to the fallacies of Fascism or Communism through the inefficiency of a Congress that could, if it would, issue sufficient money to enable wealth to be produced and consumed with a living annual wage for all who are willing to work and able to work.

Failing to do this, our present Congressmen are betraying the traditions of our fathers, the spirit of our people and the usefulness of representative government.

It is impossible to continue with the dole system forever; 10-billion dollars spent over a period of five years left us worse off than we were. Its record has taught that lesson to everyone.

And, above all, it is doubly absurd to continue with the scarcity program under the pretext that there was overproduction when, as a matter of fact, there is sinful, malicious under-consumption.

Do you doubt that statement? Permit me to prove it with official figures submitted by the very Government which advocates the policy of destruction, and bear with me while I cite New Deal statistics to prove that the chief beneficiaries of agricultural doles were the so-called princes of privilege.

Mr. Wallace, the Secretary of Agriculture, recently was asked to disclose the names of the beneficiaries of agriculture doles. He was reluctant to do so. Finally, Congress compelled him to submit only those names of persons who had received more than $10,000 of agricultural dole.

Thus, we find that 21 big rice growers in Louisiana, Arkansas, Texas and California received over $800,000 of these farm benefits--nearly $40,000 each.

Seventy-four corporations and other concerns in Louisiana received an average of $50,000 each to not produce sugar. One sugar producer received $256,000 not to raise sugar.

In the island of Puerto Rico one sugar monopoly received nearly $1,000,000 to let its lands lie fallow, and 28 other concerns received an average of $33,000 each not to produce sugar.

Three big cotton concerns in Arkansas and two in Mississippi received nearly $500,000 not to grow cotton. The State penitentiary of Mississippi was paid $43,200 not to grow cotton as if cotton growing was the business of the State penitentiary. One corporation in California was paid $157,020 and another one in New Jersey was paid $45,000 not raise hogs.

Twenty-seven beet-sugar producers in California and Colorado were paid approximately $540,000 not to produce sugar beets.

The Delta Pine and Land Company was paid more then $60,000 and the Arizona Citrus Land Company received $47,000 under the Soil Conservation Act. The Equitable Life Assurance Company was paid $80,000 of these farm benefits.

Oh, yes, the New Deal was of great assistance to the farmers of the nation in view of these official figures which I have read to you--Official figures which prove that the New Deal has been wedded to big business and to the money changers.

As far back as 1934 and 1936 I was intimating these things to the American people who could not lend credence to them because they were so fantastic.

Nevertheless, since we are in the mood to give statistics and official figures, kindly consider these facts which are now uncontradictable because this Government has been forced through its own officials to publish them.

While the Government was busied in plowing under cotton and paying monopolists and private farmers not to produce sugar and hogs and wheat and corn, what was happening in America?

It is now officially disclosed that last year we imported 1-billion 600-million dollars worth of agricultural products and substitutes valuated as such in foreign money and priced at 3-billion 200-million dollars in American money.

Specifically, during 1937 we imported 494,945 head of cattle; approximately 16,500,000 head of live hogs, 250,000 live chickens and turkeys; 191,906,000 pounds of meat and meat products; 11,110,000 pounds of butter; 181,000,000 pounds of wool; 201,000,000 pounds of cottonseed oil used as substitute for butter and lard; 319,000 pounds of coconut oil used for butter substitute; 360,000 pounds of palm oil used in the manufacture of soap instead of the fats of cattle, sheep, and hogs of this country; 119,000,000 pounds of soybeans and soybean oil; and last, but not least, 364,668,945 pounds of fish.

Last year we imported more than 312-million pounds of raw hides, more than $102-million worth of grain represented by 86-million bushels of corn; 206-thousand bushels of rye; 17-million bushels of wheat and 371-million pounds of malt barley and $2-million worth of flour and flour products.

All this was going on when we were taught that there was over-production.

Oh, yes! Billions of dollars for destruction at home forced upon us the expenditure of billions of dollars to import from abroad.

We took 40,000,000 acres of productive land out of cultivation; we regimented agriculture. It would have required millions of farmers and their families to cultivate these 40,000,000 acres and produce the farm products that were brought into this country from the West Indies, South America, India, China, Japan and other countries, and produced by underpaid labor. It would have required every acre of these 40,000,000 to produce these foreign farm products. This policy of destruction and curtailment put our own people out of work and on relief and gave the jobs to the foreigners and the poorly paid workers of all parts of the world.

Just the day before yesterday, the fifth anniversary of the New Deal, Mr. Morgenthau described the new crop-control law as a step towards more purchasing power. More purchasing power for the peon labor in China and in the West Indies and for the food monopolists, and less work and more taxes for the American laborer and farmer—so one could explain in view of the facts I have just disclosed.

My friends, be not mistaken in that I think that the sole panacea rests only with instructing Congress to coin and regulate the value of money for the welfare of all the nation. Nevertheless, the New Deal and this Congress are doomed to failure and disgrace unless they take this action.

It is regrettable that the scientists of rugged individualism cling to the error that the financial world is flat. It is not too late for the New Deal to become a new Columbus and prove that the world can enjoy a well-rounded prosperity by recognizing that work makes wealth, and by abandoning the notion that destruction makes prosperity.

Ladies and gentlemen, behind every lasting reform are the social principles of Jesus Christ.

The pagan practices current in the world today must give place to Christian practices.

Pagan usury must bow before the Christian concept of finance. Pagan destruction must give way to Christian production.

16
EDUCATION, RELIGION, AND THE COURTS IN THE 20TH CENTURY

Minersville School District v. Gobitis

and

West Va. State Bd. of Educ.

v. Barnette

What were the significant majority and minority arguments of the Supreme Court pertaining to the requirement that public school pupils must salute the flag? How did the times perhaps affect the decisions of the justices? What is the significance of these two cases?

Flag-Salute Requirement

(Held Constitutional)

Minersville School District v. Gobitis (1940)

THE ISSUE. The issue in this case was whether a school regulation requiring all children to participate in the daily flag-salute ceremony in the public classroom was in violation of the First Amendment's Free Exercise Clause insofar as children who had religious scruples against participating were concerned. Also involved was whether the requirement of participation infringed upon the due process of law guaranteed by the Fourteenth Amendment.

BACKGROUND. As stated by Justice Frankfurter:

> Lillian Gobitis, aged twelve, and her brother William, aged ten, were expelled from the public schools of Minersville, Pennsylvania, for refusing to salute the national flag as part of a daily school exercise. The local Board of Education required both teacher and pupils to participate in this ceremony. The ceremony is a familiar one. The right hand is placed on the breast and the following pledge recited in unison: 'I pledge allegiance to the flag, and to the Republic for which it stands; one nation indivisible, with liberty and justice for all.' While the words are spoken, teachers and pupils extend their right hands in salute to the flag. The Gobitis family are affiliated with the Jehovah's Witnesses, for whom the Bible as the Word of God is the supreme authority. The children had been brought up conscientiously to believe that such a gesture of respect for the flag was forbidden by command of Scripture.
>
> The Gobitis children were of an age for which Pennsylvania makes school attendance compulsory. Thus they were denied a free education, and their parents had to put them in private schools. To be relieved of the financial burden thereby entailed, their father, on behalf of the children and in his own behalf, brought this suit. He sought to enjoin the authorities from continuing to exact participation in the

flag-salute ceremony as a condition of his children's attendance at the Minersville school.

U.S. SUPREME COURT DECISION. The United States Supreme Court by an 8-1 margin upheld the Minersville School District regulation that students should salute the American flag as a condition for school attendance.

Before arriving at that decision, however, the Court heard arguments, pro and con, regarding the validity of the school regulation. Among arguments supporting the regulation was the following:

> The refusal of the children to salute the national flag at school exercises because they believed that to do so would violate the written law of Almighty God as contained in the Bible was not founded on a religious belief.

> The act of saluting the flag does not prevent a pupil, no matter what his religious belief may be, from acknowledging the spiritual sovereignty of Almighty God by rendering to God the things which are God's.

Arguments against the regulation in part said:

> To expel children from school and deny them the opportunity of an education because they refuse to violate their conscience, is wrong and is cruel and unusual punishment.

> The rule certainly abridges the privilege of the respondents and deprives them of liberty and property without due process of law.

Chief Justice Hughes and Justices Roberts, Black, Reed, Douglas, Murphy, and McReynolds concurred with the majority opinion of the court delivered by Justice Frankfurter. In part it stated:

> Centuries of strife over the erection of particular dogmas as exclusive or all-comprehending faiths led to the inclusion of a guarantee for religious freedom in the Bill of Rights. The First Amendment, and the Fourteenth through its absorption of the First,

sought to guard against repetition of those bitter religious struggles by prohibiting the establishment of a state religion and by securing to every sect the free exercise of its faith. So pervasive is the acceptance of this precious right that its scope is brought into question, as here, only when the conscience of the individual collides with the felt necessities of society. . . .

Situations like the present are phases of the profoundest problem confronting a democracy--the problem which Lincoln cast in memorable dilemma: "Must a government of necessity be too strong for the liberties of its people, or too weak to maintain its own existance?" . . . And when the issue demands judicial determination, it is not the personal notion of judges of what wise adjustment requires which must prevail. . . .

The preciousness of the family relation, the authority and independence which give dignity to parenthood, indeed the enjoyment of all freedom, presuppose the kind of ordered society which is summarized by our flag. A society which is dedicated to the preservation of these ultimate values of civilization may in self-preservation utilize the educational process for inculcating those almost unconscious feelings which bind men together in a comprehending loyalty, whatever may be their lesser differences and difficulties. That is to say, the process may be utilized so long as men's right to believe as they please, to win others to their way of belief, and their right to assemble in their chosen places of worship for the devotional ceremonies of their faith, are all fully respected.

In his dissent, Justice Stone emphasized that even though the state may exercise considerable control over pupils, that control is limited where it interferes with civil liberties guaranteed by the Constitution. In part he stated:

Concededly the constitutional guaranties of personal liberty are not always absolutes. Government has a right to survive and powers conferred upon it are not necessarily set at naught by the express prohibitions

of the Bill of Rights. It may make war and raise
armies. To that end it may compel citizens to give
military service, ... and subject them to military
training despite their religious objections. ...
It may supress religious practices dangerous to morals,
and presumably those also which are inimical to public safety, health and good order. ... But it is
a long step, and one which I am unable to take, to
the position that government may, as a supposed educational measure and as a means of disciplining the
young, compel public affirmations which violate religious conscience. ...

The Constitition expresses more than the conviction
of the people that democratic processes must be preserved at all costs. It is also an expression of
faith and a command that freedom of mind and spirit
must be preserved, which government must obey, if it
is to adhere to that justice and moderation without
which no free government can exist. For this reason
it would seem that legislation which operates to re-
press the religious freedom of small minorities,
which is admittedly within the scope of the protection of the Bill of Rights, must at least be subject to the same judicial scrutiny as legislation
which we have recently held to infringe the constitutional liberty of religious and racial minorities.

SIGNIFICANCE OF THE DECISION. The decision in this case is
significant, but academic as far as finalizing a legal prec-
edent is concerned. From the beginning of litigation there
was evidence that a judicial opinion upholding the flag-
salute requirement was doomed to a judicial overturn.

The court was compelled to make a delicate decision as to
whether or not the desire for a patriotic gesture of saluting
the flag outweighed the religious freedom expressed in the
Constitution. In this case the balance of support favored
the arguments supporting the requirement, but this was not
the end of the road for this issue.

Flag-Salute Requirement

(Held Unconstitutional)

West Virginia State Board of Education v. Barnette (1943)

THE ISSUE. The issue in this case was quite similar to that involved in the Gobitis case in that it questioned the validity of a requirement for children to salute the American flag who claimed religious scruples against doing so. One difference is that in the Gobitis case, the validity of a school district requirement was challenged, whereas, in this case, the challenge had to do with a statewide requirement.

BACKGROUND. The Gobitis decision was destined to be reversed as soon as it was given. Immediate opposition to the decision was expressed in newspapers, educational journals, law journals, and law reviews. The Jehovah's Witnesses took advantage of all the outside support for their opposition to the required flag salute when the West Virginia state legislature adopted new statutes for the teaching of patriotism in the public schools. In accordance with the statutes, the West Virginia State Board of Education adopted a regulation that the salute to the flag become "a regular part of the program of activities in the public schools," that all teachers and pupils "shall be required to participate in the salute honoring the Nation represented by the Flag; provided, that refusal to salute the Flag be regarded as an act of insubordination, and shall be dealt with accordingly."

A group of Jehovah's Witnesses from West Virginia challenged the statute in a suit seeking an injunction to restrain the enforcement of the laws and regulations against Jehovah's Witnesses.

U.S. SUPREME COURT DECISION. By a margin of 6-3 the Supreme Court upheld the District Court's ruling that the State Board rule requiring all student to salute the flag and recite the pledge of allegiance as a condition of school attendance violated the First Amendment to the Federal Constitution which guarantees the exercise of freedom of religion.

Note the concluding remarks of Justice Jackson in the majority opinion:

National unity as an end which officials may foster by persuasion and example is not in question. The problem is whether under our Constitution compulsion as here employed is a permissible means for its achievement.

Struggles to coerce uniformity of sentiment in support of some end thought essential to their time and country have been waged by many good as well as by evil men. Nationalism is a relatively recent phenomenon but at other times and places the ends have been racial or territorial security, support of a dynasty or regime, and particular plans for saving souls. As first and moderate methods to attain unity have failed, those bent on its accomplishment must resort to an ever-increasing severity. As governmental pressure toward unity becomes greater, so strife becomes more bitter as to whose unity it shall be. Probably no deeper division of our people could proceed from any provocation than from finding it necessary to choose what doctrine and whose program public educational officials shall compel youth to unite in embracing. Ultimate futility of such attempts to compel coherence is the lesson of every such effort from the Roman drive to stamp out Christianity as a disturber of its pagan unity, the Inquisition, as a means to religious and dynastic unity, the Siberian exiles as a means to Russian unity, down to the fast failing efforts of our present totalitarian enemies. Those who begin coercive elimination of dissent soon find themselves exterminating dissenters. Compulsory unification of opinion achieves only the unanimity of the graveyard. . . .

If there is any fixed star in our constitutional constellation, it is that no official, high or petty, can prescribe what shall be orthodox in politics, nationalism, religion, or other matters of opinion or force citizens to confess by word or act their faith therein. If there are any circumstances which permit an exception, they do not now occur to us.

Justice Frankfurter, who had spoken for the majority in the Gobitis case, stated his dissent in the Barnette case; in part he said:

One who belongs to the most vilified and persecuted
minority in history is not likely to be insensible
to the freedoms guaranteed by our Constitution.
Were my purely personal attitude relevant I should
whole-heartedly associate myself with the general
libertarian views in the Court's opinion, representing as they do the thought and action of a lifetime.
But as judges we are neither Jew nor Gentile, neither
Catholic nor agnostic. We owe equal attachment to
the Constitution and are equally bound by our judicial obligations whether we derive our citizenship
from the earliest or the latest immigrants to these
shores. As a member of this Court I am not justified in writing my private notions of policy into the
Constitution, no matter how deeply I may cherish
them or how mischievous I may deem their disregard.
The duty of a judge who must decide which of two
claims before the Court shall prevail, that of a
State to enact and enforce laws within its general
competence or that of an individual to refuse obedience because of the demands of conscience, is not
that of the ordinary person. It can never be emphasized too much that one's own opinion about the wisdom or evil of a law should be excluded altogether
when one is doing one's duty on the bench. The only
opinion of our own even looking in that direction
that is material is our opinion whether legislators
could in reason have enacted such a law. In the light
of all the circumstances, including the history of
this question in this Court, it would require more
daring than I possess to deny that reasonable legislators could have taken the action which is before
us for review. Most willingly, therefore, I must
differ from my brethren with regard to legislation
like this. . . .

That which to the majority may seem essential for the
welfare of the state may offend the consciences of a
minority. But, so long as no inroads are made upon
the actual exercise of religion by the minority, to
deny the political power of the majority to enact
laws concerned with civil matters, simply because
they may offend the consciences of a minority, really
means that the consciences of a minority are more
sacred and more enshrined in the Constitution than

the consciences of a majority. . . .

SIGNIFICANCE OF THE DECISION. This is another decision in which it has been ruled that, despite the desirability of a regulation imposed upon students, the regulation is illegal if it is in conflict with liberties guaranteed by the Constitution. The alleged civic achievements and desirability of a school regulation, such as the flag-salute exercise, must give way to constitutional guarantees.

Despite the Court's ruling in <u>Gobitis</u>, upholding the flag-salute requirement, the opposite ruling in <u>Barnette</u>, voiding the requirement is evidence that even the Supreme Court can be swayed by strong public opposition.

McCollum v. Bd. of Educ.

and

Zorach v. Clauson

On what bases did the Court distinguish between the two cases on a Constitutional level? What is the significance of these two cases?

Released Time for Religious Instruction

(Held Unconstitutional)

<u>McCollum</u> v. <u>Board of Education</u> (1948)

THE ISSUE. The issue in this case was whether or not public school pupils could legally be released from their regular classes to attend sectarian religious instruction during the regular school day in public school buildings, under provisions of the "Establishment Clause" of the First Amendment.

BACKGROUND. A "released-time program" as conducted in the public schools of Champaign, Illinois was offered to public school pupils in grades four to nine inclusive whose parents signed printed cards requesting that their children be permitted to attend. The classes were held weekly, the religious teachers were hired at no expense to the school authorities, and the students who did not choose to take the religious instruction were not released from public school duties.

Vashti McCollum, who was an avowed atheist, charged that the joint public school and religious group program violated the First and Fourteenth Amendments. The Circuit Court dismissed her petition, and the dismissal was affirmed by the State Supreme Court, from whence it was appealed to the U.S. Supreme Court.

U.S. SUPREME COURT DECISION. The Supreme Court ruled that religious instruction in the public school buildings during public school time as practiced in the Champaign Public Schools, was illegal under the First and Fourteenth Amendments because it amounted to an "establishment of religion."

In the majority opinion delivered by Justice Black, he stated:

> Pupils compelled by law to go to school for secular education are released in part from their legal duty upon the condition that they attend the religious classes. This is beyond all question a utilization of the tax-established and tax-supported public school system to aid religious groups to spread their faith. And it falls squarely upon the ban of the First Amendment.

The lone dissenter in the case, Justice Reed, indicated his opposition as indicated by this brief excerpt:

> Devotion to the great principle of religious liberty should not lead us into a rigid interpretation of the constitutional guarantee that conflicts with accepted habits of our people. This is an instance where, for me, the history of past practices is determinative of the meaning of a constitutional clause, not a decorous introduction to the study of its text.

SIGNIFICANCE OF THE DECISION. Never before had there been a more forceful and unequivocal denunciation of church-school entanglements than that expressed in the majority opinion of McCollum. No reservations or exceptions were cited in the decision. The Court was adamant in abiding strictly by the "separation of the church and state" principle. It left no doubt in its upholding the impregnability of the "wall of separation."

Had the Court decided differently than it did there is no doubt that numerous conflicts would have arisen in the school buildings between school authorities and religious instructors, as well as between the religious groups involved.

As has been the case in other instances, however, the losing litigants can frequently capitalize on excerpts from the dissenting opinion. It may be noted from the queries raised in Justice Reed's dissent that had certain circumstances been different, the practices in the Champaign program might have been judicially approved. In fact the decision in the Zorach case (1952) seems to confirm the possibility.

Dismissed Time for Religious Instruction

(Held Constitutional)

Zorach v. Clauson (1952)

THE ISSUE. The issue in Zorach is similar to that in the McCollum case in that it has to do with "released time." In Zorach, however, the question is whether public school children may be released from their classes to attend sectarian religious instruction during the regular school hours but away from public school buildings, under the provisions of the First Amendment.

BACKGROUND. A New York Education Law provided for such released time programs. Zorach and others, being taxpayers and residents of New York City, challenged the law on the grounds that it was essentially no different from the one involved in the McCollum case. They argued:

> The weight and influence of the school is put behind a program for religious instruction; the school is a crutch on which the churches are leaning for support in their religious training; without the cooperation of the schools this "released time" program, like the one in the McCollum case, would be futile and ineffective.

The New York Court of Appeals was not convinced by the above argument, and therefore sustained the constitutionality of the New York law. The case was then appealed to the U.S. Supreme Court.

U.S. SUPREME COURT DECISION. In a 6 to 3 decision, the Court upheld the constitutionality of the dismissed time program for religious instruction during school hours but away from public school buildings.

In the majority decision, Justice Douglas stated in part:

> New York City has a program which permits its public school to release students during the school day so that they may leave the school buildings and school grounds and go to religious centers for religious instruction or devotional exercises. A student is released on written request of his parents. Those not released stay in the classrooms. The churches make weekly reports to the schools, sending a list of children who have been released from public school but who have not reported for religious instruction.

This "released Time" program involves neither religious instruction in public school classrooms nor the expenditure of public funds. All costs, including the application blanks, are paid by the religious organizations. The case is therefore unlike <u>McCollum v. Board of Education</u>, 333 U.S. 203, which involved a "released time" program from Illinois. In that case the classrooms were turned over to religious instructors. We accordingly held that the program violated the First Amendment which (by reason of the Fourteenth Amerndment) prohibits the states from establishing religion or prohibiting its free exercise. . . .

It takes obtuse reasoning to inject any issue of the "free exercise" of religion into the present case. No one is forced to go to the religious classroom and no religious exercise or instruction is brought to the classrooms of the public schools. A student need not take religious instruction. He is left to his own desires as to the manner or time of his religious devotions, if any.

There is a suggestion that the system involves the use of coercion to get public school students into religious classrooms. There is no evidence in the record before us that supports that conclusion. The present record indeed tells us that the school authorities are neutral in this regard and do no more than release students whose parents so request. If in fact coercion were used, if it were established that any one or more teachers were using their office to persuade or force students to take the religious instruction, a wholly different case would be presented. . . .

We are a religious people whose institutions presuppose a Supreme Being. We guarantee the freedom to worship as one chooses. We make room for as wide a variety of beliefs and creeds as the spiritual needs of man deem necessary. We sponsor an attitude on the part of government that shows no partiality to any one group and that lets each flourish according to the zeal of its adherents and the appeal of its dogma. When the state encourages religious instruction or cooperates with religious authorities by adjusting the schedule of public events to sectarian needs, it follows the best of our traditions. For it then respects the religious nature of our people and accommodates the public service to their spiritual needs. To hold that it may not would be to find in the Constitution a requirement that the government show a callous indifference to religious groups. That would be preferring those who believe in no religion over those who do believe. Government may not finance religious groups nor undertake religious instruction nor blend secular and sectarian education nor use secular institutions to force one or some religion on any person. But we find no constitutional requirement which makes it necessary for government to be hostile to religion and to throw its weight against efforts to widen the effective scope of religious influence. The government must be neutral when it comes to competition between sects. . . .

In the McCollum case the classrooms were used for religious instruction and the force of the public school was used to promote that instruction. Here, as we have said, the public schools do no more than accommodate their schedules to a program of outside religious instruction. We follow the McCollum case. But we cannot expand it to cover the present released time program unless separation of Church and State means that public institutions can make no adjustments of their schedules to accommodate the religious needs of the people. We cannot read into the Bill of Rights such a philosophy of hostility to religion.

In his dissent Justice Jackson concluded with these remarks:

The day that this country ceases to be free for irreligion it will cease to be free for religion--except for the sect that can win political power. The same epithetical jurisprudence used by the Court today to beat down those who oppose pressuring children into some religion can devise as good epithets tomorrow against those who object to pressuring them into a favored religion. And, after all, if we concede to the State power and wisdom to single out "duly constituted religious" bodies as exclusive alternatives for compulsory secular instruction, it would be logical to also uphold the power and wisdom to choose the true faith among those "duly constituted." We start down a rough road when we begin to mix compulsory public education with compulsory godliness.

A number of Justices just short of a majority of the majority that promulgates today's passionate dialectics joined answering them in Illinois ex rel. McCollom v. Board of Education. The distinction attempted between that case and this is trivial, almost to the point of cynicism, magnifying its nonessential details and disparaging compulsion which was the underlying reason for invalidity. A reading of the Court's opinion in that case along with its opinion in this case will show such difference of overtones and undertones as to make clear that the McCollum case has passed like a storm in a teacup. The wall which the Court was professing to erect between Church and State has become even more warped and twisted than I expected. Today's judgment will be more interesting to students of psychology and of the judicial processes than to students of constitutional law.

SIGNIFICANCE OF THE DECISION. The decision in Zorach illustrated that the amount of religious influence injected into the public school program is what perplexes the judiciary and causes split decisions. As one of the justices stated: "The problem, like many problems in constitutional law, is one of degree." Six of the justices believed the religious influence of the New York program was not so excessive as to make it unconstitutional. The three dissenting justices, however, were of the opinion that just the slightest entanglement of church-state relations, as in the Zorach case, was sufficient reason for invalidating the program.

Engel v. Vitale

What were the primary arguments of the majority and minority opinions of the Court pertaining to the required recitation of the state prayer? What is the significance of the decision?

Requirement for Recitation of State Prayer

(Held Unconstitutional)

Engel v. Vitale (1962)

THE ISSUE. The issue here is whether state officials may constitutionally compose an official state prayer and require that it be recited in the public schools of the State at the beginning of each school day--even if the prayer is denominationally neutral and if pupils who wish to do so may remain silent or be excused from the room while the prayer is being recited.

BACKGROUND. The case was brought into focus when the State Board of Regents composed a brief prayer which they recommended for the public schools of New York: "Almighty God, we acknowledge our dependence upon Thee, and we beg Thy blessing upon us, our parents, our teachers and our Country."

The parents of ten pupils brought action in a state court, insisting that the official prayer in the public schools was contrary to the beliefs, religions, or religious practices of both themselves and their children. They further contended that the district's regulation ordering the recitation of this particular prayer was a violation of the First Amendment.

352

Despite the above charges, the recitation of the "Regents' Prayer" as required by the school district was held legal by the Court of Appeals of New York State. However, it was appealed to the U.S. Supreme Court for final judgment.

U.S. SUPREME COURT DECISION. The Court rendered its decision (8-1) that the requirement of the recital of a state-composed prayer in the public school classroom was in violation of the Establishment Clause of the First Amendment.

In speaking for the majority, Justice Black stated:

> By the time of the adoption of the Constitution, our history shows that there was a widespread awareness among many Americans of the dangers of a union of Church and State. . . . The First Amendment was added to the Constitution to stand as a guarantee that neither the power nor the prestige of the Federal Government would be used to control, support or influence the kinds of prayer the American people can say--that the people's religions must not be subjected to the pressures of government for change each time a new political administration is elected to office. Under that Amendment's prohibition against governmental establishment of religion, as reinforced by the provisions of the Fourteenth Amendment, government in this country, be it state or federal, is without power to prescribe by law any particular form of prayer which is to be used as an official prayer in carrying on any program or governmentally sponsored religious activities.
>
> There can be no doubt that New York's state prayer program officially establishes the religious beliefs embodied in the Regents' prayer. The respondents' argument to the contrary, which is largely based upon the contention that the Regents' prayer is "non-denominational" and the fact that the program, as modified and approved by state courts, does not require all pupils to recite the prayer but permits those who wish to do so to remain silent or be excused from the room, ignores the essential nature of the program's constitutional defects. Neither the fact that the prayer may be denominationally neutral, nor the fact that its observance on the part of the students is voluntary can serve to free it from the limitations of the

Establishment Clause, as it might from the Free
Exercise Clause, of the First Amendment, both of
which are operative against the States by virtue
of the Fourteenth Amendment. . . .

Justice Stewart, the lone dissenter in the case, filed a
vigorous dissent, which in part said:

> With all respect, I think the Court has misapplied
> a great constitutional principle. I cannot see how
> an "official religion" is established by letting
> those who want to say a prayer say it. On the con-
> trary, I think to deny the wish of these school
> children to join in reciting this prayer is to deny
> them the opportunity of sharing in the spiritual
> heritage of our Nation. . . .
>
> For we deal here not with the establishment of a
> state church, which would, of course, be constitu-
> tionally impermissible, but with whether school
> children who want to begin their day by joining in
> prayer must be prohibited from doing so. Moreover,
> I think that the Court's task, in this as in all
> areas of constitutional adjudication, is not respon-
> sibly aided by the uncritical invocation of metaphors
> like the "wall of separation," a phrase nowhere to be
> found in the Constitution. What is relevant to the
> issue here is not the history of an established church
> in sixteenth century England or in eighteenth century
> America, but the history of the religious tradition
> of our people, reflected in countless practices of the
> institutions and officials of our government.

SIGNIFICANCE OF THE DECISION. The decision in this case had
to do with an official state prayer--leaving doubt as to the
legality of reciting school prayers that are not officially
designed. Since the Supreme Court did not specifically in-
validate the recitation of all prayers in all situations,
some school officials and teachers have attempted to continue
the practice in a minor degree.

RELIGION DURING HOT AND COLD WARS

17

The Churches and the Clergy in World War II

RAY ABRAMS

Ray Abrams (1896-), who lives in Lansdowne, Pennsylvania, has been a student of the interaction between the clergy and warfare for nearly a half century. In 1933 he authored Preachers Present Arms which extensively documented the extent to which the clergy embraced American participation in World War I. In the article below he traces the steps by which the pacifism and neutrality of the clergy in the 1930's yielded to belligerency with the coming of a "holy war," World War II. The excerpt is from "The Churches and the Clergy in World War II," The Annals of the American Academy of Political and Social Science 256 (March 1948): 110-19, and is reproduced here with the permission of the author and The Annals. What are some of the factors which caused America's religious leaders and institutions to turn from a position of neutrality to one of belligerency by 1941? What were some of the ways in which America's religious forces helped rally support for the war? What dilemma does the church face during wartime?

When the armies of Hitler started their triumphal march into Poland on September 1, 1939, Americans, after they had partially recovered from their initial shock, gave immediate attention to trying to keep the United States out of the European conflict.

There was a widespread belief that the Neutrality Acts passed between 1935 and 1937 would help keep this country out of another European or world war. The President on September 5, 1939 issued a proclamation of neutrality, and by a second proclamation made necessary by the Neutrality--in which an embargo was placed on the shipment of war material to belligerents--travel of Americans on belligerent ships in the war zones was banned.

FROM NEUTRALITY TO BELLIGERENCY

As the war progressed in Europe it seemed evident to many Americans that a defense of the Western Hempsphere was necessary. Canada and Latin America were virtually unprotected. We could not permit the invasion and conquest of these areas. In 1941 the United States occupied Greenland and Iceland, the two governments involved having given consent. In September 1940 Great Britain received fifty "overage" destroyers from the United States and in return granted us the right to lease naval and air bases in Newfoundland, Bermuda, Bahamas, Jamaica, St. Lucia, Trinidad, Antigua, and British Guiana. By the end of 1941 the construction of these bases had proceeded rapidly.

In the meanwhile the conviction was growing in this country that Great Britain was our "first line of defense." "The British Navy alone stands between us and Hitler"--that was the phrase one heard.

Congress was called into session soon after war started, and the Neutrality Act of 1937 was revised so that the Allies might obtain arms and munitions from this country. Belligerents could purchase arms and munitions here, but on a "cash and carry" basis. By January 1941 the famous Lend-Lease Acts were introduced. After two months of heated debate the President's proposals were passed with certain amendments.

It would seem that most Americans had never really been

neutral, and it was not long before the majority came to
believe that the "Allied cause" was our cause. The Neutrality Acts were weakened and we were virtually in the war as a
partner to the Allies except in terms of armed conflict.
Dunkerque, the fall of France, and the threatened invasion
of England began to frighten large sections of the population
when they contemplated the consequences in the event of the
fall of Great Britain. Rational and influential citizens
were predicting that Hitler would be over here in three weeks.

During 1940 a total of $17.692 billion was appropriated for
national defense. A two-ocean navy was in the making. Furthermore the Selective Training and Service Act of 1940
brought in compulsory military training in peacetime. We
began to mobilize all our resources for war.

Our four-year attempt to check Japanese expansion in the
Pacific had been a failure. The sudden and unexpected attack
of the Japanese on Pearl Harbor, December 7, 1941, gave them
an initial success in the "shooting war." But this "treachery" united the people of this country as probably nothing
else could have done. On Monday, December 8 the Senate voted
to declare war against Japan 82 votes to zero, and in the
House of Representatives the vote was 388 to 1. (Only
Jeannette Rankin voted "no.")

On December 10 Germany and Italy declared war against the
United States, and the next day Congress, without a dissenting vote, passed resolutions to the effect that a state of
war with these countries existed.

President Roosevelt in his war message of December 8 said:
"No matter how long it may take us to overcome this premeditated invasion, the American people in their righteous
[italics mine] might, will win through to absolute victory."

POSITION OF THE CHURCHES, 1940-41

Keeping in mind this brief resume of some of the major trends
in this country between the time that war broke out in Europe
and the Pearl Harbor attack, what were the churches and the
forces of organized religion doing with respect to the war in
those twenty-seven months prior to December 7, 1941?

A survey of the religious periodicals and literature, of many sermons preached in that period and of material based on interviews with religious leaders indicates that the churches and the clergy were hopelessly divided in their attitudes toward the war in Europe. Moreover, there was a great deal of confusion over the causes of the war, the role that the United States should play, and what the churches should or should not do. Like the historians, the economists, the political scientists, and the political leaders of the time, the men of the cloth were to be found in many diverse camps. The editors of Fortune in January 1940 complained in an article on the "The Failure of the Church":

> We are asked to turn to the church for our enlightenment, but when we do so we find that the voice of the church is not inspired. The voice of the church, we find, is the echo of our own voices. And the result of this experience, already manifest, is disillusionment.

They even said that "so far as the record goes, the American people would do as well by their souls to follow the advice of the industrial leaders [with reference to the war] as to follow the advice of the spiritual leaders." . . .

The Religious Press

In this pre-Pearl Harbor period, of all the influential Protestant weeklies the Christian Century seems to have been among the most outspoken of the noninterventionist journals. The aims of President Roosevelt's administration were denounced in practically every issue. Dr. Charles Clayton Morrison, the editor, opposed any revision of the Neutrality Acts, the "destroyer deal," Lend-Lease, Selective Service, and so forth. By January 1941 Dr. Morrison was talking about "the President's war" and maintaining that "the President has gone on the assumption that Great Britain is fighting America's war." In October of the same year he wrote:

> . . . the obsession of our statesmen with the weird illusion that this is in any true sense America's war must be broken. America's only genuine and rational responsibility in this war is to mediate for peace--not the peace of a mere armistice, but

the peace of justice.

As late as the first week of December 1941, in the last editorial before that fatal Sunday, December 7, Dr. Morrison wrote, "Every national interest and every moral obligation to civilization dictates that this country shall keep out of the insanity of war which is in no sense America's war." He declared, "The romanticists are the interventionists. In general they pride themselves on taking a realistic view, and charge that noninterventionists are star-gazing romantics. . . ."

Other equally honest, sincere, and conscientious Christians were convinced that the Christian Century and those who supported its positions were naive romanticists and misguided Christians.

Perhaps somewhat to counteract the influence of the Christian Century, a new religious periodical started up under the name of Christianity and Crisis with Reinhold Niebuhr, a professor in Union Theological Seminary, as the chief editor. Here was expounded the interventionist position and the "Aid to Britain" program. Niebuhr frankly stated that the Neutrality Act was "one of the most immoral laws that were ever spread upon the Federal statute book." "The essence of immorality," wrote he, "is the evasion or denial of moral responsibility." According to him, "misguided idealism" was "evoked in its support" at the time of passage.

That the clergy were divided in their appraisal of the merits of the war and the part that the United States should play is further evidenced by innumerable group resolutions and recommendations of one type and another.

Before our entrance into the struggle of the nations for survival, the Fellowship of Reconciliation announced that over two thousand clergy from every state in the Union had signed a statement of "unalterable opposition to America's present threatened belligerency" and pledged themselves never to use their ministry to "bless, sanction or support war." Early in February 1941, 648 churchmen signed a statement calling for "peace without victory now." Many eminent ministers were on this list.

The files of the religious periodicals are filled with

articles and letters on both sides of the fence. Clergymen had a perfect field day in writing letters and engaging in endless discussions over finespun theological questions about religion and war.

For ten weeks beginning in early December 1940, the Christian Century ran a series on "If America Enters the War What Shall I Do?" Prominent clergy took opposite sides in the debate.

Preparedness Propaganda

Gradually, however, the social forces which were to bring America into World War II became stronger and more dynamic. Events proved much stronger than philosophical reasoning. The isolationist groups, the "America First" and "Keep America Out of the War" committees, were being offset by those who gathered around the banners of "Aid to Britain," "Defend America by Aiding the Allies," and similar organizations. Leading churchmen took an active part in several of these important propaganda groups.

In the early days of 1940 a manifesto was issued by a rather large number of influential clergymen for an "enlistment of our moral and material resources in support of the Allied nations." They believed, in general, that if "the American people are determined to take effective action toward the establishment of peace, one and only one course opens to them—the enlistment of their full national resources in assistance to Great Britain." During the next year similar and stronger statements and resolutions appeared with signatures from the clergy from practically all over the country and from the leading denominations.

In World War I, during the "preparedness era," the Episcopalians and the clergy with British and Canadian ancestry were the most conspicuous among the religious groups in arousing sympathy for Britain and promoting preparedness propaganda. To a certain extent this was true in World War II (though more research is needed on this point to determine how widespread the phenomenon was). Of the Episcopalians, Bishop William T. Manning was probably the most outspoken and seemed to be much in the limelight of publicity. He had been active before 1917 in World War I on behalf of the mother country. In World War II he followed the identical pattern. In the summer of 1941 at the convention of his diocese the Bishop announced:

> Speaking as an American, as a Christian, and as a bishop of the Christian church, I say that it is our duty as a Nation to take full part in this struggle, to give our whole strength and power to bring this world calamity and world terror to an end, and to do this now while Great Britain still stands.

This statement, it should be said, aroused considerable discussion within Episcopalian ranks. Sixty-four Episcopalians issued a pronouncement in the New York *Times* which seems to have been directed at their Bishop, repudiating the notion that the conflict across the Atlantic Ocean was a "holy war."

ADJUSTMENT TO WAR

Up to December 7, 1941, then, the forces of organized religion were divided into several camps ranging all the way from the absolute pacifists to the interventionists who wanted us to declare war at once. Each, however, appealed to the same authorities--the Bible and Jesus of Nazareth--to support his position.

The complete surprise of the Japanese attack on Pearl Harbor settled, for the time being at least, many of the finespun theological and philosophical arguments that had been going on for over two years. War was no longer a possibility. It was a reality.

Correspondence with nearly all the editors of the leading Protestant and Catholic religious periodicals reveals that they accepted the war as fact and did not attempt to hinder the all-out war effort. Most of these journals seem to have supported our Government, and some quite actively. A few stood idly by and watched the process of events.

In the case of *Unity*, a comparatively small but influential liberal religious periodical, a novel situation arose. Dr. John Haynes Holmes, who was the editor (and continued to be up to 1946), was in opposition to the war. The managing

editor, Dr. Curtis W. Reese, supoorted the war. So each of
these gentlemen wrote signed editorials and each approved
articles for publication. For the most part, both the editor
and the managing editor were in agreement on the matter of
conscientious objectors.

It will be observed that several types of adjustments or
readjustments were possible for the Christian groups. Confronted with a shooting war, religious institutions are called
upon to shift, for the time being, patterns of thought in a
manner that is not characteristic of any of our other institutions. One example of this is furnished in an editorial in
the Living Church (Episcopalian), December 17, 1941: "May
we seek always, not that God may be one our side, but that
we may be on His side, so that the victory may in the end
be His." . . .

The Holy War

One example of this is with respect to the use of the phrase
"holy war." In 1917-18 the struggle had frequently been referred to as "the most holy war of all the ages." However,
with the events that had intervened between the two wars,
the phrase had fallen into thorough disrepute.

Karl Barth, the distinguished Swiss theologian, had shocked
a great many of the faithful when, addressing the Christians
of Great Britain, he declared the war "is a righteous war
which God commands us to wage ardently."

The Archbishop of York, Dr. William Temple, solved the theological dilemma by stating: "We are fighting for Christian
civilization. I cannot use the phrase 'holy war,' for war
in its own nature is always an expression of the sin of man.
But without hesitation I speak of this as, for us, a righteous war."

The theological frame of reference is very important. Hence
among the theologians (and in one sense every clergyman must
be a theologian) it is important to know what God thinks
about the war. Once having discovered the "mind of God" on
this subject, the major premise can be stated. The rest of
the syllogism, or line of logic, is comparatively easy, particularly for a master dialectician. This helps immensely

to reassure religious folks that God is still on his throne and is greatly concerned with the triumph of righteousness.

WARTIME TRENDS

After the United States entered the war as an active belligerent the following major trends seem to be significant as far as the churches are concerned.

When compared with 1917-18, the population in World War II took the conflict and the horrors of war more in its stride. Twenty-four years before, there had been a great deal of hysteria. This time, while there was plenty of denunciation of the "Japs" and of Hitler et al., far less real excitement prevailed. One heard and saw less of the wild-eyed patriot. The clergy in their utterances reflected the same differences. A few bellicose warmongers, yes, but they were not outstanding, certainly. In general, the clergy were calm about the struggle, and, in fact, in their sermons seem to have paid relatively less attention to the current problems of the war than one might have supposed. The generalization is based on data gathered from all over the United States. The war was a grim necessity--something to be gotten over as soon as possible.

Again, a greater toleration of diverse opinions was demonstrated. The Jehovah's Witnesses fared badly, it is true. Yet, the record of civil liberties appears better this time than for the previous war. The churches regarded the pacifist or near-pacifist clergymen with more urbanity than in 1917-18. No one knows how many preachers were pacifists, but they undoubtedly numbered several thousands. A few of them were exceedingly prominent.

The conscientious objectors were more highly regarded than in World War I, when they were damned or spurned by the clergy in general. The pacifist movement of the twenties and the thirties carried right on through the war with remarkable strength. On this point Dr. F. Ernest Johnson comments: "The number of objectors has been extremely small in view of the strength of the pacifist movement, but they constitute a symbol of religious freedom, and the churches in general seem so to regard them."

Approximately 12,000 conscientious objectors served in the Civilian Public Service and in the alternate service to war. About 6,500 spent an average of thirty months in prison for their violation of the Selective Training and Service Act of 1940. They came from 240 religious denominations and sects. The Mennonite group numbered 4,665; the Church of the Brethren, 1,353; the Society of Friends, 951; the Methodist, 673; the Jehovah's Witnesses, 409, and the remainder was distributed through various denominations and small sects.

The furnishing of chaplains to the armed forces was one of the outstanding contributions of the religious bodies. The Army and the Navy recognized the importance of chaplains in maintaining the morale of the men in the service.

Since this paper is primarily concerned with attitudes rather than activities of the churches and clergy during the war period, no attempt will be made to appraise the many ways in which the religious people contributed their support to the war effort. . . .

A DILEMMA

It was a Christian soldier of three hundred years ago, Miles Standish, who is credited with saying:

> War is a terrible trade;
> But in the cause that is righteous
> Sweet is the smell of powder. . . .

Cromwell and many other stalwarts of bygone days would have agreed with the soldier of Plymouth. It is doubtful, however, whether today many followers of Jesus of Nazareth really relish war or enjoy the sweet smell of powder even in a righteous cause.

Thus times have changed--but how much? As has been observed, when groups of Christians believe that their country is fighting for its life, the attempt by force of arms to preserve its institutions becomes at least a "righteous" cause. Prayers for victory are heard over the land. The soldier dead are buried with the blessing of the Almighty. Yet between wars many of these same groups of believers in the Prince of Peace have declared that for them war is a colossal sin.

Here, then, is one of the great dilemmas of the Christian church. In time of peace, war is against God. In time of war, except for the absolute pacifists, there comes the intellectual and emotional necessity of making the war acceptable in terms of some kind of moral objective. Though war is recognized as a tragedy, fighting to preserve a Christian civilization against the "paganism" of the Axis is essentially waging war to defeat the enemies of Christ. When it became apparent that World War II was a fight to the finish, not many of even the pacifists could honestly say that it made no difference to them which side won.

Why is there often this hesitation on the part of those who believe in a sovereign God to ask him to bless their cause? Why are all manner of circumlocutions resorted to in the use of words and phrases (that in the end mean practically the same thing) to avoid labeling our cause as righteous or just? To answer that the pacifist movement has had a sobering effect upon the thought of the churches is only a step in the direction of the answer. Whatever cultural factors have been involved, the final answer must be sought in the understanding of the basic human motivations.

There is clear evidence that some of the institutional patterns that have developed to resolve the conflict within Christendom have a schizophrenic quality. An analysis of the theological arguments over war would seem to indicate that frequently the emotions and the intellect are split off from each other. Furthermore, many of the rationalizations that are used to cover up the real underlying motives are symptomatic of the unresolved conflicts and emotional turmoil within individuals themselves. For example, repressed hostility, frustrations, feelings of guilt, sadistic and masochistic tendencies, the fear of death, attachments to love objects on an infantile level, and dozens of other psychological and psychoanalytic phenomena may often lie behind attitudes toward war. The conflict over the relationship of the church to the god Mars may often be a projection of these more personal and emotional difficulties. Moreover, not infrequently debates regarding the nature of war from the Christian point of view were carried on as if in a vacuum, with little reference to reality. That fact also is diagnostic.

There is nothing new in the above statements. They are emphasized again because frequently men become so engrossed

with the more dramatic aspects of the death struggle of
civilizations that these primary considerations are forgotten.

How much longer the forces of organized religion will continue
to serve the gods of nationalism is perhaps a moot question.
At least it is evident that many drastic changes will have to
be made in man's social institutions before he can enjoy the
warless world envisioned by Isaiah: ". . . and they shall
beat their swords into plowshares, and their spears into
pruning hooks; nation shall not lift up sword against nation,
neither shall they learn war any more."

The National Council of Churches and Our Foreign Policy

ARTHUR H. DARKEN

Arthur H. Darken, educated at Yale, Union, and Columbia was an American Baptist minister in 1954 when he wrote the article which follows. In it he describes the support provided by the National Council of Churches for America's participation in the United Nations and for the early stages of the containment foreign policy after World War II. The excerpt is taken from "The National Council of Churches and Our Foreign Policy," Religion in Life 24 (1954-55): 113-26. Why did the National Council favor disarmament and noninvolvement during the 1930's? What evidence is there that the National Council provided support for the formation of the United Nations? Why does Darken call the position of the National Council after the war the "new realism?"

"My Christian conscience won't let me vote to endorse military alliances like NATO," the delegate declared. With equal passion another affirmed, "My Christian conscience will let me do no other than support the North Atlantic Treaty Alliance, to help preserve justice and freedom as well as our national security." This exchange took place at the Fourth National Conference on the Churches and World Order (1953), sponsored by the National Council of Churches. The conference voted to receive the Section report on Collective Security that supported NATO, but would not go quite that far in its final Message to the Churches.

This episode, showing wide support but not wholehearted majority approval for NATO, is symbolic of what has happened to the National Council of Churches in twenty years. The whole Federal Council of Churches, now the National Council of Churches, has responded to the changed times. They have re-examined Christianity and discovered relevant in new ways the old facts of human sin, joined with human responsibility before God who is both Judge and Redeemer. The Council has moved from a moralistic and unrealistic position to one that recognizes and faces more squarely the range of complex and ambiguous powers that make up the lives of men in the world of nations.

This author believes we must respond to the tensions and conflicts in international relations as United States citizens who take seriously the illumination of the Christian faith, that permits us neither to reject the massive political, economic, and military powers of the United States nor to accept their irresponsible use. It is their use that in large measure spells the difference between war and peace, freedom and slavery, justice and oppression for this nation and for many other lands.

From 1932 until America's entry into World War II, the Federal Council's basic concern in international affairs was to keep the peace--first for the world, and, when this was lost, to keep the United States out of the war. But, like many other America organizations, it oversimplified the problems of peace and war. It sought to secure peace by "building the will-to-peace," by joining international organizations, by convincing the world to disarm, by nonrecognition of aggression, by "eliminating the economic causes of war," and finally, by a policy of neutrality. These "answers" are now generally recognized for what they are, partial approaches to vast and complex problems, based on a utopian view of man and a view of history as progress.

I. DISARMAMENT

In 1932 the Federal Council of Churches said there was no longer any valid cause for war, and that the future belonged only to peace. The increase in communications and international trade removed barriers and made cooperation both possible and necessary. "New barriers are created from time to time, but they are no longer beyond human analysis and control. . . ." This was an unwarranted assumption, as indicated by subsequent history. While international control and reduction of armaments seemed to be the sensible way of preventing another outbreak of war, the nations would not disarm. The Geneva Conference of 1932-33 floundered on the rocks of German demands for equality of armaments with Great Britain and the United States. Future conferences were even less successful as national armaments increased instead of being reduced. Japan attacked Manchuria in 1932 and, in the same year, intensely nationalistic rearmament began in Germany. But the Council's official Bulletin devoted more space to the need for disarmament in 1932 and early 1933 than to any other international issue. It thought the tensions could best be removed by destroying and controlling the weapons of war. The Council did not see that armaments were but the outward reflection of an international malady rather than its cause.

II. THE AXIS POWERS

The Council's Executive Committee met in February, 1932, and proclaimed a three-point program to meet the Far Eastern crisis. This was more realistic than the official United States policy. The Council called for an immediate embargo on arms to both China and Japan. Secondly, they said, "We believe that the general acceptance of the principle of nonrecognition of national advantages gained by military means in violation of peace pledges will go far toward preventing resort to war." If these failed and either side resorted to force, they advocated that the United States join in a blockade of the aggressor nation.

Only the policy of nonrecognition became the official United States policy, and was subsequently adopted by the League of Nations. It was weak. Japan was not particularly worried whether anybody recognized her conquest of Manchuria as long as they didn't interfere. The other nations had been so weakened by the deep economic depression that spread across Europe and the United States, and detested the thought of war so much, that they ventured no more than this moralistic rebuke. The nations would not or could not invoke even limited economic sanctions at that time. Yet the League of Nations had to be vindicated by at least refusing recognition of this conquest.

The Council's support of an embargo shows its desire to end the fighting without involving the United States in military action. But an embargo is ineffectual unless it can be properly enforced, and this is seldom possible. The embargo would hurt the aggressor, but also the nation attacked, since it prevents both from receiving arms. The blockade, however, was the most radical suggestion the Council made in these years, for it could possibly have resulted in the military involvement of the United States. At this point the Federal Council seemed willing to sacrifice more to defend the peace and liberty of the Far East than did the United States in general.

But it was the Council's diagnosis of the Far Eastern situation, rather than its prescription for cure, that seems to have been the most responsible and realistic phase of its work before the Second World War. It pointed to Japan's desperate need for food, raw materials, and markets that had to be met if she was to survive. Similarly it called attention to China's political chaos and the ruthless conflicts amongst the war lords that prevented the nation from meeting its international obligations. It counseled friendliness and understanding, and stated, "It is idle to tell Japan she must not resort to violence to secure these legitimate ends if by following the method of peace she is going to starve."

The great omission from this analysis was, of course, the fact of Japanese aggression. While it was true the dire economic need in Japan lent support to the war forces there, it was also true the war involved Japan's imperialistic desire for the extension of her power over all East Asia. Both were important. The Council declared the Western nations were not blameless either, for they imposed high tariffs on Japanese goods and refused to permit immigrants from Japan to become citizens. This increased the economic and social problems of Japan and built hatred for the West. The Federal Council hoped for a peace that would stop aggression by all nations, and at the same time not conceal the injustice inherent in the Far Eastern situation. Justice as well as peace were at stake, and they were willing to risk a blockade to preserve them.

It is evident that a major cause of the Council's comprehensive analysis of the Sino-Japanese crisis was the expert knowledge it had available from American missionaries long active in the Far East. They knew the economic, psychological, and political situation in the area, and provided a picture of the crisis that was superior to that produced by many secular groups which issued statements on the Far East. At that time the United States had few Far Eastern exports.

On the other side of the world, Germany and Italy received much shorter shrift at the hands of the Federal Council. When Hitler rose to power in Germany, the Council's publications reflected an interest only in religious freedom and the dire fate of the Jews. Both were extremely important, but they were only part of the total situation. Almost nothing was said of the background that facilitated the rise of Hitler, except for an early interest in the canceling of German war debts in 1931, and an appeal to the United States to disarm as it had forced Germany to do after World War I. Little was said of the increasing regimentation in the German nation, the effect of German rearmament on Europe, or what United States policy should be toward Germany. When German armies began to march, the Council did not foresee the continuing aggression, and had no positive program to meet a general war in Europe. They presented only moral rebukes, urged aid to the refugees, and called on the United States to remain neutral but "work for peace." It was a narrow and fragmentary coverage as compared with that given Japan and China.

When Italy began its invasion of Ethiopia, the Council recommended economic sanctions against her, including an embargo not only on military materials but also on raw materials, like oil, that had potential military value. Other than this, it only called for a reallocation of natural resources to eliminate the economic causes of conflict. Here again, economic well-being was seen as the way to keep the peace, as though Italy's attack were but the result of that nation's desperate need for raw materials. It was, instead, the drive for the establishment of a new Roman empire under Mussolini, and the situation called for concerted, responsible use of the power at the disposal of other nations to quell the aggression. The most important material to embargo was oil, and this the nations would not do at a time when it would have been effective in preventing further aggression.

The irony of the whole emerging war situation was that the Christian churches, which live by the faith of the Bible, were seemingly unable to illumine their contemporary crisis by the biblical view of man. Pragmatic, human experience obviously bears out the biblical knowledge that man steals his brother's land because of the desire for power and control. Wars do not start because a nation lacks economic resources, has armaments, or is devoted to "nationalism." These are certainly factors upon which the aggressive desires of a government can play for support for its policies, but they do not in and of themselves create wars. While the churches seemed sensitive to the developments in the axis nations, they did not lead the American people to a much more responsible facing of the crisis than did other groups with the same knowledge of events but lacking the Christian faith. The American tradition of isolationism, compounded with pacifism, and a perhaps understandable overconfidence in the ability of England and France to defend Europe, led the churches and the American people in general to view with sadness and alarm the growing menace in Europe. It did not lead them to assess realistically the outcome in Europe and the implications for the United States.

III. NEUTRALITY AND THE WILL TO PEACE

Basic to the Council's work during this prewar period was a concern for building "the will to peace." If all nations would will peace and make it a "way of life," they would cooperate and wars would cease. An unofficial article in the Bulletin said, "Far-sighted leaders in the churches fully realize although governments can build the political structures of peace, the structure must be undergirded with a spiritual purpose and a dynamic will-to-peace. This will-to-peace is not the product of law-making. It is the product of religious education."

This was an undue emphasis on voluntarism, because the simple desire for peace can seldom stand before a challenge to the nation's honor, a thwarting of the national interest, or the ambitions of a dictator. It is further questionable whether peace is the all-consuming meaning of Christianity for international relations. Justice and freedom must receive equal attention as criteria for national action from a Christian illumination. Indeed, justice was not omitted from the Council's consideration of the Far Eastern crisis.

But, to an increasing degree, peace became the only goal, both for the Federal Council of Churches and United States in general. In 1935, the nation tried to isolate itself from the mounting international tension. Mussolini had invaded Ethiopia, Hitler marched into the Rhineland, and Japan increased her activity on the mainland of China. The United States placed embargoes on the shipment of war materials to all belligerents (except in the case of China and Japan, for they were not officially considered to be at war) and Americans were forbidden to travel on ships belonging to these nations. The Federal Council of Churches went even further and supported embargoes on raw materials of potential military value. The churches did not advocate these measures of separation from the conflict because they were unconcerned for the rest of the world. They did it in the false belief that the United States would be helping most to preserve the peace of the world if it kept out of the war. It was felt that the United States should cooperate to the extent of respecting and not interfering with the League's embargoes against the aggressors. However, it was a sort of negative responsibility, for the United States had no obligation to enforce sanctions imposed by the League.

Isolationism, or neutrality, was a strange policy for the Federal Council to embrace. Other groups, more logically, adopted it on the theory that Europe's wars did not affect us, and that we were not concerned for the fate of other nations. But the Council consistently emphasized our involvement with the destiny of other countries, and American responsibility to cooperate in keeping the peace. The policy of neutrality, however, had the effect of hurting the nations being attacked. These were even then our allies in popular sympathy, national interest, and democratic beliefs. The policy denied arms to both sides, and if England had not had control of the seas it would have hurt her even more after the addition of the "cash and carry" principle, adopted to salve our neutrality. In practice it seemed that all ideas of using American power to defend justice and freedom had been abandoned to keep the United States out of war. That this was also the temper of the nation was clearly indicated by the violent reaction to Presient Roosevelt's mild and somewhat vague "quarantine speech" of October, 1937.

It is a question just how far such an organization as the Federal Council of Churches could have departed from the popular policy even if its leaders had felt more was at stake than immediate peace for the United States. But there was not even a strong questioning of the implications for Western civilization of the negative policies they advocated.

The churches may have been somewhat uneasy about their policy, however, for the Council claimed neutrality was just a stopgap measure to be used until a world government could be built. This was the high-water mark of unrealism reached by the Federal Council in the prewar period. World government was a totally irrelevant and impossible answer to an immediate problem of political life and death. Even after the fall of Scandinavia and France, some failed to see that isolation could only result in the piecemeal conquest of the defensive nations who were our allies in spirit, thus leaving the United States in an even less secure position at the hands of the dictatorships. All considerations of responsible action in this situation had been cast aside to guarantee the purity and peace of the United States. But because God has not created us independent person, this policy could not achieve even these narrow goals.

That some Protestant leaders were aware of the religious

dimensions of the European war is indicated by the founding early in 1941 of the little biweekly, Christianity and Crisis. The lead article of the first issue said, "In the presence of the crisis the editors of this journal feel that as Christian citizens the least they can do is to advocate a policy on the part of the government of the United States of giving those who fight for freedom all the aid that it is in our power as a nation to give." Of the nature of this "crisis" the editors said, "We mean that as Protestant Christians we stand confronted with the ultimate crisis of the whole civilization of which we are a part and whose existence has made possible the survival of our type of faith and our type of church." But they were under no illusions that this was a holy war. The allies did not stand for the "final truth," but for this reason the imperative to act was not removed.

The chief editor of Christianity and Crisis, Reinhold Niebuhr, commented in answer to those who rejected aid to the allies because it meant contact with war, that we can never achieve a point of guiltlessness from which to proceed against evil. We all continually betray Christ, but our final peace ". . . is the religious peace of knowing that a divine mercy accepts our loyalty to Christ despite our continual betrayal of Him." "Life is never related to life in terms of a perfect and loving conformity of will with will. Where there is sin and selfishness there must also be a struggle for justice. And this justice is always partially an achievement of our love for the other, and partially a result of our yielding to his demands and pressures."

We have thus briefly reviewed the policy of the Federal Council until the United States entered the war, in 1941. It centered on building a superstructure of peace in a world rapidly falling into war. In many cases the Council miscalculated the feasibility of its policies in the world of nations. Disarmament was impossible in a world grappling for military security. Neutrality merely aided the axis powers, since the allies needed weapons more than did the axis. The Council made narrow analyses of what was actually involved in situations, and thus did not see the total issues. The economic needs of the axis powers were only one factor in their aggression. But in the Far Eastern crisis, the Council went far beyond the popular press and even surpassed many social scientists in its understanding of the complexities involved.

The Council's basic defects centered in four areas: (1) an overemphasis on peace and nonviolence, rather than justice or freedom, as Christian implications for the United States foreign policy objectives; (2) failure to understand the extent to which the axis aggression was a struggle for power, relatively unrelated to matters of economic justice and "living space"; (3) unwillingness to use the power possessed by the United States to restrain this evil in ways which would be effective; and (4) an imperfect appreciation of the fact that the fate of the United States was tied in with the fate of England, France, and the other allies. National power can never be neutral. God confers power that it may be used responsibly to maintain and strengthen the relative freedom and justice in the world.

IV. THE UNITED NATIONS

The Federal Council became one of the first American groups to begin serious planning for the postwar world when, in 1940, it established the Commission to Study the Bases of a Just and Durable Peace, under the chairmanship of Mr. John Foster Dulles. The Commission moved carefully, and by 1943 had agreed on its basic principles, which were issued as the Six Pillars of Peace. They called for a United Nations organization with universal membership, international agreement on national economic policies of world importance, the possibility of treaty revision as conditions changed, an organization to assure autonomy for dependent peoples, the establishment and protection of religious and intellectual freedom for all, and the conviction that the peace ultimately can only be kept by an informed and moral public opinion. Here was a clear call for the United States to abandon isolation and accept continuing responsibility for world politics as we had never done before. The Federal Council had fought hard for the League of Nations, and now was to do the same for the UN.

The Council used the Six Pillars as its guide for the discussion of the Dumbarton Oaks Proposals preparatory to the San Francisco Conference, in 1945. It accepted these proposals, because it was convinced they were the best obtainable at the time, though certainly not perfect. The Council presented its position at San Francisco; and many of its recommendations, which were likewise advocated by other groups and countries, were adopted and became part of the Charter. These included provisions for a Human Rights Commission, universal membership, plans for eventual freedom of colonial areas, the codification of international law, and an easier process of Charter amendment.

The Federal Council failed to achieve the elimination of the veto power in the Security Council and the limitation of arms. But the other changes, the Federal Council declared, brought the UN more nearly into accord with Christian principles of world order. It still needed improvements, but it was a workable basis for world cooperation for peace and justice. There were serious threats in the differences between the great powers, and the Council said a strong will to peace was needed to overcome them.

The Commission on a Just and Durable Peace spent four years developing its views and demonstrated what a responsible job the churches could do in the field of international policy-making and how they could effectively take their policy to the people. Also, while the final Charter did not embody all its wishes, the Council evidenced a real willingness to accept the best that was possible in contemporary society, and to throw support behind it. The Council did not hold out for the impossible and so risk losing the feasible. It had abandoned perfectionist ethics in world affairs, but, at the same time, kept its idealism as a goad toward greater justice and order in the world through international machinery and conscious striving for peace.

When atom bombs fell on Japan in 1945, the Federal Council immediately called for united world control of atomic energy. In the hands of the separate nations, atomic energy would precipitate total war. While noting the faults in the Acheson-Lilienthal report issued a year later, the Council supported it and called it a notable step forward. Here again the Council positively supported something that it admitted was not the perfect instrument desired, but had to be accepted and developed from there.

It is not often possible to draw sharp contrasts between the actions of great organizations like the Federal Council at two points in their history, but it is clear these decisions represented at least a trend toward realism, and proximate goals in world affairs, as compared with statements prior to

World War II. They showed a better understanding of the actual possibilities and obstacles which lie in the path to peace, justice, and order. When a group recognizes these actualities, yet doesn't lose its vision or drive, it is most apt to be successful.

V. THE SOVIET UNION AND THE NEW REALISM

After World War II many problems of foreign policy stemmed from conflict with the Soviet Union. The Federal Council of Churches has devoted much of its comment to this theme since 1945. As it became evident that more was involved in Russo-American relations than misunderstanding and mutual intolerance, the Council's policies changed. Immediately after World War II, peace seemed quite possible, the Council concluded. Compromise was unlikely between views so disparate, but peace could exist if each exerted itself to settle the avoidable conflicts and refused to impose its doctrines on others by force and violence. The churches looked to the United States to lead the way toward tolerance in world affairs, and to show Russia that intolerance would only jeopardize the peace. Yet the Council said we should not oppose the Soviets simply because they were dynamic, for all change was not evil, and "no one economic system had a monopoly of truth and virtue."

By 1948, however, the Council was convinced that war was inevitable if Russia continued its course of action. To prevent this, the United States was urged to build conditions that would keep Russia from taking reckless and dangerous actions.

> It seems that the Soviet program will be aggressively pushed to the danger point especially where the following conditions prevail: first, where economies are weak; second, where the working people can be made to believe that proletarian dictatorship offers their best hope of increased welfare; and third, where man can be terrorized.

It was in the light of these conclusions that they recommended less concentration on military policy, and more on a positive program of an economic, social, political, and moral character. This meant support for the European Recovery Plan, and for

President Truman's Point Four program of technical assistance to economically less developed areas. War would be less likely, if such a positive program were coupled with a change of mood in America. Americans, the Council maintained, should not hate the Russians, but affirm the love of God for all men, reject fatalism, and build the Christian world fellowship.

This was an invigorating and positive approach, but it had certain defects. These were all essential but long-range policies for the global conflict and especially pertinent in the economically less developed areas of the world such as Africa, the Near East, and Far East. But all discussion failed to tackle the immediate problem, which was the military strengthening and the unification of the Western world. Unless the West could offer military preponderance in the near future, there would be little time for these enlightened economic, social, and human rights programs to be effective over a long period of time, on a global level.

The Federal Council omitted almost all mention of the Greek-Turkish Aid program of 1947, the Truman Doctrine to give military as well as economic aid to these nations in their hour of peril. Surely God was also interested in these elements of foreign policy. These were fateful decisions which the American Congress and people were called upon to make, but the Council of Churches had no guidance for them, either political or theological. Similarly it paid little attention to Western European integration and the North Atlantic Treaty Organization, as these sought the West's defense both now and over a long period of time by military and economic means. The Council was now moving and moving creatively, but it had yet to take the step of giving recognition to the problems of the responsible use of military power by the United States.

It was not until the Third Study Conference on the Churches and World Order, in 1949, that the Federal Council centered its attention on the responsible use of power. The basic orientation was the recognition that America's vast power must be considered as ours under the providence of God, to be used responsibly in the development of world law, order, and community. Power could always lead to conceit and prideful boasting that would be disastrous, the report said. It would deafen us to the cries of people for deliverance from death and misery visited upon them by economic disorder and recurrent wars.

The Council reaffirmed its earlier concern for the world-wide economic and social struggle with communism and further declared, "We must maintain sufficient strength to convince Soviet Russia that attempts to impose an ideology by force cannot succeed." This was the first time a conference sponsored by the Federal Council of Churches actually called for military preparations to meet possible aggression. Some at the conference labeled any resort to military action immoral.

The Conference Message, later adopted by the Executive Committee of the Council, did not specifically call for military preparations. It proclaimed that war with Russia was not inevitable. It was even unlikely, given the proper use of the United States' powerful influence to deter the enemy in the interest of negotiation and reconciliation. The UN, it admitted, had to be developed, but it allowed for the UN's real ineffectiveness until there is world-wide acceptance of the moral principles upon which law and order are based. It was for this reason only that the Council agreed to support any regional pacts such as NATO, providing also they were in harmony with the UN Charter. . . .

More than ever before the Council recognizes the hard facts of political power, the complex nature of most problems in international relations, the ambiguous nature of man, and the perversions to which man is capable of putting God's power. From this it appears Christians can take new hope, for with a realistic view of man, proper humility, and faith in God as Judge and Redeemer of history, the vast power our nation holds can be used responsibly to God and man. As Reinhold Niebuhr said, "The message adopted by the Conference was an eloquent and mature analysis of America's position in the world and of the responsibilities which are the concomitants of our power."

RELIGIOUS RESPONSES TO THE TURBULENT 60'S

Communist America--Must It Be?

BILLY JAMES HARGIS

Billy James Hargis (1925-) is one of the foremost ultraconservative evangelists who has linked the preaching of fundamentalist Christianity with aggressive patriotism. In the late 1940's he founded the Christian Crusade, a vast complex of religious and educational institutions, which has propagated its message "for Christ and against Communism" through books, pamphlets, radio broadcasts, and preaching tours. In 1971 his American Christian College, a school dedicated to teaching "God, government, and Christian action," was opened in Tulsa, Oklahoma, the home of the Christian Crusade. In one of his recent books he referred to himself as "one of the world's foremost experts on the subject of anti-Communism." The following excerpt appears in his book Communist America--Must It Be? (Tulsa: Christian Crusade, 1960), pp. 181-85, and is used here by permission of the author. How does Hargis use the concept of self-sacrifice to support his call to anti-communist activity? What connection does Hargis make between conservative theology and conservative politics?

Epilogue--Can It Be Done Without Sacrifice?

"And behold, one came and said unto him, Good Master, what good things shall I do, that I may have eternal life? . . . Jesus said unto him, if you wilt be perfect, go and sell that thou hast, and give to the poor, and thou shalt have treasure in heaven: and come follow Me. But, when the young man heard that saying, HE WENT AWAY SORROWFUL: for he had great possessions."

From the dawn of history, men have asked God what good thing shall I do? That one spark of decency and generosity may be found in every human heart. There is not a man living, even those who have sunk hopelessly into the mire of degradation, who hasn't sometime, somewhere felt the desire to give something worthwhile to someone else.

"What good thing shall I do" is a question as old as the ages, that has always had, and will always have, one answer, that found in the book of Matthew.

Here we have the story of a young man, rich in material possessions, who wanted the assurance from Christ that his life was not totally in vain. In good faith he asks, "What can I do?" Christ's answer: "Go, and sell that thou hast and GIVE . . ." fell on deaf ears. Why, because this was NOT the answer man wanted to hear. For Christ has asked him to give to the point of personal sacrifice. Then, as now, the human weakness to find an easier way, one that does not require personal sacrifice, was too strong. The man "went away sorrowful" and his dream of giving to others remained only a dream!

It has been said that "self-sacrifice is the highest rule of grace." The Christian principles upon which our country is founded are ours through the sacrifice of others. The first founders of this nation were men and women who willingly sacrificed, not only their personal comfort and material possessions, but their VERY lives, in many instances, to establish a nation where freedom was rampart. What sustained these first citizens who faced starvation and the bitter cold of Jamestown and Plymouth? Two important things, their unwavering belief in God and His righteousness and their never ending faith that through their sacrifices a new nation, promising freedom for others, would arise.

Since 1620, the United States has faced that which threatened our freedoms without flinching. We have fought wars to protect our children's right to live in God-given liberty. The personal, self-sacrifices made in these conflicts can be counted by the silent white markers which stretch in endless rows on the rolling hills of Valley Forge, the grassy plains of Flanders and the coral-etched reef of Iwo Jima. Supreme Sacrifices they are called . . . Self-sacrifices made by men whose names you will never know . . . whose faces we will never see.

Today, this nation is engaged in a battle as fierce and urgent as any which we have ever encountered on an actual battleground. We are struggling to stamp out Communist infiltration in this nation. We have only one opportunity to win. Our defeat means the abyss of godless Communism. The battle against Communism is not a battle with guns or rockets, but a conflict for the minds, the souls and the freedom of human beings. Communism is not a respecter of persons, nor does it touch the lives of only a few. Those who have endured under Communist rule are witnesses to the fact that under its Iron Boot are ground the hopes, the dignity and the freedom of every human being.

Communism is not a political party as such. It is a ruthless movement dedicated to the destruction of Christianity. The only sure way to stamp out Communism and its ideas is through the Word of God. Communism cannot survive in a truly Christian nation. Remember, there is no freedom without God.

Had Christ shunned the cross, we would be living without hope. Christ gave his life on the cross as an act of supreme sacrifice that we might have hope . . . that we might have a Christian life. Others have given their lives that we might live in a Christian Nation.

What we do now means the difference between a Nation that lives under God or a Nation that suffers under Communism.

Why is the infiltration of Communist ideas spreading in America? Because the average citizen is not even aware of the Communist threat.

The facts that ARE printed are too often shrugged off with a casual, "It can't happen here . . . this is America." And, because THIS IS AMERICA, we have lulled ourselves into believing that we are safe and secure from any force on earth! "It can't happen here?" How many thousand Poles, Hungarians and Tibetans repeated those four simple words BEFORE they tasted the bitter dregs of Communism? The Rand Corporation, in cooperation with the Defense Department, announced recently that within the next four years Communist Russia will have the power to destroy our Air Force and to devastate 85% of our big industry and 43 of our 50 largest cities in one lightning blow. Add this to the fact that the Communists have averaged 7,000 newly enslaved subjects every hour of the day. The question is no longer "CAN the Communists overthrow us or WILL they try to overthrow us," but "WHEN will they overthrow us?"

These facts in themselves are shocking, but the fact remains that the Communist threat WITHIN is even greater and even more pressing. If the threat is so urgent why is nothing being done?

Something is being done. Thousands of Americans are now at work trying desperately to destroy Communism with the most effective weapons we possess--FACTS. But, these thousands are only a small majority of our population. Others are needed.

Each day someone says to me, in all sincerity, "Dr. Hargis, what can I do to save America from Communism? How can I help?" And, yet, when I answer them, all too often they smile, duck their head and walk away UNWILLING TO do the only thing that any of us can do, and that is sacrifice. This one word is the answer to the challenge we are faced with in America today. What can you do? First ask yourself, "Do I really want to destroy Communism from the face of the earth? Do I really want to rid our nation of Communist infiltration and to restore Constitutional government in Washington? Do I want to offset Communist influence with the gospel of Christ and freedom?" Boiled down the question is this . . . "Do I want to serve God and save America?" If you sincerely answer yes, then you have NO CHOICE but to "go and sell . . . and give . . ." and come follow Jesus Christ.

Perhaps you wonder what you as one person can do. You can take it upon yourself to act as a Committee of One to learn what Communism actually is, how it works, where it strikes. You can recognize its subtleness as the seeds of Communist thoughts, not modern thinking. You can become a spokesman for truth by discussing the facts with your neighbors, your friends, any one you can get to listen. Remember, no one can destroy what they do not see. With facts and determination, you can bring Communist infiltration out in to the open. <u>Communism only grows in the darkness of ignorance.</u>

And, you can join organized movements dedicated to exposing Communism. Unless movements like Christian Crusade are permitted to continue and grow, the doors to the churches you build now will be closed by God-hating Communists before they have a chance to develop. Your membership in such organizations will mean personal sacrifice, for you will be called upon to give your time, your energies and your whole-hearted support to fighting Communism. The reward? The knowledge that the dreams your children hold dear will be realized, the compensation that you will live to see your child grow up in freedom, knowing that he will be able to kneel in the church of his choice without the threat of reprisal. Every war takes money for ammunition. The arms in our fight against Red infiltration is truth. It takes money to print pamphlets exposing Communism. It takes funds to combat propaganda. Where does the money come from? From the pockets of Americans who are willing to sacrifice to keep their freedom. It is only through this help that such organizations are able to continue to fight against Communism for these organizations depend entirely upon the contributions received. A nation-wide campaign on every radio station, in every newspaper and on every television channel might spare us Communist defeat.

To read the truth about Communism and then to shrug and say let someone else help, is in reality, saying, "I am ready to surrender this country to Communism. It's all in vain."

Evidence indicates that we have become a nation that places more value on material possessions than on the greatest gifts of all--Christianity and country. A graphic illustration of this is shown in a newspaper account I read recently. A school teacher asked his students to list what they considered their most valuable possessions. Not one student put Christianity or country first. In fact, the words "Christianity" or "country" did not even appear on the list!

And, yet, I cannot believe that if the majority of Americans knew what is happening in their nation that you would find one Christian who would not stand up and fight openly.

I heard a man say recently, "I am willing to sacrifice all, even my life, if need be. Thank God for the man with this spirit. For if we are to survive, if we are to live FREELY under God's guidance, we cannot "turn away sorrowfully." Can it be done without sacrifice? NO. There is no hope without sacrifice. And, if we are unwilling to do our part . . . then, God have mercy on a nation whose people would not sacrifice to keep their freedom.

Civil Religion in America

ROBERT N. BELLAH

Robert N. Bellah (1927-   ) was educated at Harvard and has been a professor of sociology at the University of California since 1958. The rebirth of civil religion during the conservative era of the 1950's stimulated scholarly analyses of the civil religion phenomenon, which can be traced back to the period of the American Revolution. No analysis has been more thorough than that provided by Bellah, who, in the article from which the excerpt which follows was taken, discusses the historical roots of civil religion and how it was woven into the American cultural fabric. "Civil Religion in America" reprinted here by permission of Daedalus, Journal of the American Academy of Arts and Sciences, 96 (Winter 1967): 1-21, Boston, Mass. How does

Bellah define "civil religion"? What examples of civil religion does he discuss, and what social and political role does civil religion play? In Bellah's opinion, what negative influence has civil religion had in the past? What does he mean by the phrase "the American Israel theme"?

While some have argued that Christianity is the national faith, and others that church and synagogue celebrate only the generalized religion of "the American Way of Life," few have realized that there actually exists alongside of and rather clearly differentiated from the churches an elaborate and well-institutionalized civil religion in America. This article argues not only that there is such a thing, but also that this religion--or perhaps better, this religious dimension--has its own seriousness and integrity and requires the same care in understanding that any other religion does.

The Kennedy Inaugural

Kennedy's inaugural address of 20 January 1961 serves as an example and a clue with which to introduce this complex subject. That address began:

> We observe today not a victory of party but a celebration of freedom--symbolizing an end as well as a beginning--signifying renewal as well as change. For I have sworn before you and Almighty God the same solemn oath our forebears prescribed nearly a century and three quarters ago.
>
> The world is very different now. For man holds in his mortal hands the power to abolish all forms of human poverty and to abolish all forms of human life. And yet the same revolutionary beliefs for which our forebears fought are still at issue around the globe--

the belief that the rights of man come not from the
generosity of the state but from the hand of God.

And it concluded:

> Finally, whether you are citizens of America or
> of the world, ask of us the same high standards
> of strength and sacrifice that we shall ask of
> you. With a good conscience our only sure reward,
> with history the final judge of our deeds, let us
> go forth to lead the land we love, asking His
> blessing and His help, but knowing that here on
> earth God's work must truly be our own.

These are the three places in this brief address in which
Kennedy mentioned the name of God. If we could understand
why he mentioned God, the way in which he did it, and what
he meant to say in those three references, we would understand much about American civil religion. But this is not a
simple or obvious task, and American students of religion
would probably differ widely in their interpretation of
these passages.

Let us consider first the placing of the three references.
They occur in the two opening paragraphs and in the closing
paragraph, thus providing a sort of frame for the more concrete remarks that form the middle part of the speech. Looking beyond this particular speech, we would find that similar
references to God are almost invariably to be found in the
pronouncements of American presidents on solemn occasions,
though usually not in the working messages that the president
sends to Congress on various concrete issues. How, then, are
we to interpret this placing of references to God?

It might be argued that the passages quoted reveal the essentially irrelevant role of religion in the very secular society that is America. The placing of the references in this
speech as well as in public life generally indicates that
religion has "only a ceremonial significance"; it gets only
a sentimental nod which serves largely to placate the more
unenlightened members of the community, before a discussion
of the really serious business with which religion has nothing whatever to do. A cynical observer might even say that
an American president has to mention God or risk losing
votes. A semblance of piety is merely one of the unwritten

qualifications for the office, a bit more traditional than but not essentially different from the present-day requirement of a pleasing television personality.

But we know enough about the function of ceremonial and ritual in various societies to make us suspicious of dismissing something as unimportant because it is "only a ritual." What people say on solemn occasions need not be taken at face value, but it is often indicative of deep-seated values and commitments that are not made explicit in the course of everyday life. Following this line of argument, it is worth considering whether the very special placing of the references to God in Kennedy's address amy not reveal something rather important and serious about religion in American life.

It might be countered that the very way in which Kennedy made his references reveals the essentially vestigial place of religion today. He did not refer to any religion in particular. He did not refer to Jesus Christ, or to Moses, or to the Christian church; certainly he did not refer to the Catholic Church. In fact, his only reference was to the concept of God, a word which almost all Americans can accept but which means so many different things to so many different people that it is almost an empty sign. Is this not just another indication that America religion is considered vaguely to be a good thing, but that people care so little about it that it has lost any content whatever? Isn't Eisenhower reported to have said, "Our government makes no sense unless it is founded in a deeply felt religious faith--and I don't care what it is," and isn't that a complete negation of any real religion?

These questions are worth pursuing because they raise the issue of how civil religion relates to the political society, on the one hand, and to private religious organization, on the other. President Kennedy was a Christian, more specifically a Catholic Christian. Thus, his general references to God do not mean that he lacked a specific religious commitment. But why, then, did he not include some remark to the effect that Christ is the Lord of the world or some indication of respect for the Catholic Church? He did not because these are matters of his own private religious belief and of his relation to his own particular church; they are not matters relevant in any direct way to the conduct of his public office. Others with different religious views and commitments to different churches or denominations are equally qualified participants in the political process. The principle of separation of church and state guarantees the freedom of religious belief and association, but at the same time clearly segregates the religious sphere, which is considered to be essentially private, from the political one.

Considering the separation of church and state, how is a president justified in using the word God at all? The answer is that the separation of church and state has not denied the political realm a religious dimension. Although matters of personal religious belief, worship, and association are considered to be strictly private affairs, there are, at the same time, certain common elements of religious orientation that the great majority of American share. These have played a crucial role in the development of American institutions and still provide a religious dimension for the whole fabric of American life, including the political sphere. This public religious dimension is expressed in a set of beliefs, symbols, and rituals that I am calling the American civil religion. The inauguration of a president is an important ceremonial event in this religion. It reaffirms, among other things, the religious legitimation of the highest political authority.

Let us look more closely at what Kennedy actually said. First he said, "I have sworn before you and Almighty God the same solemn oath our forebears prescribed nearly a century and three quarters ago." The oath is the oath of office, including the acceptance of the obligation to uphold the Constitution. He swears it before the people (you) and God. Beyond the Constitution, then, the president's obligation extends not only to the people but to God. In American political theory, sovereignty rests, of course, with the people, but implicitly, and often explicitly, the ultimate sovereignty has been attributed to God. This is the meaning of the motto, "In God we trust," as well as the inclusion of the phrase "under God" in the pledge to the flag. What difference does it make that sovereignty belongs to God? Though the will of the people as expressed in majority vote is carefully institutionalized as the operative source of political authority, it is deprived of an ultimate significance. The will of the people is not itself the criterion of right and wrong. There is a higher criterion in terms of which this will can be judged; it is possible that the people may be wrong. The president's obligation extends to the higher criterion.

When Kennedy says that "the rights of man come not from the generosity of the state but from the hand of God," he is stressing this point again. It does not matter whether the state is the expression of the will of an autocratic monarch or of the "people"; the rights of man are more basic than any political structure and provide a point of revolutionary leverage from which any state structure may be radically altered. That is the basis for his reassertion of the revolutionary significance of America.

But the religious dimension in political life as recognized by Kennedy not only provides a grounding for the rights of man which makes any form of political absolutism illegitimate, it also provides a transcendent goal for the political process. This is implied in his final words that "here on earth God's work must truly be our own." What he means here is, I think, more clearly spelled out in a previous paragraph, the wording of which, incidentally, has a distinctly Biblical ring:

> Now the trumpet summons us again--not as a call to bear arms, though arms we need--not as a call to battle, though embattled we are--but a call to bear the burden of a long twilight struggle, year in and year out, "rejoicing in hope, patient in tribulation"--a struggle against the common enemies of man: tyranny, poverty, disease and war itself.

The whole address can be understood as only the most recent statement of a theme that lies very deep in the American tradition, namely the obligation, both collective and individual, to carry out God's will on earth. This was the motivating spirit of those who founded America, and it has been present in every generation since. Just below the surface throughout Kennedy's inaugural address, it becomes explicit in the closing statement that God's work must be our own. That this very activist and non-contemplative conception of the fundamental religious obligation, which has been historically associated with the Protestant position, should be enunciated so clearly in the first major statement of the first Catholic president seems to underline how deeply established it is in the American outlook. . . .

American civil religion is still very much alive. Just three years ago we participated in a vivid re-enactment of the sacrifice theme in connection with the funeral of our assassinated president. The American Israel theme is clearly behind both Kennedy's New Frontier and Johnson's Great Society. Let me give just one recent illustration of how the civil religion serves to mobilize support for the attainment of national goals. On 15 March 1965 President Johnson went before Congress to ask for a strong voting-rights bill. Early in the speech he said:

> Rarely are we met with the challenge, not to our growth or abundance, or our welfare or our security—but rather to the values and the purposes and the meaning of our beloved nation.
>
> The issue of equal rights for American Negroes is such an issue. And should we defeat every enemy, and should we double our wealth and conquer the stars and still be unequal to this issue, then we will have failed as a people and as a nation.
>
> For with a country as with a person, "What is a man profited, if he shall gain the whole world, and lose his own soul?"

And in conclusion he said:

> Above the pyramid on the great seal of the United States it says in Latin, "God has favored our undertaking."
>
> God will not favor everything that we do. It is rather our duty to divine his will. I cannot help but believe that He truly understands and that He really favors the undertaking that we begin here tonight.

The civil religion has not always been invoked in favor of worthy causes. On the domestic scene, an American-Legion type of ideology that fuses God, country, and flag has been used to attack non-conformist and liberal ideas and groups of all kinds. Still, it has been difficult to use the words of Jefferson and Lincoln to support special interests and undermine personal freedom. The defenders of slavery before the Civil War came to reject the thinking of the Declaration of Independence. Some of the most consistent of them turned against not only Jeffersonian democracy but Reformation religion; they dreamed of a South dominated by medieval chivalry and divine-right monarchy. For all the overt religiosity of the radical right today, their relation to the civil religion consensus is tenuous, as when the John Birch Society attacks the central American symbol of Democracy itself.

With respect to America's role in the world, the dangers of distortion are greater and the built-in safeguards of the tradition weaker. The theme of the American Israel was used, almost from the beginning, as a justification for the shameful treatment of the Indians so characteristic of our history. It can be overtly or implicitly linked to the idea of manifest destiny which has been used to legitimate several adventures in imperialism since the early-nineteenth century. Never has the danger been greater than today. The issue is not so much one of imperial expansion, of which we are accused, as of the tendency to assimilate all governments or parties in the world which support our immediate policies or call upon our help by invoking the notion of free institutions and democratic values. Those nations that are for the moment "on our side" become "the free world." A repressive and unstable military dictatorship in South Viet-Nam becomes "the free people of South Viet-Nam and their government." It is then part of the role of America as the New Jerusalem and "the last hope of earth" to defend such governments with treasure and eventually with blood. When our soldiers are actually dying, it becomes possible to consecrate the struggle further by invoking the great theme of sacrifice. For the majority of the American people who are unable to judge whether the people in South Viet-Nam (or wherever) are "free like us," such arguments are convincing. Fortunately, President Johnson has been less ready to assert that "God has favored our undertaking" in the case of Viet-Nam than with respect to civil rights. But others are not so hesitant. The civil religion has exercised long-term pressure for the humane solution of our greatest domestic problem, the treatment of the Negro American. It remains to be seen how relevant it can become for our role in the world at large, and whether we can effectually stand for "the revolutionary beliefs for which our forebears fought," in John F. Kennedy's words. . . .

Behind the civil religion at every point lie Biblical

archtypes: Exodus, Chosen People, Promised Land, New Jerusalem, Sacrificial Death and Rebirth. But it is also genuinely American and genuinely new. It has its own prophets and its own martyrs, its own sacred events and sacred places, its own solemn rituals and symbols. It is concerned that America be a society as perfectly in accord with the will of God as men can make it, and a light to all the nations.

It has often been used and is being used today as a cloak for petty interests and ugly passions. It is in need--as is any living faith--of continual reformation, of being measured by universal standards. But it is not evident that it is incapable of growth and new insight.

It does not make any decision for us. It does not remove us from moral ambiguity, from being, in Lincoln's phrase, an "almost chosen people." But it is a heritage of moral and religious experience from which we still have much to learn as we formulate the decisions that lie ahead.

The Jesus People

RONALD M. ENROTH

Ronald M. Enroth (1938-   ) is professor of sociology at Westmont College in Santa Barbara, California. He has written extensively on contemporary social issues which have faced the church over the past fifteen years. The rise of the counter-culture during the 1960's had a profound effect on the institutionalized church which was a target of the antiestablishment sentiment of that turbulent decade. In The Jesus People: Old-Time Religion in the Age of Aquarius co-authored by Enroth, Edward E. Ericson, and C. Breckinridge Peters, one facet of the religious counter-culture is examined, with special attention given to the reasons for its rise and its significance for the 1960's. The following excerpt from The Jesus People (Grand Rapids, Mich.: Eerdmans Publishing Co., 1972), pp. 223-39), is used by permission of the publisher. How does Enroth explain the Jesus People as part of a social movement? Why were so many people attracted to the movement in the 1960's? Why is the significance of the movement in terms of its religious impact not known at the time Enroth is writing?

The Jesus People as a Social Movement: A Great Awakening or a Gentle Stir?

Any social movement--religious, political, economic--must be understood in the context of its social and cultural setting. To comprehend fully how the movement arises and develops and where it ends up, we must first describe the "spirit of the age" within which it functions. In his book, Modern Social Movements, William Bruce Cameron notes: "The purposes of a social movement cannot be evaluated, nor the actions of members understood, unless we clearly perceive the background of the society against which they play their part. Social movements . . . are made of the stuff that is at hand" (p. 21).

The "stuff" of the sixties and seventies has been delineated, categorized, and analyzed by sociologists, journalists, philosophers, psychologists, and assorted other "people-watchers." One of the more provocative endeavors at this is Rollo May's Love and Will. Another is The Making of a Counter Culture by Theodore Roszak. We shall draw on the works of these and other commentators on the American scene in order to place the Jesus Movement in a context appropriate for analysis.

We live in an impersonal, computerized, assembly-line,

shopping-center society where all the old anchorages have been lost or weakened and where alienation has become the common malaise. Thomas Cottle, in his perceptive volume, Time's Children, speaks of "our televised and instant replay society" where few secrets are allowed and "we become frustrated when we cannot discover the exact frame on which is recorded a President's death" (pp. 86-87). It is a society in which young people especially have been subjected to a tremendous over-stimulation--by the various media, by the myriad of confusing alternatives of vocation, religion, and morals, and by the mechanisms of an economic system that provides unparalleled affluence and a seemingly endless stream of material goods for consumption.

At the same time that modern technological man has felt that he has the tools to control the universe and material possessions to make life worthwhile, he has experienced a spiritual emptiness and personal disorganization perhaps unequaled in human history. Our technical sophistication has not brought any culmination of human happiness, as Barbara Hargrove explains in her book Reformation of the Holy.

> There is a growing awareness in modern society that the basic assumptions of technical progress and scientific knowledge may be leading, not to Utopia, but to a loss of humanity if not total destruction. Not only is this so, but that awareness is compounded by the feeling that the technological machine cannot be stopped, that we are caught in an ever-descending spiral of our own making from which there is no escape (p. 281).

The introductory chapter of May's Love and Will is entitled "Our Schizoid World." "Schizoid" means "out of touch; avoiding close relationships; the inability to feel" (p. 16). He sees this schizoid orientation as a general condition of our culture and the people who comprise our society. He describes our world as one

> where numbers inexorably take over as our means of identification, like flowing lava threatening to suffocate and fossilize all breathing life in its path . . . where "normality" is defined as keeping your cool; where sex is so available that the only way to preserve any inner center is to learn to

have intercourse without committing yourself . . .
(p. 32).

Young people experience this schizoid world more directly than their elders, according to May, because "they have not had time to build up the defenses which dull the senses of their elders" (p. 32). Without the old values and symbols that served as a touchstone of orientation for past generations, today's generation is increasingly forced inward, pushed toward apathy, toward a state of affectlessness. This results in a society characterized by estrangement, indifference, anomie, and depersonalization. Ultimately, asserts May, such a process eventuates in violence. "When inward life dries up, when feeling decreases and apathy increases, when one cannot affect or even genuinely touch another person, violence flares up as a daimonic necessity for contact, a mad drive forcing touch in the most direct way possible" (pp. 30-31).

The contemporary age has been characterized as one of "new freedom" and a new morality. Our highly vaunted permissiveness in the area of male-female relations has revealed the fact that "sex for many people has become more meaningless as it is more available . . ." (May, p. 14). May continues: "What we did not see in our shortsighted liberalism in sex was that throwing the individual into an unbounded and empty sea of free choice does not in itself give freedom, but is more apt to increase inner conflicts" (p. 42).

If this is the age of liberated man and anonymous man, it is certainly the age of technocratic man. "Technocracy's Children" are the offspring of a social and economic system, writes Theodore Roszak, "which is so organized that it is inextricably beholden to expertise" (The Making of a Counter Culture, p. 19). They have come of age in a society of experts and scientism where efficiency and successful management are the order of the day. They have learned that performance counts, and the pressures to compete and succeed are often overwhelming. "One must be good in school, good at home, good at sports, good at pot and good in bed" (Cottle, p. 87).

It was in this complex social and cultural milieu that the Jesus Movement emerged. The 1960s saw armies of young people attempting to get "involved" with society's ills, trying to

effect changes in the system. Barbara Hargrove relates the
sequence of events that led to what she calls the "apocalyptic
mood" of the present:

> Failure of civil rights and poverty programs, and of
> anti-war activity increased the feeling that the
> present system could not be changed or redirected.
> By the mid-sixties the quest had begun to turn inward.
> The disastrous political campaign of 1968, with its
> assassinations, its hopes, and its riots, added to
> the disenchantment with political solutions. The
> widespread politicization of the campuses after the
> Cambodia-Kent State-Jackson State debacle in 1970
> has apparently ended in the spread of disillusion
> and alienation from political processes (p. 282).

The decade of the sixties was a period of radical cultural
disjuncture in America. It was a decade of transition, which
gave birth to the counter-culture and witnessed the emergence
of the hippie as a new social type. The hippie subculture
represented a protest against the sterile technocratic society
of the middle-class establishment. "What makes the youthful
disaffiliation of our time a cultural phenomenon, rather than
merely a political movement, is the fact that it strikes beyond ideology to the level of consciousness, seeking to
transform our deepest sense of the self, the other, the environment" (Roszak, p. 49). Roszak describes the contemporary
youth culture as being obsessed with feeling and passion as
opposed to intellect and reason. There is a searching after
visionary experience and an unprecedented penchant for occult
and magical phenomena (pp. 124-25). Perhaps most significant
of all is the counter-culture's preoccupation with drugs,
particularly the hallucinogenic drugs. In their frantic
search for new experience and meaning, the flower children
of the sixties sought to modify their consciousness through
psychedelics and to connect with a new form of reality through
pharmacological linkages. Hargrove observes that the so-
called "mind-expanding" drugs represent "symbols of membership in a new society with different cultural values" and
have been used "as a means of establishing new patterns of
perception upon which that society could be based" (p. 283).

With the demise of the Haight-Asbury scene in San Francisco
came the realization that "personal salvation and the social
revolution [cannot] be packed in a capsule" (Roszak, p. 177).

As the use of drugs (especially the so-called "hard" drugs like heroin) leveled off and even declined, interest in mystical and Eastern religions increased. As Hargrove notes:

> More and more the young are rejecting the drug-induced experience as part of the unnatural "plastic" world they seek to escape, and they turn instead to the consciousness-manipulation of Eastern religions. The greater apparent willingness of Eastern religions to treat man as a part of nature rather than as its master has much appeal in a time of awareness of Western environmental bungling (p. 283).

While some hip youth looked to Eastern mysticism, American Indian religious lore, or meditation for some kind of transcendental experience, others discovered Jesus--not in the institutional church, for organized religion held little appeal, but in the simple message of the gospel and the teachings of Christ. It is significant that these experience-oriented members of the counter-culture found meaning not only in conversion and the dramatic transformation that it entails, but also in those practices of primitive Christianity that had been all but forgotten by the historical Christian churches--healing, tongues, and other gifts of the Holy Spirit. In addition to meeting very real and deeply felt spiritual needs, the charismatic gifts experienced by many Jesus People may be thought of as ways to resolve more general inner conflicts. The teeny-boppers and flower children of the technocratic society are, more often than not, the victims of multiple inner conflicts. These tensions arise from several sources: from relations with parents and other authority figures in the establishment, from the demands for performance and achievement that haunt young people at every turn, from the desperate search for identity and the means to cope with the problems of our society.

The notion that charismatic phenomena fulfill a need in the lives of individuals who are experiencing conflict is discussed convincingly by Marvin Mayers in the September 1971 Journal of the American Scientific Affiliation. Although Mayers primarily is concerned with the attraction that charismatic groups have for some members of traditional churches, his explanation is also valid for new converts from the hip subculture:

> The established church seems to be traditional in its
> ways, impersonal in its approach to outsiders and
> even towards its own members. It appears to be like
> a machine that is interested more in keeping moving
> and keeping its gears oiled than in developing spir-
> itual insight and experience in the lives of its
> members. Especially young people want to be thought
> of not as a part of a machine, but as unique persons.
> They thus become disgruntled with the church and its
> practices. At this point they seek out more personal
> organizations, leaders who relate to them more indi-
> vidually and personally, who treat tham as valid
> persons, and who communicate personalness to them.
> Too often, in the impersonal established church the
> individual feels unwanted, rejected, alienated. Holy
> Spirit movements reverse this process. The key is
> involvement, participation, the bringing of the indi-
> vidual into the total experience (p. 92).

This no doubt explains why an increasing number of young people attend a church like Calvary Chapel (chapter four) on
weeknights and perhaps Sunday nights while attending the
church of their parents on Sunday morning--and why some
traditional church people seek out small charismatic prayer
and fellowship groups while retaining ties to the home church.

Mayers does not suggest that the individual who resolves his
conflicts through encounter with charismatic groups is necessarily emotionally disturbed. He recognizes, however, that
"there are varying stages of conflict that may or may not
result in emotional disturbance. But more, these people are
ready for a new experience; one that promises them vitality,
involvement, and participation. They are ready to flee from
some bad experience or some bad situation" (p. 92).

Many of the converts in the Jesus Movement are indeed fleeing
from bad experiences and deteriorating life situations.
Large numbers of them were heavy drug users. They had withdrawn from society. Their encounter with Jesus Christ made
them once again participating members of the human race.
Frequently, but not always, they were encouraged to get
jobs, return to school, and make amends with parents and the
law. The Jesus Movement provided the opportunity to restore
some sort of order, stability, and meaning to their lives.
It put them in touch with the supernatural and made involve-

ment in the form of witnessing a new and vital dimension to their lives.

The teen-aged runaway is one of the sad by-products of our schizoid culture. This social phenomenon represents, as Roszak points out, much more a flight _from_ than a flight _toward_. "Certainly for a youngster of seventeen, clearing out of the comfortable bosom of the middle-class family to become a beggar is a formidable gesture of dissent. One makes light of it at the expense of ignoring a significant measure of our social health" (p. 34). The tragic dimensions of this youthful exodus can only be fully understood when one talks in person to the parties involved, as we did in the course of research for this book. Thomas Cottle eloquently discusses the failure of the parental generation in his volume, Time's Children:

> No one as yet has studied the notes written by parents to their runaway children in New York's East Village or San Francisco's Haight Asbury district. . . . These pitiful missives document so well the lack of generational space and the confession of failure in parenthood and adulthood. They could almost be the letters of children who, wishing to come home, promise never again to misbehave. . . . The "Come back home--all is forgiven" notes stand as a testament to what must be seen by the young as a crumbling structure or a tragic reversal of intentionally and interpersonal competence (p. 89).

Whatever their reason for leaving home, hundreds of teenagers have been converted to Christ at places like Bethel Tabernacle in Redondo Beach, California, and have been reunited with their parents. Older teenagers and young adults have found a strong sense of family in Christian communes and with groups like the Children of God. "Their rigid discipline and strong fellowship provide a solid base for anomic young people who have found no place for themselves in the technological culture of the society" (Hargrove, p. 284).

The need for fellowship and close interaction felt by the Jesus People reflects the quest for community that characterizes the youth culture in general. Hargrove relates this quest to a more general search for religious meaning on the part of young people today.

> Young people are especially affected by the loss of strong kinship and community support, particularly since social patterns relegate them to a category somewhat separate from the rest of society. They attempt to overcome feelings of isolation by banding together in groups which can offer personal and social support. . . . One reaction to this is withdrawal into intimate groups in which effort is made to reveal and support the identities of members. Much of this kind of activity falls within broad definitions of religion, and often it is specifically labeled religious. . . .

A social movement can be defined as a large-scale, widespread, informal effort by a fairly large number of people to modify or in some way influence the existing social order. Social movements usually arise spontaneously and assume various forms. Some comprise an indefinite, shifting, unstructured membership, with the members rarely if ever meeting face to face. Other movements are more highly organized, tightly knit, intimate groups who collectively promote some program of change. The Jesus Movement is an unorganized social movement in the sense that it is composed of widely scattered subgroups that, although sharing common interests and certain basic concerns, are not united under a single leadership structure or a clearly articulated set of goals and objectives. The various subgroups are, however, internally often highly structured and influenced by very strong leaders. While they sometimes acknowledge a vague linkage with a larger movement that is not well defined--to them as least--these groups are often fiercely independent and ethnocentric. If we keep this kind of grass-roots diversity clearly in focus, it is valuable to consider the Jesus People as constituting a social movement.

Members of social movements are usually highly commited to "the cause." This commitment may become so fervent that, in effect, the person relinquishes an autonomous individual existence. The following comments by Eric Hoffer are directly applicable to a group like the Children of God:

> An individual existence, even when purposeful, seems to him futile and sinful. To live without an ardent dedication is to be adrift and abandoned. He sees in tolerance a sign of weakness, frivolity, and ignorance. He hungers for the deep assurance which comes

with total surrender--with the whole-hearted clinging to a creed and a cause. . . . He is even ready to join in a holy crusade against his former holy cause, but it must be a genuine crusade--uncompromising, intolerant, proclaiming the one and only truth (The True Believer, p. 82).

Virtually every act of membership, Toch reminds us, "involves a sacrifice of privacy and autonomy, at least in the sense that the member must accomplish some of his objectives as part of a group, rather than as an individual" (p. 133). Some students of mass movements feel that this sacrifice, in and of itself, appeals to certain kinds of people. "Although there unquestionably are some persons in some social movements whose main concern is to lose themselves in a collective enterprise, most members view their group commitments--including their sacrifices of individuality--as necessary attributes of their brand of life, rather than as ends in themselves" (p. 133).

Compared to their "unsaved" counterparts in the youth culture, most Jesus Freaks lead sober, disciplined lives. They readily submit to the restrictive rules and regimented existence of the many Christian houses and communes. For many outsiders the word commune conjures up images of unbridled freedom and permissiveness. As we have seen, this is not true in the Jesus communes. The converts recognize their need for structure and a new sense of order in their lives. Their reaction is against what Will Herberg calls "the moral laxity and putrid permissiveness that have gone so far in corrupting American middle-class, especially suburban middle-class, society" (New Guard, Nov. 1971, p. 15). For Herberg the Jesus People represent a movement seeking "to exorcise the demons and heal the putridities of [the] counter-culture, and reintegrate it into the continuing American consensus" (p. 16).

The Jesus People come from a society characterized not only by permissiveness, but one saturated with boredom. The children of technocracy are restless, dissatisfied, and bored. And as Hoffer has stated, "There is perhaps no more reliable indicator of a society's ripeness for a mass movement than the prevalence of unrelieved boredom" (p. 53). In the Jesus groups the old boredom has been replaced by a new and purposeful activism--the frantic round of witnessing excursions, the invigorating devotional exercises of speaking in tongues, group singing, and quoting memorized Scripture passages, and the satisfaction of intimate sharing.

A tightly knit group can easily lead to a tightly closed mind. We have referred again and again in the preceding chapters to the dogmatism of many Jesus groups. Social psychologists have devoted considerable attention to the phenomenon of "closed-mindedness" in their research of social movements. The implications for the Jesus Movement of Hans Toch's observations are obvious:

> The social movement that presents its inductee with authoritatively reinforced beliefs responsive to his problems unwittingly initiates a chain of events which may culminate in the confined, self-contained world of the veteran member. . . . As the believer becomes more intensely dedicated to the repair and buttressing of his current constructs, these come to assume greater personal significance for him. Moreover, supporting efforts tend to systematize beliefs. As a result, it becomes of greater import that the new data conform and extreme pains are soon taken to this end.
>
> At a given point in this process, the believer has walled himself in. Every event he encounters must be processed in terms of his beliefs. Every opportunity must be used to cement his system. At this stage, only authority can produce innovation (pp. 155-56).

Every social movement has its peculiar jargon and symbols that act as unifying factors binding the participants together. The Jesus Movement has its One Way sign, its Jesus cheers, and its favorite expressions like "Praise the Lord," "Jesus Loves You," and "Right On!" Just as the Ku Klux Klan has its elaborate regalia and secret rituals, the Jesus Movement has its own cultic uniforms and unusual activities, such as the silent vigils of the Children of God. The garb, the vigils, the beach baptisms, the bumper stickers, the huge Bibles, the music--these all provide some of the "color" of the movement, and they also serve as a means of positive identification with the movement and as a way of engendering a certain pride in belonging.

In this chapter we have outlined the major characteristics of the Jesus People as a social movement. Although other social movements demonstrate the same traits in different configurations, in the case of the Jesus Movement it must be remembered that its members find divine sanction for practices that ordinarily would be explained at the socio-psychological level only. For example, students of social behavior would seek to explain the authoritarian leader and his submissive following in terms of the human dynamics of the relationship. But the Jesus People themselves would insist that their obedience to the elder is merely a response to the clear-cut teaching of the Bible. And at every point in a sociological analysis of the movement, its participants would quote the Bible as justification of their actions and attitudes.

Part of the systematic analysis of social movements is an exploration of variables like social class, sex, age, economic status, geographic location, educational level, and racial or ethnic background. Since we conducted no formal surveys of these factors in our research on the Jesus People, we have had to limit ourselves to the impressionistic information that is presented throughout this book. For purposes of summary here, suffice it to say that the Jesus People are a highly diverse group of individuals found throughout the nation, but predominating in California and the Pacific Northwest, coming from virtually all social and economic levels, but including very few Blacks or other minority group members. The fact that few black young people are in the movement is no doubt significant and deserves additional research.

In the final analysis, the Jesus Movement is really an example of what sociologists of religion call "revitalization movements." Such movements involve more than reform or renewal; they can best be understood as revolutionary. Movements of revitalization include a reaching out into the unknown for new patterns, rather than simply a return to the more familiar. As Barbara Hargrove points out, "Revitalization is distinguished by its potential to recombine those familiar elements into creative new patterns" (p. 277).

A number of observers have compared the Jesus Revolution with the Great Awakening of mid-eighteenth-century America. Herberg, for example, feels that the Jesus People, because of their revivalistic pietism, have "placed themselves squarely in the line of 200 years of American revivalism." He